RECAPTURED AFRICANS

RECAPTURED

AFRICANS

Surviving Slave Ships,

Detention, and Dislocation

in the

Final Years of the Slave Trade

SHARLA M. FETT

The University of North Carolina Press

CHAPEL HILL

*This book was published with the assistance of the
John Hope Franklin Fund of the University of North Carolina Press.*

© 2017 The University of North Carolina Press. All rights reserved.
Designed and set in Merlo by Rebecca Evans.

Manufactured in the United States of America
The University of North Carolina Press has been a member of the
Green Press Initiative since 2003.

Cover image: Recaptive boys of the slave ship *Zeldina* in Jamaica.
Illustrated London News engraving, 20 June 1857.
Courtesy of the Huntington Library, San Marino, California.

Yvette Christiansë, "When All Else Fails" and "What the Girl Who Was a Cabin Boy
Heard or Said—Which Is Not Clear," from Yvette Christiansë, *Castaway*, 63– and 56– .
© 1999, Duke University Press. All rights reserved. Republished by permission
of the copyright holder. www.dukeupress.edu.

"Children Crying," by The Congos, from *Heart of the Congos*. Reprinted by
permission of the copyright holder. VP Records.

Portions of Chapters 3 and 5 appeared previously in somewhat different form in
Sharla M. Fett, "Middle Passages and Forced Migrations: Liberated Africans in
Nineteenth-Century U.S. Camps and Ships," *Slavery and Abolition* 31, no. 1 (2010):
75–98. Reprinted by permission of www.tandfonline.com.

Portions of Chapter 4 appeared previously in somewhat different form in Sharla M. Fett,
"'The Ship of Slavery': Atlantic Slave Trade Suppression, Liberated Africans, and Black Abolition
Politics in Antebellum New York," in *Paths of the Atlantic Slave Trade: Interactions, Identities, and
Images*, ed. Ana Lucia Araujo (New York: Cambria, 2011), 131–60. Reprinted with permission.

Library of Congress Cataloging-in-Publication Data
Names: Fett, Sharla M., author.
Title: Recaptured Africans : surviving slave ships, detention, and dislocation
in the final years of the slave trade / by Sharla M. Fett.
Description: Chapel Hill : The University of North Carolina Press, [2016] |
Includes bibliographical references and index.
Identifiers: LCCN 2016024828| ISBN 9781469630021 (cloth : alk. paper) |
ISBN 9781469630038 (ebook)
Subjects: LCSH: Slaves—United States—Social conditions—19th century. | Slaves—
United States—History—19th century. | Slave trade—United States—History—19th century.
Classification: LCC E453 .F48 2016 | DDC 306.3/620973—dc23
LC record available at https://lccn.loc.gov/2016024828

TO ELLA & JACOB

A better and more beautiful world

from *Chronicles of the Hull*

WHEN ALL ELSE FAILS

And now, be kind
stars, gods, be kind
whatever names you go by
in our many prayers
and thanksgivings
          be kind
when our fingers break
against the wood that
holds us
          be kind
when we hear our voices
fall flat out of the
childhood we lose
          be kind
in the darkness,
          be kind
when they wash us
heavily and feed us
with rough concessions
          be kind
to our yesterdays, our
back theres, the generations
we shed as we squat
in place among strangers.

To our hands, be kind,
To our ankles, our eyes
          be kind
to our memories
          even
our forgetting.

—Yvette Christiansë, *Castaway*

CONTENTS

FIGURES & MAP

TABLES

ACKNOWLEDGMENTS

This book has been long in the making. I could never have written it without the insight and support of many colleagues, friends, and family members. Many years ago at the Virginia Historical Society, Lee Shepard and Frances Pollard introduced me to the history of recaptive journeys by suggesting that I look at William Proby Young's ship log. The Ralph J. Bunche Center for African American Studies at UCLA provided an incubating space in which to begin thinking about how to tell the story of West Central African youth in the immediate wake of slave ship captivity. As the project picked up speed, a critical long-term Mellon Fellowship at the Huntington Library afforded the luxury of a year's research in a rich intellectual climate. I am also indebted to Occidental College's faculty sabbatical program and the Faculty Enrichment Grants that enabled research, travel, and precious time to think and write. My thanks as well to the many archivists and librarians who answered my queries at the South Carolina Historical Society, the South Caroliniana Library, the American Antiquarian Society, the West Virginia and Regional History Center, the Monroe County Public Library in Key West, and the National Archives and Records Administration. Thanks to Brooke Guthrie at Duke University's David M. Rubenstein Rare Book and Manuscript Library for her quick response to a key archival finding.

On my long and humbling journey to becoming an Atlantic historian, I learned from many generous colleagues. My fellow Occidental College historians Jem Axelrod, Sasha Day, Lynn Dumenil, Michael Gasper, Nina Gelbart, Jane Hong, Maryanne Horowitz, Paul Nam, Alexandra Puerto, Lisa Sousa, and Marla Stone have been a front line of support, offering insights from their own fields of research. Carol Siu and John De La Fontaine went the extra mile to assist with interlibrary loans and database access. From my year at the Huntington Library, I'm grateful for conversations with Nancy Bercaw, Roy Ritchie, LeeAnn Whites, and especially Kevin Dawson, who generously shared sources and insights in subsequent years. Ariela Gross and Judith Jackson Fossett hosted an interdisciplinary slavery studies working group at the University of Southern California that introduced me to profound scholarship on issues of legacy and redress. Elsa Barkley Brown, Adam Rothman, and Jessica Marie Johnson, along with other participants in the African American Political Culture Workshop at the University of Maryland, College Park, offered just the right critiques at a key point in my thinking about Atlantic child trafficking and recaptivity. Sandra Gunning and participants in the Neoslaveries in the Nineteenth-Century Atlantic World Symposium at the University of Michigan helped me to think comparatively about the era's many forced migrations. I'm grateful to Carla Pestana, Robin Derby, and Andrew Apter for involving me in the UCLA Atlantic History Speaker Series and to Alex Borucki for opportunities to share work with UC Irvine's History Department and Medical Humanities Initiative. Corey Malcom, director of archaeology at the Mel Fisher Maritime Museum, took time to give me a historical tour of Key West and shared his own extensive research on recaptives of the *Wildfire*, *William*, and *Bogota*. Gabrielle Foreman gave me smart writing advice and shared her passion for the broad agenda of nineteenth-century black activism. In our regular breakfast meetings, Brenda Stevenson offered warm encouragement and invigorated my comparative slavery studies with her deep knowledge. For letters of support, conference collaborations, research suggestions, and generously sharing their work in progress, I'm indebted to Rosanne Adderley, Karen Anderson, Ana Lucia Araujo, Herman Bennett, Henry Drewal, Pablo Gómez, Evelynn Hammonds, John Harris, Svend Holsoe, Tera Hunter, Walter Johnson, Suzanne Lebsock, Henry Lovejoy, Leo Marques, Joseph Miller, Jennifer Morgan, Marcus Rediker, Ellen Samuels, Marni Sandweiss, David Sartorius, Rebecca Scott, James Sidbury, Stephanie Smallwood, Steven Stowe, Lynn Thomas, Marie Tyler-McGraw, Sifu Earl White, Peter Wood, Lisa Yun, Rafia Zafar, and Michael Zeuske. Each one of these scholars has expanded my geographic and intellectual horizons and deepened my gratitude to be part of this moment of Atlantic World and Black Atlantic historiography. Any remaining errors or oversights are my own responsibility, of course.

To my longtime writing group, words cannot express my gratitude. Emily Abel, Carla Bittel, Janet Brodie, Lisa Cody, Lynn Sacco, Terri Snyder, Devra Weber, and Alice Wexler read many drafts. Over wine and delicious dinners, they listened, counseled, critiqued, and inspired. One could not ask for better or wiser writing comrades. Suchi Branfman shone a light with her art and practice. The late Stephanie M. H. Camp deserves singular mention. She extended herself in extraordinary ways, sharing resources, giving astute advice ("punch up the introduction!"), and collaborating on presentations, as we both moved into our second book projects. Her spirit and memory remain with all who loved and learned from her.

I am deeply grateful to those whose close and critical readings offered essential guidance in each phase of revision. Walter Hawthorne and a second anonymous reader at UNC Press pushed me to make a better book with their close and expert reading. I learned a great deal in responding to their suggestions. Several other colleagues read one or more manuscript chapters, and I thank the following for both frank criticism and generous encouragement: Jeannine DeLombard, Gabrielle Foreman, Lisa Lindsay, Andy Pearson, Manisha Sinha, Brenda Stevenson, Randy Sparks, and Jean Wyatt. Lynn Dumenil heroically read the entire manuscript twice. Kristin Oberiano, an outstanding senior history major, saved the day by editing notes and bibliography for the final manuscript. At UNC Press, Kate Torrey encouraged the project's early formation, and Chuck Grench patiently guided the manuscript through to production. Thanks to Jad Adkins and Kim Bryant for helpful communication and work with illustrations. I'm truly indebted to Stephanie Wenzel, who has now edited two of my book manuscripts and taught me more about writing each time.

My extended family reminds me who I am and keeps academic life in perspective. My sisters Sheryl Fett-Mekaru, Debby Desmond, and Christine Sprunger provided unwavering love and support in the midst of their own busy lives and many accomplishments. The memory of my mother, Betty Marie Dalton Fett, continues to guide me always. I thank my father, James Fett, for conversations about Congo in the 1960s and '70s; both he and Therese Sprunger have offered steady support and inspiring examples of medical compassion. To three generations of the Los Angeles Rogers family, thank you for joyous, chaotic gatherings and for knowing when to take interest and when not to ask about the progress of "the book." My beloved children, Jacob Rogers-Fett and Ella Rogers-Fett, have grown up over the course of this endeavor. Their creativity, intelligence, and commitments inspire hope and provoke new thinking. Finally, with deep love and respect, I thank John Rogers, for endless patience, superb critical advice, and many years of daily partnership that have made this book—and much more—possible.

RECAPTURED AFRICANS

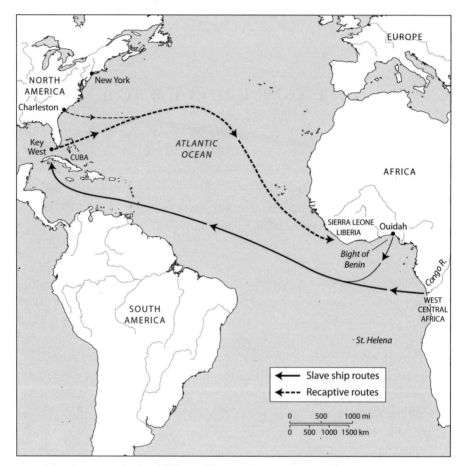

Atlantic Routes of *Echo*, *Wildfire*, *William*, and *Bogota* Receptive Shipmates. Based on
David Eltis and David Richardson, *Atlas of the Transatlantic Slave Trade* (New Haven:
Yale University Press, 2010), p. 281, map 184. Courtesy of Yale University Press.

Introduction

～

Speaking in Poughkeepsie, New York, on 2 August 1858, for the anniversary of British West Indian emancipation, Frederick Douglass condemned the hypocrisy of an American "slaveholding and slave-trading nation" that failed to consistently enforce slave trade abolition. At issue were both the expansion of U.S. domestic slavery and the continuation of an illegal transatlantic slave trade that forcibly carried off almost 1.3 million Africans even after every major slaving nation in Europe and the Americas had criminalized the traffic.[1] Douglass charged that despite the U.S. transatlantic slave trade ban signed into law in 1807, the federal government showed its true colors by refusing to allow Britain to board and inspect suspicious ships flying the American flag. Justifications for this refusal based on principles of national sovereignty could only be understood as a "refuge of lies," he insisted, when the true cause of American inconsistency resided in a fundamental contradiction between U.S. domestic and foreign policy. As Douglass eloquently put it, "A slaveholding Government cannot consistently oppose the Slave-trade; it is the logical and legitimate deduction of Slavery—and the one is as hateful as the other. They are twin monsters, both hatched in the same polluted nest."[2] The United States could not effectively prosecute slavers at sea, Douglass warned, while reinforcing the rights of slaveholders at home. Nor could the United States claim to enforce abolition in international waters while defending a domestic commerce in human beings.

For almost two-thirds of the nineteenth century, Douglass's description of the U.S. government remained apt: a slaveholding republic that criminalized international slavers while sanctioning the daily business of U.S. slave markets and overlooking American complicity in the contraband transatlantic trade. That apparent contradiction also created the conditions under which "recaptured Africans" temporarily sojourned in the United States. In the following pages, I examine the odyssey of roughly 1,800 African children, men, and women seized by the U.S. Navy from illegal slave ships headed for Cuban markets and brought temporarily into the United States. Originating in the regions of present-day Nigeria, Benin, Republic of the Congo, Democratic Republic of the Congo, and Angola, these former slave ship captives remained for weeks in federal detention in Charleston harbor in 1858 and Key West in 1860, before officials sent survivors on to Liberia. This book explores how African recaptives journeyed through the aftermath of slave ship bondage and how contending political constituencies responded to their presence. By reintroducing the term "recaptive" to historical studies of U.S. slavery, *Recaptured Africans* offers a new perspective on struggles for emancipation in the mid-nineteenth-century Atlantic World.

The state of recaptivity, a distinctive variant of slave trade captivity expressed as both social experience and racial representation, is the concern of this book. Across the globe from 1807 to 1867, naval intervention resulted in the seizure of at least 181,000 African men, women, and children. Those who survived their ordeal became known as "liberated Africans," *emancipados*, *africanos livres*, and "recaptured Africans" in Sierra Leone, the Caribbean, Cape Colony, the South Atlantic island of St. Helena, Cuba, Brazil, and Liberia.[3] In contrast to several studies of the long-term creation of communities of "liberated Africans," *Recaptured Africans* focuses instead on the immediate aftermath for African recaptives aboard four illegal slavers seized by U.S. authorities: the *Echo*, in 1858, and the *Wildfire*, *William*, and *Bogota*, in 1860.[4] The story is thus told, for the most part, in weeks, months, and years rather than in decades and centuries. Furthermore, the terminology employed— "recaptured" rather than "liberated"—signals my interest in the liminal zones between enslavement and emancipation in the nineteenth-century Atlantic World. In comparison with "liberated Africans," a term often applied by scholars to recaptives in British colonies, I use "recaptives" to emphasize the constraints of death and suffering, containment and racialization, that African shipmates endured in the course of U.S. federal detention and transportation to Liberia. "Recaptive" serves both as a more accurate descriptor of the social experience of slave ship rescue and as a useful metaphor for the conflicting representational claims made on the bodies of slave ship refugees.

Even after the U.S. Congress banned the transatlantic slave trade, the legal status of the victims of that trade remained a subject of contention. In a young republic whose Constitution protected the human property claims of slaveowners, the question of emancipation for illegally trafficked Africans inevitably hit a political nerve.[5] How would U.S. law define the status of recaptive men, women, and children who inhabited the murky realm between potential commodity and quasi-person? At first, federal lawmakers sidestepped the question by granting jurisdiction to state authorities over "any negro, mulatto, or person of colour" found aboard intercepted slavers.[6] By delegating jurisdiction to the state level and effectively permitting the sale of intercepted captives for southern state treasuries, federal law continued to treat illegally trafficked Africans as fungible commodities. In the early years of slave trade suppression, recaptured men, women, and children exited slave ships only to find themselves auctioned by state officials into the expanding cotton economies of the U.S. South.

Not until 1819 did Congress shift the legal status of recaptives further along the spectrum from property to persons by placing slave trade refugees under federal jurisdiction and prohibiting further sale. Passed in the midst of an emerging crisis over Missouri's slave or free status, the 1819 act empowered the president to deport recaptives and authorized an agent to oversee resettlement outside U.S. borders.[7] Significantly, supporters of the newly founded American Colonization Society (ACS) provided leadership in shepherding the measure through Congress, thereby creating both rationale and means for the creation of a Liberian colony in West Africa in the early 1820s.[8] From Liberia's inception onward, the policy of recaptive removal and the suppression of the transatlantic slave trade became intertwined with the emigration of free and manumitted African Americans to West Africa. Throughout the antebellum period, political tensions regarding state-national authority, commodity-person status, and Liberian colonization persisted in slave trade suppression debates. However, the 1819 law represented a genuine turning point in terms of establishing the principle of federal custody and extraterritorial removal for slave ship survivors.

Yet, legal statutes illuminate only part of mid-nineteenth-century recaptive history. In terms of legal intent, some have argued that the 1819 removal law constituted a milestone in the U.S. government's willingness "to spend money to help Africans gain their liberty."[9] Federal slave trade legislation, however, made no mention of recaptives' "liberty," nor did it describe the seizure of an illegal slave ship as an act of emancipation. Legal history thus tells only a partial story about the nature of recaptive existence following release from the holds of slave ships. To some extent, recaptives across the Atlantic World shared conditions of dispossession, displacement, and uncertainty, yet the policies of the capturing nation influenced specific experiences related to middle passage trauma, labor policies, and further displacement. In the case of the United States, temporary federal camps, the removal mandate, and apprenticeship to African American emigrant households in Liberia shaped a particular version of recaptivity. By examining the passage of African recaptives from four illegal slavers through U.S. custody, the following chapters contribute a North American case study to an expanding literature on recaptured/liberated Africans throughout the Atlantic World. Furthermore, putting recaptives at the center of the story amplifies the social and cultural dimensions of U.S. slave trade suppression.

Although overlooked in historical narratives of antebellum sectionalism confined to domestic politics, transnational slave smuggling and naval suppression exerted a significant impact on nineteenth-century U.S. public debates and popular culture. In the decades after slave trade abolition, U.S. naval efforts to intercept illegal slavers failed to stem the participation of American sailors, slave ships, and financiers in the trafficking of African captives to Brazil and Cuba. Accounts of suspicious vessels seized by U.S. warships appeared regularly in the American press. Tensions over British interception of American ships ignited diplomatic protests over rights of search and U.S. sovereignty.[10] American newspapers across the political spectrum avidly followed the trials of slave ship crews and captains in major seaport cities. Two bestsellers of the 1850s were, in fact, memoirs written by a U.S. Africa Squadron commander and a notorious retired transatlantic slave smuggler.[11] Broad public familiarity with slave trade enforcement enabled Frederick Douglass to condemn the American institution of chattel slavery as a "system of piracy," a clear invocation of U.S. piracy statutes that defined maritime human trafficking as a capital crime.[12] Once we recognize the extensive public impact of the slave trade and its suppression, we are able to see antebellum slavery debates more accurately within an Atlantic political geography.

The patterns of wind and current that brought the *Echo*, *Wildfire*, *William*, and *Bogota* within range of the U.S. Navy also drew recaptives into an evolving Euro-American debate on the racial destiny of Africans and their descendants. The representation of African recaptives in American newspapers and magazines illustrated the influence of both racial science and African exploration literature on U.S. slavery debates. Recaptives arriving in southern ports such as Charleston, South Carolina, encountered an American public that could perceive them only through the caricatures of slave or savage. Let them stay in the hands of benevolent American planters, argued one South Carolina editorialist, where recaptive Africans could have "all the liberty they could use."[13] Racialization through ethnography, proslavery rhetoric, and colonizationist discourses impaired the American public's ability to grasp the nature of recaptive struggles for physical and social survival. Furthermore, recaptive debates in U.S. newspapers employed a hardening racial ideology in arguments about black labor, global commerce, and African colonization. Consequently, the history of recaptives in the United States provides an instructive example of early U.S. imperialism decades in advance of its traditionally narrated late nineteenth-century rise.[14]

—

Surrounded on all sides by proslavery demagogues, federal guards, and curious sightseers, traumatized shipmates sought to survive their displacement along Atlantic routes of forced migration by pursuing the tentative repair of their fractured worlds. The approach I have taken to recuperate a history of recaptivity as lived experience has necessarily been shaped by the limitations of existing sources. On one hand, government officials and local eyewitnesses obsessively documented recaptives of the *Echo*, *Wildfire*, *William*, and *Bogota* as bodies to be fed, buried, counted, guarded, controlled, and transported.[15] Obviously slanted toward bureaucratic concerns, the records of naval officers, U.S. marshals, and other government agents provide detailed information on mortality rates, legal proceedings, and local arrangements for sheltering recaptives. Records of the ACS as well as the daily journals and correspondence of appointed federal agents offer glimpses of daily conditions on Liberian-bound ships and the survival strategies of slave trade refugees recrossing the Atlantic. Still, the archive of evidence on U.S. slave trade suppression is marked by a virtual erasure of first-person testimony from these specific recaptive adults and youth. The absence of any reliable first-person evidence threatens to silence key aspects of the social experience of recaptives, such as individual memories of homeland, social affiliations, spiritual practice, and intellectual frameworks for understanding such extended journeys. Compared to detailed linguistic and ethnographic evidence (however distorted or misunderstood) kept by officials in Havana, Freetown, St. Helena, and Rio de Janeiro, U.S. records on recaptives in Charleston and Key West lack all but the most generic observations on appearance and language.[16] As a result, we can be fairly sure of the places from which the *Bogota* or *Wildfire*, for example, left the African coast but less certain about particular recaptives' origins and routes into Atlantic enslavement. As I discuss below, superficial and caricatured treatment of ethnicity in U.S. slave trade suppression sources poses significant obstacles for accessing the frames of reference through which African men, women, and children interpreted their experiences of enslavement and recaptivity.

Faced with archives that reflect the historical devaluation of enslaved

African lives, historians must make decisions about how to use partial and fragmentary evidence. In this book, I situate existing primary evidence within a rich and growing body of scholarship on saltwater slavery (enslavement on the sea) and liberated African studies that offers insight into the question of what it meant to be a recaptured African in the last decade of the transatlantic slave trade.[17] Through this lens, the outlines, if not the fine grain, of recaptive experiences become visible by careful contextualization. First, and fundamentally, recaptivity must be understood as a phase of forced migration, geographically and conceptually linked to Atlantic routes of enslavement. The term "serial displacement," elaborated by historians of the Atlantic slave trade, reminds us that the time spent by recaptured Africans in U.S. custody was just one phase of dislocation within an extended process of upheaval, terror, and physical deprivation. Each recaptive seized by U.S. naval patrols had already traveled thousands of miles, some having passed through a succession of owners, traders, and brokers in West and West Central Africa before embarking on transatlantic slave ships.[18] Depending on age, gender, and conditions of capture, most recaptives had also experienced the breaking and remaking of their social worlds many times over, in shifting familial, labor, and commercial contexts.[19] Within this framework, recaptive camps and government removal ships can be understood as "transit zones," temporary detention spaces through which refugees of the slave trade passed after already enduring many stages of enslavement. Borrowed from twentieth-century research on the movements of refugees and displaced persons, the term "transit zone" emphasizes transience, insecurity, alienation, and potential for further trauma.[20] Whereas federal law treated recaptives as a population in the process of exiting the slave trade, the question of where that exit led remained unanswered within the immediate environs of the transit zone.

A large number of slave ship recaptives in the 1850s proved particularly vulnerable due to their young age. Although definitions of childhood and children varied across societies, demographic research clearly indicates the increase in enslaved young people embarked on transatlantic slavers in the nineteenth century. The proportion of children younger than fifteen years sold to foreign traders from all regions of Africa rose over time, from 22.7 percent in the eighteenth century to 46.1 percent between 1810 and 1867. Even more to the point, captives embarked near the mouth of the Congo River, including those enslaved on the *Echo*, *Wildfire*, and *William*, came from regions where the proportion of children under fifteen surpassed 50 percent in the same decades.[21] By necessity, any study of nineteenth-century recaptives from the West Central African region must confront the particular crisis of these slave trade "orphans," primarily male youth. How might the young age of recaptives have defined their vulnerability and, perhaps, their ability to adapt to protracted displacement?[22] Furthermore, how might the expectations of recaptive groups containing a larger numbers of adults, such as the shipmates of the Ouidah-embarked *Bogota* in 1860, have been shaped by their arrival in the Key West camp already inhabited by large numbers of younger West Central African recaptives? Asking such questions, informed by pathbreaking arguments on African children in slavery and diaspora, illuminates the possible social experience of recaptive communities, even when the perspective of individual recaptives has been lost.[23]

Shipmates who shared and survived the experience of saltwater slavery forged powerful social bonds with one another.[24] In his study of 1821 Yoruba survivors of the *Emilia*, Walter Hawthorne argues that "social death was followed by 'social reincarnation,'" growing out of ties between shipmates. Enslaved Africans arriving throughout the Americas used specific terms to acknowledge the deep significance of connections forged with those who shared their ocean terrors: *malungo* in Brazil, *sippi* and *máti* in Surinam, *malongue* in Trinidad, and *batiment* in Haiti.[25] Shipmate bonds proved equally powerful for recaptive Africans, many of whom had more control over maintaining their shipmate connections than did enslaved Africans in the Americas.[26] The people at the center of this study made a second Atlantic crossing in company with shipmates who had already shared a common first middle passage. A critical reading of the daily ship journals of white government agents reveals recaptive shipmates' assertion of sociability, aesthetic creativity, and survival strategies on the voyage to Liberia. Moreover, the deep alienation of a few who were separated from their original shipmates and placed with a different group of recaptives traveling to Liberia underscores the continuing power of shipmate relations throughout the period of recaptivity.

Finally, the official reports and receipts left by U.S. and ACS agents in Liberia suggest how, throughout successive forced migrations, recaptives underwent a complex process of "ethnogenesis" that transformed shipmate relations and common regions of origin into broader networks and identifications. As many Africanist scholars have emphasized, enslaved people did not think of themselves as "Africans" or their homelands as "Africa."[27] These terms, though used in historical writing today, were generated by centuries of interaction between the diverse people and polities of the Atlantic Basin. Like enslaved communities in the Americas, recaptives were also forced by circumstances to construct new collective identities and communities. David Northrup has written, for example, of the heightened awareness of being

"African" that developed among liberated Africans in Sierra Leone.[28] The present study, focused on immediate aftermath, does not address the long-term development and impact of "Congoes" in Liberia. In fact, much of that history remains to be written. However, *Recaptured Africans* does examine the initial period of apprenticeship, which reveals the continued subordination of recaptive children and adults to Liberian colonial interests. Ongoing struggles for collective belonging allowed some recaptives to build networks of family, church, and neighborhood despite limited political and economic rights.

Taken together, the reconstruction of social bonds in the midst of death and displacement demonstrates a powerful repudiation of the threat of "social death" imposed by the transatlantic market in human commodities. Vincent Brown incisively challenges historians to understand social death not as a fixed condition but as a "productive peril" that generated a politics of struggle among the enslaved.[29] Brown's argument about slavery and "political life" revisits Orlando Patterson's classic definition of slavery as social death, defined by an institutionalized set of social relations that constitute *"the permanent, violent domination of natally alienated and generally dishonored persons."*[30] Recent studies by Atlantic historians including James Sweet, Walter Hawthorne, and John Edwin Mason reject the idea of social death as a permanent condition, instead placing emphasis on the creation of cultural, religious, and political affiliations that foster social "reincarnation" or "resurrection."[31] In these pages, I argue that the critical work of slave trade refugees in the first days and months of recaptivity entailed just such a work of reconstruction. However, as this story shows, those struggling for a life beyond survival in the aftermath of the middle passage repeatedly confronted grim realities of death and loss. From the elemental effort to remain alive in federal camps to the politics of space and resources that developed aboard recaptive ships, and finally to collective efforts to escape apprenticeship or form new families in Liberia, both adults and children re-created fragile social groupings that defied the social annihilation imposed by slave traders and would-be rescuers.

⁓

In contrast to the partial and fragmented archive on recaptive social experience, evidence for the racial representation of recaptive Africans while under U.S. federal jurisdiction fills the historical record. Proslavery southern nationalists, colonizationists, and abolitionists generated a noisy public debate over U.S. slave trade suppression policies and took an interest in the 1858 and 1860 arrivals of recaptured Africans. Newspaper reports and visual images of recaptives in the illustrated weeklies depicted slave trade refugees as racially exotic subjects. Congressional subsidies passed to fund the removal of recaptive shipmates exacerbated the long-running debate among African American activists, slave trade revivalists, and abolitionist circles over U.S. support for Liberian colonization. Black activists already involved in protest over the illegal transatlantic trade to Cuba asserted the humanity and rights of young recaptives. Finally, ACS officials and the U.S. agent for recaptured Africans in Liberia generated copious records on the transition of recaptives into Liberian apprenticeships. To understand the dual nature of recaptivity as both social experience and racial representation requires reading many of these sources against their grain.

As the first large group of recaptives to arrive in the United States for several decades, the 1858 shipmates of the *Echo* sailed directly into the sights of slave trade revivalists eager to capitalize on their presence. Accounts of court proceedings, such as those against the *Echo* crew in South Carolina in 1859, as well as newspaper editorials, speeches, and pamphlets reflect the intense politicization of slave trade refugees and convey the arguments of transatlantic slave trade advocates. Charleston lawyer and newspaper editor Leonidas Spratt, for example, identified the same contradiction between foreign slave trade suppression and domestic slavery that Frederick Douglass condemned in his 1858 speech.[32] In Spratt's designs, however, Douglass's monstrous twins became the dual progenitors of southern wealth and political power. Unlike his more moderate southern colleagues who accepted the transatlantic slave trade prohibition, Spratt and his fellow thinkers condemned the federal slave trade ban for casting a shadow of moral doubt on American slaveholding. "*Slavery itself must be wrong*," he declared in mock outrage, "when the ships and seamen of our country are kept upon the seas to preclude the means to its formation. By no dexterity can we dodge the logical accuracy of this conclusion."[33] The assertion was purely rhetorical, of course, for Spratt ardently embraced the proslavery position; following his own logic, he sounded the reactionary call to reopen the transatlantic slave trade, eviscerate slave trade suppression laws, and thereby ensure slavery's future.

Yet, Charleston's slave trade revivalists made clear, the true context for the debate over the fate of slave trade refugees was the wider arena of global abolition. Radical proslavery spokesmen thus used recaptives to fight not only a sectional battle for states' rights but also a hemispheric one against Atlantic emancipation. Following the massive 1791 St. Domingue slave uprising that led to Haitian independence, southern U.S. planters began to build a defensive case against the threat of abolition. The expansion of cotton cultivation across the Deep South in the early nineteenth century gave planters a strong economic stake in proslavery arguments.[34] After British colonial emancipation, the introduction of an apprenticeship system in the West Indies in 1834, and the milestone of full legal emancipation in 1838, proslavery advocates in the United States operated in continuous backlash against British abolitionism.[35] Gradual emancipation in newly independent Latin American countries, such as Peru, Mexico, and Venezuela, and the abolition of slavery in the French Caribbean by 1848 only served to deepen the U.S. proslavery defense.[36]

As a result, slave trade revivalists sought not only to reenslave African recaptives but to harness them as symbols for the larger global advancement of "slave racial capitalism."[37] Global production of cotton, sugar, and coffee directed toward consumer markets in the industrializing regions of Europe and the Americas characterized the period of "second slavery," a concept of global economy developed by historian Dale Tomich.[38] Cuban annexationists, Nicaraguan filibusters, and "Dixie nationalists" with their eyes on Brazil spun visions of a slaveholding empire that would hold back the tide of emancipation and capitalize on this world market.[39] Walter Johnson's recent analysis of slavery and capitalism in the lower Mississippi Valley demonstrates how "slaveholders sought to project their power outward in the shape of pro-slavery imperialism in the 1850s."[40] Many proslavery imperialists fought for open and unregulated access to a transatlantic traffic in African enslaved laborers. Thus, the presence of slave trade recaptives in federal custody gave proslavery spokesmen an opportunity to confront the tensions between U.S. slave trade suppression efforts and slaveholder aspirations for territorial expansion into the southern hemisphere.

As I discovered in the course of researching this book, the political debate over the fate of slave trade recaptives occurred not only between government officials but also in popular print culture. *Recaptured Africans* is therefore distinctive as a study that incorporates cultural politics into the history of U.S. slave trade suppression. Public display and racialized representations in print and visual images constituted part of the process of "recapture" for slave trade refugees in U.S. custody. We might ask how captive youth who sat on the *Wildfire*'s deck in view of a *Harper's Weekly* journalist or photographer in Key West experienced these intrusions. How might they have related the curiosity of soldiers and white visitors in the camps to previous experiences of being examined and probed as slave trade commodities? We do not know enough about recaptive responses to being viewed as spectacle, but it is clear that antebellum print treatment of recaptive Africans drew on the conventions of nineteenth-century travel accounts as much or more than on the abolitionist tropes of the middle passage.[41] The publication of slaver memoirs and naval adventures along the African coast heightened public appetites for ethnographic fare that portrayed African bodies, social organization, and perceived behavior as evidence of human inequality.

For a select group of southern white elite men, slave trade refugees, encamped under federal protection, created a desire to engage in firsthand observation of the racial differences that structured their worldview. Racial science of the nineteenth century increasingly represented African-descended people as biologically unable to claim forms of social belonging and autonomous personhood that Euro-Americans deemed essential for those deserving full political rights.[42] The theory of polygenesis, or separate human origins, grew in popularity with the escalation of U.S. slavery debates in the 1850s. Although the obvious contradictions of polygenesis with the biblical creation story put off many otherwise sympathetic southerners, proslavery physicians from both North and South popularized the idea of inherent and natural difference between people of African descent ("the Negro race") and white European descendants.[43] Developments in racial science and proslavery ideology in the 1850s manufactured a slave trade spectacle out of the human misery of hundreds of slave ship survivors. Moreover, the racialization of recaptives, particularly in Charleston, but also in Key West, implicitly asserted that slave trade refugees were inherently incapable of benefiting from a free status. Both African travel literature and theories of racial science combined to frame recaptive shipmates of the *Echo*, *Wildfire*, *William*, and *Bogota* as racialized ethnological subjects, specimens of "interior" Africa, and objects of white rescue. In the following pages, I ask what the print culture representations of recaptives can tell us about hardening theories of racial destiny and white supremacy that would serve not only the proslavery South but also future forms of colonialism. Just as importantly, I ask what alternative perceptions of African recaptives in the United States were eclipsed by the prevailing narrative of white rescue premised on either enslavement or colonization.

Free black abolitionists generated one such counternarrative of human rights that challenged the escalating arguments for polygenesis and racial inequality. By analyzing the sustained protest against the illegal slave trade in the New York black press of the 1850s, *Recaptured Africans* reveals an understudied dimension of free black transatlantic activism.[44] Northern leaders such as Frederick Douglass and the "fugitive blacksmith" minister James W. C. Pennington called attention to the human costs of the illegal slave trade with a critique of U.S. law and proslavery economics. Both men strongly condemned American complicity in illegal slaving as well as the federal policy of removal to Liberia that funneled money to the ACS. By recognizing young recaptives as human sufferers with freedom rights, African American activists asserted the common origins of humankind and uplifted Enlightenment principles (however unrealized) of human equality. At the same time, black activists also sought to recruit young recaptives for missionary projects aimed at the Christian regeneration of the African continent. Demonstrating this complex agenda, Pennington's activism illustrates how black abolitionists in the New York area took on the illegal transatlantic trade and U.S. recaptive policy.

Finally, an extensive body of evidence was generated by the officials who oversaw the detention, transportation, and apprenticeship of recaptives in Liberia. Even after declaring itself an independent republic in 1847, Liberia figured prominently in American slavery debates and continued to serve as justification for an American naval presence along the West African coast. In contrast to proslavery advocates and most abolitionists, the ACS viewed the unprecedented waves of recaptives between 1858 and 1861 as both a daunting challenge and a potential boost to Liberian "commerce, civilization, and Christianity."[45] ACS and U.S. government records thus reflect paternalistic responses to a humanitarian crisis while revealing the colonial racial hierarchy of Liberian apprenticeships. By carefully reading bureaucratic records and receipts against correspondence from ACS, American, and Liberian officials, we can glimpse the strategies of recaptive men, women, and children as they attempted to survive and build a future among strangers.

Situating the United States within the wider nineteenth-century transatlantic slave trade, this book begins with the racial politics of federal recaptive policies. Chapter 1 examines the precedents established by the deportation of African shipmates from the *Antelope*, *General Páez*, *Fenix*, and *Pons* in the period between the passage of the 1819 removal law and 1845. The first chapter also charts the emergence of a literary genre of "slave trade ethnography" in slaver and naval narratives that contributed to the racial representation of recaptives in 1850s print culture. Chapter 2 follows the *Echo* recaptives' arrival in Charleston in 1858. While West Central African shipmates sought to survive their physical trauma and social crisis in the confines of Fort Sumter, local attempts at ethnological inquiry and slave trade tourism thrived in a proslavery atmosphere. Chapter 3 turns to the recaptive camp at Fort Taylor, Key West, in the summer of 1860. It examines how recaptives reconstituted a tenuous social life amidst death under the gaze of popular illustrated news stories that turned suffering into spectacle.

In the second half of the book, although racial representation remains relevant as a context for recaptive struggles, the analysis turns to the social experience of recaptive Africans as historical subjects of forced migration caught up in the uneven processes of Atlantic emancipation. Chapter 4 explores how James Pennington and other African American activists in the New York area advocated for recaptured Africans with a radical formulation of equal rights based on human unity. Chapter 5 considers recaptives as forced migrants on their passage to Liberia, a journey that echoed the middle passage but also served as the matrix for new shipmate relationships. Finally, Chapter 6 explores how these former slave ship captives—embarked from Ouidah and the Congo River region—began the next phase of their displacement in Liberian apprenticeships. Just as they had throughout the entire Atlantic odyssey, shipmate relations played a crucial role in the future social worlds built by recaptives now called "Congoes" in Liberia.

Africans recaptured from the mid-nineteenth-century slave trade, as this study shows, journeyed through a dangerous liminal space between enslavement and an uncertain future. By dwelling on the bleak spaces adjacent, but not identical, to enslaved captivity, *Recaptured Africans* explores the meaning of recapture for slave ship survivors in U.S. custody. The following pages thus present a bifurcated view of recaptivity as a confrontation with both the alienation of enslavement and a racially caricatured representation of "native Africans" in need of white rescue. An existential gap opened between the urgency of recaptives' fragile shipmate bonds and the inability of almost any American observers to recognize the survival imperatives of those same bonds. That gap in human comprehension was also a spawn, to paraphrase Frederick Douglass, of the slaveholding republic's polluted nest. In the racialized representation of American print culture, slave trade survivors could only exit the status of human commodity through the door of ethnographic spectacle. Other routes of exit—such as that of the civic personhood fought for by free blacks and abolitionists in northern states—were foreclosed by recaptives' legal status as outsiders mandated for removal and the increasingly biological definitions of race that turned slave trade refugees into traveling specimens of "interior" Africa. Remarkably, those who survived this vast oceanic circuit drew on shipmate bonds and the social resources of their past to painstakingly craft a new collective existence in Liberian "Congo" communities. With one foot in saltwater slavery and one foot on alien ground, recaptive voyagers outlined the borderlands that foreshadowed the future perils of a postemancipation Atlantic World.

1

Recaptives of a Slaveholding Republic

For if the influence of economic motives on the action of
mankind ever had clearer illustration it was in the modern
history of the African race, and particularly in America.

—W. E. B. Du Bois, "Apologia," in 1954 reprint of
*The Suppression of the African Slave-Trade, to the
United States of America* [1896]

At the age of eighty-six, W. E. B. Du Bois took a rare opportunity to reflect back over sixty years of his own scholarship to his Harvard dissertation on the suppression of the transatlantic slave trade to the United States. Du Bois's carefully researched study, published in 1896, framed the troubled enforcement of U.S. slave trade abolition laws as a moral challenge to a nation whose highest court had just enshrined the *Plessy v. Ferguson* decision. In the conclusion to the original work, Du Bois had demanded, "How far in a State can a recognized moral wrong safely be compromised?"[1] By 1954, however, Du Bois critiqued as simplistic the idea that human behavior was motivated by "a series of conscious moral judgments." From his mid-twentieth-century vantage point, Du Bois remained proud of the study but regretted his "ignorance" of Freudian and Marxist theory. From Freud, he implied, he would have borrowed the insight of complex psychological responses to the politics of abolition that contributed to the persistence of racial inequality. Informed by Marx, he wrote, he would have substituted a focus on "moral lassitude" with an analysis of "the willingness of a privileged class of Americans to get power and comfort at the expense of degrading a class of black slaves."[2] For the mature Du Bois, the suppression of the slave trade could be understood not as a narrow encounter between individual conscience and the law but, rather, as the product of entangled histories of global labor, racial subordination, and economic interest.[3]

These entangled histories generated a new kind of captive experience for African children, men, and women seized by the United States from illegal slave ships in the era of second slavery. "Second slavery," a concept first introduced by historian Dale Tomich, aims to shift our understanding of nineteenth-century slavery from a national to a global framework.[4] From this vantage point, antebellum U.S. slavery constituted part of a larger "second cycle of slavery," stretching from roughly 1804 to the 1880s and linking sites of production where slavery persisted as a dominant form of labor. Following the Haitian and British emancipations, U.S., Brazilian, and Cuban slaveholders accelerated plantation production to meet the demands of consumers in industrializing societies. The expansion of sugar, cotton, and coffee production would not have been possible without a thriving contraband transatlantic slave trade that forcibly disembarked at least 2.8 million Africans primarily in Cuba and Brazil, facilitated in part by U.S. resources.[5] The small number of recaptured Africans diverted from this slave trade by U.S. intervention thus entered a society increasingly defined by the racial politics and economic interests of second slavery.

U.S. transatlantic slave trade laws reflected the internal contradictions of suppression policies developed by a second slavery nation. As this chapter will show, U.S. policies on recaptured Africans evolved over time, treating recaptives first as saleable property and then as potentially dangerous foreigners designated for exclusion. From 1808 to 1819, recaptives brought into the United States found themselves at the mercy of state laws, treated as moveable property, and subject to continued enslavement. In 1819, federal law shifted responsibility for slave ship recaptives to federal jurisdiction but required the government to transport all recaptives beyond U.S. borders. Even then, many slave trade refugees endured years of detention in the United States under protracted legal proceedings resulting from sectional, political party, and international disputes. Colonizationists spoke about recaptive removal using the humanitarian rhetoric of repatriation, but few recaptives ever saw their homelands again. Throughout the 1840s and much of the 1850s, recaptive policy remained an abstract issue due to the rarity of slave ship interceptions by the United States. Only in the 1858–62 period did more aggressive naval enforcement bring thousands of recaptives into U.S. custody, including nearly 1,800 Africans who arrived under intense scrutiny in Charleston and Key West. By examining the entire evolution of U.S. recaptive policy with its distinctive emphasis on federal removal, we can begin to understand how shipmates from the *Echo*, *Wildfire*, *William*, and *Bogota* slave ships were appropriated as symbols in the heated slavery debates of the late antebellum period.

The contested politics of recaptivity drew heavily on representations of Africans and the illegal slave trade in Anglo-American print culture. Specifically, the wide circulation of African travel accounts in 1850s popular print culture generated a literary genre I call "slave trade ethnography," which significantly shaped Americans' interpretation of the unfamiliar figure of the slave trade recaptive.[6] Naval accounts such as Commander Andrew Hull Foote's *Africa and the American Flag* and slaver narratives like *Captain Canot, or Twenty Years of an African Slaver*, both published in 1854, fed the appetite of readers for ethnographic fare.[7] In addition to recounting travel adventures, these works painted an ahistorical portrait of African "customs and manners" and positioned slave trade victims as objects of white rescue.[8] Furthermore, by depicting Africans—and, by extension, slave trade recaptives—as permanently dependent and civically incapacitated, regardless of age, slave trade ethnography obscured the very real presence of child captives in the late transatlantic slave trade. Such representations of illegally trafficked Africans in U.S. print culture form part of the broader cultural history of second slavery.

U.S. Slave Trade Suppression in the Era of Second Slavery

African recaptives came into U.S. custody in the late 1850s through transatlantic routes developed over decades of contraband slaving. The financial integration of nineteenth-century trade in "legitimate" goods and contraband people proves the fallacy of a sharp break between slavery and free labor. As mercantilist restrictions on shipping and commerce gave way to free trade ideals, global capital flows linked illicit slaving and legal commerce.[9] Americans became leading consumers of Brazilian coffee and Cuban molasses, grown and processed by illegally trafficked African laborers.[10] Moreover, emerging trade routes linked commerce from U.S. ports such as New York and Baltimore to an internationally diverse group of merchants and slavers along the West African coast.[11] British credit financed the modern infrastructure of "railroad, steamship, and steam mills" necessary to move sugar, coffee, and cotton to European markets.[12] Both U.S. and British legislators balked at regulations that would have prevented the sale of ships or trade goods to parties either indirectly or directly involved with transatlantic slave trading.[13] Observing the ability of known slavers to buy American goods and access British credit, naval officer Horatio Bridge wondered "how far either Old or New England can be pronounced free from the guilt and odium of the slave trade, while, with so little indirectness, they both share its profits and contribute essential aid to its prosecution."[14] Despite the early slave trade abolitions, the global flow of capital financed human and nonhuman commodities well into the nineteenth century.

Historians have long argued that the rise of African commercial goods deemed "legitimate" developed in symbiosis with a continued slave trade from and within Africa.[15] Increasing African exportation of palm oil, peanuts, and ivory frequently relied on slave labor to gather or grow and transport these "legitimate" commodities. The labor requirements of the new palm oil industry in Ouidah, for example, actually stimulated demand for enslaved workers, leading to an expansion of internal slavery in Dahomey.[16] In West Central Africa, enslaved captives transported tons of ivory in Ovimbundu caravans trekking from the central highlands to the Angolan coast.[17] Nineteenth-century Bobangi traders on the Congo River used their wealth gained from ivory sales to buy slaves and build large lineages of enslaved wives and children.[18] Luso-African planters in Angola also utilized slave labor to produce sugar and cotton for overseas markets.[19] This entanglement of "legitimate" exports with the slave trade and African systems of slavery contributed to the persistence of the transatlantic slave trade despite international action taken against it.[20]

U.S. participation in transatlantic slaving during the entire period of illegality similarly relied on overlapping networks of legal and contraband trade. As recent work by historian Leonardo Marques shows, despite fairly successful curtailment of the incoming slave trade by 1820, U.S. crews, equipment, and ships proved deeply complicit in slave trafficking to Cuba and Brazil.[21] High demand for fast clipper ships from Spanish and Portuguese slave trading firms, for example, reinvigorated the U.S. shipbuilding industry, particularly in Baltimore. Of almost 1,700 documented slaving voyages in the 1830s, 63 percent occurred on ships built in the United States. From 1836 to 1850, during the period of heaviest Brazilian contraband trade, U.S. ships and crews played a major role in the illegal slave trade by carrying equipment and trading goods to the African coast for purchase by Spanish and Portuguese slave traders.[22] In the last phase of the illegal transatlantic trade following effective Brazilian slave trade abolition in 1851, U.S. port cities like New York and New Orleans served as headquarters for international slave trading firms, who availed themselves of lax customs enforcement and the cover of legitimate commerce to launch slave voyages and launder money.[23] Finally, in those same years, the U.S. flag became the standard under which contraband traders could move their human cargo without British intervention. What made these financial and legal machinations possible was the consistent refusal of the United States to sign mutual search rights treaties with Great Britain.

The British-led international campaign that historians now call slave trade suppression aimed explicitly to cultivate new commercial ties while eradicating the banned traffic in human captives. Even before the landmark 1807 abolition of the British transatlantic slave trade, British antislavery advocates had envisioned increased commerce with Africa made possible by the end of the slave trade and the extraction of new commodities.[24] Maritime dominance and colonial wealth gave Britain the resources to extend its empire to the African continent by degrees throughout the nineteenth century. The 1841 Niger Expedition championed by Thomas Fowell Buxton, for example, illustrated the tight ideological and economic connections between slave trade suppression and Europe's greater access to African agricultural and mineral resources.[25] Furthermore, the British naval attack on Lagos in 1851 and subsequent annexation of the West African port city a decade later demonstrated the antislavery rationale for a new era of commodity production and commercial expansion. Historian Kristin Mann succinctly captures the imperialist ethos of the Lagos occupation: "Foreign commerce, it was felt, would bring not only material progress but also moral uplift. In West Africa, the final campaign to end the slave trade and the drive for commercial expansion were intimately related and mutually compatible."[26]

Interception of suspicious ships at sea rather than coastal raids, however, remained the dominant European strategy of slave trade suppression. From 1815 forward, Britain used its rising maritime dominance to pursue a "treaty network" organized around the strategies of mutual rights of search, mixed-commission courts, and joint naval cruising, supplemented by slave trade abolition treaties with African rulers.[27] After the conclusion of the Napoleonic Wars and the Congress of Vienna, Britain urged the United States, as it had other European nations, to join multilateral treaties allowing mutual rights of search of suspicious vessels at sea. In 1815 and 1817, Portugal and Spain, respectively, signed treaties to ban the transatlantic slave trade north of the equator. Britain's continued pursuit of suppression through international treaties in the 1820s and '30s established the British navy's right to board suspicious vessels flying the flag of Spain and newly independent Brazil in 1826. In the wake of the 1833 British Slavery Abolition Act, antislavery members of Parliament pursued "equipment articles" that defined certain items of cargo, such as extra water or surplus rations, as evidence of illegal intent and legitimate grounds for seizure of a suspect ship, even in the absence of enslaved captives.[28] Mixed-commission courts set up in Havana and Sierra Leone addressed complex international maritime disputes created by the seizure of suspected slavers. By 1839, the powerful British Royal Navy had also asserted its right to board ships flying the Portuguese flag in the southern hemisphere as well.[29] Finally, British officials used military force, naval blockades, and diplomacy to secure a series of agreements with slave trading polities, such as the Kingdom of Dahomey, to end the slave trade and encourage alternative forms of commerce.[30]

Until Abraham Lincoln's administration, however, the United States refused to grant right-of-search privileges or sign bilateral treaties sought by Britain.[31] The financial interests of intransigent U.S. slave traders had a hand in early resistance to negotiations with Britain. For example, in 1819, an amendment removing mutual search rights from an Anglo-American treaty came from Senator James DeWolf, brother to George DeWolf, an active slave trader in the Rhode Island merchant family.[32] Moreover, with recent memories of the 1812 war fought against British infringements on U.S. ships, many Americans agreed with John Quincy Adams's feelings that granting rights of search to Britain would be "making slaves of ourselves."[33] Naval commander Andrew Hull Foote likewise defended the principle that "the deck of an American vessel under its flag, is the territory of the United States, and no other authority but that of the United States must ever be allowed to exercise jurisdiction over it."[34] In 1842, the U.S. government took a small step toward international cooperation with Britain when it signed the Webster-Ashburton Treaty, whose section 8 established a joint cruising agreement for British vessels and U.S. Africa Squadron ships with a minimum force each of eighty guns.[35]

In the shadow of British maritime power, U.S. businessmen also sought to forge their own legal trade relations with West African merchants. The volume of U.S. maritime trade to West Africa grew over the course of the nineteenth century, although often entangled with the banned traffic in human captives.[36] During the 1850s, Congress entertained requests to subsidize West African inland explorations intended to lead toward the expansion of U.S. business firms supported by a line of steamers carrying U.S. mail. The support of Boston merchant William Sturgis, Southern Baptist missionary Thomas Jefferson Bowen, naval commander William Lynch, and American Colonization Society (ACS) secretary Ralph Gurley for a U.S.-sponsored expedition illustrated the convergence of U.S. military, church, and business interests in West Africa during the mid-nineteenth century.[37] Indeed, Africa Squadron officers from 1842 through 1859 received instructions from the secretary of the navy that actually placed slave trade suppression second to the primary assignment of protecting "the right of our citizens engaged in lawful commerce."[38] Specifically, naval military instructions sought to shield

U.S. merchant ships from being boarded by British antislavery patrols. Overall, U.S. responses to multilateral treaties demonstrate how free trade ideals and concerns of national sovereignty served as obstacles to an effective international effort to end the slave trade.[39]

By midcentury it was a matter of common knowledge among critics that the U.S. refusal to sign mutual search treaties created a wide loophole for slavers working the international contraband trade. As vessels bearing first the Spanish and then the Portuguese flag became subject to British search and seizure, slave ships increasingly displayed the U.S. flag to ward off British boarding parties.[40] Frederick Douglass denounced the situation in 1858 when he charged that the "stealers of men . . . have only to run up the stars and stripes, when pursued by an honest man-of-war, to be safe from pursuit."[41] The hypocrisy of the situation grated hard on former Africa Squadron officer Robert Wilson Shufeldt, who struggled to reconcile his view of the United States as a virtuous republic with the clearance of clandestine slavers from American harbors: "She sails out of port some bright morning with the American flag, that beautiful emblem of liberty to the oppressed—flaunting to the breeze—& speeds on a mission—the horrors & cruelties of which my pen can not describe."[42] Of course, American warships *could* seize slave ships flying the U.S. flag, but the tiny Africa Squadron could not operate effectively along hundreds of miles of African coastline.[43] From the USS *Yorktown*, naval surgeon John Fox articulated the frustration of many Africa Squadron personnel longing for a prize capture when he wrote to his wife, Elizabeth, "We are perfectly useless here so far as the slave trade is concerned."[44] A *New York Times* correspondent, observing the operation of slavers near the mouth of the Congo River in 1860, compared the successful interception of an illegal slave ship by an American cruiser to "an angel's visit—a thing of many fews and far betweens."[45]

Only in the late 1850s, when the illegal transatlantic trade flowed primarily to Cuba, did the United States augment its abolition enforcement efforts. In 1859, navy secretary Isaac Toucey almost doubled the size of the Africa Squadron by establishing a force of eight vessels, including four smaller steamships capable of moving well in shallow coastal waters.[46] Democratic president James Buchanan also ordered ships from the U.S. Home Squadron to cruise along Cuba's northern coast. In so doing, the Buchanan administration sought to defuse Whig and Republican outcries over several developments: slave trade revivalism lodged in the southern wing of the Democratic Party, United States filibustering in Cuba and Central America, and the recent successful landing of the slaver *Wanderer* in Georgia. Furthermore, Buchanan used the

Home Squadron deployments to counter British diplomatic pressure on the American government to curb the participation of U.S. ships and citizens in the illegal traffic to Cuba.[47] By the summer of 1860, the naval steamers *Crusader, Wyandotte, Mohawk,* and *Water Witch* alternated patrols to maintain a presence along the Cuban coast, while resupplying at Key West and Pensacola.[48]

As a result, naval patrols seized ten suspected slavers carrying almost three-quarters of all recaptured Africans ever to enter U.S. custody.[49] Four of these vessels carried the recaptive shipmates at the center of this study: numerous young West Central Africans on the *Echo, Wildfire,* and *William* and an older group mostly comprised of Yoruba-speaking war captives on the *Bogota.* The arrival of all of these recaptives on U.S. soil forced federal officials to enact a removal policy whose precedent had been in place since the 1820s but seldom utilized.

Implementing Recaptive Removal Policy, 1819–1845

Although there is a lively historiographic debate evaluating U.S. slave trade suppression, remarkably little sustained attention is given to the treatment of African recaptives in U.S. hands.[50] In part, this is due to the small size of the population in question. All of the world's naval patrols together managed to divert only 6 percent of illegally trafficked Africans. Of these, only a tiny fraction (roughly 3 percent of all African captives intercepted) came under U.S. control.[51] Despite their small numbers, however, recaptives represented a significant political legal category, whose midway position between enslavement and free status sparked congressional debate and state-federal tensions.[52] Furthermore, the sudden arrival of so many traumatized people presenting urgent human needs posed significant logistical challenges to government officials operating without an established concept of refugees or displaced persons.[53] Indeed, the continued tendency of U.S. officials to see recaptives much like the domestically enslaved—as potential property and exploitable labor—often pushed humanitarian concerns to the side. African recaptives newly removed from slave ships consequently experienced further displacement and separation, often-lethal living conditions, and even reenslavement.

In the years immediately following the 1807 Act to Prohibit the Importation of Slaves, U.S. law treated recaptive status as virtually indistinguishable from that of chattel slavery. During early national legislative debates, states' rights Jeffersonians resisted both the concession to federal power and the potential for adding to the free black population represented by slave trade regulation statutes. As a result, the abolition law came at the cost of provisions that would leave the disposition of recaptive Africans to state and territorial legislatures, which in most cases meant the auctioning of recaptives to southern planters for the benefit of state treasuries and the expanding plantation economy.[54] In the words of one of the provision's congressional opponents: "We punish the criminal, and then step into his place, and complete the crime."[55] State and territorial laws across the South established their own instructions concerning the sale of recaptive Africans and the distribution of resulting funds.[56] The absence of federal records for this period, however, makes it difficult to determine how states and territories applied the law to actual recaptives.[57] In some protracted court cases, it appears that local officials and their planter associates quietly took possession of Africans awaiting disposition.[58]

The shift to a federal removal policy occurred during sensitive U.S. diplomatic discussions with Spain for Florida and Britain's negotiations on international slave trade suppression treaties. In 1817, U.S. federal troops attacked a thriving hub of privateers and slave smugglers on Amelia Island in East Florida.[59] The attack revealed how the illegal slave trade was caught up in early U.S. efforts to establish diplomatic relations with Europe. As historian Eliga Gould has argued, the new American republic sought recognition as a sovereign power according to "the law of nations."[60] Under President James Monroe's administration, Congress therefore passed several supplementary transatlantic slave trade laws that served as the legal apparatus for U.S. policy up to the Abraham Lincoln administration. An 1820 statute—observed only in the breach—defined American citizens' participation in the African slave trade as piracy, and therefore a capital crime. Most relevant for recaptives, an 1819 act shifted responsibility for recaptive disposition from state to federal jurisdiction. Section 2 of the 1819 Act in Addition to the Acts Prohibiting the Slave Trade empowered the president to remove all Africans found on illegal slavers "beyond the limits of the United States." The act also asserted U.S. sovereignty abroad by authorizing naval patrols and the appointment of a U.S. recaptured African agent on the African coast.[61] In legal terms, the prohibition against the selling of seized Africans by state governments placed recaptives beyond the commodification of chattel slavery. Notably, it did so without mention of the "liberated" status by which such recaptives would become known in British rhetoric.

In terms of domestic slavery politics, the 1819 language of removal also reflected contentious debates over race and civic capacity in the antebellum United States.[62] As early as the 1780s, Thomas Jefferson had listed historical resentments and natural difference as arguments against measures to "incorporate the blacks into the state."[63] Early national debates over American slavery raised the question of the status of free blacks, who in those very years were building a collective voice for inclusion in U.S. citizenship.[64] White fears of political disruption caused by free blacks merged with the heightened white alarm over the possibility of southern slave revolts in the aftermath of the Haitian Revolution.[65] The ACS, founded in 1816 and composed of many leading statesmen of the day, built upon these anxieties to craft a colonizationist agenda for an experimental black settlement in West Africa that would protect the whiteness of citizenship at home. Colonization offered moderate antislavery advocates the opportunity for gradual abolition and a "free soil" colony in West Africa. In turn, moderate southern slaveholders found reassurance in the promised removal of free blacks, whom they had long considered a destabilizing element for the enslaved population.[66] Antipathy against civic inclusion of people of color in the United States deepened alongside the shift from environmental theories of difference to biological theories of race applied not only to free African Americans but to Native Americans and Mexicans as well.[67] Indeed, it is no coincidence that the movement for Indian removal emerged within a decade of the 1819 African recaptive removal mandate.

Nor was there any coincidence in the timing of the 1819 act to align with initial U.S. forays into colonization that would eventually result in the ACS settlement of Liberia. The ACS, argues historian Eric Burin, used the question of recaptive disposition as "a new tool with which to pry open the federal coffers."[68] The 1819 bill's author, Virginia congressman Charles Fenton Mercer, also served as an ACS manager. A small portion of the $100,000 appropriation, included in Mercer's provisions, would give the ACS the resources it needed to establish a colonial foothold in West Africa.[69] Initial attempts by eighty-six African American emigrants to settle at Sherbo Island, just south of the British colony of Freetown, Sierra Leone, failed due to high mortality and political dissent. Late in 1821, ACS agent Eli Ayres and U.S. Navy lieutenant Robert Stockton forced through a treaty with Dei leader King Peter in an infamous scene of pistol diplomacy.[70] Black American emigrants and white missionaries struggled with heavy mortality as well as militant resistance from Dei and other indigenous polities they displaced and whose trade they disrupted. By 1823, however, a tiny colony of roughly 150 people lived in the settlement that came to be known as Monrovia.[71] American slave trade suppression legislation thus represented a crucial funding stream for the ACS, while the removal policy promised a source of new immigrants for the Liberian project.

Due to the slow pace of U.S. slave trade intervention, however, the primary migrants to Liberia over the course of the mid-nineteenth century came from the United States. Between 1820 and 1850, the ACS and the separate Maryland Colonization Society sent almost 7,000 free and manumitted black American emigrants to Liberia.[72] Although Liberia declared its independence as a black republic in 1847, the settler population remained closely tied to the ACS, which continued to post agents, send emigrant ships, and recruit support for colonization in the United States. Larger numbers of formerly enslaved emigrants arrived in Liberia during the 1850s, often with fewer resources than free African American emigrants who came from the northern states. The Liberian outpost, designed as an asylum for recaptive Africans, thus emerged as a colonial society with its own order of class and caste.[73]

The cases of the *Antelope*, *Fenix*, and *General Páez* represent early precedents for later recaptive removals to Liberia. As the following discussion demonstrates, African men, women, and children seized by the United States from suspect ships continued to be treated as latent property and exploitable laborers. Historian Rebecca Scott notes that even people of color with clear free status in one part of the Atlantic World were vulnerable to having others "find property in their persons" once they traveled to another location.[74] The liminal status of recaptives held in the expanding slaveholding republic of the United States proved at least as vulnerable. The removal mandate ostensibly protected recaptives from reenslavement in southern states, yet district courts often struggled with the question of whether Africans seized on particular ships qualified for federally funded removal and colonization under the 1819 statute.

The well-known case of the *Antelope* illuminates the difficulties of applying and implementing the removal mandate. Registered to a Spanish owner in Cuba but under the control of a privateer crew commissioned by South American revolutionary forces, the *Antelope* became embroiled in a maritime legal dispute with Spanish and Portuguese claimants over the disposition of African captives.[75] On 29 June 1820, the revenue cutter *Dallas* seized the *Antelope* on the northeast coast of Florida with 280 enslaved Africans embarked from Cabinda, a slaving port just north of the Congo River. By late July, U.S. marshal John Morel took custody of 258 Africans (an unaccounted-for reduction from the original number), whom he corralled in hastily built sheds at Savannah's racetrack. While a seven-year legal battle wound its way to the U.S. Supreme Court, district court judge William Davies ordered 51 of the most "prime" captives to labor on the city fortifications. Marshal Morel brought more than 100 young captives to his own plantation and hired out most of the rest to Savannah elites, including doctors, judges, and a toll road contractor. By the end of 1820, almost 50 had died and at least 1 young man had fled or been kidnapped.[76] Having already endured captivity in West Central Africa, pirate ship attacks, and the middle passage, the *Antelope* shipmates now lived under conditions that differed little from those of other enslaved Africans in Georgia.

Treated as virtual property even before the trial, young captives from the *Antelope* experienced further threat of enslavement in a May 1821 Sixth Circuit Court decision. Despite U.S. attorney Richard Habersham's continued attempts to argue for the free status of all *Antelope* captives, Judge William Johnson ordered the division of 204 *Antelope* survivors into three groups: Spanish property, Portuguese property, and 16 men and boys designated as recaptives subject to U.S. removal law.[77] Underscoring the commodification implicit in the judicial ruling, officials used a lottery to select the small group of African shipmates released from the Portuguese and Spanish claims.[78] Yet their ordeal was far from over. Not until March 1827 did the Supreme Court make its final decision, leaving 39 recaptives enslaved with the Spanish and releasing the remaining 131 survivors to American authorities for removal.[79]

The group of former *Antelope* shipmates, now including a second generation of infants and children, sailed to Liberia on the ACS ship *Norfolk* in July 1827, to become some of the first inhabitants of the recaptive town known as New Georgia.[80] Among the *Norfolk* travelers, at least three families of *Antelope* women and children left behind husbands and fathers, designated as Spanish property but eventually enslaved in Georgia.[81] In the ACS rosters, twenty-three of the migrants bore Habersham's last name, a sign of their sojourn in the wilderness of the American legal system. Indicative as well of their travails as Atlantic captives, not to mention the high mortality endemic to Liberian emigrant society, only 23 percent of the original *Antelope* shipmates remained alive in New Georgia by 1844.[82]

Legal disputes also produced long detention periods and further journeying for 82 African captives seized near Haiti by the USS *Grampus* aboard the schooner *Fenix* on 5 June 1830.[83] Like the *Antelope*, the *Fenix* was also registered to a Spanish owner. Because the *Grampus* intervened after the *Fenix*'s alleged act of "piratical aggression" on the U.S. brig *Kremlin*, District Attorney John Slidell brought suit against the ship for violation of an 1819 piracy statute rather than the 1819 slave trade law. Attorney General John Macpherson Berrien, who had been involved with the *Antelope* trials as well, argued that a Spanish ship "manned and navigated by Spaniards" could not be prosecuted under the 1819 slave trade act and thus U.S. officials could not avail themselves of the removal provision to transport the *Fenix* recaptives to Liberia. Meanwhile, recaptives languished on the ship as it sailed from Key West to Pensacola. The surviving shipmates were finally allowed to leave the crowded schooner six weeks after naval seizure, and U.S. marshal John Nicholson placed them with nearby slaveowners, where they were expected to labor in return for provision.[84]

Once again, lawyers argued over which statutes applied because the *Fenix* had been seized as a pirate ship, not as a slaver. The Spanish owner of the vessel attempted, unsuccessfully in this case, to make a claim on the ship's African captives. Alfred Hennen, a noted New Orleans jurist and past vice president of the Louisiana Colonization Society, filed a motion of habeas corpus for the African shipmates, on the grounds that they were "free men."[85] On 30 July, Samuel H. Harper of the U.S. Eastern District Court of Louisiana issued an ex parte decision rejecting Hennen's writ. Harper first argued that "foreign negroes, however introduced," must "in *all cases* either be sent home, or in some way be excluded from the United States."[86] Citing Louisiana's own laws excluding new arrivals of free people of color, Harper asserted that "slavery would be a blessing" in comparison with allowing recaptives to remain in the country, subject to hostile black codes. Second, he noted that ongoing court proceedings also required the detention of the "African negroes." Ultimately, in a March 1831 decision, Justice Harper rejected the Spanish claim and turned the remaining 62 recaptives over to federal authorities for removal "beyond the limits of the United States." Congress then appropriated $6,000 for the navy's transport of *Fenix* survivors to Liberia.[87] Four more years passed, however, before only 37 of 82 original shipmates of the *Fenix* sailed on the ACS ship *Louisiana* for Monrovia, where they also received lands in New Georgia. How many had perished in New Orleans and how many remained behind in slavery is not clear.[88]

Removal rarely held out hope for repatriation of African captives to their specific homelands, as the cases of the *Antelope* and *Fenix* attest. One exceptional instance, however, occurred in August 1822, when the schooner *General Páez* arrived in Baltimore carrying fourteen Africans recently seized from a slave ship by privateer Captain John Chase.[89] Although Chase claimed the men as legitimate crew members, Baltimore abolitionists and colonization society members attempted to gain custody of the Africans by charging Chase with violating U.S. slave trade laws.[90] Over more than a year of legal maneuvering, the West African men and boys were held first in the city's poorhouse and later in a Baltimore jail.[91] In the spring of 1823, the U.S. district court judge ruled that federal slave trade laws did not apply to a privateering vessel such as *General Páez*, and thus Africans found aboard the ship could not be considered recaptives under the 1819 law.[92] Yet the Monroe administration, under increasing pressure from the British and seeking to craft a response consistent with the newly issued doctrine of hemispheric influence, still faced the question of the stranded Africans' future. Furthermore, with Liberian colonization now considered more viable, ACS agents such as Eli Ayers hoped to garner government support by engineering an African return.

What happened next illuminates the conditions necessary for a process even remotely approximating repatriation and the reasons for most recaptives' permanent exile. In early 1823, Richard Wilkinson, an Anglo-Baga trader from the Rio Pongo trading region, arrived on business in Baltimore. Wilkinson soon agreed to act as interpreter in an interview between ten of the *General Páez* shipmates, U.S. naval agent James Beatty, ACS advocate and Federalist statesman Robert Goodloe Harper, and U.S. attorney Elias Glenn.[93] Although fearful of betrayal at first, each African man or boy responded affirmatively to the offer to sail at government expense to Liberia. One man named Dowrey, for example, explained that he could walk to his home from Cape Mesurado in only three days. Like the rest of his shipmates he strongly favored repatriation, however difficult the voyage: "I wish to go home, I wish to see my father, my wife and children." Another man named Cubangerie inquired, "Why do you ask this over and over? Do you not know that nothing is so dear as a man's home?"[94] No doubt much was lost in translation and filtered through the American interviewers' ideal of an African nuclear family.[95] Yet the men clearly conveyed the sense that freedom could only be fully realized through restoration of kin. Their answers may also have been strategic, revealing the men's understanding that their best chance for return depended on articulating their familial claims and their former free status. One young boy for whom Wilkinson could not translate remained in Baltimore, but ten older shipmates left Baltimore in October 1823 on Wilkinson's ship *Fidelity*. They disembarked at Cape Mesurado, where ACS leaders reported they were reunited with "friends."[96] To what extent they reunited with the specific family members named in their interviews remains uncertain.

Overall, in its first decades of implementation, the 1819 law created an alternative to reenslavement for slave trade recaptives, yet it functioned more as a deportation order than a repatriation policy.[97] Although U.S. courts ultimately ruled that neither the *Antelope*, the *Fenix*, nor the *General Páez* came under the 1819 slave trade act, officials nonetheless followed a policy of removal (with the exception of the *Antelope* shipmates designated for Spanish claims). As Judge Samuel H. Harper put it in his *Fenix* decision, African recaptives would be "kept, supported and removed beyond the limits of the United States."[98] These African voyages to Liberia foreshadowed how recaptive settlement could serve ACS interests in establishing the organization's colonial footprint. Only the much-celebrated group of *Amistad* shipmates, freed by a U.S. Supreme Court ruling in 1841, followed a path of difficult repatriation similar to that of the *General Páez* recaptives.[99] In both the *General Páez* and *Amistad* cases, adequate translators helped recaptives gain a voice in the proceedings. Furthermore, each of these two shipmate groups was smaller and included adult men, compared with the hundreds of destitute youth of the *Echo*, *Wildfire*, and *William*. Finally, in each case a vested interest beyond the recaptives' repatriation came into play: Wilkinson's interest in strengthening Baltimore trade networks with Rio Pongo and the ACS's bid for recognition in the first case and, in the second, the Union Missionary Society's interest in establishing their West African mission.[100]

One other important earlier journey anticipated a final dimension of American recaptive policies in the 1858–62 period. Following the deployment of a small U.S. Africa Squadron, a prize crew from the USS *Yorktown* boarded the slaver *Pons* in 1845 and discovered 900 young captives recently embarked from Cabinda. This time there was no question as to the disposition of weakened captives who had received no food in the three days since their voyage began. As naval commander Charles Bell explained, he chose the shortest course by which recaptives could be removed from their terrible imprisonment.[101] The prize crew sailed for Monrovia, Liberia, before taking the vessel to Philadelphia for trial.[102] Thus recaptives of the *Pons* endured a shortened middle passage, sailing under U.S. naval supervision for a sixteen-day journey to Liberia. This voyage set the U.S. precedent for transporting recaptives seized near the African coast in later years, while those taken from slavers on the approach to Cuba entered Charleston and Key West under intense public scrutiny and political controversy.

Slave Trade Ethnography of the 1850s

In contrast to the earlier slaver cases, the shipmates of the *Echo*, *Wildfire*, *William*, and *Bogota* entered a late antebellum U.S. society far more likely and able to sensationalize their presence. The development of an Anglo-American Dark Continent mythology of African superstition, ignorance, and savagery has been deeply explored by numerous historical and literary scholars.[103] More to the point for the American reception of U.S. recaptives, however, was the impact of popular interest in the illegal slave trade, which created a tension between the iconography of suffering middle passage victims and prevalent racial images of debased, barbaric "Africans." Several converging print culture trends made possible this juxtaposition of abject suffering and inherent depravity. First, the advent of the penny press and new illustration technologies allowed a much wider dissemination of newspapers, pamphlets, and books to mid-nineteenth-century readers. Second, these readers avidly consumed a fresh round of English-language missionary and exploration accounts of Africa published during the 1840s and '50s. David Livingstone's *Missionary Travels and Researches in South Africa* (1857), for example, was widely read and discussed on both sides of the Atlantic.[104] Third, the popularization of a brand of racial science known as the "American school of ethnology" challenged older theories of environmental difference and reinforced concepts of permanent, biological inequality among humans.[105] Together with the political turmoil that followed the Compromise of 1850, these converging cultural trends fed a genre of slave trade ethnography that obscured the social crisis of slave ship recaptives.

Despite U.S. historians' tendency to tell a domestically focused story of 1850s sectional politics, American newspapers in the period regularly covered all aspects of the clandestine transatlantic trade. High-profile trials in New York, Charleston, and Savannah not only popularized knowledge of illegal slaving and maritime law but also romanticized the outlaw figure of the slave trader.[106] In 1854, for example, accused slave captain James Smith of the brig *Julia Moulton* gave a markedly unrepentant and widely reprinted interview from his jail cell in the New York Tombs. Smith, according to the account, spoke "with the freedom and pride of an old soldier relating his battles."[107] These slaver trials, as scholar Jeannine DeLombard argues, crucially shaped discourse on "questions of national sovereignty and U.S. citizenship." Journalistic coverage of U.S. sailors and captains who toyed with the American flag as disguise and denied their own nationality to avoid prosecution under American laws forced readers to confront the uses and abuses of national citizenship.[108]

Furthermore, the covert landing of the *Wanderer* and the *Clotilda* in Georgia and Alabama, respectively, proffered the specter of the transatlantic slave trade's revival not just abroad but in the United States as well. In late November 1858, the *Wanderer*'s Captain William Corrie smuggled more than 300 West Central African boys across the bar at Jekyll Island. Rumors began to circulate through Lowcountry newspapers of slaveowners purchasing "wild Africans."[109] The trials that followed made headlines but produced no convictions. The case against the *Wanderer*'s owner Charles Augustus Lafayette

Lamar and his partners ended in mistrial in Savannah. Just one month after a Charleston jury returned a "Not Guilty" verdict on the *Echo* crew, U.S. district court judge Andrew Magrath nullified the 1820 federal piracy statute, and Captain Corrie walked free in Charleston.[110] In response, a satirical piece in New York's black-owned *Weekly Anglo-African* parodied the Democratic Convention of 1860 as a parade of "choice Southern melodies" that included the "'The Little Wanderer'—a new melody by Lamar."[111] The states' rights challenge to federal law heightened the visibility of these trials and tied the illegal slave trade to heated sectional politics.

Inciting more rumors of a revived African slave trade, the schooner *Clotilda* slipped up the Alabama River in July 1860 with 110 captives purchased at the Dahomean port of Ouidah. Timothy Meaher, the Mobile entrepreneur who funded the clandestine voyage, evaded federal officials and quickly put the smuggled captives to work in his cotton fields.[112] A defiant *Mobile Register* congratulated Meaher, taking a jab at federal recaptive policy for good measure. An editorial reassured readers that the "sons of Afric," safely stashed in Alabama, were "not likely to undergo what the imported darkies so detest— *deportation*." A reprint of the *Register*'s editorial in a San Francisco newspaper within just a few weeks indicated the national scope of interest in the story.[113] Closer to the scene of the crime, the *Charleston Daily Courier* posted news of the *Clotilda* within days.[114] Defiant acts of slave smuggling evoked cheers, curiosity, and outrage, reflecting the broad spectrum of public opinion and heightened awareness of the illegal transatlantic slave trade.

Given the controversy surrounding the illegal slave trade at midcentury, it is hardly surprising that memoirs and travel narratives from both naval officers and former slavers found an avid readership. To begin with the naval accounts, the creation of the U.S. Africa Squadron sent a whole cadre of American men into naval service along the western coast of Africa. Many of them shared one memoirist's belief that "the West Coast of Africa is a fresher field for the scribbling tourist, than most other parts of the world."[115] Throughout the 1840s and '50s, private letters, official reports, personal journals, and serialized travel accounts of naval officers circulated news of the slave trade and African travel.[116] Accounts of Africa Squadron activity along the western African coastline appeared in the aftermath of U.S. annexation of Mexican territory and in the decade of the Ostend Manifesto's belligerent claim on Cuba. Within this context of nation-building and expansionism, American naval forces deployed in the name of slave trade suppression constituted an early projection of U.S. power abroad, however weak and limited.[117] At the same time, naval narratives functioned for American readers as "cultural resources," which, as Mary Renda's study of U.S. Navy marine occupation of Haiti has demonstrated, articulated "new versions of Americanness" and ideas about "the U.S. role in the world."[118]

The best known of such accounts was Andrew H. Foote's widely reviewed 1854 volume, *Africa and the American Flag*. Commander of the U.S. naval brig *Perry* during an 1850–51 tour of duty, Foote aimed primarily to strengthen support for the U.S. Africa Squadron in a period when states' rights and proslavery advocates sought to remove Article 8 of the Webster-Ashburton Treaty. He also wrote the volume in general support of Liberian colonization and the defense of U.S. sovereignty at sea.[119] The combination of Foote's own travels along the western coast of Africa with excerpted missionary and exploration accounts appealed to readers as much for the "novelty" of its material on African "manners and customs" as for its analysis of the slave trade.[120] In this sense, *Africa and the American Flag* functioned as a work of slave trade ethnography and shared certain similarities with accounts by slave traders.

Even more than naval officers, the outlaw figure of the nineteenth-century slaver piqued public curiosity, eliciting both admiration and disgust. Slaver accounts in the 1850s emerged from a genre of "sea literature" that included stories of pirates, sailors, and castaways.[121] The most widely read and reviewed of the slaver narratives was Theodor Canot's *Captain Canot, or Twenty Years of an African Slaver* (1854), edited by Brantz Mayer. Born in Tuscany, Italy, in 1804, Theophilus Conneau shipped aboard his first slaver from Havana in his early twenties, eventually emerging as a well-known slave trader on the Upper Guinea under the name Theodor Canot.[122] During the 1840s, Canot came under increasing pressure to transition to legal commerce. U.S. courts eventually condemned and destroyed his slaving vessels.[123] By 1853, Maryland colonizationist leader Robert Hall introduced Canot to writer Brantz Mayer, and the two men began their literary collaboration.[124] Mayer, whose expansionist views had been shaped by diplomatic service during the U.S.–Mexico War, saw Canot's story as a golden opportunity to explore the question of Liberian colonization.[125] The edited version of Canot's memoir appeared in 1854 to laudable reviews and frequent excerpting by literary, religious, and political periodicals.[126]

Considered together, both naval and slaver texts illustrated the twisting racial logic by which encampments of slave trade refugees could be represented as venues of white imperial benevolence and ethnological exhibit. Both made use of literary conventions of sentience and suffering developed in the eighteenth-century abolitionist movement. Olaudah Equiano, for example, exemplified this strategic appeal to empathy when he wrote in 1789,

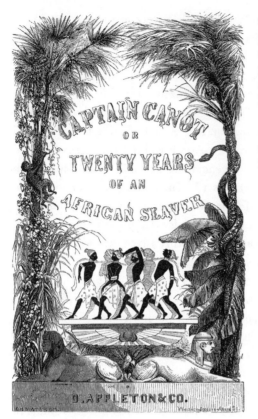

FIGURE 1.1 Egyptian iconography, palm trees, and tropical animals on the title page of *Captain Canot* portrayed this slave-trading memoir as an exotic African adventure. Brantz Mayer, *Captain Canot or Twenty Years of an African Slaver* (New York: Appleton, 1854). Courtesy of the Huntington Library, San Marino, California.

"Such a tendency has the slave-trade to debauch men's minds, and harden them to every feeling of humanity!"[127] Foote's and Canot's publications clearly draw upon the conventions of middle passage horrors. Yet, by the mid-nineteenth century, these phrases threatened to become stock tropes, liable to manipulation. Enlightenment treatments of the "noble savage" shifted to the "savage savage," and gothic elements began to appear alongside appeals to sentiment in slave trade literature.[128] Thus both Foote and Canot, while using the respectable discourse of ethnographic inquiry, indulged in exotic tales of human sacrifice and barbarous violence.

In *Africa and the American Flag*, Foote gave lengthy descriptions of the suffering of African children, women, and men whose illegal trafficking the USS *Perry* aimed to suppress. During Foote's assignment, however, the Africa Squadron failed to seize even a single slaver loaded with captives. Nevertheless, Foote and his publisher understood that the narrative would lack emotional impact without descriptions of the slave trade's human victims. *Africa and the American Flag* found its abject images in the heartrending story of the failed British interception of the *Veloz* in the 1830s and in naval accounts of the *Pons* capture in 1845. Both excerpts focused particularly on the suffering of children increasingly trafficked in the nineteenth century. Borrowing from British reports, for example, Foote excerpted Robert Walsh's account of hundreds of "poor suffering creatures" packed so tightly below the *Veloz's* deck that they could not even move. "There were found some children next to the sides of the ship, in the places most remote from air and light," recounted a witness. "The little creatures seemed indifferent as to life or death; and when they were carried on deck, many of them could not stand."[129] Similar descriptions on the *Pons* from Captain Charles Bell warned readers that "none but an eye witness can form a conception of the horrors these poor creatures must endure in their transit across the ocean." The pathos of the *Pons* recaptives appeared most starkly in Foote's account, excerpted from a Liberian newspaper, of a dying young boy being tended by two brothers "of the same tribe."[130]

Perhaps more surprising was how the slaver Canot also invoked the horrors engineered by his own trade. Contracted to manage a voyage between the Rio Pongo and Havana, Canot described loading the small slaver *Areostatico* with 108 boys and girls fifteen years or younger. As he stowed his captives aboard, Canot wrote, "I confess I could not imagine how this little army was to be packed or draw breath in a hold but *twenty-two inches high!*" Eventually, as Canot related, young people were forced to spoon into each other, "like *sardines* in a can" throughout the weeks-long passage to Cuba.[131] Canot flipped the tropes of middle passage horror, however, by charging abolition, not illegal traffickers, with responsibility. Whenever possible, he claimed, he employed "systematic order, purity, and neatness" to "preserve the cargo."[132] Nonetheless, Canot insisted that the criminalization of the trade added to the suffering of its captives by encouraging haste, secrecy, and crowding. Moreover, Canot used his purported ethnographic expertise to assert that the chaining of African captives to the rough slave deck represented only a "slight inconvenience" to people used to lying on hard mats and dirt floors.[133] Other published slaver narratives indulged the gothic body horror of the middle passage to a greater degree than Canot, but they, too, held legal abolition of the trade responsible for increasing human suffering of African captives.[134]

Canot placed the heaviest responsibility for the slave trade, however, on what he perceived to be an inherent racial trait of African depravity. For example, Canot explained his African business partners' resistance to "legitimate" trade as an inability to suppress slaving as a "natural appetite or function."[135] Further illustrating this "appetite" (while overlooking his role in stimulating it), Canot recounted an upriver slaving voyage in which the mere glimpse of European trading goods incited local inhabitants to sell kin and neighbors. "Every man cudgelled his brain," exclaimed Canot, "for an excuse to kidnap his neighbor, so as to share my commerce."[136] Although Canot conceded that contemporary slavery in Africa had been heavily shaped by white "avarice and temptation," he nevertheless portrayed slavery as an African "national institution" that reflected "indigenous barbarity."[137] The claims of slavery as Africa's original creation were hardly new, but in the context of the mid-nineteenth century they now served to justify both colonization through slave trade suppression and reopening the transatlantic trade.[138] In a passage often quoted by slave trade revivalists, Canot asserted, "Africans have been bondsmen every where: and the oldest monuments bear their images linked with menial toils and absolute servitude." Cementing his argument that slavery was a natural condition of African life, he claimed that "five-sixths of the population is in chains."[139] The *North American Review* confirmed American mainstream receptivity to this idea when a reviewer of *Captain Canot* remarked, "We might as soon expect the leopard to change his skin, as the Ethiopian to wipe out the foul spot of servitude."[140]

Notably, the naval memoir *Africa and the American Flag* ascribed a similar set of uncivil attributes uniquely marking Africa as "the great slave-land of the world."[141] Like many Western writers, Foote viewed African systems of slavery as manifestations of ancient cruelty and perceived civilization deficit, rather than as institutions with their own history and politics.[142] Drawing an implicit line between his civilized readers and his literary "natives," Foote professed his inability to understand "the eagerness to share in cruelty which glows in a negro's bosom."[143] In a blanket summary of this widespread assumption, Foote declared, "Africa is guilty of the slavery under which she suffered; for her people made it, as well as suffered it."[144] Foote's generalizations about African slave-making as an ethnographic fact revealed the shifting terrain of antislavery rhetoric in the era of the illegal transatlantic slave trade. In the eighteenth century, abolitionists such as Olaudah Equiano could invert racial hierarchies to condemn the atrocities of the savage slaveholder.[145] By the 1850s, with the transatlantic slave trade technically outlawed in Europe and the Americas, the antislavery naval officer seemed to be returning responsibility to the African continent.

Foote's ruminations on African civic incapacity reflected a sentiment commonly expressed by Africa Squadron personnel, which had serious implications for how slave trade recaptives would be viewed and treated. For example, after a tour of Monrovia, Liberia, in 1858, ordinary seaman Henry Eason, serving on the USS *Marion*, confided in his journal that "free negroes" would be much better off remaining as American slaves "then to live as they do here, continually fighting & quarrelling among themselves."[146] Thomas Aloysius Dornin, commander of the USS *San Jacinto* and USS *Constellation*, echoed sailor Eason's sentiments when Dornin's ship picked up a pair of African canoe men stranded without paddles at sea. The seamen feared for their safety on unfamiliar shores and so urged Dornin to land them near their home coast. Dornin commented on their request in his journal, "Such is the happy accord existing among this Free & Happy Race out here in their own country."[147] Typical for their linkage of blackness and continental Africa with social disorder, both Eason's and Dornin's remarks reveal racial assumptions shared among white naval personnel holding otherwise differing views on U.S. slavery.

Together, naval and slaver accounts of the 1850s formed a body of slave trade ethnography that argued the need for global white rescue. As we have seen, both Foote and Canot wrote accounts that contrasted the horrors of the middle passage against the horrors of the mythic Dark Continent. A *Boston Post* reviewer described the moral confusion induced by reading *Captain Canot* when he exclaimed that the volume's "descriptions of negro manners, religion and social life, are absolutely horrible." Weighing perceived African customs against the travesty of the slave trade, the Boston reviewer admitted, "At one moment he [the reader] would be thankful to see all Africa packed off in slave ships—yea, anything to terminate the dreadful abominations of its people."[148] Only the trope of white rescue could resolve such painful tensions. Both naval and slaver narratives engaged in fantasies of gallant intervention—not just through naval interception of slave ships but also by redeeming human sacrifice victims or, in Canot's case, cleverly rescuing an enslaved Fullah "princess."[149] Slave trade ethnography as a genre suggested the need for rescue that extended beyond the seizure of enslaved captives from illegal slavers to the cultural and moral redemption of Africans perceived as naturally inferior.

Within both slaver and naval narratives, themes of white rescue and African depravity overshadowed the historical facts of the nineteenth-century slave trade, chief among them the predominance of children. As future chapters discuss in depth, most recaptives taken into U.S. custody came from regions where young males under the age of fifteen comprised up to half the captives sold to foreign traders. Yet, the presence of children in slaver and naval narratives remained elusive, flitting in and out of view. When Canot or Foote drew upon abolitionist middle passage discourses, as in the examples above of the *Areostatico* or the *Veloz*, the suffering of boys and girls vividly underscored the brutal packing of illegal slavers. When it came to the portions of their narratives that emphasized Africa as the original "slave-land," however, those same children were harder to find. Rather, the narrative of racialized civic incapacity and dependence on white colonial oversight overshadowed considerations of youth and vulnerability based on age.[150] Because both Foote and Canot were advertised and reviewed most notably for the novelty of their African ethnographic description, the overriding impression imparted by the narratives was one of all Africans as figuratively childlike in their dependence.[151] As cultural resources that shaped American views of the nineteenth-century transatlantic slave trade, both slaver and naval narratives therefore diminished the significance of actual children among the recaptives who entered U.S. ports.

Reviews and other contemporary references suggest that American readers drew two different versions of rescue from Foote and Canot, which recirculated in solutions offered for African recaptives detained in the United States. On one hand, *Africa and the American Flag* used the claim about Africa's original sin of slavery to argue for the urgent regeneration of "the African" specifically through the colonizationist experiment of Liberian self-governance.[152] Foote gave measured support to Liberia's historical mission "to vivify [Africa] with liberty and self-government."[153] Like many supporters of Liberia, he believed stronger slave trade suppression would usher in a new age of African commerce and civilization. Yet Foote took the long view on black self-determination. He argued, for instance, that "much kind watchfulness" would be required to prevent independent Liberian citizens from "sinking back to become mere Africans."[154] In this way, Foote's narrative situated slave trade recaptives within an antislavery history of African uplift that nevertheless maintained powerful racialized constraints.

From Foote's nationalist perspective, the mission of slave trade suppression proved entirely consistent with—and, indeed, necessary for—American commercial ambition. "The reduction, or annihilation of the slave-trade, is opening the whole of these vast regions to science and legal commerce," *Africa and the American Flag* pronounced. "Let America take her right share in them."[155] Foote's promise of expanding markets resonated with his readers. A Philadelphia reviewer, for example, praised the admiral's memoir for its enlightening discussion of the "fruitful field of commerce" opening in Africa in which "first comers will be first served."[156] The ACS similarly attached the promise of profits to its civilization mission. "Africa has great commercial resources," argued the *African Repository*, further adding, "The teachers of her civilization will be richly rewarded."[157] Foote's volume thus clearly anticipated the aspects of "the colonizing structure" summarized by scholar V. Y. Mudimbe: "the domination of physical space, the reformation of *natives'* minds, and the integration of local economic histories into the Western perspective."[158] Recaptives, upon arrival in Liberia, would be placed precisely within this colonizing structure.

In contrast to the colonizationist agenda, advocates of proslavery empire argued for the reopening of the transatlantic slave trade itself as a mode of rescue. Deep South commercial conventions debated and publicized the issue, while lawmakers in Mississippi and Louisiana debated plans to import African laborers thinly disguised as "apprentices."[159] Fueled by "the global reach of the cotton economy," as Walter Johnson argues, proslavery imperialists defended a theory of expanding slaveocracy that challenged the idea of emancipation as a sign of human progress.[160] As one might expect, slave trade revivalists derided both Liberian colonization and the slave trade laws as exercises in "false philanthropy" and abuses of U.S. federal power.[161] Frequently invoking the leopard and its proverbial spots, proslavery advocates adamantly opposed the transport of slave trade refugees to Liberia and sought to reclaim recaptives from federal power. Virginian Edmund Ruffin, for example, used Foote's discussion of the *Pons* recaptives in Liberia to argue that apprenticeship to black emigrants constituted the worst form of bondage, that is, the "'apprenticeship' of savage negroes" to a "negro master."[162] Revivalists in southern hot spots like Charleston targeted recaptives as useful pawns in the political battle against federal intervention in both the slave trade and domestic slavery.

Analyzed together, slaver narratives and naval memoirs shed light on how the cultural manifestations of the illegal slave trade shaped U.S. antebellum debates on race and slavery in the Atlantic World.[163] In truth, slave trade literature had little immediate relevance for recaptive youth and adults as they struggled to survive the aftermath of the middle passage. Yet the works of slave trade ethnography produced by slaver and naval authors alike mattered because they painted a portrait for American readers about who slave ship recaptives were and where they belonged within a global racial hierarchy. With the arrival of actual recaptives on the slavers *Echo*, *Wildfire*, *William*, and *Bogota*, newspapers across the country posed the presence of slave trade survivors as a problem for the white nation to solve. The varying answers to that question offered an Atlantic World antecedent to Frederick Douglass's 1863 warning that emancipation by "law and the sword" could only go so far against "pride of race" and "prejudice of color."[164]

—

As implemented in the years between 1807 and 1861, U.S. policies toward African recaptives demonstrated the political tensions inherent in an expanding slaveholding republic's campaign of transatlantic slave trade suppression. The place of the United States in the global second slavery economy depended on a domestic system of enslaved labor and an interstate trade in human property. Outlawing the transatlantic slave trade, as the United States did at the national level in 1807, was not necessarily a blow to those domestic institutions of servitude. In fact, during the years after the Anglo-American transatlantic slave trade abolition laws, both slavery and the U.S. internal slave trade expanded.[165] Yet actively suppressing the slave trade and especially "liberating" the captives of illegal slavers proved to be inherently controversial in the United States because these policies exacerbated sectional tensions and interfered with the free flow of capital through legal and illegal commerce. Moreover, the resulting trials of seized ships produced opportunities, such as the *Antelope* Supreme Court cases, for asserting the slave trade's fundamental immorality. As Georgia senator John Macpherson Berrien argued in 1825, the Constitution had for twenty years endorsed the slave trade and "its fruits yet lie at the foundation of that compact."[166] Antislavery arguments against the transatlantic trade, Berrien warned the justices, therefore cut at the very origins of the U.S. republic. With the rising campaign to reopen the transatlantic slave trade, issues surrounding slave trade suppression become even more contentious.

Overall, only a few hundred African recaptives of the illegal trade came under federal custody in the 1820s and '30s. In the early cases, such as the *Antelope*, *Fenix*, and *General Páez*, the courts did not even agree that the 1819 law applied. Yet the eventual transportation of recaptives from these vessels to Liberia set precedents for later implementation of the removal policy. Though placed by law beyond the reach of the U.S. slave market after 1819, recaptive African children, women, and men found themselves leased and hired to southern planters and detained in southern jails and workhouses. The mark of their long sojourn through the United States could be seen in the elite American surnames by which they were known in Liberian records. None of these early slave trade refugees gave formal testimony in a courtroom, and only the shipmates of the *General Páez* had even a limited say in their future destination. Although some officials, such as Richard Habersham, dedicated themselves to implementing the removal policy, the experience for African captives was largely one of detention and forced migration, albeit in some rare cases accompanied by hope of eventual repatriation.

Increasingly, as the United States entered the 1850s, the ethnographic framing of Africa and Africans in Anglo-American print culture threatened to blind observers (as well as the extant archive) to recaptive struggles with loss of kin, psychic trauma, and vast dislocation. This oversight resulted not from a silence on the illegal slave trade but from its sensational treatment in the popular press. Indeed, the cultural impact of the illegal slave trade has not yet been sufficiently recognized in present historiography on the antebellum U.S. politics of race and slavery. During the 1850s, popular demand for maritime and travel narratives resulted in both widespread newspaper coverage of illegal slaving and published slaver and navy accounts focusing on African adventures. Slave trade ethnography, constructed out of dual images of the suffering recaptive and the inherently (possibly unredeemable) savage African, made the slave trade into a spectacle and slave trade refugees into objects of exoticism. Thus, when naval escorts directed the *Echo* into Charleston harbor carrying 306 West Central African recaptives, many white Americans viewed the ship's arrival with more curiosity and opportunism than compassion. Strands of racial science, proslavery politics, and nineteenth-century popular amusements merged to create a distinctive slave trade spectatorship that generated new forms of commodification from the presence of slave ship recaptives.

2

Proslavery Waters

What I mean is that I lost my family, and I don't seem to have life,
so can I say that I survived? It is by the grace of God that I'm
still breathing, how can I say that I survived? I would have survived
if one of my children survived, but all of them were killed.
I would say I survived if I had something to sustain me.

—Karoli, *Voices of Rwanda* Archive, *Listening on the Edge:*
Oral History in the Aftermath of Crisis, 2014

But the wicked carried us away in captivity
Required from us a song.

—Melodians, "Rivers of Babylon," 1970

The gulf between slave trade survival and slave trade ethnology became evident soon after *Echo* shipmates arrived at Fort Sumter at the port of Charleston, South Carolina. For eight weeks, hundreds of West Central African captives had been packed in a low-ceilinged slave deck, on a treacherous passage that killed almost a third of their number. Disembarking from the *Echo* in a much-weakened state, recaptives came face to face with a delegation of Lowcountry slaveholding elite. The group of planters, merchants, lawyers, and doctors, according to the *Charleston Mercury*, "were much gratified at the spectacle represented by these savages, who appeared in fine spirits, and entertained their visitors with a display of their abilities in dancing and singing."[1] No one on that morning of 31 August 1858 recorded what the dancers thought about the party of white onlookers. It is a silence that further deepens the significance of South Carolina slaveholders' assumption that the ragged group of slave ship survivors performed for them alone. The encounter and its subsequent depiction in Charleston's proslavery newspaper reveal the power of the ethnographic gaze to transform a social crisis into an exotic spectacle.

The *Mercury*'s account of this event, however one-sided, calls attention to a critical question raised by historians of transatlantic slaving, namely, how did enslaved Africans make meaning of the crisis in which they found themselves?[2] The first section of this chapter contributes to the larger historical question of Atlantic enslaved perspectives by treating the experience of recaptivity as an extension of saltwater enslavement. Despite barriers of language, physical depletion, and fear, *Echo* shipmates, like other recaptives around the Atlantic Basin, sought to understand what the interruption of the slaving voyage meant for their collective survival and possible future. By listening to recaptive testimony from elsewhere in Atlantic slave trade suppression and reading the *Echo* evidence against its grain, it is possible to ask what the three-week detention of slave ship survivors at Fort Sumter meant within a longer experience of terrifying and unpredictable dislocation. Such a vantage point broadens the history of U.S. slave trade suppression from one primarily concerned with naval maneuvers, legal decisions, and political conflict to a social history that illuminates African shipmates' forced migrations in the era of second slavery.[3]

At the same time, white Charlestonians' racialized expectations of black civil incapacity and permanent dependence sharply curtailed the ability of recaptives to order their fractured worlds.[4] The second half of this chapter examines how proslavery ethnography created a "potential imaginary museum" of recaptive representations in two overlapping arenas.[5] First, Charleston's place in the South as a seat of scientific and medical inquiry encouraged the application of ethnology and polygenesis as frames of proslavery knowledge that cemented the racialization of *Echo* shipmates. The *Echo* case illustrates how advocates of transatlantic slave trade revival utilized pre-Darwinian racial taxonomy to portray slave ship refugees as a permanently subordinated group. Second, as the political controversy over the *Echo* crew and African recaptives grew, proslavery propaganda spilled into public exhibition of the *Echo* shipmates. Steamboat operators capitalized on the presence of recaptive Africans at Fort Sumter by advertising novel opportunities for white entertainment and racial voyeurism. Both elite politics and popular spectatorship limited the chances of *Echo* shipmates for surviving their ordeal. Their use as pawns in a political battle waged by proslavery imperialists against federal authorities ultimately heightened the difficulty of their struggle by intensifying their isolation in the fort and hurrying their removal to Liberia in a weakened state.

Recaptivity as Social Crisis

On the morning of 21 August 1858, just hours from being smuggled into Cuba's thriving plantation economy, the enslaved captives of the *Echo* suddenly became "recaptured Africans" by the authority of the U.S. government. In doing so, they passed from the hands of an international ring of human traffickers into the custody of a slaveholding republic. After Brazil's illegal traffic finally ended, a network of illegal slavers forcibly shipped almost 200,000 more African captives to Cuba before the arrival of the last documented voyage in 1866.[6] The *Echo*'s slaving voyage had begun in March 1858, when New Orleans customs officials cleared the ship under Rhode Island sea captain Edward Townsend, ostensibly bound for the Caribbean island of St. Thomas. Equipment such as wood decking and large cookers hidden in the brig's hold revealed the voyage's true purpose. Even the name of the ship was a ruse, for Townsend had painted over the ship's true name of *Putnam* and rechristened the slaver as the *Echo*. Built in Baltimore and collectively financed by U.S., Spanish, and Portuguese businessmen in New York, New Orleans, and Havana, the vessel symbolized the wider criminal conspiracy that abducted thousands of young African captives across the Atlantic.[7] Had the *Echo* slavers been successful, their human cargo would have joined nearly 15,400 other predominantly young enslaved Africans smuggled into Cuba in 1858 alone.[8]

Placing shipmates of the *Echo* within these 1850s routes of transatlantic enslavement illuminates the social crisis of recaptivity as part of a more extended experience of global dislocation.[9] The crisis of *Echo* recaptives in U.S. custody began months and even years before their forced passage to the Americas, as slavers tore young people from familiar institutions of collective identity, lineage, and kinship.[10] For example, Kongo children grew up within densely intersecting social networks of clans, houses, and lineages, where *nkazi*, or the descent group heads, spoke for those under their authority.[11] Enslavement ruptured these connections and imposed a terrible condition of kinlessness. Therefore, as historian Joseph Miller argues, survival beyond the barest existence "meant constant rebuilding of new connections out of the succession of transitory circumstances through which most found themselves propelled, a recurrently thwarted effort to find places of their own, to belong, somehow, somewhere."[12] If we are to truly understand the social experience of recaptivity, the moment of slave ship "rescue" must be considered as inaugurating yet another period in which captive men, women, and children sought to gain a foothold in their shattered world through reestablishing social connections. Yet, circumstances of physical debility, spiritual and social alienation, and forced mobility shadowed recaptives long after disembarking a slave ship. *Echo* shipmates at Fort Sumter entered this new social crisis with bodies depleted by slave ship confinement in a hostile proslavery environment, surrounded by white authorities who proved unable to conceptualize either the past losses or the current struggles of the recaptives.

From the perspective of enslaved captives, the seizure of the *Echo* marked another phase in a series of forced transitions that had wrenched recaptives from their place within extended kinship affiliations in West Central African societies. Thomas Rainey, the Portuguese-speaking U.S. agent who accompanied *Echo* recaptives to Liberia, reported among the surviving shipmates a majority of "Congos, some Kabendas, some Miquombas, many from the interior tribes of the provinces of Loanda and Loango."[13] These generalized ethnonyms and the recaptives' embarkation point near the Congo River pointed to a common region of origin for many young captives sold to Cuba in the middle decades of the nineteenth century. Indeed, 60.6 percent of all enslaved captives arriving in Cuba between 1841 and 1865 embarked from the coastal region of West Central Africa.[14] More specifically, slave traders as well as agents for so-called African apprentices gravitated northward to the unregulated regions of Cabinda and the Congo River estuary, in response to intensified British patrols near the Portuguese colonial ports of Luanda and Benguela.[15] Seaman Henry Eason, assigned to the U.S. Africa Squadron in 1858, observed one such barracoon at Loango, where for $40 per head a French trader kept "600 young negroes, of both sexes, who were to be sold for slaves, to any vessel who chose to come for them."[16] *Echo* slavers used the terms "Congo" and "Miquombas" to designate people of the Lower Congo region and "Kabendas" for captives drawn from the coastal region surrounding Cabinda Bay.[17] Rainey's report thus identifies many of the *Echo* shipmates as Kikongo (or related dialect) speakers from societies along the banks of the lower Congo River, from northern Angolan regions, or from the Loango province surrounding Cabinda. Many of these captives would have been conveyed to the coast through networks of traders who acted as middlemen supplying foreign traders at the coast.[18]

Each man, woman, and child loaded onto the *Echo* had become enslaved through various mechanisms of pawnship, debt, judicial sentence, or abduction that ensnared their societies' most vulnerable members. Increasingly after 1830, the massive extension of European commerce and credit into the Central African interior increased debt and put pressure on older political traditions.[19] Within societies where individual identity derived primarily from descent groups, the "doctrine of collective responsibility" meant that less powerful dependents of a family lineage sometimes paid the price when an elder was sentenced or fined.[20] Dependents in large corporate lineages, pawned as collateral for an elder's debt or in substitution for a legal penalty, sometimes experienced sale to coastal slave traders before their relatives could redeem them.[21] For example, Nanga, a young Angolan recaptive interviewed in Sierra Leone, recalled how his family pawned him to recover his maternal uncle who had received a sentence of enslavement as punishment for adultery. Before his mother could redeem him as she intended, he was sold to Portuguese slave traders in Luanda.[22] Still other young people arrived at the Cabinda barracoons with recent memories of sudden abduction, raids, and the deaths of other family members.[23] Sale to foreign slavers tore young people from networks of kinship and dependence that structured their place in society and cast them into a disorienting and isolated journey. In other words, slave trade commodification generated an existential crisis that could not easily be healed.

Many of the *Echo*'s captives had not been drawn from deep in the "interior," as some American newspapers speculated, but from port towns and coastal regions where residents became increasingly vulnerable to transatlantic enslavement in the nineteenth century.[24] Even when legally protected from enslavement by the colonial law of "original freedom," as historian Mariana Candido has shown, Angolan subjects of local rulers could be seized, branded, and swiftly loaded onto a slaver's vessel.[25] Although Cabinda Bay lay north of Portuguese territory, coastal people there proved similarly susceptible to enslavement. Three men among the *Echo* recaptives had worked for local slavers before being caught up along with the captives they tended in the barracoons.[26] These men most likely numbered among the *Echo*'s "Kabendas," since Cabinda maritime and shore workers did much of the labor that kept human captives and legal trade flowing through that port at midcentury.[27] Although individuals enslaved from the coast may not have had to endure the grueling overland travel experienced by captives from the interior, they were nevertheless suddenly severed from their familial, social, and political identities.

Crammed into waiting pens known as barracoons near Cabinda, men, women, and children turned to their fellow captives, even those who were strangers to them, in a desperate bid for information.[28] Recent studies of western Africa's integration into the Atlantic economy make clear that new social affiliations emerged among diverse groups of captives brought together through the paths of enslavement in African coastal regions.[29] Especially in the lower Congo River region, the similarity of related "Bantu" languages (a term coined by Europeans in the same period as the *Echo*'s embarkation) and a shared cosmology facilitated rapport among captives of different regions.[30] Here in the midst of social isolation, despair, and uncertainty, enslaved captives began to build the communal networks through which they might comprehend their ordeal. Death and departure, however, constantly undercut the fragile connections established in the coastal barracoons.

Furthermore, the prevalence of children and youth among captives forced onto slave ships along the West Central African coast critically shaped shipmates' social relations and resources for survival. The *Echo* was no exception, for once the shipmates surfaced in the U.S. historical record as recaptives, observers described them as "all young," "majority boys," and comprised mostly of male youth "apparently from eight to sixteen years of age."[31] An increasingly sophisticated accounting of the nineteenth-century transatlantic slave trade clearly indicates a "child-dominated" traffic from West Central Africa primarily to Cuba in the years of the *Echo*'s capture. Even when allowing for historical differences in how a child was defined, it is clear that the proportion of captive youth in the transatlantic slave trade climbed upward during the nineteenth century.[32] West Central African ports embarked an estimated 53 percent of captives under age fifteen, with male youth predominating.[33] Why this was so has yet to be fully understood. Historians generally agree that the retention of enslaved females for agricultural production and to expand the wealth and lineages of powerful men within Africa contributed to gender ratios skewed toward males in the transatlantic trade.[34] Yet the rising proportion of children in the late transatlantic slave trade poses many still-unanswered questions. This increasing percentage of enslaved children occurred during a transitional period in West Central African history that enlarged the wealth of European merchants as well as certain elite African elders at the expense of vulnerable dependents, primarily boys and young men, but also young women as well. Scholars point to both international slaver demand and internal African influences on the age and gender of captives sold into the transatlantic trade. Arguments include the demands of international slavers for "malleable" young captives with a maximum "workable life span," the depletion of adult males from African regions heavily impacted by slaving, pricing incentives in both American and Africans markets, the reliance of African systems of slavery on women's productive and reproductive labor, and competition for adult men from internal African slave markets.[35]

Due to the nature of the evidence, the story of the *Echo* cannot settle these ongoing debates on *why* illegal slavers from Congo to Cuba carried so many youth, but it can illuminate another set of pressing questions about the strategies and priorities of young slave trade refugees. Maintaining the visibility of youth in the recaptive history of *Echo* shipmates merges two lines of inquiry in recent Atlantic historiography: the nature of child enslavement and the efforts of the enslaved to rebuild their social worlds. Attending to young recaptive shipmates along their Atlantic journey thus allows us to ask how age, alongside other factors such as gender, region of origin, and experiences of capture, shaped the strategies of recaptives for social belonging. Present-day readers might choose to see seizure of an illegal slave ship as the first step in a passage from slavery to freedom. Yet it is far more likely that the youthful majority of *Echo* recaptives, coming from societies in which individuals derived identity through networks of kin and other corporate affiliations, prioritized the criteria of security and collective belonging over individual legal categories of "slave" versus "free."[36] Historian Marcia Wright, drawing on published narratives of women and children in nineteenth-century Central Africa, identifies a "psychological drama" of childhood enslavement, in which, as she put it, "the terrors of cruelty were eclipsed by the terrors of abandonment." Wright shows how resilient women and children captives in East Central Africa acquired relative security and resources through kinship and domestic structures that tied them to powerful elders.[37] Wright's insights can be extrapolated to the young West Central African *Echo* shipmates. While legal frameworks may highlight recaptives' rescue from Cuban slave markets, the immediate concerns of recaptive shipmates had more to do with the search for information, security, and social belonging that attended the aftermath of slave ship seizure. The imperative of the search for security would continue through the many phases of the journeys of recaptive children.

From the first moments of embarkation from Cabinda, age and gender determined how information would flow among the *Echo*'s enslaved captives. In July 1858, Cabinda maritime workers hustled naked and newly branded captives onto the massive lighters that carried them to the slave ship.[38] At the waiting ship, *Echo* crewmembers sent the smaller number of women and girls, along with the younger boys, to a forward slave deck. At least two of the women were pregnant or carrying very young infants.[39] Sailors drove the men and older boys to the rear of the slave deck. In both the male and female sections of the ship, it is probable that captives familiar with Portuguese colonial towns in Angola could communicate some of their understanding of the transatlantic slave trade. Most likely, some of these individuals had already witnessed the capture and shipping of family and friends before their own ordeal began.[40] Other young captives may have been completely disoriented, as was the child captive Samuel Ajayi Crowther, who reported his embarkation by Portuguese slavers at Lagos: "Being a veteran of slavery, . . . and having no more hope of ever going to my country again, I patiently took whatever came; although it was not without a great fear and trembling that I received, for the first time, the touch of a White man."[41] On the *Echo*, those who trusted one another enough responded with plans of insurrection in the first days at sea. U.S. defense attorneys in the *Echo* crew's trial later claimed that some of the captives attempted to "rise upon the crew" and were kept shackled below in the hold for the rest of the voyage.[42] Unfortunately, little else is known of this attempted uprising.

In the last weeks of the *Echo*'s passage, however, sickness and exhaustion made movement, let alone planning revolt, difficult. With less than four feet of headroom, the cramped captives could only sit with knees drawn to the chin or sleep spooned against one another; those placed under the hatchways breathed fresher air but, according to the ship's coxswain, "were exposed to all weathers."[43] Freshly branded letters, half an inch long each, on shoulders and backs increased the captives' bodily suffering.[44] With no medical attention, and fed on an unchanging diet of rice and beans, both adults and children quickly developed dysentery, eye infections, and skin lesions.[45] Excrement, urine, and vomit spread across the slave deck, and the stench of the airless quarters increased daily. Six weeks into the voyage, as the *Echo* passed along the north coast of Cuba, the vessel "was filthy to the last degree." The USS *Dolphin*'s surgeon later testified that two boxes of medical supplies had been found aboard the *Echo*, but no effort was made to separate the sick from the well.[46] Estimates from trial records and interviews with the crew indicate that 132 captives, or 29 percent of those embarked, did not live to see the crew of the U.S. Navy brig *Dolphin* board the *Echo*.

Just what *Echo* shipmates understood about the consequences of slave ship seizure bears directly upon how they understood their subsequent internment in Fort Sumter. Viewed from the perspective of scholarship on Kongo cosmology, the events of the middle passage took place beyond the *kalunga* line, between this world and the spirit world, a symbolic threshold associated with rivers and the sea.[47] West Central Africans frequently associated this crisis of saltwater enslavement as the work of witches who, as historian Monica Schuler put it, "visibly sucked the life out of [their] victims."[48] Moreover, accusations of witchcraft in parts of Africa ranging from Upper Guinea to Angola directly resulted in enslavement. According to historian Roquinaldo Ferreira, an accusation of witchcraft and the ensuing trial by ordeal could lead to the enslavement of either the accused or the accuser, along with family members.[49] As deaths mounted among the *Echo* shipmates in U.S. custody, recaptivity could have simply been perceived as a continuity of malevolent consumption.[50]

Recaptives also incorporated into their broader Kongo frameworks specific information gleaned from circuits of commerce and migration between the Americas and the places on the African western coast where the transatlantic slave trade persisted into the late 1850s.[51] Histories of U.S. slave trade suppression have generally treated slave ship captives as silent and passive subjects of naval pursuit.[52] However, even when physically restrained, enslaved captives would have endeavored to understand what the interruption of their terrible passage portended. There is good reason to believe that many African captives on nineteenth-century slaving vessels had been exposed to the possibilities of interception. For example, even before the *Echo* left Cabinda, captives may have gained clues about the illegality of the vessel from the words and actions of the Cabinda mariners who were trained to deflect British suspicions as they conveyed captives from shore to ship.[53] Once under way, and already alert to clues such as the changing color of the water, some captives noted the crew's constant watch for British patrols, a hint that the slavers had enemies of their own. Cudjo Lewis, a young Yoruba man taken to Alabama from Ouidah in 1860, later described the captain's continuous watch on the horizon and his rapid orders to force African captives down into the hold when he spied a possible British cruiser.[54] Slave ship sailors sometimes directly communicated a threat of recapture to their captives. According to the narrative of Joseph Wright, enslaved in the 1820s in the Yoruba city of Oba, Portuguese sailors departing Lagos told the enslaved boys that the British would eat them if "we suffered them to prize us."[55] Such experiences aboard other slavers suggest that at least some *Echo* recaptives would have understood that their voyage could be interrupted, even if the outcome was not clear.

The moment of a ship's seizure by naval cruiser clearly signaled to enslaved captives a shift in power that could prove either advantageous or lethal. The danger lay in the fact that slavers, especially in proximity to naval cruisers, depended to some degree on the silence of enslaved captives in the hold to avoid detection.[56] Mahommah Gardo Baquaqua, embarked at Ouidah in 1844, recalled that as the ship approached the shore at Pernambuco, "we were given to understand that we were to remain perfectly silent, and not make any out-cry, otherwise our lives were in danger."[57] Compounding the terror of a chase near the Cuban coast in 1860, slavers reportedly killed six of the *William* shipmates to silence them as the U.S. steamer *Wyandotte* approached within hearing distance.[58] A less direct but equally deadly threat was the denial of food or water during pursuits at sea that could last a day or longer. Suffocation and heat exhaustion also threatened the lives of captives confined below decks with covered hatches.[59] As in the case of the *Echo*'s captives, the approach of a naval gunboat could mean hours in stifling heat and darkness before a boarding officer lifted the hatches and declared them "prize negroes."[60]

When naval prize crews boarded a slaver, further uncertainty plagued recaptives waiting on the slave deck. Crowther, for example related his initial dread of British seamen, whom he regarded as simply "new conquerors" in a long line of captors.[61] Crowther's narrative alerts us to read with some skepticism the many self-congratulatory U.S. and British accounts of African captives exulting at the sight of naval officers. Yet reports of slave ship seizures in the Atlantic and Indian Oceans do suggest that recaptives understood they might influence the outcome of a naval seizure with their own testimony. This was particularly true during the 1820s when Anglo-Portuguese treaties banned only the slave trade originating north of the equatorial line.[62] In the case of a naval seizure, Joseph Wright reported, his captors gave threatening instructions to say that the ship had been at sea for a month, thus making a southern hemisphere embarkation more plausible and concealing their recent departure from Lagos. During the British boarding of the previously mentioned *Veloz*, some captives asserted their origins at Badagry (north of the equator) but were tragically overruled by the Brazilian captain's testimony that he had adhered to the current restriction to Angolan slaving ports.[63] When slavers were successfully seized, some recaptives found gratification in seeing the tables turned on their captors.[64] Crowther, for instance, reacted strongly to seeing his enslaver come aboard the British ship in fetters. He recalled, "Thinking that I should no more get into his hand, I had the boldness to strike him on the head." Yet Crowther also described much doubt and uncertainty, reporting his shipmates' continual suspicion of being reenslaved even after disembarking in Sierra Leone as "liberated Africans."[65]

A similar range of responses also characterized the *Echo* shipmates' first hours with the U.S. Navy prize crew. Those on the main deck would have observed and been able to relay the news that the slaver's crew had been seized and confined below.[66] Some recaptives took this moment of discovery to defy the violently enforced rules of access to food and drink imposed by slavers.[67] As First Lieutenant Joseph Bradford put it, when the Africans realized they had "new masters," some "destroyed large quantities of water and provision" in attempting to slake their thirst. Efforts to satisfy even the most urgent physical needs, however, were not long tolerated by naval officers, for

Bradford soon "restored their former masters,"—meaning that he unchained arrested members of the slaving crew to exert control over recaptives—"and they had to resort to the fiercest cruelty before they could break up these practices of the slaves."[68] The moment in which *Echo* shipmates battled their former captors for water under the gaze of U.S. naval officers foreshadowed recaptives' struggle for survival in the hands of authorities who deemed them barbaric and in need of control.

In the days immediately after the *Echo* was boarded by officers of the USS *Dolphin*, recaptives confined to the slave deck under supervision by some of the slaver crew would have seen little evidence of their altered legal status. The seized slaver sailed another six days to reach Charleston, during which time the daily routines and spatial packing of recaptives remained very similar to that of the middle passage. "A pint of water is given to each, morning and evening," explained an eyewitness. At night they slept "spoon-fashion, on their sides," and "at day light they are dashed with buckets of water."[69] Reported to be "without medical assistance of any kind," the recaptives lost another twelve of their shipmates during their passage to Charleston. With cases of yellow fever appearing in the city, Charleston officials took no chances on a shipload of sickly African passengers. Against Lieutenant Bradford's protests, the port physician held the *Echo* in quarantine on Sullivan's Island, where slave ships had arrived with their enslaved human cargo for over a century and a half.[70] Like the hundreds of thousands of enslaved captives who preceded them, *Echo* shipmates ended their transatlantic crossing uncertain of what future catastrophes awaited them.

Unlike the earlier generations of enslaved captives quickly dispersed through Charleston's slave market, however, *Echo* recaptives continued their journey together as a shipmate group struggling to comprehend and survive their situation. After two days at Sullivan's Island, the recaptives disembarked at Fort Pinckney and within twenty-four hours had been transferred again, this time to Fort Sumter.[71] At the massive granite fortification farther out in the harbor, federal authorities supplied shipmates with blankets, rice, and beans. Shipmates may have had shelter from summer thunderstorms in the brick barracks still under construction but little else in the way of material comfort.[72] It was here at Fort Sumter that the first white visitors from Charleston witnessed the skeletal forms of recaptives ravaged by ophthalmia, edema, and dysentery. A child of "six or eight years," observed lying near death on the fort's stone wharf, revealed the absolute vulnerability of young isolated captives unable to secure protection and care.[73] As days went on, authorities at the fort improvised a hospital area where Charleston physicians States Lee

Lockwood and Thomas L. Ogier tended to the sick and dying.[74] Lockwood later testified at the trial of the *Echo* crew that the condition of African captives "in point of physical strength, was very much enfeebled, and this was the case of the whole ship's cargo of them."[75] Death and disease strained the social resources of the surviving *Echo* shipmates, who remained for one another the only familiar touchstone in a seemingly endless progression of captors, dislocations, and carceral spaces.

In the aftermath of the middle passage, physical and psychic trauma severely curtailed the ability of recaptives to strengthen the social fabric of their fragile shipmate relations. Whereas recent Atlantic World scholarship has emphasized enslaved and recaptive shipmates' defiance of enslavement's "social death," the recaptive camps at Fort Sumter (and later at Key West) force us also to see those who lost that struggle, those who had been pushed too far in body and soul.[76] Atlantic slave traders tested the limits of human endurance with calculations of how little water and food could profitably convey a human cargo across the sea.[77] Fear of detection and high slave prices in Cuba further degraded the condition of midcentury slave ships, where rations and people were hurriedly loaded into ship spaces not originally constructed for mass human transport.[78] What historian Rosanne Adderley has argued for liberated African settlements in the Bahamas merits repeating for *Echo* shipmates: "One cannot overemphasize how much these Africans, although emancipated, continued to suffer medically as victims of the Atlantic slave trade."[79] The recaptive community included not only survivors with reserves of physical and mental resilience but also individuals on the brink of death, whom scholars of contemporary trauma might call "a walking fatality."[80] Recognizing the many registers of aftermath for slave ship survivors requires an acknowledgment of despair and resignation as well as hope and struggle.

Even in these dismal circumstances, however, recaptives enslaved in the coastal regions near slaving ports like Cabinda possessed language skills and knowledge of legal processes to advocate on their own behalf. Notably, according to one observer, the three adult maritime workers soon informed Charleston officials that "they were not purchased, but that the white men brought them away without their consent."[81] Making their claim in Portuguese and Spanish through *Echo* crewmember Frank (Franco) Lear, the men distinguished their enslavement as illegitimate within the legal frameworks of slavery prevailing near Cabinda. Political tradition of the Loango Coast throughout the era of the transatlantic trade forbad the enslavement of individuals born in Loango, except for those enslaved through criminal conviction—a loophole increasingly abused in the last decades of the slave trade.[82] Although their claims made little difference to their status as recaptives within U.S. suppression law, the Cabinda barracoon workers nevertheless drew upon their own legal frameworks in an attempt to shape their fate. In doing so, they refuted the proslavery imperialist claim of the ubiquity of slavery throughout western Africa. At the same time, in their protest they implicitly acquiesced to the concept of legitimate enslavement, and in doing so, they drew a line between themselves and the youthful Congo captives who were also their shipmates.[83]

The age, gender, former occupations, and language abilities of the three Cabinda men gave them authority among *Echo* recaptives recognized by both other shipmates and Charleston authorities. Their presence is thus significant to our understanding of the hierarchies and social networks that developed among slave ship survivors. From this vantage point, the newspaper report of recaptives singing and dancing, with which this chapter began, acquires additional meaning. A white observer for the *Mercury* referred to one of the three Cabinda barracoon workers as "the principal negro," describing him as a large man who was apparently able to bring together separate linguistic groups. Despite their "evident inability to converse generally with each other," the observer noted, disparate groupings of recaptives became "united" under the man's leadership when they sang together.[84] The scene as described for the *Mercury* is ambiguous, for although one paternalistic account assumed that recaptives sang and danced to entertain white observers, the report of recaptives singing under the headman's leadership made no mention that recaptives sang for the benefit of white onlookers. Whether or not the Charleston onlookers' arrival triggered the performance, the re-creation of West Central African music and movement in a U.S. federal fort carried much larger importance as an expressive vehicle through which shipmate networks could be forged.[85]

By lifting their voices and moving their bodies together, former captives of the *Echo* reconfigured their space of confinement at Fort Sumter, even in the shadow of death and the middle passage. Becoming "united" in song would not have been an easy process, however, for the same adult leaders organizing the rhythms of recaptive life at the fort existed in the memories of most *Echo* shipmates as workers in the Cabinda barracoons. They had cooked for and fed the captives at Cabinda, but they may also have guarded, branded, and beat them. Thus, the recaptive shipmates' community encompassed conflict and cooperation, animosity and trust. Alongside these complicated human dynamics, however, new possibilities for social identity emerged. No longer segregated by age or gender at Fort Sumter and with more room to move than in the cramped slave deck, "Congos," "Kabendas," and "Miquombas" congregated in smaller groups comprised of those with whom they could best communicate. In the basic element of song and dance, however, they also began to cement the larger collective identity of recaptive shipmates that they would take with them back across the Atlantic to Liberia.

From Cabinda to Charleston, the bare materials that youth and adults would use to reclaim social identity were their own bodies in combination with memories of past experience. African bodies, however, also became the object of public attention as news of the arrival of "wild Africans" spread. The *Mercury* observed that, in addition to stirring up intense "speculation" on the repercussions of the *Echo*'s capture for states' rights politics, "much curiosity is also excited, and many are anxious for an opportunity to observe the African in his native state."[86] As recaptives struggled daily to assert legible meaning over their alienating journey, their bodies were subjected to ethnographic scrutiny by white slaveholders who sought to claim them as both savages and slaves.

Slave Trade Recaptives as Ethnographic Subjects

In ordering his prize crew to Charleston harbor, Lieutenant John Maffitt virtually ensured that both the *Echo* and its recaptives would ignite public controversy.[87] While only a vocal minority of white Charlestonians urged the reopening of the transatlantic slave trade, a much larger contingent embraced strong states' rights opposition to any federal intervention in slaveholder property rights. The prospect of a slaving crew prosecuted by U.S. district attorney James Conner and of *Echo* shipmates held in custody of a U.S. marshal at a federal fort ignited strong states' rights protest in the city's newspapers and courts. Furthermore, with the spike in cotton and slave prices and the passage of the Kansas-Nebraska Act, the slave trade revival movement had gathered steam.[88] In 1856, South Carolina governor James H. Adams supported the revivalist position in a speech to the state legislature, prompting the establishment of house and senate committees to study the question.[89] In the year before the *Echo*'s seizure, both committee reports (including a positive house report) were published, and the issue energized the 1858 state elections.[90] Almost as if the heated debate had conjured up both a slave ship and 300 recaptives for their own benefit, slave trade revivalists greeted the arrival of the *Echo* shipmates as an opportunity to confront "Federal usurpation."[91]

Historian Manisha Sinha has skillfully charted the significance of the trial of the *Echo*'s crew for South Carolina's counterrevolutionary proslavery movement. The successful defense of *Echo* crewmembers gave slave trade revivalists—led by newspaper editor Leonidas Spratt—a public platform for repudiating the constitutionality of the 1820 piracy law. Furthermore, the eventual acquittal of the *Echo* crew paved the way for U.S. district judge Andrew Magrath to nullify the 1820 piracy law one year later in the case of the *Wanderer* captain William Corrie.[92] Echoing some of Spratt's arguments in the *Echo* trial, Magrath depicted the transatlantic trade as a regulated "business" rather than as a theft of African captives' liberty.[93] As Sinha argues, Magrath's judicial decision boldly extended slaveowners' extraterritorial rights in human property beyond national boundaries "to span the high seas and even the continent of Africa."[94] Leading slave trade advocates attempted to apply this logic to the case of the *Echo* not only by setting slavers free from federal law but by rejecting federal custody of the *Echo*'s African survivors.

Initial efforts to gain legal possession of the *Echo* recaptives soon faltered. Days after the slave ship's appearance, slave trade advocates unsuccessfully sought to gain custody of *Echo* recaptives under the terms of South Carolina's Negro Seamen's Act.[95] Next, Spratt and fellow attorney F. D. Richardson attempted, on the pretense of seeking to serve as the recaptives' counsel, to use a writ of habeas corpus to "liberate" *Echo* shipmates from federal control.[96] District Attorney Conner rejected both of these legal maneuvers, but southern citizens continued to seek a slaveholders' alternative to Liberian removal. The *Courier* republished the arguments of the *Richmond Whig*, regretting that recaptives "are to be sent back into their native barbarism" and recommending they be allowed to stay in Charleston, where they "would have good masters, and plenty of good food and clothing; and would be made useful to themselves and to the world."[97] From St. Bartholomew's Parish, planter J. Fraser Mathewes voiced his willingness "to take under my charge as apprentices fifty of the cargo," removing them from their "disagreeable" circumstances to "enjoy all the comforts of a plantation life."[98] Despite rumors and threats, however, no one proved ready to force the issue, and *Echo* recaptives remained at Fort Sumter, beyond the reach of state laws and white planters.[99]

Even so, federal authority could not prevent another sort of "recapture," that of *Echo* shipmates within a popularized discourse of proslavery ethnology. Noting the distances that usually prevented white Americans from "seeing the native African in his native condition," the *Courier* urged Charlestonians to make use of the "opportunity to extend and apply our ethnological information." With a sideways dig at the federal custodial role, the editorial called for a "committee of savans sufficiently versed in the ethnology and ethnography of Africa and the African tribes, to give us a report on the varieties now confined in the U.S. hotel."[100] Such attempts at the ethnological interrogation of recaptives occurred outside the realms of law and formal politics, yet they nevertheless reveal how popular discourses of race shaped the political culture of slave trade suppression. Historians' primary focus on the *Echo* trials and state nullification of the federal piracy statute, while valuable in its own right, has overshadowed the significance of the illegal slave trade's broader cultural impact.[101] The *Courier*'s call for "ethnological information" deeply implicated the science of race in debates over the nineteenth-century transatlantic slave trade. Slave trade suppression thus became one of the many sites for "making race" in 1850s America, one that situated the meaning of race not in a national framework but in terms of U.S. international relations to the Atlantic World and particularly to Africa.[102] As the *Courier* suggests, white Charlestonians sought direct access to recaptives in a manner scripted by contemporary missionary and African exploration accounts. In short, Charleston's short-lived obsession with *Echo* shipmates as ethnological evidence demonstrates how proslavery imperialism advanced its claims not only with constitutional and economic arguments but also by exhibiting the very bodies of African recaptives whom revivalists sought to possess.

Of course, these shipmates were not the first to be put on display. Marcus Rediker has clearly demonstrated that *Amistad* shipmates, on trial for their freedom after a slave ship revolt in 1839, also experienced display for political and entertainment purposes. In jail, they were subjected to phrenological readings, caricatured in engravings, sketched, and painted.[103] Once the shipmates were freed by the courts, their 1841 fundraising tour of northeastern venues prompted one self-styled "Native African" editorialist to disparage the exhibitions of Bible-reading "Mendi" as demeaning "puppet shows." Speaking on behalf of the *Amistad* Africans, the anonymous critic held that *Amistad* shipmates recoiled from being displayed to curious onlookers like "a giraffe of their native plains."[104] Even so, the northeastern reformers' presumption that Africans were even capable of acquiring and performing Christian "civilization" sharply distinguished the *Amistad* case from the proslavery and polygenist assumptions made about recaptives almost two decades later.[105]

By the 1850s, the popularization of ethnology in the late antebellum United States offered slave trade revivalists additional scientific justifications for racial inequality. Formally articulated as a field of research by the Philadelphia physician and naturalist Samuel George Morton, American ethnology was neither southern nor necessarily proslavery in its inception. Instead, Morton built on the work of Johann Friedrich Blumenbach and other eighteenth-century naturalists to develop measurements of physical difference (cranial measurements, for example) that could be used to create hierarchies of civilization and scientific classification.[106] Morton's 1839 *Crania Americana* quite typically placed white or "Caucasian" men at the top of the ladder of humanity, with the "highest intellectual endowments," and "Ethiopians" (sub-Saharan Africans) at the bottom.[107] American ethnologists used these observations to develop the theory of polygenesis, an idea already present in European scientific thought, which attributed differences of morality, intelligence, and physiology to multiple human origins. Predictably, polygeny's challenge to the biblical narrative of unitary human creation provoked ongoing opposition by the nation's clergy.[108] However, as the contemporary writer Louisa McCord phrased it, ethnological researchers increasingly rejected the "literal and cramped interpretation of Genesis."[109] For example, the Mobile physician Josiah C. Nott collaborated in 1854 with Egyptologist George Gliddon to publish *Types of Mankind*, which argued for the "multiplicity of species in the human genus."[110] Not only did the volume sell widely, but Nott's authorship also signaled the important role of southern physicians in popularizing ethnological arguments for proslavery purposes.[111]

As illegal slavers flocked to Cabinda barracoons in the 1850s, Charleston's learned men expanded their interest in racial science. The Lowcountry region with a historical black majority produced a preeminent circle of naturalists deeply involved in ethnological debates.[112] Charleston also featured the South's leading natural history museum, the College of Charleston, and the Medical College of Charleston. In 1850, the American Association for the Advancement of Science (AAAS) recognized Charleston's scientific reputation by holding its annual meeting in the city. Harvard naturalist Louis Agassiz, in attendance at the 1850 AAAS meeting, took the opportunity to travel to Robert W. Gibbes's plantations near Columbia, South Carolina, for a closer view of Gibbes's enslaved laborers. More specifically, Gibbes had promised Agassiz access to the bodies of African-born individuals and their children. "The writer," Agassiz later wrote in a scientific article on plural origins, "has examined closely many native Africans belonging to different tribes, and has learned readily to distinguish their nations."[113] Following his upcountry visit, Agassiz commissioned a now infamous set of daguerreotypes with intentions of documenting perceived African racial typologies, including "Guinea," "Mandingo," and "Congo."[114] Seven enslaved men and women stripped naked in a Columbia daguerreotypist's studio foreshadowed the future ethnological interest of South Carolinians in West Central African slave ship refugees.

In practical terms, however, Charleston's proslavery apologists showed most interest in using ethnology to refute the colonizationist vision of African "civilization, commerce, and Christianity." For example, the *Courier* suggested that local gentlemen could examine *Echo* recaptives in order "to test the Arcadian reports of Livingstone, and Bowen, and Wilson." In doing so, the editors issued a specific challenge to prominent missionary-explorers who employed ethnographic discourse to argue that certain "types" of Africans were constitutionally more amenable to the Western civilizing mission than others. At the forefront of these, Southern Baptist missionary Thomas Jefferson Bowen published *Central Africa: Adventures and Missionary Labors in Several Countries in the Interior of Africa* in Charleston just a year before the *Echo*'s seizure. Bowen had worked and traveled in Yorubaland but fell short of his goal to establish missions in the Sokoto Caliphate (Bowen's "Central Africa"). Based on his own ethnological distinctions among African groups, Bowen believed that the "interior tribes" were "more civilized, and are superior as to race" in comparison with coastal societies.[115] Bowen explicitly refuted slave trade revivalists' argument that all "negroes" were biologically destined for enslavement. Instead, he passionately asserted an alternative redemption of Africa through Christian conversion and the commercialization of interior groups he deemed "far in advance of the Guinea negroes."[116] Interestingly, Bowen cited David Livingstone's writings on southern Africa as verifying his case for slave trade suppression and colonization of interior regions of western Africa. In the later years of his life, Bowen actively lobbied for U.S. congressional funding of an American expedition on the Niger River and even worked with free black emigrationists to advance black American colonization near Abeokuta.[117] Though firmly invested in a vision of global white dominance, he nevertheless refuted the revivalists' assertions about slavery as black racial destiny, and he opposed the idea of the slave trade as a mode of rescue from an unredeemable continent. Charleston's outspoken revivalists took up the gauntlet, seeking to depict Bowen as "a very bad reasoner" whose "optics present Africa to him *couleur de rose*."[118]

All this cultural freight accompanied the expedition of federal officials and Lowcountry elite to Fort Sumter on 31 August 1858, the day after hundreds of young *Echo* shipmates had been installed there. Although U.S. marshal Daniel Hamilton had initially chartered the steamer to take much-needed provisions to the fort, the names of other powerful white men, published in the *Mercury* the next day, suggested a range of expectations and motives. Lutheran minister, naturalist, and AAAS member John Bachman had written extensively on the question of human origins. His 1850 publication, *The Doctrine of the Unity of the Human Race*, and his published refutations of Nott, Gliddon, and Agassiz set forth staunchly monogenist, but also proslavery, views.[119] Thomas L. Ogier, physician to the *Echo* receptives and past president of the Medical Society of South Carolina, also accompanied the party, as did cotton planter J. Fraser Mathewes, who had volunteered to take fifty receptives as "apprentices."[120] Regardless of the particular questions each had in mind, all had determined to see the *Echo* shipmates for themselves.

Elite white sightseers encountering receptive Africans for the first time especially wanted to see the "Congo tribe." The general geographic label was realistic, given the *Echo*'s point of embarkation. Yet, "Congo" as an ethnonym also carried cultural weight as a designation of racial degradation within midcentury U.S. ethnological discourse and popular press. Nott and Gliddon repeatedly referred to the "Congos" in the most derogatory terms as the "purest negro type."[121] Reports of slave trade suppression in American newspapers consistently described receptives from West Africa to be "much superior to the Congos" in both strength and intellect.[122] Beneath these midcentury racial labels lay older ethnic designations that South Carolina planters from earlier centuries had used for large numbers of people forcibly transported from West Central Africa to work the Lowcountry rice plantations of the Carolinas and Georgia. The expectations that "Congos" comprised a docile labor force prevailed in Carolina slave markets in the early eighteenth century, only to be upset by the Stono Rebellion in 1739.[123] "Congo" thus resonated with the newer science of human pluralism but also with the older language of the slave market that these Lowcountry elites hoped to revive.

And so, from the perspective of one unnamed member of the visiting party, we see a group of white men survey the crowd of emaciated receptives, noting, like Agassiz, what they perceive to be "the difference of tribes." Of course, visitors to Fort Sumter were not entirely oblivious to the suffering of the *Echo*'s shipmates. Some noted with pity the signs of emaciation, disease, and impending death. Many whose letters appeared in the *Mercury* concluded that these "horrors" could be amended with a well-regulated and legal slave trade. Yet the white visitors also imagined themselves as figurative explorers of Africa. They gestured with signs to the assembled receptives and spoke in Portuguese with both the Cabinda "principal negro" and "Frank," the slave crew translator. "Upon our party asking the sailor to show us the Congo tribe," wrote the observer, "the negro brought three men, who took their places before us; and I distinctly heard him say 'Congo.'"[124] The moment crystallized the gulf of representation and social experience inherent in the condition of receptivity. The young men faced their appraisers, having been scrutinized many times in the past by those who had power to shape their futures. The white observers eagerly scanned their bodies, intent upon the arguments they could build from teeth, face, and limbs.

In naming "Congos" and searching for racial variation, the Charleston observers treated the slave trade as a sort of scientific collection process. Slaving—and by extension the "recapture" of human cargos—drew together "types" of Africans in much closer proximity than could otherwise be found on the African continent. This was exactly the view that German zoologist Hermann Burmeister advanced in his broadly read 1853 publication, *The Black Man: The Comparative Anatomy and Psychology of the African Negro*, based on the author's travels in Brazil. As Burmeister argued, Brazil (with its illegal slave trade continuing through 1850) was the best place to study "the African negro" because "the varieties of the African race so mingled together there."[125] The white Charleston visitors engaged in similar acts of ethnographic correlation, attempting to connect the individuals before them with Euro-American writing on different parts of Africa. The author of the previous description of "Congo" recaptives, for instance, noted that since his return from the Fort Sumter excursion, he found himself "somewhat at a loss for references," since he had access only to works by Bowen, Livingstone, and the German explorer Heinrich Barth, whose geographic focus did not coincide with the *Echo* recaptives' homelands. In the end, this observer decided to "leave the ethnological questions to the learned."[126] Nevertheless, his remarks reflect how proslavery South Carolina white elites viewed *Echo* recaptives as ethnographic specimens that could reinforce their argument for a revived flow of enslaved Africans into the Lowcountry.

The interaction of white elites with *Echo* shipmates on the grounds of Fort Sumter also reveals the centrality of visual experience to the ongoing making of race in the U.S. history of slave trade suppression. Visual culture, historian Stephanie Camp reminds us, played a formative role in the development of European racial ideologies.[127] In the nineteenth century, men of science like Morton, Nott, and Gliddon using the "natural history method" placed great faith in their ability to see into bodies, far below skin color. "The science of ethnology," scholar Molly Rogers argues, "was above all a science of looking."[128] Given this fact, and the political uses that slave trade revivalists wanted to make of recaptives' bodies, it is notable that none of the city leaders on the 31 August excursion thought to take along a photographist.[129] Instead, slave trade revivalists, such as College of Charleston professor Frederick A. Porcher, relied on their reputation to lend authority to their conclusions. In a series of editorials written in the *Mercury*, Porcher held up his firsthand observations against abolitionist accounts of the "far famed horrors of the 'middle passage.'" The *Dolphin*'s capture of the *Echo*, wrote Porcher, "has permitted us to see the sons of Africa in *puris naturalibus* [state of nature]." Having seen for himself, Porcher proclaimed, "We now know that they would, in every respect, be improved by removal to this country."[130] Having dispensed with the abolitionists, Porcher next turned to the missionaries. Dismissing Bowen's colonizationist vision as a "chimera," Porcher asserted the common proslavery view of black racial destiny, arguing that "a successful voyage of an African slaver does more for civilization than all the missionaries that are spending their lives on the African continent."[131]

Slave trade spectatorship extended far beyond elite proslavery interests, however, for antebellum racial ideology was made in the pursuit of entertainment as often as in scientific discourse. An emergent mode of scientific inquiry, ethnology did not have clear professional boundaries, and amateur interests frequently shaded into modes of popular amusement.[132] A letter to the *Carolina Spartan* testified to the crowd appeal of the *Echo* shipmates when it claimed, "Very many of the younger portion of our citizens have availed themselves of the opportunity of seeing real *live Africans*." Indicating an awareness of the ethnographic images that photographic technology was starting to make possible, the *Spartan*'s correspondent wished that a local photographer had been present: "What an excellent chance they have, of taking a grouped picture of some half dozen of these wild negroes; and what an interesting sun-sketch would it prove to be to our country friends, who have no opportunity of seeing the originals!"[133] This enthusiastic endorsement of slave trade spectatorship points to yet another way in which slave trade survivors were drawn into the circuits of popular consumption in a slaveholding nation. By 1860, when recaptives landed at Key West, the visual representation of slave ship refugees as exotic ethnographic subjects would be fully realized in national illustrated weeklies.

Ethnographic curiosity directed at the Africans in Fort Sumter partook of a long history of public display of black and brown bodies for white popular entertainment mixed with varying degrees of scientific purpose. Scholars have given considerable attention to the story of the Khoekhoe woman Saartjie Baartman, privately examined and publicly exhibited to European audiences as the "Hottentot Venus" by Louis Agassiz's mentor Georges Cuvier.[134] In Europe, photography created a visual index of physical difference that could be used by scientists and displayed for popular consumption.[135] In the antebellum United States, poor and enslaved African Americans had long been subjected to exposure in medical school amphitheaters, and their racialized images were popularized on the minstrel stage. Indeed, the greatest showman of the century, P. T. Barnum, began his rise to fame by exhibiting an aging enslaved woman, Joice Heth, as George Washington's 161-year-old former nurse.[136] Popular interest in *Echo* recaptives similarly reflected what cultural historian Susan Pearson calls the "complex dynamic of objectification and identification" that characterized the spectrum of nineteenth-century racial display, from the "freak" exhibit to the use of patients as medical specimens.[137] Holding that such exhibition could be instructive as well as entertaining, the *Charleston Mercury* praised the "beneficial" value of allowing "all classes, black and white, to see and judge for themselves of the natural condition and calibre of these poor wretches fresh from their native land."[138] By implication, the *Mercury* held that all Charlestonians, including free and enslaved blacks, would readily perceive the merits of southern slavery by viewing slave ship survivors whose degraded "caliber" seemed to be rooted not only in their history of enslavement but in their essential natures.

In addition to midcentury slave trade and missionary literature, Charleston's maritime connections to slave trade suppression also contributed to the public excitement about recaptives at Fort Sumter. As residents of a significant Atlantic port, Charlestonians had a number of friends and relatives who served in the U.S. Navy, some of them in the Africa Squadron. Though an Africa Squadron cruise could be a hardship, young seamen also viewed it as an adventure and an opportunity to collect exotic souvenirs. Horatio Bridge, for example, observed that after a raid on a West African coastal town, U.S. marines gathered several "household utensils" that they intended to bring home as "trophies and curiosities."[139] During his 1859 cruise on the *Marion*, seaman Henry Eason noted in his journal that he had purchased a parrot from traders near Loango.[140] In this manner, the material culture of the African coast made its way into the homes of Charleston families. In November 1858, when the sloop-of-war *Marion* arrived in Charleston with the suspected slave ship *Brothers* in tow, the commanding lieutenant brought with him "several curiosities," including an elephant tusk and an "African spear," sent by fellow officers to their friends and family.[141] Within this context, the white public would have seen both the *Echo* and its recaptive shipmates as a particularly sensational form of African "curiosity."

Soon after its arrival, the *Echo* itself became a sort of museum, offering local visitors a peek at a genuine slave ship, rarely openly identified as such in U.S. ports by midcentury. After disembarking crew and recaptives, navy seamen securely moored the brig near the new Custom House to await its legal condemnation as a prize ship. The *Mercury* announced that wharf superintendent E. B. White would "undoubtedly gratify the reasonable wishes of parties, who may desire to observe the interior arrangements of a slaver."[142] Whereas Quakers in Philadelphia posted abolitionist broadsides about the cramped dimensions of the *Pons* slaver in 1846, the *Echo*'s display had more of a carnival feel.[143] Even 200 miles away in upcountry Spartanburg, correspondents reported on the large numbers of sightseers who flocked to the *Echo* for the "gratification of curiosity."[144] The language of gratification signaled a certain thrilling pleasure that, in the smallest measure, recognized enslaved Africans' physical ordeal while still reveling in the sight of the ship.[145] Nevertheless, the presence of recaptive Africans proved far more alluring than the slave ship, and the majority of public attention remained on recaptive youth and adults.

The exposure of *Echo* recaptives to hundreds of curious viewers, given the heightened slave trade debates of the time, is best understood as an act of public possession that merged popular entertainment with proslavery political culture. The most public access to the ship and its forced passengers came in the quarantine period before the naval prize crew turned African recaptives over to U.S. marshal Hamilton. Charlestonians reportedly deluged mayor Charles Macbeth with requests to board the ship. (Macbeth and several aldermen had visited the *Echo* themselves on the day after its arrival.) In evident disregard of quarantine rules and despite the threat of yellow fever from the city, one viewer reported that "very many went and very great was the curiosity and interest exhibited" during the two days when recaptives remained on the quarantined ship at Sullivan's Island.[146] After recaptives disembarked at the more remote Fort Sumter, tensions rose over the issue of their military guards.

Yet access to black bodies constituted a core prerogative of white mastery in southern slave society. For Frederick Porcher, "monstrous" federal suppression laws interfered with that access. Regarding *Echo* recaptives, he charged that "many a gentleman has repressed his curiosity to visit them from his unwillingness to encounter a mortifying repulse" from distrustful federal authorities.[147] In fact, it appeared that federal guards continued to allow small expeditions of wealthy white men to visit the fort and interact with African shipmates. Berkley Grimball, for example, exercised his entitlement with two private trips to the fort that he made in the company of fathers and sons of several elite families. Planter Charles Manigault similarly chartered his own exploratory expedition, which included two African-born elders (one owned by Manigault and the other loaned from a city slaveholder) intended to serve as translators. According to the account, however, the old man and woman "found none of their tribe and could not make themselves understood at all." Instead, West Central African shipmates laughed at the apparently

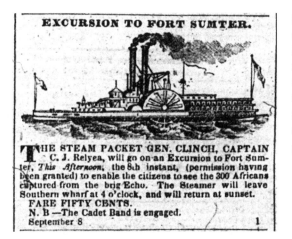

FIGURE 2.1 Excursion advertisement, *Charleston Daily Courier*. For a fare of fifty cents, the steam packet *General Clinch* offered Charleston sightseers a chance to view recaptives of the *Echo* under federal guard at Fort Sumter.

unintelligible speech of the enslaved translators.[148] Much is submerged in this account, including the perspectives of the elderly enslaved man and woman. However, the trip highlights Manigault's power to assemble this experimental encounter in hopes of further investigating the language and origins of *Echo* shipmates.

At the same time, public interest also inspired commercial ventures exploiting slave trade refugees as a visual spectacle. White leisure activities that consumed black bodies as part of a picturesque landscape were not entirely novel. Indeed, steamboats regularly offered pleasure excursions up and down the Ashley and Cooper Rivers. The *General Clinch*'s advertisements, for example, invited sightseers to witness the "mysteries of rice harvesting" in which "these periodical drum beatings and negro songs indicate that it is more a frolic than arduous work among the negroes."[149] Such excursions served as part of the social reproduction of race that naturalized the black labor enriching Lowcountry planters. Trips to Fort Sumter could likewise reinforce the racial ethnography of slave trade revivalists. The steamers *Osiris* and *General Clinch* both advertised steamboat excursions scheduled for 8 September "to enable the citizens to see the 300 Africans captured from the brig Echo."[150] (See fig. 2.1.) Notably, these ventures depended on the ethnographic lens for their unique promise. Unlike the *Echo*, which was exhibited specifically as a slave ship, *Echo* recaptives were not exhibited as victims of the slave trade but as "native" specimens of Africa. For only 25 cents and to the music of the local Cadet Band, the *Mercury* exclaimed, the excursion "will afford the shortest trip on record to Africa."[151] The steamboat advertisement effectively replaced the middle passage with an exotic transatlantic voyage for sightseers. For the price of the ticket, white Charlestonians could figuratively become a Bowen, a Livingstone, or a slaver and see with their own eyes what the revivalist debate was about.

Consequently, when weather and federal orders combined to foil the excursions of 8 September, some Charleston elites decried the tour's failure as an assault on southern honor. The passengers who turned up at the Southern wharf that day faced heavy rain showers and high waves. The captain of the *Osiris* wisely canceled its promised trip and rescheduled for the following day, but the *General Clinch* forged ahead through the choppy water.[152] Whether due to rough seas or federal suspicion of local slaveholders' motives, the soldiers at Fort Sumter did not allow eager passengers to disembark and tour the grounds.[153] Instead, the steamboat pulled up near the wharf, and the officers "in charge of the negros then paraded them outside the Fort, with the design of affording an opportunity for all to see."[154] *Echo* shipmates may have wondered what new separations awaited them as they were ushered through Fort Sumter's gates and exhibited on the rain-swept wharf. Curious sightseers, like disappointed explorers unable to penetrate an imagined African interior, had to satisfy themselves with a distant view. Moreover, the vocal faction of *General Clinch* passengers clearly objected to the "forms and ceremonies" of the federal guard as an "offensive exhibition of distrust on the part of the government officials."[155]

Accusations that the *General Clinch* agent had failed to deliver on his exhibitionist promise quickly evolved into political controversy. On the return trip, a group led by Professor Porcher organized a committee of protest against the tour restrictions and passed several indignant resolutions.[156] In light of the prevailing political excitement surrounding the *Echo*, limited access to African recaptives granted to sightseers by U.S. soldiers joined the list of federal insults against "the Southern people." From Porcher's perspective, the federal authority that denied access to Fort Sumter paralleled the federal ban on slaveholders' access to the transatlantic slave trade. The laws and treaties of trade suppression, he argued, were responsible for restricting southern states' rights to African bodies, whether to satisfy ethnographic curiosity or for plantation labor demands. In short, Porcher's politicization of an episode of frustrated slave trade tourism assumed a racial destiny of continued commodification for recaptive Africans. Ultimately, however, the federal removal law of 1819 denied southern slaveholders permanent possession of recaptive bodies. After three weeks at Fort Sumter, the enormous naval steamer *Niagara* arrived to load the surviving shipmates for another devastating transatlantic passage.[157]

The question of African racial destiny lingered weeks after the surviving

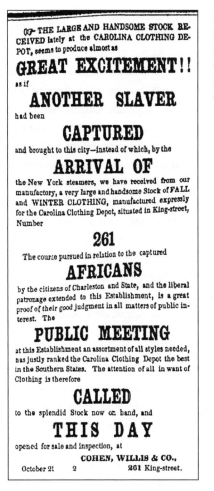

FIGURE 2.2 *Charleston Mercury* advertisement, 21 October 1858. Charleston
merchants sought to capitalize on public
excitement over the slave ship *Echo* with
this advertisement for their "handsome
stock" of fall and winter clothing.

Echo shipmates had departed for Liberia. A sign of the popular impact of recaptives at Fort Sumter appeared in the form of an advertisement posted in the
Mercury on 21 October. "GREAT EXCITEMENT!! ANOTHER SLAVER CAPTURED /
ARRIVAL OF 261 AFRICANS / PUBLIC MEETING CALLED THIS DAY," trumpeted
the eye-catching boldface headlines (see fig. 2.2). On second glance—and
reading literally between the headlines—curious readers detected another
message in smaller typeface: A "large and handsome stock" of "Carolina
clothing" had arrived from New York, and "the good judgment" shown
by Charleston's citizens "in relation to the captured Africans" would be no
less demonstrated by patronizing the establishment of Cohen, Willis & Co.
on King Street. By associating the excitement generated by the arrival of
recaptive Africans with an opportunity to shop, the Charleston clothing

merchants drew the *Echo* shipmates into yet another system of valuation, that of slaveholding consumer culture, in which enslaved black bodies became exchangeable for other material goods. At the top of the column, the phrase "THE LARGE AND HANDSOME STOCK" appeared in an intermediate typeface, smaller than the slave trade headlines but larger than the clothing descriptions. Ambivalence about the kind of "large and handsome stock" being promised would not have been lost on a southern antebellum reader.

While the ad played on the pun of African "stock," it also reflected a central theme in slave trade suppression politics, for its cleverness depended on an implicit opposition to the category of "legitimate" commerce. As alluded to earlier, advocates of slave trade suppression and colonization placed great faith in the ability of "lawful" commerce such as trade in ivory and palm oil to eradicate both the African internal and the international slave trade. Missionary Thomas Jefferson Bowen put it precisely: "The little palm nut is the greatest enemy that has ever reared its head against the slave trade."[158] Slave trade revivalists, however, rejected the legal demarcation entirely. Asserting the right to human property on racial grounds, Spratt and others argued that the federal government had no right to ban the illegal slave trade any more than it had the right to ban the shipment of any other product from one country to another.[159] Enslaved Africans could be reputably compared to "Carolina clothing" and great "excitement" generated by the prospects of acquiring both. Lying just below the surface of this equivalence between clothing and African bodies was another parallel drawn by slave trade revivalists between the U.S. domestic slave trade and the transatlantic trade they desired to renew.[160] With a wink to a time when foreign slave ships openly advertised their wares at the Charleston wharf (and to a future when that might again be so), Cohen, Willis & Co. capitalized on *Echo* recaptives' recent presence to capture consumers' attention.

———

Historian Beatriz Mamigonian notes that the category of "liberated African" arose as a "by-product of the suppression activities," leading to the treatment of liberated Africans in most places under British influence as part of a broader imperial "abolitionist experiment."[161] Recaptives at Fort Sumter were equally "by-products" of slave trade suppression, coming into custody of U.S. authorities ill prepared to shelter and feed them. Yet, the arrival of the *Echo* shipmates in a hotbed of U.S. slave trade revivalism resulted in the adamant rejection of their potentially "liberated" status. Rather, Charleston slave trade revivalists sought access to recaptive bodies to assert the natural existence of human inequality and chattel slavery. Despite some acknowledgment of abject medical suffering, public discussion of recaptives primarily treated them as ethnographic subjects whose bodies revealed not the ravages of slave ship captivity but the barbarity of people intrinsically suited for enslavement.

Exhibition of recaptives via elite inspection and steamboat excursions revealed an early form of imperial visual culture, which by the 1890s would be more widely institutionalized in world fairs and museum exhibits. Charleston's version of exhibition extended the imaginations of Lowcountry white audiences. Instead of merely reading about Africa in midcentury exploration literature, Charlestonians could now see living Africans in their "native condition." The display of *Echo* shipmates is an important part of the *Echo* story because it illuminates both the cultural politics of race and the political culture of proslavery imperialism. Furthermore, the very fact that white Charleston sightseers paid to see slave ship recaptives as a form of entertainment vividly illustrates the human cost of slave trade suppression policies carried out by a slaveholding republic. The animosity of slave trade revivalists to federal authority contributed to the urgency of the shipmates' removal, thus sending recaptives on another ocean crossing long before their bodies had time to recover from their first traumatic passage.

While scholars of nineteenth-century racial spectatorship in other contexts have explored the ability of racial subjects to gaze back and engage in "performative act[s] of self-determination," there is very little evidence available to explore this line of analysis with *Echo* shipmates.[162] Rather, it is more accurate to think of West Central African slave ship survivors at Fort Sumter as engaged in a parallel struggle for survival and meaning in the midst of the obscenity of their racial display. Under federal guard and popular gaze, recaptives constituted a collective of shipmates, a nascent and emerging community. The relationships forged within and across language groups, between younger and older, were the raw materials out of which recaptives sought to make their ordeal legible. Their struggle would be repeated two years later in another federal camp, this time among a larger and more diverse group of shipmates in Key West, Florida. By the time recaptives arrived in Key West, slave trade revival politics had faded in the face of impending national division and the fractious presidential campaigns. Nevertheless, the American public continued its fascination with recaptive Africans as exotic spectacles for mass consumption. Once again, the sensation of "native Africans" in the popular press would submerge the social ordeal of slave ship survivors. Yet, recaptives continued to wage their parallel struggle, building shipmate bonds in order to lend their own meanings to the category of "recaptive."

3

Suffering and Spectacle

What is to come even a bird with a long neck
cannot see, but our Lord only.
—*Narrative of the Travels of Ali Eisami*,
Sierra Leone, ca. 1850

Beginning in May 1860, a transient settlement of slave ship refugees sprang up on the southernmost tip of the Florida Keys.[1] The Key West "African Depot," as U.S. marshal Fernando Moreno called it, resulted from newly vigilant U.S. Home Squadron patrols near the Cuban coast that intercepted three ships trafficking in contraband human cargo: the *Wildfire* (26 April), the *William* (9 May), and the *Bogota* (23 May). Despite having orders from the secretary of the navy to bring any recaptives seized to the healthier ports of New England, Lieutenant T. Augustus Craven of the U.S. steamer *Mohawk* determined that the longer journey would prove lethal for most of the young recaptives crowded below deck. Craven thus took the *Wildfire* to Key West and established a precedent for the other two captured slave ships.[2] Two years earlier, Moreno had turned the *Echo* away from Key West, sending the seized slaver on to Charleston.[3] By the summer of 1860, however, the largest group of "recaptured Africans" to enter U.S. ports waited on the southernmost Florida key for their mandated removal to Liberia.

To a certain extent, the Key West Depot resembled many of the temporary encampments of diverse groups of recaptives located across the Atlantic World in sites that included Freetown, St. Helena, and Rio de Janeiro.[4] In Key West, the 1860 surge in U.S. slave ship interceptions brought together recaptives from two different regions of Africa. West Central Africans from the *Wildfire* and the *William* had already been encamped for a month in Key West when a predominantly adult group of recaptives from the Bight of Benin arrived in the *Bogota*. The *New Orleans Picayune* remarked on the *Bogota* ship-mates, "They are of distinct tribe, or tribes, from the others, having no affinity in common with them—each to the other was quite a subject of curiosity and wonder."[5] As death continued to erode their numbers, hundreds of slave trade refugees made their survival intelligible primarily through relationships to their immediate shipmates and others with whom they shared language, geographic origins, and—in exceptional cases—kinship. In this sense, an analysis of recaptives at Key West expands the discussion of the reconstruc-tion of social life initiated with the story of the *Echo* shipmates.

Detained by a nation whose majority feared free blacks and upheld the constitutionality of human property, recaptives in U.S. custody found virtu-ally no recognition of their social crisis in the outside world. Instead, condi-tions within the African Depot reflected the underlying racial politics of slave trade suppression implemented by a slaveholding republic. From the highest levels of government, federal officials viewed the supervision of recaptives as a difficult, expensive, and disagreeable task.[6] Furthermore, predatory planters from the Gulf States stalked Key West, threatening abduction and reenslave-ment. At ground level, federal officials and other local residents sought to meet the physical needs of recaptives, who numbered roughly half the size of Key West's total population.[7] Yet the spectacular qualities of the African Depot also quickly attracted the interest of sightseers and the popular press.

From the first moments of recaptivity in the Florida Keys, slave ship survivors came under the scrutiny of a wider American public. The depot's location just outside Fort Taylor and less than a mile from the small town of Key West gave journalists greater access to recaptives than Fort Sumter had afforded. The *Savannah Republican* provided a glimpse of the sensational tone of press coverage: "The African village presents a very curious spectacle: 1480 wild Africans dancing and singing night and day."[8] From Salt Lake, Utah, to Manitowoc, Wisconsin, distant news editors concocted rabid headlines about "Raw Darkies" in Florida or simply reprinted other papers' stories.[9] New York–based illustrated weeklies rushed to cover Key West as well, adding visual imagery to pages of newsprint. *Harper's Weekly* produced a three-quarter-page engraving of *Wildfire* shipmates posed on the deck of the slave ship. Artists from *Frank Leslie's Illustrated Newspaper* drew up sketches of young people, too weak to walk, carried off the *William* by horse-drawn carts. Departing from South Carolina's earlier slave trade revivalist agenda, illustrated news of Key West slave trade survivors emphasized white national benevolence and African exoticism, while passing lightly over recaptive sur-vival struggles. Recaptives in Key West thus endured a peculiar kind of visibility in which popular ethnographic conventions shrouded the crisis of recaptive life and death.

Routes to Recaptivity

Like the *Echo* in 1858, the slavers *Wildfire*, *William*, and *Bogota* followed the narrowing routes of contraband slaving in the waning years of the trans-atlantic trade. Built in Amesbury, Massachusetts, the *Wildfire* left New York City with an American captain sailing along the dominant slaving route for the Congo River region. The *William* had been purchased in New York in 1859 and sent to Mobile, and then on to Cuba.[10] In Havana, outfitters readied the *William* for a slaving voyage to the Congo River. Like the *Echo* before them, both the *William* and the *Wildfire* relied on multiple investors who circulated and laundered capital through Havana and New York businesses to feed the illicit trade. The money and men behind the *Bogota* also had New York con-nections, but the barque had been built in Honfleur, in northwestern France. Captained by a Frenchman, the *Bogota* cleared from New York headed for the West African port of Ouidah.[11] No slavers associated with these three voy-ages were ever convicted; some, as foreigners, could not even be tried under U.S. laws.[12] Long after the slavers had been released, their African captives remained in U.S. custody and subject to American slave trade legislation.

Recaptives who disembarked the *Wildfire* and the *William* in Key West resembled 1858 *Echo* shipmates in terms of both their young age and origins in West Central Africa. To an even greater extent than the *Echo*'s embarkation port of Cabinda, the Congo River's trading posts served as gathering points for the majority of West Central African captives in the last years of illegal transatlantic slaving.[13] Of the estimated 75,865 slaves embarked by foreign slavers from Congo regional ports between 1856 and 1860, 55.5 percent came from barracoons on the Congo River, compared with 31.6 percent from the Loango Coast that included Cabinda.[14] A rash of new trading posts spread along the river in the 1850s as American, Portuguese, Angolan, and Spanish traders defied naval warships in search of quick profits from Cuban slave sales. Illicit networks connecting Havana, New York, and Benguela financed the unregulated and decentralized satellite loading depots just out of view of naval cruisers on the Atlantic coast.[15]

Situating the Key West African Depot as an outgrowth of 1850s Congo-to-Cuba slave routes further reinforces our understanding of child captives' vulnerability on both sides of the Atlantic.[16] One government agent in Key West reported roughly 50 adults among the *William*'s 355 survivors, with over

300 others being children and youth between the ages of five and fourteen.[17] News correspondents who boarded the *Wildfire* soon after its arrival in Florida also confirmed roughly three-quarters of the shipmates to be "boys aged from ten to sixteen years."[18] These comments reveal observers' basic recognition of recaptives' young age, despite the absence of clearly articulated criteria for designating childhood. Like recaptives of the *Echo*, these young people found themselves uprooted from their dependent places in home societies by mechanisms of debt, warfare, criminal sentencing, and abduction that intensified as the expansion of the nineteenth-century Atlantic commercial economy made inroads into African polities.[19] Young West Central Africans experienced great vulnerability as Cuban slave prices rose. Some, who had been locally enslaved for years or even from birth, were now shunted to foreign slavers.[20] Historian Jelmer Vos's research on French indenture recruitment suggests that many enslaved youth originated from villages close to the Congo River and particularly from the port of Boma.[21] Other *Wildfire* boys had been taken during raids and witnessed the violent deaths of their parents during attacks on their towns.[22]

Thrust onto illegal slave ships through a variety of mechanisms, many young captives from the *Wildfire* and the *William* shared broad social and cultural affinities as well as histories of traumatic loss. The existence of multiple states in West Central Africa as well as the undocumented and decentralized nature of the late slave trade poses difficulties for the task of identifying specific homelands for the majority of these shipmates.[23] After speaking with recaptives through translators, *Harper's Weekly* correspondents identified many of the *Wildfire* recaptives as "Congos." The term suggests both the embarkation point and the route of captivity through Vili trading networks on the northern banks of the Congo toward the coast.[24] Slave traders also crossed the Congo River from the southern side at Manianga, Isangila, and Inga to bring their captives to barracoons on the Loango Coast and near the river's mouth.[25] In general, most West Central African recaptives spoke "Bantu" languages that shared enough in common to be mutually intelligible. One agent reported that among the *Wildfire* survivors, linguistic variations suggested "portions of three tribes" whose differing dialects were "not so marked as to prevent intercommunication."[26]

Regardless of their different routes to the barracoons, all faced the terrifying rupture that arrived with the rush and din of embarking slave ships. In 1860, seaman Lucius Vermilyea described how, after traders assembled their captives for shipment, barracoon workers drove frightened people, 80 to 100 at a time, into large coastal boats that plied deadly currents and high waves on their way to the waiting ships. The slaver *Montauk*, according to Vermilyea, loaded more than 1,000 captives in less than three hours. On the open upper deck, sailors packed 350 boys and girls "in nude condition" side by side, "leaving scarcely room for seamen to get to the wheel without stepping on them."[27] Crammed together on slave decks and in improvised storage spaces, terrified enslaved shipmates absorbed the rumors that ran through the ship about what might happen next.

The very bodies of these recaptives, prized as commodities by contraband traders, testified to interrupted lives and ruptured social relationships. For young men and women imprisoned in the *Wildfire* and the *William*, transatlantic enslavement and abduction interrupted stages of initiation by which they would have reached social maturity within their home societies.[28] As the *Harper's* correspondent observed, some of the older men and women from the *Wildfire* bore marks of initiation, whereas many youthful recaptives did not. Four or five of the women, according to *Harper's*, "were a good deal tattooed on the back and arms." These nuanced signs of belonging and status appeared on some of the women, alongside the "merchant's mark" branded into their arms. In addition, many adults and adolescents also had dental modifications similar to those described for the *Echo* shipmates, with the two front teeth either sharpened "to a point" or with portions chipped away.[29] Such deliberate shaping of appearance, also identified in skeletal remains from a St. Helena recaptive cemetery, would have been immediately intelligible to recaptives from common regions.[30] Furthermore, the journalist's explicit observation of altered teeth among "boys and girls" confirmed particular rites of beautification and initiation these young recaptives had already undergone in the now interrupted process of coming of age.

With so many young people in the West Central African captive population, adult men and women assumed particular authority as hierarchies formed among shipmates. A *Harper's* correspondent remarked, for example, that Madia, an unbaptized "pagan" of about twenty years with a "fine personal appearance," possessed significant status, judging from the "deference that seemed to be paid to her by some of her companions" (see fig. 3.1). Although the correspondent did not elaborate on the basis of Madia's evident authority, the brief remark suggests an internal social hierarchy commonly understood by West Central African shipmates but obscured to outside observers. Madia's ability to command respect or fear could have derived from spiritual authority, as was the case of documented healers forcibly transported into American slave societies.[31] Furthermore, witchcraft charges could have resulted in a woman of higher status being sent into Atlantic exile, for existing

FIGURE 3.1 "The Princess Madia," *Harper's Weekly* engraving, 2 June 1860. Courtesy of the Huntington Library, San Marino, California.

THE PRINCESS MADIA.—[From a Daguerreotype.]

prohibitions against the enslavement of freeborn Kongo subjects accused of witchcraft had weakened considerably by the eighteenth century.[32] It is also possible that Madia's companions recognized her as a high-born woman, for even the nobility could find themselves enslaved due to political rivalries caused by the rapidly transforming state economies in nineteenth-century Loango and Kongo.[33] In a recaptive population skewed unnaturally toward youth, Madia's mature age may have further reinforced authority based on either social class or ritual expertise. However, it is also significant that *Harper's* noted only "some" *Wildfire* recaptives deferred to Madia, hinting at the presence of subsets of shipmates who were most recognizable to one another among hundreds of strangers.

Several recaptives of the *Wildfire*, by virtue of their exposure to Luso-African culture in Luanda, served as translators in conversations with Key West journalists and government authorities.[34] According to *Harper's Weekly*, the recaptives, who gave their names as Francisco, Salvador, Constantia, Antonia, and Amelia, "did not belong to the same tribe that the rest do." All had been baptized by Catholic priests in Luanda and spoke some Portuguese.[35] Luanda's many languages afforded some captives the chance to gain language skills that were particularly useful on contraband slave ships where at least some of the crew invariably spoke Portuguese and Spanish.

The presence of *Wildfire* recaptives associated with Luanda further confirms recent scholarly revisions of the concept of an advancing inland "slaving frontier." Rather than positing African slave raids progressively far inland, historians now find that many nineteenth-century transatlantic captives originated in towns and villages closer to the coast.[36] As a center of Luso-African commerce with a population of more than 12,000 by the 1850s, the port of Luanda operated as one such site of enslavement.[37] Historian Roquinaldo Ferreira argues that Luanda proved dangerous to both free and locally enslaved residents, who were kidnapped and sold to foreign slavers despite regulations against wrongful enslavement.[38] Nineteenth-century Portuguese sources reported the common sight of mothers "banging old kitchen pots on the streets of the city" to seek help in the search for their kidnapped children.[39] Once the Brazilian slave trade closed in 1850, coastal traders simply moved captives like Francisco and Constantia up the coast to the Congo River through trade networks stretching from Benguela to Cabinda.[40]

The young *Wildfire* shipmate Constantia traveled this pathway from Luanda into Atlantic enslavement. According to the *Harper's* interviewer, "She does not remember her father; she was stolen away when she was young, and was sold by her brother." Constantia's story illustrated the climate of insecurity prevailing in and near Luanda, where young people could be not only kidnapped but also sold or pawned, sometimes by their own relatives.[41] Constantia's interview with *Harper's* also revealed her own gendered survival strategies as an isolated young, female recaptive. Representing herself as fatherless and in need of protection can be understood as a strategy congruent with her hopes for acquiring some minimal protection as a domestic dependent within a new household.[42] Like the others enslaved through Luanda, Constantia seems to have used her exposure to Luso-African culture and her facility in Portuguese to communicate her story and perhaps gain some advantage in her state of exile.

Francisco, another *Wildfire* shipmate from Luanda, employed language skills to assert his value for new federal captors in Key West. As the only adult male among the Luanda affiliates, Francisco survived, in part, by using his cultural capital to gain authority over other recaptives. Through an interpreter, Francisco explained to the *Harper's* correspondent that he "was a slave in Africa." Rather than returning there, he continued, he would prefer to be "a slave to the white man in this country."[43] Physician and special government agent William Proby Young observed that Francisco quickly acquired some English and emerged as a "supervisor of the crowd" in the sprawling camp that swelled from 500 to over 1,300 people between May and mid-July 1860.

According to Young, "Just before the time for their meals [Francisco] would collect them in squads of ten and beat upon a drum while they kept time by clapping their hands and singing."[44] As Francisco facilitated the depot's daily food distribution, he secured his relationship to fellow shipmates and his usefulness to U.S. officials. His statement of preference for American enslavement can be interpreted in a number of ways, including a mistranslation, fear of another Atlantic crossing, or a perceptive attempt to gain the favor and protection of American officials. In the fragmentary evidence on Constantia, Francisco, and other Africans singled out for attention by American observers, we can catch a glimpse of how recaptives sought to assert their position within shipmate groups and gain some modicum of control over their perilous situation.

At the end of May 1860, the geographic origins of recaptives in Key West's impromptu wayside station expanded with the arrival of a third ship. Up to that point, the camp was a West Central African transit zone peaking at 1,020 people and declining as the sickest shipmates died. Kikongo rang out, possibly merging with occasional Umbundu or Kimbundu spoken alongside the English and Spanish of the guards and camp workers and the Portuguese of the slave crew translator. On 25 May, however, news arrived of a third slaver, intercepted by the USS *Crusader* near Nuevitas on the northern coastline of Cuba. Aboard the French-built *Bogota*, U.S. naval authorities found more than 400 captive men and women embarked from Ouidah, the only location north of the equator still operating as a slaving port in 1860.[45] Their arrival brought the encampment's total population to 1,350.[46] "The Depot is now full," wrote marshal Moreno, "and not a foot of room to spare for the accommodation of any more Africans until the present occupants are removed."[47] Yoruba, Hausa, and Fon now sounded through the camp as well.[48]

In contrast to West Central Africans in Key West, the *Bogota* shipmates arrived with immediate memories of violent abduction particular to political upheavals in and around the Kingdom of Dahomey.[49] Dahomey emerged as a powerful West African state in the mid-seventeenth century and gained direct access to the transatlantic trade by conquering the port city of Ouidah in 1727.[50] Many of the *Bogota*'s shipmates had been taken as prisoners of war in Dahomean military campaigns early in 1860.[51] During attacks on Yoruba-speaking towns to the north and east of Dahomey's capital, Abomey, the king's army took thousands of captives.[52] In a long-standing tradition, returning Dahomean soldiers ritually sold their prisoners of war to the king. Captives not deemed useful to Dahomean society were then marched to Ouidah for transatlantic sale.[53] Despite British diplomatic pressure to replace slave trading with palm oil exports, a brief revival of Dahomean royal support for the slave trade occurred between 1857 and 1863. During those years, eleven recorded voyages carried away over 6,800 enslaved captives.[54] Compared with West Central African mechanisms of enslavement, Dahomey's military raids resulted in many more adults—primarily men—among the *Bogota* shipmates. Children and elders were often killed in such attacks, and women were more likely to be retained internally. Meanwhile, royal officials sent young men, along with a small number of women and girls, on to coastal traders.

Memories of wartime devastation haunted many West African recaptives arriving in Key West, further deepening the alienation of transatlantic enslavement. Cudjo Lewis, an enslaved Yoruba man smuggled from Ouidah into Mobile Bay on the *Clotilda*, vividly recounted the sudden violence of his initial capture.[55] Half a century later, trauma still suffused Lewis's recounting. At dawn, formidable Dahomean forces had attacked Lewis's town, killing scores and taking the strongest as captives. During the forced march to the coast, Lewis recalled the sight of triumphant soldiers displaying the heads of dead townspeople as war trophies.[56] The threat of social death did not begin with the middle passage for Lewis but deepened with each successive move farther from home. *Bogota* recaptives most certainly also grieved similar losses even as they formed tentative new shipmate relations under the shadow of disease and mortality at Key West.

Other *Bogota* captives arrived in Ouidah's slave warehouses not as prisoners of war but as victims of pawnship practices or random kidnappings. As one of the last slaving ports in West Africa, Ouidah served as a collection point for many sorts of captives arriving from the hinterlands of the Bight of Benin. Sources from Liberia later identified *Bogota* recaptives as including, in addition to Yoruba and Hausa speakers, some Fon speakers from Dahomey and possibly at least a few individuals from the Bariba and Miyobe groups located in the northern regions of present-day Benin and Togo.[57] James Grymes, a white physician hired to attend *Bogota* shipmates on their voyage to Liberia, heard through an interpreter one man's story of being captured and taken to Ouidah while "carrying a letter from some one in 'Paw-Paw.'"[58] If the man had been abducted near one of the coastal centers of Little Popo or Grand Popo, he would then have had to travel fifteen to thirty miles eastward before being locked in an Ouidah warehouse.[59] Grymes recorded the man's description of a "large house," to which "they kept bringing others in, day & night."[60] In Ouidah's slave pens, captives traded stories of home and hoped for the unlikely ransom by relatives. According to another account from Ouidah, boys among the confined captives sometimes found the resilience to play games, although being confined with adult men could also result in injury and abuse.[61] The arrival of foreign slavers, however, shattered tenuous alliances and most remaining kinship ties. As the anonymous *Bogota* man told Grymes, the buyers in Ouidah "ruthlessly divided families and relatives."[62]

Like their West Central African counterparts, *Bogota* shipmates arrived at Key West with a similarly terrifying experience of embarkation. Once a sale had been negotiated in Ouidah, traders pushed men, women, and children from the warehouses and drove them on foot or by boat through the lagoon between Ouidah and the coast. Just before departure, men working for the slave merchants burned their captives' flesh with marks of ownership that allowed various investors to track their portion of slave sales.[63] Mahommah Gardo Baquaqua, a Dendi-speaking youth sold to slavers in Ouidah during the 1840s, vividly recalled the searing iron brand that slavers pressed into his back.[64] When captives arrived at the ocean, hired canoe men from the Gold Coast paddled them through the rough, shark-filled surf and over treacherous sandbars to the waiting ships.[65] There, a final humiliating ritual of embarkation took place. According to Cudjo Lewis, the maritime workers stripped the remaining clothes from slaves as they scrambled from canoe to ship, imposing another stamp of dishonor and degradation.[66] In similar fashion, the men, women, and children of the *Bogota* passed into the cramped interior of the ship, filled with fear, anger, and pain. They also carried within themselves the social identities and cultural knowledge by which some would laboriously begin to heal the wounds of their ordeal.

In contrast to the Congo River cohort of recaptives, rough demographic outlines indicate that *Bogota* shipmates included a much larger proportion of mature men and women. A government agent reporting on *Bogota* survivors embarking for Liberia tallied 266 men (69.5 percent of the total), 19 boys (5 percent), 86 women (22.5 percent), and 12 girls (3 percent).[67] These numbers are significant because, as in many places, age factored heavily in shaping a person's place and influence within West African society. Age could identify cohorts for initiation and hierarchies of obligation and power and could indicate readiness for marriage and childbearing.[68] For recaptives in motion across the Atlantic, age shaped the repertoire of skills, leadership, and knowledge necessary for forging meaningful social ties among shipmates. Stripped of much of the material culture, institutions, and relationships that defined their past lives, many *Bogota* recaptives nevertheless carried experiences of mature participation in home communities, made visible in precise dental modifications and elaborate scarification adorning both faces and bodies.[69] In the months to come, the more mature profile of *Bogota* survivors would influence the character of shipmate relations, the perception of survivors by U.S. authorities, and the prospects for survivors once they landed in Liberia.

Receptive Life in the Shadow of Death

As one of many temporary bases for recaptive Africans around the Atlantic World, the Key West Depot dictated the material constraints under which recaptives built their fragile shipmate collectives. Like other such holding areas, Key West's depot shared problems of crowding, disease, and scarce provisions. For example, the encampment at Rupert's Valley, on the South Atlantic island of St. Helena from 1841 to 1867, often exceeded its capacity of 500 people. In the peak months of March and April 1850, almost 1,300 recaptives filled Rupert's Valley's rough shelters.[70] Key West's recaptive camp had a much shorter life, and its U.S. agents were less prepared for their task than St. Helena officials. Yet recaptive shipmates in both places waited in limbo for the next phase of their displacement. The depot's inmates had not yet entered new labor contracts of apprenticeship, and their days in Key West were filled with uncertainty. Psychologists studying refugee trauma in twentieth-century camps have analyzed the stress of suspended existence on refugees who inhabit one or more intermediate locations between the initial rupture from home and a designated resettlement area.[71] Looking at refugee experiences from a different discipline, medical anthropologists have analyzed the ways in which violence, loss of kin, and a fractured sense of identity result not only in mental trauma but "somatization," in which the experience of displacement manifests in culturally specific physical distress.[72] The scholarly insight that transit zones can become sites of "secondary traumatic experience" proves useful in thinking about recaptives' existence in the aftermath of slave ship interception.[73] Key West's slave trade refugees countered the alienation of their liminal existence through daily relations with fellow shipmates.

As the depot's population grew, U.S. authorities focused primarily on the daunting logistics of housing and feeding survivors, burying the dead, and maintaining control over the recaptive camp. With each new arrival of African shipmates (on 30 April, 12 May, and 25 May), the camp next to Fort Taylor evolved as a settlement defined primarily by the routines and restrictions of military oversight.[74] In early May, U.S. marshal Moreno described to Secretary of the Interior Jacob Thompson his construction of a 140-foot-long wooden building and a kitchen on three acres of shore near Fort Taylor, surrounded by a six-foot-high fence that extended into the surf.[75] He sent the most desperately ill individuals from the *Wildfire* to a makeshift hospital in a carpenter shop near the fort.[76] Moreno's initial optimism dwindled along with the island's resources. "I must call the Attention of the Department to the great necessity of removing these Africans from here at the Earliest possible moment," he wrote in mid-May. "Their continuance here for a period of two or three months will exhaust the supply of water on this island."[77] By June, the combined population of three groups of shipmates strained the depot's capacity for basic provisions of safety, medical care, and nutrition. Although the outdoor spaces alleviated crowding during the day, in the nine rooms of the expanded barracks, each child and adult would have had just enough room to lie down.[78]

An ambiguous blend of protection and incarceration characterized government oversight of the recaptive camp. Well aware of the politics of slave trade revival and the value of African captives in the Deep South and Havana slave markets, Moreno took measures to prevent either "escape or recapture" and established contingency plans for any "Emergency."[79] A naval marine unit from the USS *Wyandotte* and an army unit from Fort Taylor with two small artillery pieces provided armed guard outside the camp.[80] The danger was real, for several planters from South Carolina and Florida attempted to bribe the guards and spirit away recaptives (or "rescue" them, as one paper put it) on a clandestine steamer.[81] Lowcountry planter Richard T. Morrison, described as "a principle of the party," told Young that had their plans not been foiled by rumors of stiff federal resistance, "I should have had every one of them. I'd give $50,000 cash to have them landed on the Coast of Carolina."[82] Whether or not recaptives were aware of this additional danger, the security measures in place contributed to the guarded atmosphere of the depot.

Moreno's equal concern with an internal "African" threat led him to amplify the "geography of containment" imposed upon the depot. If, as historian Stephanie Camp has argued, the "spatial impulse" lay at the center of American enslavement, constrained movement and regimented routines also defined recaptive existence in Key West.[83] The encampment featured barracks segregated by age and gender, regulated mealtimes and rations, and physical punishment in the form of stocks for individuals regarded as unruly.[84] Moreno established a military guard along the camp's external perimeter and employed a civilian guard inside the camp that he deemed "absolutely necessary to direct and keep the Africans in good discipline." In addition, he employed a Spanish "passenger" from the slaver whose services, remarked Moreno, have been "invaluable to me in controling these people."[85] Upon the *Bogota*'s arrival, the marshal allowed women and children to disembark within

FIGURE 3.2 Sketch of 1860 Key West "African Depot" by unknown artist.
Records of the Office of the Secretary of the Interior Relating to the Suppression
of the African Slave Trade and Negro Colonization, 1854–1872. Courtesy of the
National Archives and Records Administration, College Park, Maryland.

three days but kept the men on board the anchored slaver for an additional
five days until the guard could be strengthened. Moreno explained his actions
by warning that the "stout" men "of gigantic proportion" on the *Bogota* were
"much more savage than the Congo negroes." In addition, Moreno pleaded
for military reinforcements "for the purpose of aiding me in guarding and
keeping these Africans under subjection." Although existing records make no
mention of recaptive protest against their confinement at Key West, Moreno
feared an "outbreak" would overwhelm the depot's armed guards.[86] As the
recaptive population grew, the marshal sought increased militarization that
replicated certain conditions of captivity—indeed, some observers called
the camp a "barracoon."[87]

Despite its obvious carceral features, the depot's environment also allowed recaptive shipmates to move and interact, to some extent, on their
own volition. Mobility within the depot's boundaries differed significantly
from exhausting overland marches or the whip-imposed immobility of captives in a fetid slave deck. A sketch preserved in Moreno's records conveys a
sense of open space on the white sand beach that *Wildfire* recaptives at first
found unsettling (see fig. 3.2). *Harper's Weekly* reported that upon entering
the newly constructed wooden barracks, the *Wildfire* shipmates "all arranged
themselves along the sides of the building as they had been accustomed to
do on the decks of the vessel, and squatted down in the same manner."[88]
Aboard the *Wildfire*, reported *Harper's*, enslaved boys and young men had

been conditioned to occupy only the edges of the deck, so as to leave a central aisle for crewmembers to pass.[89] Only after several hours did Moreno's men manage to communicate the possibility of moving freely around the buildings and toward the nearby ocean, where recaptives could bathe each morning. The account offered a stark reminder that recaptivity entailed a fundamental readjustment of the body as a first step in reasserting social life.

In the bare environment of the depot, recaptives' bodies became the first resource of collective expression. Echoing white observers at Fort Sumter in 1858, two physicians appointed as government agents remarked on the sound and style of recaptive musical expression. William Proby Young compared the refrain of West Central African recaptives as they clapped and sang to Francisco's drumming to an American evangelical "Camp Meeting."[90] Several weeks later, John Moore McCalla commented on *Bogota* shipmates "going through their wild dances preparatory to taking supper." According to Mc-Calla, one man seated on a wooden barrel sounded out a drum rhythm that accompanied and organized the distribution of food. Indulging his sense of the exotic, McCalla found some young women "extremely graceful and wild" and other dancers "ludicrous beyond description."[91] No doubt McCalla's words reflect characteristic Victorian assumptions about uncivilized bodies, but he also unwittingly recorded the collective act of displaced people from multiple localities and language groups engaging in common expression.

Recaptives' free movement to music served more than the utilitarian purpose of a call to meals. It is true that slave ship crews often forced captives to dance to reinvigorate their stiffened limbs, and the Key West dance could also have had overtones of coercion.[92] Yet a "somatic approach" to "enslaved bodies in space," as Camp would put it, offers an alternative interpretation of how recaptives may have danced to gather courage, summon ancestors, or grieve the dead, thus creating an intelligible world among marooned slave trade refugees. By engaging in clandestine parties in the antebellum South, Camp argues, bondsmen and -women asserted their "third bodies"—not the bodies dominated by slaveholders or suffused with pain, but the transcendent body capable of pleasure, beauty, and meaning.[93] Extending this powerful analysis to recaptives in American custody suggests one of the ways in which diverse groups of destitute shipmates collectively manifested this "third body," an expression made all the more necessary by suffering and death. By the time McCalla made his observations, only the West African shipmates of the *Bogota* remained in the depot. Yet even among this single shipmate group, it seemed to him as if "no two seemed to go through the same series of motions or to be singing the same words." The remark clearly reflected McCalla's incomprehension of West African polyphony. Yet he may also have been observing how people of different languages and traditions came together to improvise a collective present out of the fragments of individual pasts.[94] Expressions of social identity that could be enacted with few resources other than the body itself, aided by memory and imagination, would remain critical to the daily existence of survivors as they embarked on their second Atlantic crossing.

Whereas most shipmate bonds had been formed in exile, a rare recovery of lost kin prompted celebration among West Central African recaptives and drew the attention of the American press. According to one widely circulated account, a "middle aged" woman, who had arrived with her three children in the *Wildfire*, discovered among the *William*'s shipmates four young women "whom she claimed as her daughters."[95] Both slave ships had loaded captives in March 1860 from the same barracoons near the mouth of the Congo River, making possible a remarkable reunion of seven women and girls torn from one another in previous captive journeys.[96] The newspaper account's assumption of sentimentalized nuclear family bonds obscured the subtleties of the women's reclaimed kinship; these women could have been joined as mother and daughters or by local residence, extended lineage, or ritual family.[97] Yet fellow shipmates clearly understood the magnitude of the moment. A journalist wrote that "shouts rose from three hundred voices" as the woman embraced her reclaimed daughters. The older woman who anchored her social identity strongly in her role as a mother and elder kinswoman recovered a familiar social mooring. Young and vulnerable female recaptives regained a reassuring adult presence and tangible evidence of their former lives. The strength of their connection became further evident in the fact that the four younger women left their *William* shipmates to travel with their maternal elder on the *Wildfire* recaptives' Liberian passage.[98] Even so, the exceptional nature of their reunion highlights the enormity of recaptives' social alienation and the imperative of building shipmate networks.

For most recaptives, the collective basis of identity in family and lineage had been irrevocably ruptured. Shared experiences of illness and death instead served as the foundation from which recaptives built their social worlds in the wake of illegal slave ships.[99] Numerous recaptives arrived in Key West weak and emaciated, wracked by dysentery, blinded by ophthalmia, and suffering from skin and respiratory infections.[100] Due perhaps to the condition in which captives embarked at Ouidah, *Bogota* shipmates had experienced relatively fewer deaths and less sickness in the middle passage than their young West Central African counterparts. Young Congo shipmates of the *William*, however, arrived in such a state of extremity that many required transportation in horse-drawn carts from the government wharf to the camp's buildings.[101] At the depot, the effects of weeks at sea in crowded, filthy quarters with little water and food proved difficult to reverse.[102] Daniel Whitehurst, a Virginia native and army physician with prior experience in Liberia, headed a team of three doctors hired by Moreno.[103] Concerned most to defend his record in supervising the depot, Moreno told his superiors in Washington that after recaptives had embarked for Liberia, he took great satisfaction in knowing that he had been relieved of his "responsible charge *without loss except from natural causes*."[104]

Congregating large numbers of people already suffering from a slave ship voyage, however, produced devastating results in recaptive camps throughout the Atlantic. In one extreme example, the recaptive hospital in Sierra Leone between 1838 and 1850 showed an average annual mortality of 50 percent.[105] Key West recaptives experienced a lower overall rate of mortality (18.9 percent), but the deaths were compressed into a period of only eighty days and affected every shipmate group.[106] During the entire period of occupation, only four days passed without the report of one or more deaths. On 28 May, the only recorded birth in the camps took place; one fragile life joined the camp as seven slid away. From that day until 7 July, in a period during which almost 200 people passed away, several days took a toll of six, seven, or eight lives each. The losses peaked on 20 June, when U.S. marshal Moreno recorded the deaths of one *Bogota* male, eight *William* males, one *William* female, one *Wildfire* male, and one *Wildfire* female. None of the recaptives had much control over how the deceased were buried. In Florida's summer heat, dead bodies quickly decomposed and thus had to be promptly removed for burial. Daniel Davis, a Key West master carpenter, oversaw the laborers who interred bodies in shallow graves on a southern shore removed from both the camp and the main Key West cemetery.[107] Tally sheets drawn up by Moreno listed 294 deaths and bore the signatures of the hospital steward and three attending physicians and a signed statement by the master carpenter. Perfunctory burial procedures addressed concerns for public health and official documentation.

Consequently, as with all enslaved Africans in motion across the Atlantic, the inability to properly bury and honor the dead deepened the social crisis faced by Key West recaptives. To borrow historian Vincent Brown's phrasing, the Key West camp represented one of many "gasping new societies" in which hundreds of recaptive shipmates attempted to make their loss comprehensible through meaningful acknowledgment of death in an alien environment.[108] Over many years, enslaved and recaptive Africans in the Americas gradually adapted familiar burial rites to their New World circumstances, but recaptives in Key West did not have this kind of time.[109] In their immediate crisis, they were unable to enact collective rituals, which in both West and West Central Africa soothed the transition of a living relative into the realm of ancestors. An honorable burial helped family members ensure the positive intervention of an ancestor in the lives of his or her kin.[110] In the transient Key West and Fort Sumter government camps, however, physical depletion, impending removal, and few resources precluded the necessary rites. A closer sampling of burial practices from nineteenth-century West Central and West Africa clearly illustrates the threat to the critical relations between the living and the dead posed by the bleak conditions of U.S. recaptive camps.

Each group of recaptives experienced the alienation of death through Atlantic dislocation in culturally specific ways. Although the following burial rites are neither static nor definitive for the regions discussed, their material, social, and intellectual complexity highlights the impoverishment of burial practice for marooned recaptives. In the nineteenth-century Yoruba homelands of many *Bogota* shipmates, families buried their dead in tombs dug under their houses. Several other rituals, distinguished by the gender, age, and wealth of the deceased, followed in the three months after the burial. Relatives marked these consecrated months of mourning by abstaining from bathing, shaving, and hairdressing. During ceremonies of farewell, an elaborately masked Egũgun—the embodiment of the deceased ancestor by an initiate— accepted gifts from grieving family members and blessed the mourners. The Egũgun representing a mature woman with children, for example, received a calabash symbolizing the hearth on which she would cook in the afterlife. In each of these ceremonies, the Egũgun was attended by assistants and elders who helped facilitate the family's giving of gifts and blessings.[111] Clearly, however, even a superficial consideration of proper Yoruba rites exposes the diminishment of burial at Key West: the missing crowd of grieving relatives, the absence of ritual specialists, and the lack of crucial material gifts. Above all, the twenty-eight *Bogota* shipmates who died awaiting Liberian transport would forever remain interred far from the homes of their kin.

Hundreds of West Central African recaptives also found little consolation in the shallow sandy graves dug for their deceased on Key West's southern shore.[112] Kongo cosmology, which outlined the realm of the dead in mirrored opposition to the living, revealed the manner in which recaptives expected the newly dead to influence the lives of the living. In their homelands, Kongo mourners interred the dead near other deceased kin in cemeteries located a distance from their inhabited towns. "Corporate cults of the dead" required the living to know where their kin were buried and to attend to their graves ritually in hopes that their ancestors would act constructively on behalf of the living.[113] In the case of young infants who died, however, parents and relatives intentionally buried the infants poorly in order to discourage the soul of an infant from returning in the form of future dead children.[114]

In the Luso-African coastal environment known to Francisco, Constantia, and their Luanda-affiliated shipmates, both free and enslaved Angolans created ritual space to soothe the deceased soul and ensure spiritual protection. Angolan religious authorities known as *gangas* (from *nganga*) led free and enslaved residents of colonial Luanda in ceremonies aimed to keep the spirits of the dead from afflicting the living. *Gangas* also officiated at *entambes*, eight-day wakes held at the home of the deceased that allowed relatives to mourn and usher the souls of their dead (*zumbi*) to "eternal rest."[115] Any recaptives who had spent significant time in Luanda's Catholic missions would also have seen Christian funerals as well. Proper burial locations, specific rituals, and spiritual frameworks differed from Yoruba funerary rites, but West Central African recaptives also sought the necessary continuity of relationship between the living and their dead kin and the correct observance of burial practices.

Despite the impossibility of an acceptable burial, when given the chance, surviving shipmates drew on past experience to mourn in ways that would meaningfully recognize lives lost.[116] Newspapers noted, in particular, the burial for a six-week-old infant of a young mother from the *Wildfire*. The pair had, in fact, been portrayed to the nation in a *Harper's* illustration, "The Only Baby among the Africans" (discussed below), but the child did not survive long in the depot.[117] In mid-May, the mother and seventeen of her fellow shipmates gathered at the southern shore soon to be designated by Key West residents as the "African cemetery."[118] The mourning party interred the baby in a "handsome coffin," quite possibly built by master carpenter Davis. According to the *Key of the Gulf*, the woman's companions echoed her "plaintive song" with "low chauntings [*sic*] and loud wails of grief." The mourners' distress may also have been deepened by fears of how the infant's spirit would fare so far from ancestral terrain. Once the coffin was placed in the ground, each mourner "threw in its handful of earth, and amid the deepest sorrow they returned in silence back."[119] The ceremony, filtered through the words of an American journalist, nevertheless conveys the collective creativity recaptives harnessed to bury their dead. The call and response of the mourners mirrored forms of West Central African collective expression. At the same time, the Christian custom of dirt-throwing, which acknowledged the "dust to dust" nature of human mortality, could easily have been adopted from Luso-African regions of the Angolan coast. Improvised attempts to reclaim the dead from an alienated burial served as one of the early collective rituals devised by Key West shipmates.[120]

Examining recaptivity through the life and death of the body illuminates the human cost of slave trade suppression and underscores the crucial nature of daily relations among African shipmates in Key West. From the perspective of government authorities, the African Depot created a never-ending problem of basic human needs for food, shelter, medicine, and burial. For recaptives, social belonging and affiliation also constituted a basic survival need, for only in connection to the world of shipmates could the alienation of their displacement be meaningfully contained. Loss of family, unknown landscapes, physical pain, and spiritual disorder became partially intelligible, if not bearable, through common understandings of misfortune, illness, and death. And the need of recaptives to find belonging, protection, and community with shipmates became all the more urgent in light of most U.S. officials' inability to see beyond their basic life or death status.[121] Further amplifying the duality of recaptive experiences, popular press coverage took a sensationalistic approach to the presence of African shipmates under federal protection.

Representing Key West Recaptives in Illustrated Weeklies

The rise of illustrated weeklies made possible the mass distribution of recaptive images that reinforced narratives of rescue and African exoticism purveyed in slaver and naval accounts. An earlier tradition of illustrated warships capturing illegal slavers rarely depicted the human victims of the illegal trade. Images of recaptive Africans, however, began to appear in the pages of Anglo-American illustrated newspapers in the 1850s.[122] These engravings and the text that accompanied them conveyed multilayered messages that mixed humanitarianism and civilizing discourses with ethnographic voyeurism. Take, for instance, the *Harper's Weekly* correspondent touring the deck of the *Wildfire* who sympathetically noted "decided evidences of suffering" among diseased and malnourished recaptives. "But *notwithstanding their sufferings*," he continued "we could not be otherwise than interested and amused at their strange looks, motions, and actions."[123] A large engraving of naked shipmates on the *Wildfire*'s upper deck placed directly above these words invited readers to examine the remarkable sight for themselves. Together, image and words performed a deft pivot from sympathy to spectatorship, effectively curtailing a discussion of recaptive social crisis and future legal status. Instead, illustrated news images of recaptives at Key West conveyed two potentially compatible messages to American readers. First, they situated recaptives as beneficiaries of U.S. benevolence, while avoiding the issue of complicity in the illegal slave trade. A second powerful message, implicit in the first, depicted the arrival of recaptives in Key West primarily as a rare opportunity for ethnographic observation. In both cases, the illegal slave trade and its suppression influenced the visual culture of nineteenth-century Anglo-American race formation.[124] Even exceptional imagery of female recaptives ultimately demonstrated the novelty value of slave trade refugees on American soil.

The portrayal of recaptives in mid-nineteenth-century illustrated newspapers differed in purpose from other attempts to represent recaptive bodies in administrative records. Ironically, liberated African registers elsewhere in the Atlantic World noted some of the same somatic features, such as teeth, skin markings, and hairstyles, used by the weeklies to convey recaptives' racial inferiority. The scarification marks, brands, heights, and weights recorded in mixed-commission registries served the state by securing individual identity and regulating the line between enslaved and liberated blacks.[125] For example, "Ruperto," of the Congo Luango *nación* and liberated from the slave ship *Águila*, appears in the 1832 Havana Liberated African registers as a seven-year-old boy, forty-one inches in height, with the African name "Fana." Officials designated Ruperto's twelve-year-old shipmate "Bembe" (also called "Josefa") as belonging to the *nación* Congo Musundí and measuring fifty inches tall.[126] Liberated African registers in Rio de Janeiro and Freetown noted similar information along with facial scars and bodily tattoos.[127] By the 1860s, British officials documenting captives of the Indian Ocean trade took photographs on board captured slavers.[128] The United States, with its much lower number of slave ship seizures and its unilateral approach to slave trade suppression, kept no such records identifying individuals for legal purposes.[129] Rather, visual images of Key West's African Depot fed public appetites for tales of national strength at sea while placing recaptives firmly beyond the pale of "civilization."

The ability of illustrated weeklies to turn a particular moment in U.S. slave trade suppression into a generic encounter with "native Africans" derived in part from the geographical distance between most *Harper's* readers and the Key West depot.[130] To be sure, recaptives attracted local attention as well. One correspondent in Key West during the first week of the excitement claimed that, as "the only attraction on the Key," the camp drew large numbers of local visitors daily.[131] Yet unlike remote readers of national weeklies, the residents of Key West, numbering almost 3,000, encountered the temporary encampment as more than a spectacle.[132] For carpenters, gravediggers, and locals tapped for guard duty, the sudden appearance of hundreds of recaptives provided unanticipated employment opportunities. Some of Key West's women enacted principles of female benevolence by collecting women's clothing to supplement the shirts and pants Moreno provided for African men and boys.[133] Still others worried that diseases carried from the "filthy holds of the slavers" would incubate in the crowded camp and spread from recaptive bodies to their own.[134] Furthermore, although the number of recaptured Africans at the depot marked a unique event in the island's history, the familiarity of residents with accused slavers and shipwrecked migrants most likely tempered the novelty of the event.[135] A few old-timers may even have remembered the shipwrecked Africans from the slave ship *Guerrero* who stayed on the island in 1822 while awaiting a court decision on their next move.[136] Though varied, the reactions of Key West residents remained rooted in local conditions of health, community, and economy. In contrast, *Harper's* images used the alchemy of antebellum markets to turn the misery of the slave trade into spectacular images for national print culture.

The distinctiveness of the illustration of recaptives and the illegal slave trade in the U.S. news becomes clearer when examined alongside images in similar British publications. Established in 1842, the *Illustrated London News* introduced new technologies of pictorial reporting that by the 1850s had established middle-class readers' expectations of being able to see as well as read about current events.[137] Aware of the news value of photographs or sketches of captures, navy seamen and civilian observers often sent such images to editors of illustrated papers.[138] For instance, when the British warship *Arab* seized the schooner *Zeldina* near Cuba and brought it to Jamaica's Port Royal, "J.S." quickly sent off photographs and written descriptions of 370 recaptives to the *Illustrated London News*.[139] Juxtaposing abolitionist rhetoric with engraved images, the newspaper clearly framed recaptives as abject sufferers of that "horror of horrors," the middle passage. Using the language of commodification, the written text explicitly guided readers' perception of an illustration of young West Central African boys sitting in close formation (fig. 3.3): "The sad group of boys in the Engraving tells how they were packed—like so many bales of goods, closely wedged in!" Furthermore, the writer supplied a history for the *Zeldina* survivors as "ill-treated African youths . . . so cruelly torn from their native country." Though sightseers flocked to the grounds of Fort Augustus in Jamaica as they did in Key West, the *Illustrated*

SLAVES PACKED BELOW AND ON DECK.

FIGURE 3.3 Recaptive boys of the slave ship *Zeldina* in Jamaica. *Illustrated London News* engraving, 20 June 1857. Courtesy of the Huntington Library, San Marino, California.

London News couched the story in terms of sympathy and "humanitarian attention."[140]

At the same time, British humanitarianism, as scholars have argued, emerged from a particular moment of postemancipation commerce, free labor values, and imperial maritime power, presenting itself as a moral and benevolent force.[141] The *Zeldina* engraving most similar to the *Harper's* engraving of *Wildfire* recaptives implicitly celebrated British postemancipation guardianship over recaptive youth (fig. 3.4).[142] *Illustrated London News* artists placed *Zeldina* recaptives physically within a double ring of British protection, symbolized first by the figures of colonial authorities and then by the buildings of Fort Augusta. Small tags, visible around the necks of many recaptives, conveyed the efficiency of British imperial bureaucracy in assigning each recaptive a tin ticket stamped with an individual number documenting his "liberated African" status.[143] Stock gestures chosen by staff artists reinforced the paternalistic message. Toward the center of the engraving, a white figure rested his hand on an African man's shoulder, directing the man's gaze upward toward his free future under British supervision. A uniformed

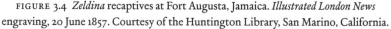

GROUP OF SLAVES ON THE PARADE, FORT AUGUSTA.

FIGURE 3.4 *Zeldina* recaptives at Fort Augusta, Jamaica. *Illustrated London News* engraving, 20 June 1857. Courtesy of the Huntington Library, San Marino, California.

soldier dominating the left side of the frame made a similar motion. Depicting *Zeldina* survivors as passive recipients of British rescue, the scene also situated recaptives in a civilizing narrative of imperial authority.[144]

Leading illustrated weeklies in the United States also conveyed naval strength in enforcing the slave trade laws, but the political realities of the slaveholding republic dictated different terms of discourse. As sectional tensions mounted in the 1860 presidential election, stories that asserted national unity and the rule of law in southern ports encouraged both northern and southern readers, in the words of one print culture historian, "to think, act, and feel nationally."[145] *Frank Leslie's Illustrated Newspaper* reporters, for instance, dramatically recounted the U.S. steamer *Wyandotte*'s seizure of the *William*.[146] Radiating national benevolence, the front page illustration depicted a long line of wagons carrying the "poor Africans" in orderly procession to the camp, "where every care was taken to provide for their cleanliness and comfort" (fig. 3.5).[147] Even with the American-built and -owned slave ship *William* anchored prominently in the background, words and image offered readers a sanitized narrative of U.S. vigilance in the suppression of the slave trade. Similarly, *Harper's Weekly* engravers portrayed the armed

LANDING OF THE CARGO OF SLAVES CAPTURED ON BOARD THE AMERICAN BARK WILLIAMS BY THE U. S. STEAMER WYANDOTTE—DISEMBARKATION AT KEY WEST.—PHOTOGRAPHED BY DAVID LAWRENCE.

FIGURE 3.5 *William* shipmates disembarking at Key West. *Frank Leslie's Illustrated Newspaper* engraving, 23 June 1860. The caption reads, "Landing of the cargo of slaves captured on board the American bark Williams by the U.S. steamer Wyandotte—disembarkation at Key West.—Photographed by David Lawrence." Courtesy of the Huntington Library, San Marino, California.

military guard, rendered to the left in strong white and black lines, standing before the barracks in which "the Africans are confined" (fig. 3.6).[148] Another group of white men pictured on the right (probably the civilian guard hired by Moreno) represented the local contribution to protecting both African recaptives and Key West residents. In contrast to the open rupture between federal policy and radical proslavery Charlestonians two summers earlier, such illustrations depicted a law-abiding and humane slaveholding republic to middle-class American readers in a volatile political climate.

Despite their implicit support of U.S. slave trade suppression, the New York news illustrations avoided abolitionist overtones in their depiction of recaptive subjects. Occupying fully three-quarters of the page, *Harper's* striking woodcut engraving "The Africans of the Slave Bark 'Wildfire'" best illus-

THE BARRACOON AT KEY WEST, WHERE THE AFRICANS ARE CONFINED.—[FROM A DAGUERREOTYPE.]

FIGURE 3.6 "The Barracoon at Key West," *Harper's Weekly* engraving, 2 June 1860. Courtesy of the Huntington Library, San Marino, California.

trates this point (fig. 3.7). The image shows a crowd of young male recaptives seated on the captured ship's wooden deck. A canvas covering, commonly known as "the house," shaded the men and boys on an otherwise exposed deck, while crudely sketched female figures appeared on a raised platform behind them.[149] The image captured a particularly uncertain time for recaptives as they remained on board the ship, moored at the government wharf for four days, awaiting the completion of hastily erected barracks.[150] Although the young men at the front of the image have distinctive features, the overall effect is one of an anonymous sea of thin bodies packed tightly into the confines of the ship. The nakedness of these bodies further distanced African recaptives from the presumably well-clothed white reader and evoked conventional associations of nudity with inherent barbarism, rather than holding slave traders responsible for stripping their captives.[151] In contrast with the British imperial setting depicted for *Zeldina* shipmates at Fort Augustus, no government officials or Key West landscapes appeared within the frame to remind readers how these captive figures arrived in their current state. Rather, recaptives appear as anonymous representatives of "native Africa," suspended in time within the confines of the ship's deck.

Slave trade commodification relied on the anonymity and interchangeability of bodies, but so did nineteenth-century ethnographic conventions in

THE AFRICANS OF THE SLAVE BARK "WILDFIRE."—[From our own Correspondent.]

THE SLAVE DECK OF THE BARK "WILDFIRE," BROUGHT INTO KEY WEST ON APRIL 30, 1860.—[From a Daguerreotype.]

FIGURE 3.7 "The Africans of the Slave Bark 'Wildfire.'—[From our own Correspondent.] The Slave Deck of the Bark 'Wildfire,' Brought into Key West on April 30, 1860.—[From a Daguerreotype.]" *Harper's Weekly* engraving, 2 June 1860. Courtesy of the Huntington Library, San Marino, California.

which *Harper's* took part. The technology of photography and mass-produced illustrations became a new tool in the production of scientific racism focused on the idea of human "types."[152] "The type," writes art critic Brian Wallis, "represented an average example of a racial group, an abstraction, though not necessarily the ideal, that defined the general form or character of individuals within the group; it subsumed individuality."[153] Like the previously discussed Agassiz photographs of enslaved men and women in South Carolina, typological photographs consisted of one or two figures intended to represent a racially defined group for use in academic and medical literature. Many illustrated weeklies adopted this convention for a more popular use.[154] The *Illustrated London News*, for example, presented a pictorial survey of ethnographic types living in Sierra Leone during the 1850s. Written text next to the image of a "young *Congo* or *Angola* lad—a liberated African" informed the reader that Congos/Angolans were "apparently not an ambitious race of people," yet they were "much esteemed as both soldiers and servants."[155] The use of one illustrated figure to represent the traits of a "race" or tribe demonstrated how mass-produced weeklies used images of recaptives to make ethnographic claims.

Artist John McNevin, responsible for creating the *Wildfire* image that *Harper's* staff workers then engraved, would have been familiar with the Anglo-American visual conventions of both abolition persuasion and ethnographic display. Trained as an artist in Dublin, Ireland, McNevin completed a series of paintings of the 1851 Crystal Palace Exhibition in London and illustrated the Crimean War; thus he was familiar with conventions of imperial spectacle and power.[156] McNevin served as the pictorial reporter on the Crimean War for the *Illustrated London News* before immigrating to New York to become a *Harper's Weekly* artist and book illustrator, known for his epic historical and wartime subject matter.[157] It is not known whether he had drawn African subjects before taking on the *Wildfire* image, whose caption indicated "From a Daguerreotype." He could easily have seen the 1857 *Zeldina* images in the paper where he formerly worked.[158] Though little more is known about McNevin's views on slavery, his artistic eye captured the sensational potential of the *Wildfire* shipmates' presence and displayed their image for the avid consumption of *Harper's* readers.

As "A Journal of Civilization," however, *Harper's Weekly* emphasized themes that drew readers' attention away from the enslavement of the *Wildfire* shipmates and portrayed them instead as exotic specimens usually seen only by intrepid white travelers. The correspondent proved more interested in markings of "tribe" (filed teeth, tattoos, hair, etc.) than in the dislocations of the slave trade.[159] Recall that a British correspondent directed the *Illustrated London News* audience to imagine the horrors of the middle passage in the physical posture of the *Zeldina* boys. In contrast, *Harper's* informed readers, "Travelers describe the natives of Congo as being small of stature" and "possessed of little energy either of mind or body." Indeed, noted the article, "Negro indolence is carried with them to the utmost excess."[160] This ethnographic claim, printed directly adjacent to the image of a desolate young

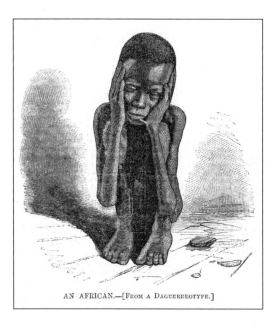

FIGURE 3.8 "An African," *Harper's Weekly* engraving, 2 June 1860. Courtesy of the Huntington Library, San Marino, California.

AN AFRICAN.—[FROM A DAGUERREOTYPE.]

recaptive ("An African") squatting on the ship deck (fig. 3.8), effaced the social experience of forced migration and overlooked the American investors who produced enslaved children's displacement.[161] Rather, the article used the *Wildfire* as a vehicle to convey readers to faraway Africa.[162]

As an exceptional category of recaptive due to their smaller numbers, women received more ambiguous depiction. *Harper's Weekly* illustrations situated recaptive women in a liminal space between female dependence and inherent racial inferiority by depicting them as the only clothed figures and the only recaptives with familial ties. "The Only Baby among the Africans" (fig. 3.9), for example, combined the genre of ethnographic representation with a second popular genre of domestic portraiture, prized by middle-class consumers as tokens of sentimental attachment and legally validated personhood.[163] Abolitionist literature frequently invoked the slave trade's violation of mother-child bonds as evidence of the system's inherent evil. Several mid-nineteenth-century book illustrations of transatlantic slaving, for example, depicted enslaved infants at their mother's breast as icons of innocence in the fundamentally corrupt setting of the slave ship.[164] The *Harper's* image of mother and child thus had the potential to resonate with the sympathetic newspaper descriptions of mother-daughter reunion and infant burial, previously discussed.

Crucially, however, the artist's depiction of the recaptive mother's partial clothing limited the identification of *Harper's* readers with the woman's

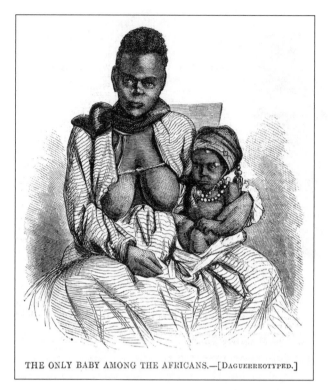

FIGURE 3.9 "The Only Baby among the Africans," *Harper's Weekly* engraving, 2 June 1860. Courtesy of the Huntington Library, San Marino, California.

THE ONLY BABY AMONG THE AFRICANS.—[Daguerreotyped.]

maternal suffering. Most obviously, the woman's bared breasts evoked a truly overdetermined set of associations between race, reproduction, and womanhood.[165] The recaptive mother, though presumably no longer defined as slavers' property, remained exposed in the image, as did other non-Western women in nineteenth-century newsweeklies or enslaved women at auction.[166] Prominently revealed, the woman's breasts exposed her black female body in contrast to white middle-class women's conventions of sexual propriety. Although the illustration did not possess the anonymity of a typological photo, the way in which the woman's blouse was staged to expose her ample breasts called attention to her radical distance from both middle-class white mother-child portraiture and abolitionist morality.[167] Even recaptive women's exceptional portrayal turned in the end toward ethnographic exhibit.

The representation of Key West recaptives in illustrated weeklies and daily newspapers used the consequences of slave trade suppression to generate a print culture product for mass consumption. Critical race studies scholars have offered the useful metaphor of "alchemy" to analyze the production of "race" in U.S. history from elements of genealogy, law, and property claims.[168] Illustrated weekly coverage of the Key West Depot performed the alchemy of race with engravings of destitute but exotic strangers from a "Dark Continent" known to middle-class readers through missionary, naval, and slaver accounts. Mass-produced images made recaptives peculiarly visible outside U.S. domestic circuits of value; destined for removal, they would be neither human property in the American South nor low-wage laborers in the North. The sensational news coverage of the African Depot thus performed a distinct kind of alchemy that transformed misery, isolation, and death into didactic entertainment and newspaper sales. The ethnographic framing of recaptive experience made it more difficult for most Americans to think in terms of human rights in the wake of a slave ship and thus contributed to the visual culture of racial inequality in a postemancipation world.

How pointless the attentions of reporters and sightseers must have seemed to *Wildfire*, *William*, and *Bogota* shipmates confronting the physical and social crisis of their Florida detention. As mortality figures rose, recaptives mourned their dead and attempted to guard shipmate bonds they had begun to forge in previous phases of their captivity. Removal threatened new separations, but remarkably, most of the original shipmates seem to have remained together when three ships arrived one after the other to transport recaptives to Liberia. Secretary of the Interior Jacob Thompson simply instructed Moreno to distribute the depot population by thirds on each of the chartered vessels.[169] Yet agent William Proby Young clearly identified *Wildfire* shipmates embarked together on the *Castilian*.[170] Likewise, the agent James Grymes recorded traveling with men and women first taken across the sea in the *Bogota*, and physician Webster Lindsly wrote that all but thirteen recaptive passengers on the *South Shore* had shared a lethal passage in the *William*.[171] Did recaptives exert what little influence they had to ensure these continuous shipmate groupings? Though the answer is not definitive, we do know that a few individuals separated from their shipmates bore an additional burden of social isolation while traveling to Liberia. As agent Webster Lindsly reported, several of the *Wildfire* recaptives transported with *William* shipmates "were unable to communicate with the rest of the company," despite shared West Central African origins.[172] In an environment of extreme scarcity, pervasive uncertainty, and continued illness, shipmate relations served as vital bonds of identification.

As antebellum news coverage of the Key West African Depot shows, few constituencies in the United States could perceive recaptives as a displaced group in social crisis. When it came to the representation of recaptivity, the ethnography of race and the contentious politics of slavery created almost no space in contemporary discourse for a discussion of the common humanity or effective freedom of slave ship survivors in U.S. custody. One important exception, however, was that of free black activists in the New York region well acquainted with the open secret of their city as a financial center for the contraband slave trade. Black transatlantic activism centered in New York linked the illegal slave trade and the Liberian removal of recaptives to broader visions of emancipation and black progress. The following chapter shifts focus to one of New York's African American activists who took up the cause of young recaptive Africans during the summer of 1860.

4

A Human Rights Counterpoint

A shrewd lawyer once said that he could drive a coach and four
through any law ever yet made in America. Laws in America are made
to drive coaches and fours through at any time, or a ship,
or a fleet of ships either, when necessary.
— *Weekly Anglo-African*, 23 June 1860

Taking the *Echo*, *Wildfire*, *William*, and *Bogota* altogether, it will be
found that they have conveyed to our shores about two thousand living
Africans, *wrongfully* and *wickedly* torn from their homes. How many
they buried on the middle—that most awful and destructive
of all passages—no tongues but the guilty parties can tell.
—J. W. C. Pennington, 20 July 1860

Brought together by the Atlantic slave routes of two different centuries, a unique gathering took place on 16 August 1860 in a Lower East Side city jail: three West Central African recaptive boys and a fifty-three-year-old Presbyterian minister whose grandfather had crossed the ocean in shackles during the mid-eighteenth century. The youths had been brought by naval officers to New York and detained as witnesses after their discovery aboard the *William R. Kibby*, a slave ship abandoned near the Cuban coast. James W. C. Pennington (fig. 4.1) accompanied a *New York Times* reporter to the airless quarters the three boys occupied on the second floor of the Eldridge Street jail.[1] There, Pennington attempted to communicate with the youth through hand signs, counting exercises, and prayer.[2] The minister must have been deeply moved, for he himself had experienced capture and incarceration when he fled from his Maryland owner at age twenty. His interests, however, also extended to finding an interpreter so that he could call attention to the

boys as victims of the ongoing slave trade. In other words, Pennington not
only personally identified with the human condition of recaptivity but also
mounted a systemic protest of the illegal slave trade.

James Pennington's advocacy on behalf of recaptive Africans in Manhattan
and Key West during the summer of 1860 illuminates an overlooked area of
protest against the resurging illegal slave trade within circles of New York
black abolitionists. By first examining African American activists' arguments
against the illegal slave trade and then turning more specifically to Pennington's efforts on behalf of recaptives, this chapter argues that protest against
the illegal slave trade shaped African American formulations of a concept of
human rights in a climate of hardening inequality and racial determinism.[3]
As Mia Bay and Patrick Rael have shown, assertions by black radicals about
human equality could not entirely escape the "ideological parameters" of
antebellum public discourse.[4] Pennington's vision of justice for the *William R.*

Kibby boys, for example, assumed the desirability of Christian conversion and Western education that came under the umbrella of "civilization." Nonetheless, African American critiques of the illegal trade and recaptive policies diverged sharply from both Charleston's proslavery rhetoric and the national illustrated weeklies' assumption of U.S. federal benevolence in Key West. Pennington and other activists of the New York region forced the concept of recaptives' common humanity into a prevailing discourse that depicted recaptives, for the most part, as either potential slaves or permanent savages. In doing so, they voiced significant opposition to the entrenchment of biological determinism taking hold of nineteenth-century U.S. racial ideology. The examination of northern black responses to recaptives in U.S. custody thus expands the history of the illegal slave trade and adds another transatlantic dimension to the study of late antebellum northern black politics.

Alongside writing and speaking against all forms of the slave trade, New York's free black activists had a history of direct action on behalf of enslaved Africans arriving in the city's harbor. Long a center of African American life and labor, New York City was home to the largest population of urban free blacks in the antebellum North, many of whom supported abolitionist organizations.[5] As far back as the 1799 New York gradual emancipation law, black protest against the transatlantic slave trade intertwined with the movement to fully end slavery and secure equal rights for African Americans.[6] Once federal law had abolished international slave trading (1807), established a removal policy for recaptive Africans (1819), and imposed a capital piracy sentence for slavers (1820), African American activists condemned the persistence of transatlantic slaving as a poignant symbol of the hypocrisies of the slaveholding republic. Throughout the antebellum period, therefore, New York abolitionists applied lessons of "practical abolition" learned in aiding fugitives from domestic slavery to assist captive Africans as well. In 1836, for example, a constable arrested the fearless organizer David Ruggles for his part in an attempted rescue of enslaved Africans held aboard the *Brilliante*, a Brazilian ship docked in the harbor.[7] Nine years later, members of the New York Vigilance Committee filed a writ of habeas corpus to release West African captive Mahommah Gardo Baquaqua and his fellow crewmember from the Brazilian ship *Lembrança*. When New York courts refused the men's freedom claim, Vigilance Committee members helped Baquaqua and his comrade escape from the same Eldridge Street jail where the three young *William R. Kibby* recaptives would later be detained.[8] Pennington's visit to the three detained African children in 1860 partook of these traditions of principled protest and practical action. Political engagement on the issue of slave trade suppression thus constituted an important thread of transatlantic activism in which black intellectuals like James Pennington connected their own history, rights, and destiny to those of Africans trafficked by illegal slavers.

"Other Days Surround Us":
The Illegal Slave Trade and Radical Black Politics of the 1850s

With its reputation as "the great slave-ship mart of this continent," New York City served as a crucible of African American protest against the illegal transatlantic slave trade.[9] During the 1850s, both the financing and outfitting center for illegal slavers shifted northward from New Orleans and Baltimore to New York City.[10] As a Democratic stronghold with tight business ties to southern planters, New York extended its commercial networks beyond the American South to Havana and the West African coast.[11] The sheer volume of whaling voyages and legitimate West African trade leaving New York's port provided ideal coverage for the criminal intentions of outbound slave traders.[12] Evidence from condemned prize ships clearly reveals New York's central role in the late illegal trade. At least nineteen of the forty-one ships seized by the United States as suspected slavers between 1850 and 1862 began their voyages in New York.[13] It was at a pier on the East River, in fact, where the *Wildfire* loaded cargo to buy Francisco, Madia, Constantia, and other young Africans who would eventually land as recaptives in Key West.[14] Furthermore, New York's taverns and boardinghouses served as prime recruiting grounds for sailors who embarked, sometimes knowingly and sometimes not, as crewmen for clandestine slavers. Lucius Vermilyea, for instance, signed up at the Randall and Robinson shipping office in 1860 for a voyage on the *Montauk*, a "Long Island whaler." The *Montauk*'s other crewmembers, recalled Vermilyea, hailed from New York City and were "perfectly aware of what the business of the ship was to be."[15] New England abolitionist Charles Lenox Remond made the city's reputation clear when, in an 1857 debate with Frederick Douglass, he charged that New York exerted "more capital and enterprise . . . in the prosecution of the slave trade, and in the maintenance of Slavery, than in any city of the Union."[16]

By invoking New York's function as an essential node in illegal slaving networks, black intellectuals sharpened their critical appraisal of the U.S. justice system as fundamentally corrupt. A thriving array of African American churches, schools, mutual aid societies, theater, and newspapers nurtured this northern urban culture of protest.[17] After the passage of the 1850 Fugitive Slave Act heightened the threat of kidnappings and the devastating 1857

Dred Scott ruling denied African American citizenship, slaveholders' commercial interests appeared to be holding both state and federal legislation hostage.[18] The literary *Anglo-African Magazine* and the *Weekly Anglo-African*, two black-owned New York periodicals founded in 1859, urgently called attention to the illegal slave trade as another sign of the slaveholding republic's hypocrisy.[19] "Talk of government and laws! These, then, would be a ridicule truly," scoffed a *Weekly Anglo-African* editorial on the reinvigorated slave trade in June 1860.[20] The writer may have been thinking about New York customs officers who casually cleared questionable vessels for departure.[21] Or perhaps he had in mind the U.S. Circuit Court of the New York Southern District, where Judges Samuel Rossiter Betts and Samuel Nelsen exercised well-known leniency resulting in numerous acquittals of accused slavers.[22] Undoubtedly, the writers also remembered the infamous 1854 case of Captain James Smith, who, despite being the first defendant ever convicted by a New York jury under the piracy law, received a reduced two-year sentence and eventually a presidential pardon.[23]

Regardless of existing laws, American law enforcement appeared to be on the side of slavery at home and abroad. As the *Weekly Anglo-African* editors concluded, "If the people are pirates the law will be the law of pirates."[24] Two federal appointees in New York added to this impression. Just a month before the *Weekly Anglo-African* editors ridiculed U.S. "government and laws," the aforementioned Judge Betts had ordered the return of two fugitive men to Maryland slaveowners, an event labeled as "slave-hunting" by the *Weekly*.[25] Moreover, the U.S. federal marshal Isaiah Rynders avidly pursued fugitive slaves while looking the other way when suspicious ships equipped as slavers left New York harbor.[26] In strictly legal terms, the status of fugitive slaves starkly contrasted with that of slave trade recaptives. U.S. law defined fugitive slaves as outlaws within U.S. boundaries. In contrast, slave trade suppression codes defined recaptives as lawful charges of the government who were mandated for removal outside the nation. However, in terms of social experience, fugitives and recaptives shared common conditions of social isolation, physical suffering, and racialized suspicion from white state authorities. Drawing lessons from the vulnerability of black mobility under both domestic and transatlantic slavery laws, New York black activists extended the accusation of piracy from illegal slavers to the entire U.S. justice system.

In their analysis of the intersection between law and commerce, *Anglo-African* contributors developed a clear counterpoint to the vision of a slaveholding empire emanating from South Carolina and the Gulf States.[27] For example, the activist educator William J. Wilson, writing under the pseudonym

"Ethiop," explained the slave trade revival movement as the outcome of Anglo-American tendencies to subordinate principles to profit.[28] Responding to Charleston judge Magrath's nullification of the piracy clause in the trial of *Wanderer* captain William Corrie, Wilson observed that slave trade revivalists seemed to be calling out the contradictions of American suppression law.[29] Since Anglo-America already legally condoned the internal slave trade and chattel slavery, he asked, why shouldn't "this wonderfully democratic country of ours" prove its consistency by opening the transatlantic slave trade to everyone? In a satirical celebration of American freedom rhetoric, Wilson challenged, "Let us be free. Free to buy slaves, free to sell slaves. Free to import, free to export. Free to bind, free to loose, free to flog, free to kill. We love freedom." Although Wilson concluded by invoking a future society with "the most perfect and fullest equality," the righteous anger seething below his satire reflected the dire circumstances of the 1850s.[30] African American protestors had exposed the contradictions of the slaveholding republic since its inception, but *Weekly Anglo-African* editors now warned their readers of the heightened danger: "But we live now in other times. Other days surround us."[31]

The southern call for slave trade revival directly threatened northern African Americans' sense of collective progress and prompted calls for community education. At the *Anglo-African* office on the Lower East Side, founder Thomas Hamilton maintained a reading room that included several genres of literature on the transatlantic slave trade. Pamphlets regularly advertised for sale by the *Weekly Anglo-African* included reprints from the *Anglo-African Magazine* by "Ethiop," James Pennington, and the Liberian-based writer Edward Wilmot Blyden.[32] The *Weekly Anglo-African* also serialized Martin Delany's novel *Blake; or the Huts of America*, whose revolutionary plot began with a U.S.–Cuban illegal slaving scheme.[33] Even sensationalist slaver literature such as the cheap, racy novel *Revelations of a Slave Smuggler* found a spot in the *Anglo-African* reading room as a "thrilling" account of middle passage horror.[34] The *Weekly Anglo-African*'s contributions to New York print culture thus encouraged African American readers to educate themselves about the transatlantic slave trade not as a painful chapter of history but, rather, as a present threat reasserting itself in new forms.[35]

Furthermore, as an 1859 letter to the *Anglo-African Magazine* argued, education imparted an "imperative duty" to act. The anonymous author of this letter warned that after 200 years of painful advance to "freedom and hope," the revived slave trade would open "the flood-gates of oppression" and sweep "our race . . . down to a deeper gulf of degradation." Employing the idea of

African Americans as a "redeemer race" destined to counter the aggressive sensibilities of Anglo-Saxons, the letter placed a distinctive responsibility on the shoulders of its African American audience.[36] Who but free people of color, asked the author, could speak for voiceless enslaved brethren in the South as well as for "our fellow-men in Africa, marked as future victims of a hellish trade?" Who would protest "in behalf of our common humanity, against the consummation of this astounding crime?" Who else, the letter concluded, "but we, the free colored inhabitants of these United States." Calling on "our leading men" to organize a congressional petition against slave trade revival and for better enforcement through U.S. cooperation with Britain, the writer asserted a platform of global activism that joined African descendants in North America to African captives of illegal slavers.

Reflecting this diasporic vision, black activists also extended their censure of the transatlantic slave trade to coercive systems of African apprenticeship created under the guise of free labor. Speaking to the British and Foreign Anti-Slavery Society in 1843, James Pennington criticized the British policy of recruiting recaptive Africans in Sierra Leone for apprenticed labor on West Indian plantations as simply a "new form of slave trading."[37] Likewise, the Liberian emigrant Edward Wilmot Blyden, in an essay for the *Anglo-African Magazine*, charged that French apprenticeship schemes shared similarities with U.S. slave trade revival in their coercion of vulnerable African youth.[38] Using the legal fiction of the contract, Blyden charged, French emigration ships on the Liberian coast embarked African boys and young men who were, in actuality, abducted or forced to sign up by village headmen seeking to fulfill labor agreements with French agents. In Blyden's analysis, both French labor recruiters and the North American slave trade revivalists represented the death throes of the "giant oppression" of slavery. It is true that other American critics also condemned coercive British and French labor policies as a way to defend the benevolence of American slavery or the superiority of U.S. suppression policies. Yet, black radical analysis of postemancipation labor did not originate in these proslavery or nationalist concerns. Rather, Pennington's and Blyden's condemnation of apprenticeship and emigrant labor schemes grew out of their own bitter experiences of the barriers encountered by free black communities in the wake of northern state emancipations.[39] Their awareness of the condition of Africans and their descendants living in various Atlantic zones of emancipation, enslavement, recaptivity, and apprenticeship revealed an expansive transatlantic perspective on black freedom struggles. And it was from that vantage point that James Pennington would worry about the vulnerability of young recaptives under the U.S. policy of removal.

Closely connected to the question of persisting racial inequality, the contentious issue of colonization also informed African American views of U.S. slave trade suppression. Dating back to an 1817 mass meeting in Philadelphia's Bethel A.M.E. Church held to protest the founding of the American Colonization Society (ACS), northern black communities consistently condemned the racist underpinnings of the colonization movement.[40] In 1827, the first black newspaper, *Freedom's Journal*, published letters and editorials that opposed the colonization of free blacks but nevertheless considered Liberia's potential to serve as a "home" and "asylum" for recaptured Africans.[41] As the interracial abolitionist movement gained momentum in the 1830s and 1840s, however, opposition to the ACS and Liberian colonization grew even more adamant.[42] James Pennington stood firmly in this camp, once comparing the prospects of freedom through colonization in Africa to "feeding a hungry man with a long spoon."[43] When New York's Governor Washington Hunt called for state funding of the ACS in 1852, Pennington joined other black activists in the Committee of Thirteen to prepare a public protest against Hunt's plan.[44] The 1853 Colored National Convention in Rochester, New York, also created a committee to study the issue, which Pennington chaired. A small number of free African Americans weighed their odds and opted for a future in Liberia, but overall, most looked on the colonization movement with skepticism, even after Liberia's independence in 1847.[45] For that reason, U.S. recaptive policies, which relied on congressional appropriations to the ACS for recaptive transport and subsistence, generated little enthusiasm in northern free black communities.[46]

During the 1850s, however, questions about the fate of slave ship recaptives acquired new relevance in the context of renewed debates over the prospects for African Americans in the United States. As the Dred Scott decision and proslavery reactionary politics dimmed hopes for achieving equal citizenship, some free black leaders warmed to the idea of independent emigration to West Africa, as well as Canada, the Caribbean, and Central America.[47] A few, such as Martin Delany and Robert Campbell, mounted West African explorations of their own, seeking to form treaties with indigenous rulers and prepare a place for autonomous black settlement.[48] In 1858, Pennington's fellow Presbyterian cleric and outspoken activist Henry Highland Garnet founded the African Civilization Society, aimed at economic development and Christian conversion of western Africa through a Niger Valley settlement.[49] Just one month before discussions of the *Wildfire* recaptives began to appear in the news, an intense confrontation occurred in New York's Zion Church between Garnet and opponents of the African Civilization Society.[50]

While Garnet defended the integrity of his plan, the abolitionist business-man George Downing led opponents in a set of resolutions condemning the African Civilization Society as deceptively furthering the political aim of "shipping off the negro."[51] Although Pennington may have originally voiced support for Garnet's organization, by 1860 Pennington placed himself firmly in the opposition.[52] As we shall see in Pennington's case, the hot button issues of Liberian colonization and African emigration strongly influenced his response to U.S. slave trade suppression policy.

Reinforcing legislative and judicial attacks on African Americans in the 1850s, the popularization of ethnology further shaped black protest against the illegal slave trade. The spread of ethnological arguments in popular print culture galvanized black clergy and scientists in defense of the unity of the "human family."[53] "Black ethnology," to use Mia Bay's phrase, opposed poly-genist assertions of permanent black inferiority with biblical creation accounts and Enlightenment theories about the environmental causes of human variation.[54] In the wake of Samuel Morton's publications on cranial capacity and racial hierarchy, several black intellectuals published defenses of a single human creation and the equality of human souls. Pennington's 1841 *Text Book of the Origin and History, &C. &C. of the Colored People*, for example, refuted "the Jefferson school" using scripture and history to show that "no man is any thing more than a man, and no man less than a man."[55] In a speech to the Troy Female Benevolent Society, Garnet affirmed, "There is but one race, as there was but one Adam."[56] Frederick Douglass, in a well-known 1854 commencement address, asserted the equality of all humans against the scientific theories of "the Notts, the Gliddens, the Agassiz, and Mortons."[57] During the first years of the Civil War, Douglass refused to endorse a Central American colonization proposal with the objection that all colonization schemes were predicated on an "ethnological apology," which he decried as the most damaging of all proslavery defenses.[58] Antebellum free black intellectuals asserted arguments of human equality not only in their own self-defense but also on behalf of Africans and their descendants globally, including those caught up in the nineteenth-century transatlantic slave trade.

Egalitarian arguments for the unity of human nature served as an important underlying theme in the African American counterpoint to transatlantic slave trade revivalist arguments. Historians such as Mia Bay, Joanne Pope Melish, and Patrick Rael have assessed the limitations of black ethnological arguments and debated the extent to which black northern intellectuals "internalized the core premises of racial science."[59] Some African American intellectuals, as such scholarship shows, invoked essentialist notions of racial difference and employed condescending—even derogatory—language to discuss native-born Africans. Yet, however off-putting the rhetoric for today's readers, it is important to understand the fundamental nature of what was at stake in antebellum black ethnological arguments. As proslavery expansionists harnessed racial science to their vision of slaveholding empire, African American intellectuals asserted a radical alternative future predicated on the principles of human unity and black redemption.

A case in point was the Glasgow-trained physician James McCune Smith, who demonstrated both the radicalism and the contradictions of black ethnological counterargument. As a coeditor of the *Anglo-African Magazine*, McCune Smith penned erudite essays aimed at dismantling the science of racial determinism that supported systems of slavery and "caste."[60] Specifically, McCune Smith developed a physiological explanation of how various climates influenced both human physical variation and intellectual ability.[61] Both the limitations and the emancipatory potential of these arguments were illustrated one February evening in 1849, at the twelfth annual meeting of New York's Colored Orphan Asylum. Before an audience of students and benefactors, McCune Smith, the orphanage's medical director, lectured on a young Khoekhoe youth named Henry who had come to the asylum on a circuitous route that led from the massacre of his family in southern Africa to his rescue by a white English trader who lodged him with the American consul in Cape Town. The consul eventually traveled to New York, bringing Henry with him and placing him in the Colored Orphan Asylum.[62]

As a physician, McCune Smith was closely attuned to the ethnological debates of his day. After Henry demonstrated his English-language abilities to the audience, McCune Smith lectured on the climate and geography of Henry's homeland, as well as the "Bushman" culture. Using a form of black engagement with racial science that Patrick Rael calls "concession," McCune Smith shaped a narrative of uplift by describing Henry's origins in "circumstances which perpetuate the lowest grade of Barbarism to which the human family can be sunk."[63] Clearly, McCune Smith's wording reflected familiar assumptions about the superiority of Western civilization and the inferior position of nineteenth-century African societies. Even so, it is important to note the insistence on "the human family," lodged in the heart of McCune Smith's most derogatory remarks. Even tropical climate and geographic isolation from the West, McCune Smith insisted, could not "erase from one of God's human creatures the stamp of humanity." Henry's newfound literacy, McCune Smith implied, was a reflection of that very humanity. Though McCune Smith assumed great distance between himself and Henry, he also urged his audience to see in this young boy "another link in the grand chain of facts and arguments which go to prove the unity of the human race."[64]

As James McCune Smith's address revealed, black intellectuals' defense of human unity articulated a concept of "human rights" with as much emphasis on the *human* as on the rights. To understand what African American assertions of the human family had to do with illegally trafficked and recaptive Africans, one only needs to recall the intensity of ethnological inquiry aimed at *Echo* shipmates to justify the natural basis of their enslavement. Both the sensational representation of *Wildfire* "Africans" in *Harper's Weekly* and the *Herald's* blatant mocking of *Echo* recaptives as filthy "black animals" were made possible by antebellum white discourses of race that created a gulf of identification between most white readers and slave trade refugees. Despite the contradictions and condescension of their ethnological arguments, northern black leaders agreed upon a central principle of common origins. To be clear, the claim of a common human family was not a unique African American perspective, for millions of white Americans also shared the monogenist assumption. Yet black radical abolitionists (and a small number of their white comrades) followed the radical logic of shared origins to a theory of human rights that extended the notion of black uplift to the most exploited victims of the slave trade. "Human rights stand upon a common basis," Frederick Douglass declared in his famous speech on ethnological science, and therefore belonged to "*all* the human family."[65] Pennington, as we shall see, employed the idea of human rights, developed across four decades of activism, in his advocacy for recaptive youth.

Although alarmed responses to slave trade revival appeared in abolitionist newspapers across the country, the reputation of New York's port intensified the issue and elicited a strong regional critique of the slave trade. Centered in the publications of the *Anglo-African*, black activists examined the global markets that connected enslaved plantation workers, nineteenth-century slave ship captives, and struggling northern free black communities. In a political climate where Charleston's counterrevolutionary theorists depicted slavery as both the creation and the destiny of Africa's inhabitants, black intellectuals who protested the illegal slave trade linked their own fortunes to the uplift of those most vulnerable to the threat of slavery's expansion.[66] Issues of fugitive recapture, colonization, emigration, and polygenesis all intersected with the illegal slave trade's threat to African American progress and hope. Yet, although black New Yorkers spoke out regularly against the illegal slave trade, few black leaders moved their protest into advocacy for recaptives caught up in the belated flurry of U.S. slave trade suppression efforts. James

Pennington seems to have been the exception in 1860, when he entered the public arena to intervene on behalf of recaptives in Key West and in New York's Eldridge Street jail.

James W. C. Pennington and the Crisis of Recaptivity

When James Pennington spoke out about the condition of recaptive Africans in Key West and New York, he acted from deeply held convictions about black historical struggles for progress and justice. He responded to news of the *Wildfire*'s arrival in Key West by publishing two letters that questioned the priorities of U.S. suppression policy and elevated the issue of justice for recaptive Africans. Pennington's choice of *The World*, a newly established white-owned and moderate religious New York daily, as a platform for his ideas suggests the desire to reach an interracial reformist audience.[67] His subsequent visit to three jailed African boys in New York extended the focus on recaptives as overlooked casualties of the illegal slave trade. These initiatives of an activist minister and former fugitive slave applied an expansive concept of human rights to those made vulnerable by their mobility across treacherous boundaries of slavery and freedom.

Motivated by more than simple charity, Pennington believed that slave trade recaptives had a role to play in a historical project of black uplift. According to his biographer Richard Blackett, Pennington adapted French philosopher Auguste Comte's law of progress to the historical travails of African descendants around the world. His speeches and writings emphasized the possibility of black progress through self-improvement and the exertion of moral power—or "Christian Zeal"—against sin and oppression.[68] As Pennington phrased it, "Our trials, as a people, have been peculiar and severe." In his 1859 essay for the *Anglo-African Magazine* titled "The Great Conflict Requires Great Faith," Pennington painted a millennial view of history, in which good would eventually prevail in its struggle with evil. As a Christian activist, he exhorted his readers to maintain "holy courage" and trust that the coming confrontation between liberty and slavery would culminate in the "year of jubilee."[69] Not limited to the condition of African Americans, Pennington's vision of history also had a part for recaptives of the illegal trade to play in the ongoing battle for black redemption and justice.

In addition to Pennington's theological convictions, his personal experience with the physical violence and social isolation of enslavement uniquely shaped his concern for the condition of recaptive youth. Born into slavery in 1807 on Maryland's eastern shore, Pennington knew family separation, physical violence, fear, and hunger from an early age.[70] After acquiring blacksmithing and carpentry skills, the young Pennington determined to emancipate himself when he came of age. Escaping over dangerous terrain, he arrived in New York City in 1827, just as the state extinguished legal slavery. With this fortuitous timing, Pennington merged his life with what historian Graham Hodges has called New York City's rising "freedom generation."[71] He soon found work as a coachman and embarked on a fierce pursuit of knowledge that eventually led him to audit classes at Yale's School of Divinity. Despite Pennington's own exodus from Maryland, his family remained enslaved, and for much of his adult life the threat of recapture under fugitive slave law hung over him. Nevertheless, Pennington married a free black woman named Harriet. Together they had a son, and Pennington immersed himself in abolition and teaching, eventually becoming a prominent Presbyterian pastor.[72] Pennington settled first in Brooklyn and then took a teaching job at a school for African American students in Newtown, Long Island. He went on to pastor the Talcott Street Colored Congregational Church in Hartford, Connecticut, and the Shiloh Presbyterian Church in New York City. In 1849, he published his narrative *The Fugitive Blacksmith* and received an honorary doctorate of divinity from the University of Heidelberg. By the 1850s, his political and moral vision embraced not only immediate abolition and full equality but also deep concern about the persistence of the transatlantic slave trade.[73]

International travel as an abolitionist further expanded Pennington's view of slavery in world history and informed his critique of the illegal slave trade. His travels to international conferences in London, Paris, and Frankfurt as well as lectures to abolitionist societies in England and Scotland deepened his understanding of emancipation and its relationship to the "second slavery" of the United States.[74] During his trip to England in 1849, Pennington encountered a fugitive man, "about my color and size," from New Orleans, who—after multiple escape attempts and lashings—had managed to sail to Liverpool. Pointing to the persistent insecurity of this self-emancipated passenger, Pennington wrote, "Here you see American slavery reaching forth its blood-stained hand all over the world, feeling after its victim, and seizing by the throat, all who dare aid him."[75] Pennington's obvious identification with the man as a fellow fugitive indicated his understanding of both slaveholder power and black insecurity as transatlantic problems. In a later article for the *Anglo-African Magazine* titled "A Review of Slavery and the Slave Trade," Pennington further expanded his historical analysis of "that commerce of the human species" that reached back to the Romans and extended forward in racialized form to his immediate family.[76] Both scholarship and international activism developed Pennington's broad historical and geographic framework for contemplating the crisis of slave trade recaptives.

Although Pennington is not considered among the early architects of black nationalism, his message of African redemption and the importance of black self-determination nevertheless reiterated some classical black nationalist themes.[77] On a tour of Jamaican churches in 1846, Pennington told U.S. mission supporters, "The people are becoming very desirous to see black men in their pulpits." Furthermore, he urged U.S. missions that any educational plan proposed to Jamaican church congregations "must come from their colored brethren or the abolitionists."[78] As the title of one of Pennington's essays suggests, the jubilee would be brought about through "The Self-Redeeming Power of the Colored Races of the World." Common goals, he believed, should unite African descendants across the boundaries of nation. "The free colored men of the North look further than the South," he proclaimed, and in return, "colored men of other localities in the world are exchanging views with us." As the battle over slavery gathered steam in the United States, Pennington noted, "the minds of the colored people of the world are coming earnestly to a thinking point."[79] Over the course of his career, Pennington developed the idea that the responsibility for black self-redemption extended to the entire African continent. Not only that, but the very laws of nature ensured continued improvement in the condition of all people of African descent, as defined by Pennington's ideas of Christianity, self-governance, literacy, and collective pride. Slave trade recaptives would have been part of this diaspora of people of color, which inspired in Pennington a sense of both affiliation and duty.

Prior personal involvement with African captives of the transatlantic trade deeply influenced Pennington's 1860 interventions. The seizure of the *Amistad* in 1839 and the extended freedom suit of the self-liberated shipmates at district and Supreme Court levels served as formative events in developing Pennington's ideas about African redemption. When a U.S. Supreme Court decision finally ordered the release of the *Amistad* shipmates in 1841, Pennington rallied his modest congregation to the cause of their repatriation. The Talcott Street Colored Congregational Church hosted the founding meeting of the Union Missionary Society, which aimed to use the shipmates' African return to establish a mission known as the Mendi mission. As the church's minister, Pennington mentored Henry and Tamar Wilson, a husband-and-wife missionary team with respective origins in Barbados and the Connecticut town of Brooklyn. In a speech at New York's Zion Chapel commissioning the missionary couple for their travels to Sierra Leone, Pennington contemplated what he believed to be God's providential hand in history. Imagine, he invited his listeners, the moment that linked the *Amistad* hero Cinque's "bitter farewell" to Africa with Henry Wilson's early missionary training in Berbice.[80] His rhetorical mapping of Cinque and Henry as contrasting black travelers across zones of enslavement and emancipation vividly illustrated Pennington's global vision of African-descended people engaged in a historical project of self-redemption. Pennington's personal contact with the *Amistad* shipmates thus shaped his conviction that free people of color should involve themselves in the future of the African continent through missions, not colonization.[81]

Building on ideas cultivated in the *Amistad* case, Pennington developed with other black abolitionists a critique of colonialism that went far beyond simply opposing the ACS.[82] Notwithstanding the occasional reference to Africa's "benighted and afflicted shores," Pennington (who once described himself as "3rd generation from pure Mandingo stock") tended to identify with the African continent more positively and engage in less condescending rhetoric than some other African American leaders.[83] In his 1843 speech against British recruitment of West African laborers for Caribbean plantations, Pennington opposed the extraction of people from a continent possessing rich natural resources and "room enough for all its inhabitants."[84] Neither did he support the emigration of African Americans to Liberia, whose founding Pennington classified in the category with every other European "system of Colonization."[85] More than once, Pennington referenced the sixteenth-century Dominican friar Bartolomé de las Casas's fiery condemnation of colonization and indigenous slavery.[86] What we might call today an anticolonial ideology developed more fully in direct opposition to the ACS when Pennington chaired the Committee on Colonization at the 1853 Rochester Colored National Convention. As author of the committee report, Pennington invoked the historical examples of Dutch settler impositions and British appropriation of indigenous land in South Africa. As for Liberia, he charged, "the condition of the natives is worse, rather than better, since the domination of these self-styled pioneers of African civilization."[87] Opposition to the ACS entailed a defense not only of the rights of African Americans in the United States but also of the rights of indigenous polities in Liberia.

Closer to home, Pennington's immediate experience with a different sort of recapture enhanced his sensitivity to the insecurity of slave ship refugees in U.S. custody. For years of his ministry, Pennington hid the fact of his fugitive status from even his wife Harriet and closest associates. (Harriet Pennington died of an illness in 1846, and by the time James remarried Elmira Way two years later, he had publicly established his identity as a fugitive from slavery.)[88] He traveled frequently to avoid slave-catchers and worried deeply about family members still in slavery, some of whom were sold away after his escape.[89] Only in May 1851 did an arranged purchase from the estate of Pennington's ex-master, Frisby Tilghman, put the stamp of legality on the free life Pennington had seized for himself more than twenty years earlier.[90]

Personal experience moved Pennington to direct action on behalf of others in similarly vulnerable situations. Soon after arriving in Brooklyn in 1827, the young Pennington joined the New York Vigilance Committee, an organization known for providing both legal aid and direct physical intervention to protect fugitives from being returned into slavery. Harriet and James Pennington's Hartford home served for several years as a safe house for numerous passengers on the Underground Railroad.[91] Of course, the legal status of fugitive slaves contrasted with that of the slave trade recaptives in whom Pennington later took interest; the former fled the reach of the federal government, while the latter ostensibly received protection from federal authority. Yet Pennington would have understood that certain experiences of the fugitive, such as the enduring traumas of enslavement and the difficulties of reconstructing secure social and family ties, shadowed African recaptives as well.

A catastrophic family event in 1854 further emphasized the fragility of the free life Pennington had built for himself in the North. In May of that year, Pennington's brother, Stephen Pembroke, and his two nephews, Robert and Jacob, made their escape from Sharpsburg, Maryland, moving through the Underground Railroad first to Philadelphia and then toward New York. There, at the safe house to which Pennington had conveyed them, slave-catchers captured the three fugitives and secured their forced return to Maryland. After extended negotiations and great expense, abolitionist supporters managed to arrange the purchase of Pennington's brother, but his nephews were sold away to North Carolina.[92] Philadelphia's Underground Railroad organizer William Still later suggested that Pennington, overwhelmed by the emotional reunion, failed to anticipate the fugitives' dangerous situation.[93] News of the calamity rippled through a distressed northern fugitive aid network, but no one could have grieved over the recapture of the Pembroke men more than their brother and uncle, James Pennington. Compounding the emotional toll of these events, other personal difficulties soon threatened to destroy the respectable reputation Pennington had worked his entire adult life to establish.

A close examination of Pennington's biography in the five years prior to the *World* editorials and the visit to the jailed boys from the *William R. Kibby* places Pennington's activism against the illegal slave trade at a critical moment of his life and career. In 1854, rumors began to surface that Pennington, a living symbol of moral rectitude, had broken his temperance vows. Added to the accusations of intemperance, growing debts and allegations of financial irregularities loomed over Pennington.[94] At the end of 1855, the Shiloh Presbyterian congregation requested his resignation, and he returned temporarily to the Talcott Street Colored Congregational Church in Hartford and then to the Newtown, Long Island, community where he had first begun to teach. A lull in his usually prolific writing and organizing ensued between 1856 and 1858.[95] In order to support his family and provide for his ailing wife Elmira, James Pennington felt it necessary to ask for financial assistance from several abolitionist friends to supplement his small teaching salary. "I do not know in my own case whether most to blame the South for enslaving me, or the North for oppressing me," he wrote to Gerrit Smith, "for since I have been North few men have been required to make more bricks with less straw than myself."[96] The biblical allusion to the bondage of northern poverty is telling. When in 1860 Pennington revived his activism and publicly challenged U.S. slave trade suppression policy, he did so with a painful sense of how blurred the lines between slavery and freedom could be.[97]

The cause of slave trade recaptives not only offered Pennington an opportunity to reassert his voice as a national abolitionist leader, but it also brought together the scholarly, religious, and political strands of the minister's activism. In the 13 and 20 July letters to the *World*, Pennington first tackled the larger picture of slave trade suppression before turning to the more immediate issue of how best to redress African recaptives' wrongs. Citing both the recent congressional appropriation of $250,000 and government contracts with the ACS for recaptive settlement in Liberia, Pennington charged that U.S. slave trade suppression had become "a brisk business" that failed to prioritize the immediate cessation of the transatlantic traffic. Prize ships served as "a golden vein" for naval officers, the ACS thrived on federal contracts, and "guilty slavers are never punished as *pirates* as they should be."[98] Everyone profited, implied Pennington, except the direct victims of the trade. He rejected a sentimental or sensationalist view of the illegal trade, focusing instead on the institutional structures that kept U.S. slave trade suppression operational but ineffective. His incisive criticism offered a counternarrative to the benevolent claims of white rescue that permeated naval accounts such as Foote's *Africa and the American Flag*.[99] For Pennington, slave trade suppression had become yet another business in which whites profited through the exploitation of African bodies.

Turning to recaptives themselves, Pennington went on to challenge the wisdom of federal removal policy for "hundreds of these poor young Africans brought into *Key West*." He questioned the "justice and humanity of hurrying them back, either to run the risk of dying on the return passage, or to be thrown upon a strange part of that immense continent where they will never reach their own homes." In contrast to federal policy that recorded recaptives' ages only to calculate per capita government subsistence, Pennington perceived the heightened social vulnerability of child captives. In contrast to the illustrated weeklies' spectacle of suffering and savagery, Pennington shifted the focus of debate to questions of justice and brought recaptives into the human family, with an insistence on full equality. His ongoing study of the colonization issue had deepened Pennington's understanding that Liberia was "home" to neither the *Bogota*'s Yoruba shipmates nor the West Central African recaptives of the *Wildfire* and the *William*. Three decades of battle against colonization shaped Pennington's opposition to a recaptive removal mandate that originated with white American fears of sharing citizenship with free blacks.

Instead, Pennington offered an alternative plan from his past that targeted his northern, churchgoing audience. In a labor-hungry nation like the United States, he argued, there was no reason to subject the already traumatized slave trade refugees to yet another displacement. Why couldn't the farm families of the "East, West and North" take in "some of the young strangers and train them here?" he asked. Pennington called for a guardian committee to assist the placement of recaptives with American families in free states.[100] He based the merits of this approach on the example of the *Amistad* case, in which a committee had worked to house the freed *Amistad* shipmates in Farmington, Connecticut, "under christian and other instructions" in advance of return to West Africa. Pennington, who had been stationed as pastor nine miles away in Hartford at the time, assured his readers that he had visited the *Amistad* shipmates often and could testify to the harmony of their arrangements. In a subsequent rebuttal, although Pennington backed away from opposing the Liberian settlement of Key West recaptives, he continued to defend the idea of placing future recaptives with northern U.S. families, at least as an intermediate step in preparation for African repatriation.[101] By questioning the plan for apprenticeship with Americo-Liberian settler families, Pennington sought to overturn a federal policy of expedience that treated recaptives as permanent strangers in need of quick deportation.

Pennington's interventions on behalf of recaptive policy also reflected his thinking as a Christian minister about the role recaptives could play in redeeming and uplifting the African continent through missionary work that was free of colonial abuse, although this idea was not apparent on the surface of his editorials. In 1841 Pennington had viewed the liberation of the "citizens of Mendi" as a providential opportunity to send missionaries to Africa "without countenancing Colonization." In a letter to the *Colored American* editor Charles Ray, Pennington had expressed hope that a school could be established in Farmington so that "other persons may be placed there when taken from slavers, and be taught something of civilization and Christianity before they return." Such an institution would be a site of cultural exchange in which "pious young men of this country" interested in African missions could acquire necessary African-language skills and other important information from recaptives.[102] Ray supported Pennington's proposition as a means to establish a mission station in the "interior of Africa," purified from economic exploitation, free of European deception, and "disconnected, too, with *powder and ball and rum, colonization and slavery.*"[103] Two decades after Pennington had first proposed such a collaborative missionary endeavor, he sought to turn the seeming resurgence of the illegal slave trade toward a policy he believed would elevate the condition of African-descended peoples everywhere.

The *World*'s readers, many of whom advocated colonization, moved quickly to disagree. Resettlement in Liberia represented the "most humane disposal of them," countered a former naval officer. Not only would recaptives "enjoy all of the christianizing and humanizing influences [in Liberia] that they would in our own country," he wrote, but they would also achieve the "privileges of citizenship" and thus be better off even than the "*nominal* freemen" of the U.S. North.[104] Refuting Pennington's labor arguments, another reader responded that U.S. labor demands would easily be met by the poor and oppressed of Europe and asserted, "The white man will not labor beside the African in this land."[105] Although the *World* editors worried about the ability of Liberia's population of African American emigrants to absorb "such an accession of barbarism," they also rejected the idea that recaptives could thrive as free people of color in the United States. They pointed out that the *World* had published another letter by Pennington just the previous week about his violent ejection from the segregated New York City public streetcars. "If such is the treatment extended to black doctors of divinity, born on the Chesapeake," they queried, "what might black heathen, fresh from the Senegambia, expect?"[106]

Participants in this debate challenged not only Pennington's ideas but also his credentials as a free man of color expressing anticolonizationist views. The former naval officer conceded that he could understand opposition to Liberian resettlement coming from self-interested slaveholders, but he expressed surprise that "a leading man of the colored race" should take this position.[107] From New England, the *Springfield Republican* chided Pennington and other educated free blacks for "cling[ing] to white society" and failing to build their own civilization in "their native country."[108] Another critic (perhaps a supporter of black emigration) found Pennington's opinion an odd position for an "*intelligent* colored man" to hold. Referencing the geographical findings of recent African explorations, this contributor noted that "the hills and valleys of the Niger, and the tablelands of Yoruba, may not be 'home, sweet home' to Mr. Pennington, but it was to his fathers, if not to him." Questioning Pennington's own sense of identity, this writer mocked the minister's inability to understand that "Africa [is] the land and home of the African."[109] These responses, which shifted from the proper destiny of recaptive Africans in U.S. custody toward a larger argument about what free African Americans should call home, reveals the entanglement of slave trade suppression policies with antebellum racial politics.

Despite the Key West Depot's distance from Pennington's New York, the city soon had its own encounter with a tiny group of slave trade recaptives. On 23 July 1860, the U.S. steamer *Crusader*, cruising north of the Cuban coastline, seized the *William R. Kibby*, which had been abandoned after disembarking roughly 600 captives from the Congo River barracoons.[110] After the *Crusader* towed the presumably empty slaver to Key West, navy seamen cleaning the ship made the surprising discovery of three African boys secreted below deck. The naked and terrified youngsters had somehow evaded both slavers and the naval prize crew by hiding themselves for seven days in the pitch-dark forepeak of the brig and subsisting on leftover bread rations.[111] By that point, all recaptives had departed from Key West for Liberia and the admiralty court's judge was temporarily off the island. Naval lieutenant Duncan sailed the *William R. Kibby* to New York, taking the boys along to serve—provided interpreters could be located—"as witnesses against the vessel." Upon reaching New York, Duncan gave custody of the boys, Tony, Pablo, and Suguilo, to the Democratic Party strongman and U.S. marshal Isaiah Rynders pending their eventual removal to Liberia.[112] The boys, described variously between the ages of eight and fourteen, soon found themselves sharing a single bed in a small cell in the Eldridge Street jail.[113]

Pennington may have reflected on his long experience with America's prisons and jails as he made his way to Eldridge Street in search of the *William R. Kibby* stowaways. Beginning with the stages of captivity that marked his own flight from slavery in Maryland, Pennington had become intimately familiar with America's carceral spaces during his years of fugitive slave activism.[114] As a newly arrived abolitionist pastor at Talcott Street Colored Congregational Church in 1840, he would have been well aware of the *Amistad* shipmates' confinement in New Haven and Hartford jails.[115] In 1852, Pennington and the white lawyer John Jay collaborated in a clever legal ruse that spirited fugitive slave Nicholas Dudley (alias James Snowden) from the state prison of Sing-Sing to a free life in Canada hours before his former owner arrived to claim him as property. Although Jay secured the pardon that enabled Dudley's early release, it was Pennington who met Dudley at the gates of Sing-Sing and walked several miles with him along the route toward the Canadian border.[116] The jailing of Tony, Pablo, and Suguilo must have resonated with Pennington's knowledge of how northern jails in general—and Eldridge in particular—often served the interests of slaveholders and their allies. Jailing nominally freed recaptive boys cast the shadow of criminality on their rescue from illegal slavers and ignored their vulnerability as young people displaced by the illegal trade. Ultimately, Pennington sought to call attention to their plight and win a more secure existence for the three boys.

First, however, Pennington needed to surmount the gulf of language that separated him from the recaptive youth. A seaman of color also lodged in the same jail cell confirmed that neither Tony, Pablo, nor Suguilo knew Spanish or Portuguese. Pennington then attempted to communicate with the youth by asking them to count to ten in their native language. Although Pennington did not know it at the time, the boys' response in Kikongo (or a closely related dialect) confirmed their reported origins in the Lower Congo.[117] Later, the boys repeated the words of the Lord's Prayer at Pennington's prompting. As a lifelong educator of young African Americans, Pennington may have been attempting to demonstrate the boys' potential for learning in addition to hoping they could contribute to the ship owner's arrest, yet he did not manage to break through the language barrier. Two weeks later, the *Times* reporter returned with an African-born porter, Henry Carter, who tried in vain to find a common tongue by singing a "nursery song," listing "tribe" names, speaking a "Mandingo dialect," and reciting verses of the Koran in Arabic.[118] Considered within the broader history of U.S. recaptives, these abortive communication attempts highlighted the boys' isolation as recaptives without a larger group of shipmates with whom they could identify.[119]

From the viewpoint of Pennington and other New York abolitionists, Pablo, Tony, and Suguilo belonged in a protective, educational environment such as the Colored Orphan Asylum, not a jail.[120] Yet the federally mandated removal law frustrated these objectives and led to a confrontation that underscored the hostile world through which young recaptives traveled. In the course of a discussion about financial responsibility for the *William R. Kibby* recaptives' expenses, Secretary of the Interior Jacob Thompson had written to Rynders asking for clarification of whether the boys were merely legal witnesses, "destitute foundlings," or African captives seized on an illegal slaver. In reality, all three conditions applied, but clarification of their status as slave ship recaptives eventually took precedence. Thompson, following the 1819 removal policy, ordered Rynders to ship the boys to Liberia at his earliest opportunity.[121] As their departure date grew nearer, the white abolitionist Lewis Tappan and his grandson William Barney visited the marshal's office to make a final plea for the boys' placement in the Colored Orphan Asylum. Rynders, who had risen to fame in the 1840s as a "polling place thug" for the Democratic machine, threw Tappan and Barney out of his office.[122] According-ing to a sworn affidavit Tappan later published in the *Evening Post*, Rynders cursed Tappan's philanthropic meddling and declared, "I have been annoyed enough about these dammed infernal niggers."[123] No doubt, antipathy based on past skirmishes with Tappan over fugitive slaves contributed to the New York marshal's violent response. At the same time, his racial characterization of recaptives as troublesome black youth also revealed how northern racial politics impinged on the three young slave trade refugees in U.S. custody.

The run-in with Rynders brought the *William R. Kibby* recaptives' three-month stay in the Eldridge Street jail to a close. In November 1860, Tony, Pablo, and Suguilo embarked from Baltimore for Liberia on the ACS emigrant ship *Mary Caroline Stevens* in the custody of white missionary C. Colden Hoff-man.[124] After a safe and uneventful passage, they joined thousands of other newly arrived recaptives to begin a new chapter of their lives as "Congoes" in Liberia. By then, the lower South's response to Lincoln's election in the United States had considerably heightened the imminent prospect of seces-sion and civil war. Within months of the *Mary Caroline Stevens*'s departure, James Pennington began a new phase of international activism as he prepared to sail for England to solicit British abolitionists' support for the Union cause. In 1870, he died from a sudden illness while working in Florida with a freed-men's mission.[125]

—

James Pennington's arguments on behalf of recaptives in Key West and New York City built upon his long-standing commitment to human rights and black self-redemption shaped by past experience with the *Amistad* shipmates and West African missions. Despite the fact that Pennington's language reflected the assumed hierarchies of nineteenth-century Christian benevolence, his interventions proved strikingly free of the ethnographic voyeurism discussed in earlier chapters. Departing from the racial exoticism that characterized much of the mainstream press coverage on recaptives in U.S. custody, Pennington's *World* editorials placed young people freed from illegal slavers within the longer historical campaign for transatlantic abolition. Linking the *Wildfire* and its fellow slavers to the *Amistad*, Pennington viewed recaptive shipmates as victims *"wrongfully* and *wickedly* torn from their homes" by a global system of stolen labor and lives. He thus addressed their condition as refugees and forced migrants—"young strangers"—without homes and in perilous health. Furthermore, he drew attention to the structural obstacles to effective suppression presented by U.S. policies that valued African lives less than the prize money they represented. In summary, action on behalf of recaptive Africans expressed Pennington's conviction that "taking for granted that certain portions of the human family are incapable of, or not worth the effort of attempting to civilize, is a dangerous state or church policy."[126]

Yet Pennington's activism on behalf of recaptives should be understood not just in terms of his individual biography but also as a reflection of an overlooked theme in antebellum black politics. Perhaps because of the emphasis on trials and slave ships, rather than recaptives, historians have tended to treat the nineteenth-century slave trade—including its suppression and threatened revival—as tangential to or entirely separate from the concerns of northern antebellum black protest.[127] A closer look, however, demonstrates what can be gained from examining how northern black activists confronted the illegal transatlantic trade. One insight offered by this chapter is a deeper understanding of regional political cultures of northern black abolitionism. The burgeoning literature on African American abolitionism and northern black communities in recent years affords us an opportunity to explore the subtleties of emphasis and strategy that distinguished particular regions.[128] Although news of the illegal slave trade circulated across the northern abolitionist press, New York's black activists seem to have been particularly galvanized by the city's complicity in transatlantic slaving. Promulgating their ideas in the *Anglo-African* publications, black intellectuals in New York drew explicit connections between the beleaguered condition of northern free blacks and the threat of transatlantic slave trade revitalization.

Following the thread of black protest against the transatlantic slave trade also makes visible on certain counterintuitive parallels between recaptivity and the fugitivity to which New York's activists responded. Early eighteenth-century narratives by African abolitionists such as Olaudah Equiano sought to transform a world where neither the transatlantic slave trade nor slavery as a system of property and labor had yet been criminalized.[129] In comparison, members of New York's "freedom generation" had, in their lifetimes, seen the emergence of a nation and a world crosscut by shifting zones of slavery and emancipation. People of color traveled through this partial geography of emancipation at their peril, whether crossing the Ohio River or the Atlantic Ocean. Located in a city known for its support of the Fugitive Slave Act and the real threat of kidnapping, New York's black activists understood how treacherous journeys across these boundaries could be. They knew all too well that there was no safe ground, no clear "free soil" where men, women, and children of color could claim their liberty without a struggle. Knowledge of the dangers of black mobility deepened Pennington's concern for recaptives whose vulnerability did not cease once in the hands of federal authorities like Isaiah Rynders. Decades of "practical abolition" mobilized against slave hunters at home and collective engagement with the transatlantic politics of emancipation prepared New York activists to speak out against the terrible human cost of the slavers regularly departing their port city.

Awareness of the illegal slave trade and its proslavery advocates further shaped black abolitionist demands for racial justice couched as a human right. As targets of hardening theories of racial determinism in the 1840s and '50s, free African Americans held a distinctive stake in debates concerning the "family of man." The embrace of polygenist ethnology by slave trade revivalists such as Frederick Porcher and Leonidas Spratt in South Carolina served to sharpen black intellectuals' egalitarian counterarguments. The *Weekly Anglo-African* articulated this broad vision of human equality in November 1860 in an article about Queen Victoria's knighting of Edward Jordan, a Jamaican man of color. Astutely invoking the political landscape of the 1850s, the writer concluded the review of Sir Edward Jordan's accomplishments with the following admonition: "We only add here that he is a negro—one of the same blood with those whom our Chief Justice declares to have no rights that white men are bound to respect—one of the same material of common human nature with those who are bought and sold as merchandise in Richmond and New Orleans—one who has no more title to be a man than if he had come *from Congo in a slave ship.*"[130] The Dred Scott decision, the domestic slave trade, and the illegal traffic in West Central African youth had in common the complicity of U.S. law, whether through enforcement or neglect. In the wake of the summer's wave of recaptive arrivals, the Congo captive became for the *Anglo-African* a vibrant symbol through which to assert black entitlement to human rights across the nineteenth-century Atlantic.

Informed by the wealth of his life experiences, James Pennington recognized not just the political symbolism of the recaptive but also the immediate social crisis of recaptive children, men, and women. In the name of "justice and humanity," he warned of further suffering for recaptive Africans in Key West facing an imminent second ocean crossing. In this last prediction, Pennington showed tragic foresight. The politically expedient removal of recaptives from Charleston and Key West sent slave trade refugees in fragile states of health back across the Atlantic. Admittedly, there were no easy answers to Pennington's call for justice and humanity for slave trade recaptives. Even if recaptives had been temporarily and adequately sheltered in the United States according to Pennington's proposal, questions of repatriation and redress would still have remained. Furthermore, black abolitionists' articulation of shared human rights could not address the socially specific crisis faced by recaptives in their Atlantic odyssey. In this respect, African American advocacy reached its practical limits. On their own, slave ship survivors in transit to Liberia responded to the social crisis of death and loss by building shipmate communities through the day-to-day art of innovation amidst scarcity.

5

Surviving Recaptive Transport

> We are the finished. We are the people
> at the railing, peering into the water,
> waiting for the Great White Whale, waiting
> for the shark of many jaws. We are the
> jokers who laugh like fire falling into
> water.
>
> —Yvette Christiansë, "What the Girl Who
> Was a Cabin Boy Heard or Said—Which
> Is Not Clear," from *Castaway*

Almost seven weeks into the *Castilian*'s crossing from Key West to Liberia, a group of women recaptives brought a companion in great distress to the ship's white American doctor, William Proby Young. As Young noted in his journal later that day, the women gestured to their shipmate's abdomen and breasts, exclaiming, "Picanini," to indicate her pregnancy. Within hours, the afflicted woman began to hemorrhage and soon "was delivered of a foetus between 6 and 7 months old." Young stanched the bleeding with a cloth tampon and treated her with laudanum, giving strictest instructions to the ship's black nurse that she should stay in the hospital. Privately he confided to his journal, "It is hardly possible she can recover." To his surprise, Young discovered the next morning that female recaptives, led by the spokeswoman Bomba, had insisted on moving their shipmate out of the foul-smelling sickroom and back to the women's quarters below. For the next two days, Bomba watched over the woman and relayed news of her condition to the doctor. Though Young prevailed in the end by moving the patient back to the hospital, recaptive women played an active role in her care, quite possibly contributing to her survival in the critical period immediately following her miscarriage.[1]

The interaction between recaptive women shipmates and the government-appointed physician William P. Young vividly illustrates how slave ship refugees responded to the social crisis of recaptivity in the midst of death and debility. Far from depicting recaptives as passive victims of their ordeal, the incident reveals African women organizing collective care on behalf of a companion and negotiating shipboard authority in the figure of the white physician and the space of the designated "hospital." The women's actions convey what Vincent Brown has so aptly called the "politics of survival, existential struggle transcending resistance to enslavement."[2] Bomba's authoritative actions and the women's refusal to leave their weakened companion enacted a recaptive politics of survival that asserted the social world of shipmates over Young's idea of black patient care. The forced policy of recaptive removal, however, often compounded the difficulties of reconstructing such social bonds. Another ocean voyage, following in the wake of the middle passage, extended recaptives' physical trauma and deepened the threat of alienation, even as shipmates created a temporary society at sea. For this reason, the movement of recaptive shipmates through the death-filled journeys of government-chartered ships illuminates the intertwined nature of trauma and resilience as well as the power relations underlying recaptive survival strategies.[3]

An exploration of the existential struggle for survival on four recaptive voyages to Liberia provides new insight into the historical processes of "retention, reinvention, and remembering" in the Black Atlantic (see Table 1).[4] We have already considered recaptive worlds in the short-term camps of Fort Sumter and Key West, in which shipmates turned to one another to mourn the dead and carry on daily life under federal guard. Recaptive transport ships traveling for Liberia under the American flag can be seen as federal camps afloat, in which the authority of both ship captains and government-appointed physicians determined daily routines and rations. Coercive regimes of discipline, provision, medical care, and spatial confinement replicated some of the conditions of slave ships. In important respects, however, as historian Walter Hawthorne has observed for the *Emilia* shipmates in Brazilian custody in 1821, recaptives en route to Liberia "had no one but themselves."[5] Between moments of externally imposed authority, recaptives were often left to their own devices. How they filled long days and nights of sea travel can tell us much about recaptive politics of survival. Read carefully, partial evidence kept by American agents aboard these ships reveals a range of culturally specific practices of mourning, healing, and beautification through which recaptive shipmates improvised a social world that could carry them

TABLE 1 Dual Voyages of Recaptive Shipmates in U.S. Custody, 1858 and 1860

Embarked*	Slaver Seized	Recaptive Transport
Putnam/Echo embarked Cabinda, 8 July 1858.	Seized 21 August 1858, by USS *Dolphin*. Disembarked at Fort Sumter, Charleston harbor, 30 August 1858.	USS *Niagara*, 21 September 1858, from Ft. Sumter. Arrived Monrovia, Liberia, 8 November 1858. U.S. Agent: Thomas Rainey
Wildfire embarked Congo River, 12 March 1860.	Seized 26 April 1860, by USS *Mohawk*. Disembarked Key West, 4 May 1860.	*Castilian*, 30 June 1860, from Key West. Arrived Cape Mount, Liberia, 27 August 1860. U.S. Agent: William P. Young
William embarked Congo River, 10 March 1860.	Seized 9 May 1860, by USS *Wyandotte*. Disembarked Key West, 16 May 1860.	*South Shore*, 15 July 1860, from Key West. Arrived Grand Bassa, Liberia, 6 September 1860.** U.S. Agent: Webster Lindsly
Bogota embarked Ouidah, 8 April 1860.	Seized 23 May 1860, by USS *Crusader*. Disembarked Key West, 28 May (women and children)–2 June 1860 (men).	*Star of the Union*, 19 July 1860, from Key West. Arrived Sinoe, Liberia, 5 September 1860. U.S. Agents: John M. McCalla, James Grymes

*All embarkation dates were reported by slave ship captains and crew to U.S. officials and cannot be independently verified.

**Including thirteen *Wildfire* shipmates who sailed with the *South Shore* to Liberia.

Sources: Woodruff, *Report of the Trials*, 8; Log of United States Naval Ship *Niagara*, 21 September–8 November 1858, LNS; Log of United States Steamer *Mohawk*, 26 April 1860, LNS; Log of United States Steamer *Wyandotte*, 9 May 1860, LNS; Log of United States Steamer *Crusader*, 23 May 1860, LNS; *Voyages*, IDs #4284, #4362, #4364, #4363; Young Ship Log; McCalla Journal; Grymes Report; *H.R. Ex. Doc. No. 7*, 615–20.

to the next phase of their journey. Shipmate bonds proved vital, not only for enslaved Africans in the Americas but also for recaptives in motion across the Atlantic.

Not all recaptives had equal access to resources that enabled them to reconstruct new forms of affiliation and belonging. Later sections of this chapter demonstrate that although recaptives of all ages suffered the traumas of displacement, youth and adults waged their politics of survival differently. Specifically, the West African group of older recaptives sold in Ouidah had deeper reservoirs of knowledge and skill to offer one another on their Liberian return. Survivors of Congo River enslavement, most of whom were children and adolescents, pursued a more basic path to survival, seeking protection under more powerful adults and, failing that, in their own numbers. Evidence from U.S. recaptive voyages thus extends and tests Benjamin Lawrance's assertion, based on a study of six children of the *Amistad*, that

FIGURE 5.1 William Proby Young sketched this image of himself as he sailed from New York to Key West in June 1860. He fashioned himself in the tradition of intrepid African explorers with the caption "Ye unshorn phys^n to the Congos as he appeareth in his red plaid woolen shirt." Courtesy of the Virginia Historical Society, Richmond.

"ethnicity and identity had little meaning to child slaves" and that recaptive African "orphans" prized security over the fictions of legal freedom.[6]

Ironically, the very ethnographic objectification that surrounded recaptives in the United States also generated much of the evidence on shipmate interaction aboard recaptive transports. Physicians William P. Young, Webster Lindsly, John Moore McCalla, and James Grymes all made observations that revealed their familiarity with the "manners and customs" genre of mid-century African exploration literature. Each of the upper South white doctors hired as federal agents expressed a certain degree of humanitarian motivation, but the opportunity for adventurous travel also influenced their acceptance of the job. Perhaps thinking of David Livingstone, Young adorned the front of his personal journal with a sketch of himself captioned, "Ye unshorn phys^n to the Congos" (fig. 5.1).[7] In addition to keeping a daily journal, Young capitalized on the exotic element of his trip by writing a colorful letter that was reprinted by several East Coast newspapers.[8] In a similar vein of tropical fantasy, Young's counterpart John McCalla packed a "fancy dress" and other items he hoped to trade with "natives on the coast."[9] James Grymes also included lengthy ethnographic observations in his medical reports submitted to the American Colonization Society (ACS) and the federal government.[10] Without a doubt, racial assumptions and imperial frames of reference shaped the observations of white agents and must be factored into any use of their writing as evidence for recaptive shipmate relations. Nevertheless, their ship journals and physician reports, in addition to a journalist's account and the official USS *Niagara* log, provide the only existing daily record of U.S. recaptive transport voyages. Despite their obvious biases, these records attend to the myriad details of everyday life and death, revealing valuable insights about the social worlds of individual recaptives and their survival strategies.

"Emancipation of Itself Will Not Do": Recaptive Voyages in Comparative Perspective

The 1858 and 1860 recaptive voyages considered here belong to a broader Atlantic history of migration forced upon recaptives after their seizure on illegal slave ships.[11] The vast majority of slave trade refugees had little to no say in their subsequent journeys. Extended movement under circumstances ranging from difficult to lethal must thus be considered as one of the key attributes of recaptivity that profoundly shaped the possibilities for survival, protection, and community formation in the first weeks and months after the interruption of a slaving voyage. When navy vessels intercepted slavers at sea, recaptives often endured weeks of further confinement in the slave decks before being allowed to disembark. Once landed in temporary receiving areas, thousands of recaptives soon found themselves shipped to distant locations for resettlement according to the policies of the capturing nation. Situating U.S. recaptives within the context of other forced migrations of nineteenth-century slave trade refugees illuminates both the commonalities of recaptive survival struggles and the distinct impact of American removal policies.

For captives seized on slavers far from an adjudicating port, the voyage of a slaver in the hands of a naval prize crew often extended the suffering and mortality of the middle passage. In one horrific instance publicized by a British chaplain in 1844, a British prize crew took fifty days to sail the slaver *Progresso* from the Mozambique Channel to the Cape of Good Hope, a voyage marked by sailor abuse, slave deck revolt, and 163 recaptive deaths.[12] Captives of slave ships seized along the western coast of Africa also experienced extended voyages and further deprivation caused by inexperienced crews, insufficient provisions, and countervailing winds and currents as prize ships sailed for Sierra Leone and Liberia.[13] In fact, British officials began using St. Helena in 1840 as a transit site in part to reduce the long days spent by recaptives on seized slaving vessels.[14] Although prize ships intercepted by the U.S. Navy near Cuba reached Key West and Charleston within just a few days, recaptives aboard four other slavers seized that same summer on the African coast by the U.S. Africa Squadron endured greater additional time at sea. The USS *Mohican*, for example, captured the slaver *Erie* near the Congo River on 8 August 1860, but it took almost two more weeks to bring 900 "wretched and emaciated" children, men, and women to Monrovia, during which time at least thirty more deaths occurred despite medical attention provided by the prize crew.[15] The *Pons*, in 1845, had an even more terrible two-week passage from Cabinda to Monrovia, resulting in the deaths of 150 young people and the suicide of one male recaptive.[16] Even after naval captors took control of illegal slave ships, African recaptives continued to endure middle passage conditions.

In other cases, the extended confinement of slave ship refugees resulted from international disagreements in mixed-commission courts.[17] During the 1820s and 1830s, multilateral slave trade suppression treaties created significant tensions between British abolitionism and the interests of second slavery societies like Cuba and Brazil.[18] As Beatriz Mamigonian and Rosanne Adderley have argued, British officials imbued the category of "liberated African" with free labor and abolitionist meanings, even as they sought to take advantage of a potential new reservoir of labor.[19] The resulting international controversies prolonged the uncertainty for recaptives waiting to disembark seized slave ships. In 1839, for instance, 500 recaptives aboard the slavers *Diligente* and *Feliz* anchored for weeks at Rio de Janeiro while Brazilian and British authorities negotiated the rules for mixed-commission adjudication. Held as diplomatic "bargaining pieces," African shipmates waiting in the harbor became virtual slave ship prisoners, suffering from perilous health and the dangers of abduction while British officials threatened to send the ships to the British colony of Demerara. The conflict eventually resolved with the disembarkation of recaptives as *africanos livres* in Rio de Janeiro, but many recaptives did indeed find themselves quickly loaded onto ships for other unfamiliar destinations.[20]

British plantation labor demands initiated most of the recaptive journeys that followed quickly on the heels of slave ship passages. Labor agents routinely targeted the recaptive yard in Sierra Leone and transit camps in St. Helena for coerced emigrant labor to the West Indies and Cape Colony.[21] Additionally, some male recaptives were pressured or compelled into military service.[22] The shift in venue for most slave ship hearings from mixed commissions to British vice-admiralty courts gave British authorities full authorization to structure recaptive policies that steered slave ship refugees toward West Indian migration. In Trinidad, for example, planters sought apprenticed African laborers to boost the flagging production of post-abolition sugar plantations.[23] In all, transport ships carried roughly 30,000 liberated Africans as emigrant laborers to postemancipation Caribbean colonies. British officials from the 1830s to the 1860s made a variety of arrangements, including private subcontracting, military transports, and monopoly contract, to transport apprenticed African recaptives.[24] Recaptives who had already experienced the terrors of a slave ship distrusted these emigrant vessels for obvious reasons, and many refused labor recruiters. Notwithstanding their fears, when confronted with undesirable alternatives, thousands of malnourished, diseased, and exhausted people recrossed the Atlantic on voyages that ruptured shipmate bonds and forced recaptives to forge new social ties in distant plantation communities.[25]

A different political context, however, produced the recaptive journeys to Liberia under U.S. federal jurisdiction after 1819. The entrenchment of antebellum proslavery ideology discouraged any association between American recaptive policies and abolitionism. Nor did the United States follow other second slavery societies like Cuba and Brazil in classifying *emancipados* as a special category of domestic black laborers who were neither free nor enslaved.[26] Although rare individuals like African American abolitionist James Pennington supported humane asylum in northern homes, no one advocated for recaptives' incorporation as citizens of the United States. One reprinted piece in the *Charleston Mercury* flatly asserted, "Emancipation of itself will not do."[27] To "turn them loose as free negroes," other pundits opined, would only exacerbate sectional conflict and introduce "barbarism," yet repatriation to specific African homelands would prove too complicated and costly.[28] The 1819 law compelling American presidents to remove slave ship recaptives beyond the nation's borders thus remained in force under President James Buchanan, reflecting U.S. unilateral suppression policy and internal fears about the status of a free black population.[29]

Two other unusual journeys of slave ship survivors prove the exception to the rule of alienated and dangerous recaptive voyages. The *Amistad* shipmates, for example, sailed with American missionaries for Freetown after more than two years in the United States. On a crossing that Marcus Rediker calls "reversing the Middle Passage," thirty-five African adults and children traveled as conventional free passengers aboard the *Gentleman*, without incident of death or flogging. As passenger Kinna wrote to Lewis Tappan, "We have been on great water. Not any danger fell upon us."[30] In 1860, Tony, Pablo, and Suguilo, the recaptive boys from the slaver *William R. Kibby*, also experienced a safe passage with other emigrant passengers to Liberia following months in New York's Eldridge Street jail. At the conclusion of thirty-three days at sea, the missionary C. Colden Hoffman, who took charge of the boys, wrote, "We have had a good voyage and a pleasant one; no accident has occurred, and no serious sickness."[31] In both cases, small groups of African passengers who had some time to recover physically from their middle passage ordeal traveled with sympathetic advocates and, in the case of the *Amistad* company, played a part in arrangements for the voyage. Larger cohorts of recaptive Africans in U.S. custody, however, traveled in circumstances far more coercive and lethal.

Despite the optimistic spin on the recaptive transports imparted by some elements of the American press, inexperience and hurried preparations compounded the difficulties of recaptive journeys. With a removal policy firmly established, the American government rushed to arrange transportation from southern ports where federal custody of recaptive Africans inflamed states' rights politics. In 1858, Secretary of the Navy Isaac Toucey ordered the steamer *Niagara*, the nation's largest wooden warship, to carry the *Echo*'s survivors. "Put the Negroes on board outside the bar [not in the harbor]," Secretary of the Interior Jacob Thompson directed the federal marshal in Charleston. "Let there be no delay."[32] The appearance of the *Niagara* drew the ire of South Carolina slave trade revivalists, yet major national papers celebrated the steamer's Liberian mission as both modern and benevolent. In the *Niagara*'s "spacious apartments," the *New York Times* reassured readers, "the poor negroes will find abundant room, and none of the horrors of the middle passage."[33] The journey to Monrovia under steam power was expected to last no more than three weeks, though as it turned out, sailing against a southerly wind pushed the voyage to seven.[34] Furthermore, the *Echo* shipmates would travel in comfort with food and blankets on the spar deck like other "lower class passengers."[35] President Buchanan appointed Thomas Rainey, a New York–based scientist and ocean steamship enthusiast with North Carolina roots, as special U.S. agent in charge of recaptured Africans during the crossing.[36] The *Niagara*'s crew also included a surgeon and an assistant surgeon to serve the medical needs of the ship's 300 sailors and 50 marines.[37] Press coverage suggested that the *Echo* captives would travel in comfort and protection. As the 26 percent mortality rate of the *Niagara*'s voyage revealed, however, these expectations proved tragically naive.

Responding to the Key West encampment two years later, Secretary Thompson and U.S. marshal Moreno also pursued a "speedy removal" of recaptive shipmates to Liberia. Thompson gave orders for the inspection and certification of "A1" quality ships for the Liberian voyage.[38] The recaptive voyages in 1860 reflected close collaboration between the federal officials and the ACS to implement recaptive policy. Working in concert with ACS secretary William McLain, Thompson appointed four doctors from Washington, D.C., to accompany the ships as government agents. William Proby Young, a twenty-six-year-old Virginia native, sailed on the *Castilian* with the survivors of the *Wildfire*. Webster Lindsly, the twenty-four-year-old son of ACS Executive Committee member Harvey Lindsly, received an appointment to oversee the ailing *William* youth on the *South Shore*. Kentucky-born John Moore McCalla, accompanied by another Virginia physician, James W. Grymes, sailed on the *Star of the Union* with the *Bogota* shipmates.[39] The ACS and government officials also worked together to assemble medical supplies and provisions for each journey. Compared with the slavers on which Key West recaptives had been taken from Africa, each of the chartered ships proved to be significantly larger. For example, captive shipmates who had crossed the Atlantic in the 300-ton barque *Bogota* departed Key West in the *Star of the Union*, a 1,057-ton clipper ship stocked with cases of medicine and food stores.[40] Despite these practical preparations and the good health of the ships' crews, however, recaptive shipmates experienced high mortality rates, sometimes even higher than those of the middle passage.

Middle Passages and Coercive Recaptive Transport

The anomie, violence, and coercion that marked recaptives' journeys to Liberia suggest continuities with earlier phases of enslavement and displacement. Historians Marcus Rediker, Cassandra Pybus, and Emma Christopher have urged scholars to ask how that "epitome" of forced migration, the transatlantic middle passage, might provide insight into the "many middle passages" of a wide range of subordinated peoples set in motion by shifting global economies.[41] The middle passage nature of the four Liberian transports considered here surfaces in the physical depletion of recaptive bodies, the racial disparagement of the crews, the snap of the rope whip, and the clank of shackles. Though the law of slave trade suppression clearly mattered to setting these journeys in motion, legal categories mattered less at sea. Rather, the gritty realities of daily maritime travel served as the matrix from which recaptives forged their "politics of survival."

Embarkation in itself proved coercive, for despite the severe conditions of temporary federal camps, many sources reported the fear and grim resignation with which recaptives faced their impending journeys. None of these journalistic descriptions can be taken at face value, however, since secondhand reports by white observers varied wildly, from tearful pleas to remain as slaves of "civilized" American planters to calm satisfaction with their return accommodations.[42] What can be discerned is that, at least in Key West, recaptives received the misleading assurance that they would "*soon return to their own Country*" by voicing a preference to stay where they were.[43] Another correspondent in Key West noted the unusual quiet and "stolid indifference" with which *Wildfire* shipmates boarded the waiting *Castilian*, "mute, listless and many sobbing."[44] Yet another observer emphasized the distress shown by *William* shipmates: "They begged on their knees, threw themselves down, and by signs, in every possible way, communicated their repugnance to going back. Such as had picked up a few English words, spoke for themselves and the rest, asking the physician and the marshal to allow them to remain, and let the citizens do whatever they wished with them."[45] It is hardly necessary to accept the proslavery political agenda of some invested observers to consider the terror that another voyage evoked in young people who had experienced long, suffocating weeks packed into the deck of an illegal slaver. Reports of those who attempted to convey their alarm using English acquired during weeks in the Key West camp indicate the emotional distress caused by the approaching recaptive transport ships.

The process of loading the transports could also amplify distress. The *Niagara*'s imposing size, for example, inspired wonder even for navy seamen such as Henry Eason, who, when glimpsing the *Niagara* at sea, described it as looking "like a floating island."[46] The boarding conditions for *Echo* shipmates in rough waters near Charleston on a Sunday afternoon in September could easily have converted wonder to terror. High waves made it impossible for the steamboat *General Clinch* (of Fort Sumter excursion fame) to convey African passengers to the *Niagara* until the supervising officials devised a precarious method of loading groups of recaptives through the stern port of the *Niagara* in a cargo tub. In a process lasting well into the evening, all 271 adults and young people (including 2 infants) went aboard the naval steamship, enduring an "exportation" in "tubfulls," as the *Mercury* phrased it.[47] In Key West, authorities loading young recaptives aboard the *South Shore* used a leaky boat that capsized, drowning two people before the journey even began.[48] Such measures reflected a view of African recaptives as a "cargo" to be moved as quickly as possible from camp to ship.[49]

Given the large numbers of children and the existing gulf of communication, it is likely that many recaptives entered their assigned transport ships not fully comprehending the purpose of their journey.[50] Language barriers, both with the crew and government agents and among recaptive shipmates, contributed to the sense of disorientation and may have compounded tensions between recaptives and crew. U.S. agents relied primarily on speakers of Portuguese or Spanish to bridge the gap between English and indigenous African languages. Among the white U.S. agents, only Thomas Rainey spoke some Portuguese as a result of his previous travels to Brazil. Rainey also had the help of a Portuguese-speaking *Echo* crewmember, known under the name of Frank Lear, who accompanied the *Niagara* as interpreter and "overseer."[51] On the *Castilian*, Constantia, Francisco, and others who had spent extended time in Luanda used their knowledge of Portuguese and Spanish to translate for fellow shipmates.[52] One crewmember on the *Star of the Union* spoke Spanish, and other "interpreters" (perhaps among the recaptives) contributed to the task of daily communication.[53] The evolving linguistic abilities of all shipmates as they lived with one another and came into contact with crewmembers also added to the ship as a multilingual site.[54] During the previously mentioned medical crisis over the miscarrying woman, for example, the women's use of both the word "picanini" and hand signs demonstrated the improvisation necessary to communicate across language barriers.[55]

Linguistic obstacles nevertheless contributed to conflict and isolation during the weeks at sea. In the *Castilian*'s hospital, the black nurse George, who had been hired by the ACS for his stated ability to "talk Congo," had great difficulty communicating with his recaptive charges.[56] On the *Star of the Union*, the physician James Grymes also noted the mutual incomprehension of several languages spoken in the West African shipmates' quarters. "Those even who assumed to be interpreters scarcely comprehended the most commonplace words," he wrote, "and when signs failed to convince, all hope was lost."[57] Most poignantly, two or three recaptives from the *Wildfire* found themselves separated from their shipmates, placed aboard the *South Shore*, and "unable to communicate with the rest of the company" for the duration of the fifty-three-day journey.[58] As in the middle passage, linguistic isolation added to the experience of alienation even as new language abilities slowly began to bridge that gap.

Restricted movement and confined spaces evoked other continuities with slave ships. In clear contrast to the first middle passage, in which captives lay spooned together and naked on a dark slave deck with less than four feet of vertical clearance, the passengers on Liberian transports had greater personal freedom to move and congregate in designated areas. Nevertheless, sleeping quarters remained segregated by gender, and the ship's spaces were cordoned into permissible and restricted areas. For example, the *Niagara*'s captain John S. Chauncey ordered the creation of separate male, female, and sick sections on the expansive spar deck of the massive steamer and established strict "police regulations" to control the movements of African passengers.[59] A rope barrier stretching across the deck demarcated the permissible areas for recaptives on the *Castilian*.[60] Below deck, in the men's and women's sleeping areas on the *Star of the Union*, the air hung still and close. Especially when rainstorms forced the closing of the vessel's "three small hatches," wrote Grymes, the atmosphere became "oppressive and sickening."[61] On other ships, where passengers embarked in poorer health, similar conditions resulted in "many slow and torturing deaths" that unfolded over weeks of grinding monotony.[62] In terms of spatial confinement and regulation, conditions on the Liberian voyages thus bore some similarity to those on slave ships as well as on many of the forced transoceanic migrations of convicts and indentured and contracted laborers in the mid-nineteenth century.[63]

Closely supervised mess times, which in some cases borrowed from slave ship equipment and routines, also reflected the imposed discipline of recaptive journeys. According to Grymes, the *Star of the Union* shipmates "were watered" twice daily from a common barrel (although they could then drink "as much as desired"), while the crew distributed salted meat and rice in buckets morning and afternoon. The government doctors Grymes and McCalla devised a feeding system comprised of numbered wooden tags hung around each person's neck to organize the shipmates by "gangs" of ten.[64] Significantly, Grymes also reported that the tag system doubled as a means of surveillance by which unruly recaptives could be "easily remembered and detected."[65] In making arrangements for the *Star of the Union*'s galley, Grymes consulted a Key West sea captain "well acquainted with the customs etc. of the Africans" to arrange for cooking rice that would resemble West African diets. In reality, the captain's advice more accurately conveyed the customs of transatlantic slavers, for the system of feeding recaptives twice daily from large buckets of rice and salted meat closely resembled the arrangements on many slave ships.[66] In fact, the boiler that cooked massive amounts of rice each day had been taken from the galley of the slave ship *William* in Key West. The forty-gallon sheet-iron cooker, as Grymes put it, perfectly suited "our 'peculiar passengers.'"[67]

Despite Grymes's satisfaction with the galley, months of poor diet and exposure to the elements resulted in widespread disease and high levels of mortality on Liberian journeys. As Webster Lindsly's report to the ACS clearly indicates, young people who embarked sickly and weak from the *William* suffered most from these cumulative effects. Lindsly described the "whole company" of child recaptives aboard the *South Shore* as exhibiting a "cachetic" condition, wasted away "by long confinement, vitiated air, improper food and want of exercise." Of the 355 who boarded at Key West, Lindsly estimated that 80 had been in the depot hospital. Two-thirds of the rest remained "in a diseased condition," with ailments like dysentery, edema, and ophthalmic blindness.[68] Without the careful ministrations of Paul Hall, a black nurse hired for the journey, Lindsly reported, the death toll would have been even higher.[69] Scurvy, whose long-term cause lay in the nutritional deficits of the middle passage and U.S. camps, plagued African shipmates on the Liberian passage. On the *South Shore*, Captain Lathrop released a stash of fresh potatoes to ameliorate the suffering, but recaptives on other ships did not have access to the crew's fresh food stores.[70] Although some government doctors took pains to place the entire blame for the mortality on the ravages of the illegal slave trade, others saw the removal mandate as complicit in recaptive deaths.[71] According to James Grymes, physician to the *Bogota* shipmates, "It seemed as if the change from land to shipboard the second time, was fatal to many of those, who had been sick or convalescing at Key West."[72] In effect, recaptives struggled to survive not only their present journey but also the physical imprint of the former middle passage.

Coercion persisted even in the medical care supervised by physician agents. The ACS charged the physicians they contracted to "give constant and earnest attention" for the "health and comfort" of recaptive passengers.[73] Reflecting common racial assumptions, however, these white southern doctors tended to expect their African patients to be ignorant, intransigent, and duplicitous.[74] William Young began his duties on the *Castilian* by asserting that the Africans "will not take doses without compulsion." The ship's nurse George reportedly carried out Young's conviction in the *Castilian*'s hospital with a rope whip. When a "juvenile" refused to swallow the paregoric Young had prescribed for his "belly ache," the doctor by his own account threatened to summon George and his rope to force the issue.[75] Likewise when a headman's wife fell ill, McCalla remarked that he and Grymes "had a rich time making her take a dose of Castor oil."[76] Confidence in Western medicine, compounded by a language gulf, led the ships' doctors to force treatments on African patients. Young people without strength to refuse may have been particular targets of such treatments. William Young, for example, reported the eye surgery he performed on a "terribly scared" young girl, who endured the procedure "held upon the carpenter's bench" that served as makeshift operating table.[77] In such cases, the doctors may well have viewed themselves as merely doing their jobs, while recaptives would have experienced alien medical procedures as resembling other forms of violence imposed on their enslaved and recaptive bodies.

The harsh nature of maritime discipline aboard recaptive vessels further linked the Liberian voyages and past middle passages. The *Niagara*'s log indicates that Captain Chauncey regularly held public courts-martial for sailors and issued sentences of solitary confinement in double irons as well as bread-and-water diets for infractions among the enlisted men.[78] Amidst frequent notices of death and burial, the *Niagara*'s log said little about discipline of African passengers, but near the end of the voyage an officer briefly noted, "Confined two female Africans in single irons for fighting."[79] We will return to the conflict between these two women below, but for now, the entry raises the question of what it meant for these unnamed African women to find themselves incarcerated and chained around wrists or ankles. On the *Castilian*, Young noted with indignation the treatment of six "fellows," some of whom were either too young or too emaciated to fit the shackles placed on their wrists. For the act of stealing bread from other passengers, the *Castilian*'s captain ordered the young men chained to the mast overnight on the open deck and then "*lashed* with a cowhide" that raised "thick welts" and drew blood.[80] Several other recaptive boys or young men, accused of stealing biscuits and other personal items, were forced to scrub the deck under a "freely applied" cat-o'-nine-tails wielded by the headman Francisco.[81]

Furthermore, recaptive women and youths may have been particular targets of arbitrary violence, both because of their physical vulnerability and because recaptive men were appointed to "overseer" roles. Young noted that crewmembers and Francisco used both the cat-o'-nine-tails and the cowhide whip frequently and randomly on African passengers, whether for failing to follow orders or simply for making too much noise.[82] On one occasion, Young had to clean and suture a badly infected cut on Bimba, a male recaptive who had been hit in the mouth by the ship's mate.[83] Notably, no ship log, journal, or physician's report directly mentioned incidents of sexual assault. However, shortly after Bimba's injury, a woman whom Young called "Ghost" was admitted to the hospital and died shortly thereafter with an infected eye wound caused by a rope's blow to her head.[84] Deaths and injuries resulting from arbitrary violence highlighted the political dimensions of survival in which the racialized norms of physical coercion could prove as deadly as the slave ship's diseases.

Young's and McCalla's daily records provide some sense of how, even among white agents charged with recaptives' well-being, an environment of casual racial disdain set the tenor of daily shipboard relations between white American and recaptive African passengers. With some exceptions, white agents and crew amused themselves at the African passengers' expense, laughing at their eating manners and, in one case, encouraging them to scramble for biscuits thrown onto the ship's deck. The "greedy, animal like manner" of the Africans, wrote U.S. agent John McCalla, "was disgusting to behold."[85] Agents and crew of the *Castilian* joined in bestowing nicknames that mocked attributes of individual men and women. They dubbed a talkative young

TABLE 2 Recaptive Death and Survival in Circuits of Slave Trade Suppression, 1858 and 1860

Slave Ship/U.S. Ship to Liberia	Sold from African Coast	Naval Seizure	U.S. Landing	Embarked U.S.	Liberian Landing
Echo/Niagara 1858, Charleston	450	318	306	271	200
Wildfire/Castilian 1860, Key West	650	550	507	400*	308
William/South Shore 1860, Key West	744	570	513	355*	233
Bogota/Star of the Union 1860, Key West	418	411	411	383	337
TOTAL	2,262	1,849	1,737	1,409	1,078

*Thirteen *Wildfire* shipmates from the Key West hospital did not board the *Castilian*, sailing later instead with the *South Shore*. In this table, they are included in the 355 recaptives listed for the *South Shore*.

Sources: Young Ship Log; McCalla Journal; reel 177B, folder Letters Rec'd "Liberated Africans," ACSR; Letters Received from John Seys, reel 10, RSI; John Seys, Certificate of Receipt of Liberated Africans, reel 3, RSI; Howard, *American Slavers and the Federal Law*, 223–54.

man "Parson" and the woman who received the fatal blow from a rope whip "Ghost" because she wore a long white shift. Some of these names reflected sexual overtones and sailors' scrutiny of the bodies of recaptive woman. For example, the *Castilian*'s crew renamed "Eta" as "Great Briton" and called another recaptive woman "Snowball" for her dark complexion. Young also noted the christening of "Topsey, a mischievous looking wench."[86] Even before the trip, Young had privately expressed his belief that recaptives would be better off enslaved in the United States. Echoing New York marshal Rynders's feelings for the *William R. Kibby* boys, Young summed up the general disdain for recaptive passengers as the *Castilian* neared the Liberian coastline: "Nearly every one is sick of the business who has been brought into contact with the niggers."[87] Even Grymes and Lindsly, who wrote eloquently about the voyage's traumatic impact, also described African passengers as lacking entirely in "moral sense" and found the men in particular to be "mostly lazy and seemingly good for nothing."[88] The Liberian-bound ships, like the slave ships of Marcus Rediker's analysis, "produced 'race,'" with direct results for daily shipboard life.[89]

The compound impact of physical suffering, fear, and violence overwhelmed some recaptives' desire to survive. After a month at sea, a fifteen-year-old girl attempted to throw herself over the *Castilian*'s rail, despite the

TABLE 3 Percentage Mortality on Slave Ships, in U.S. Camps, and on Transport Ships to Liberia

Name of Slave Ship/ U.S. Ship to Liberia	Middle Passage to U.S. Camps	In U.S. Camps	Voyage to Liberia	Total Atlantic Circuit
Echo/Niagara	32.0	11.4	26.2	55.6
Wildfire/Castilian	22.0	18.5	23.0	52.6
William/South Shore	31.0	33.3	34.4	68.7
Bogota/Star of the Union	1.7	6.8	12.0	19.4
Shipmates Combined	23.2	18.9	23.5	52.3

Note: Percentage mortality is based on the total number of recaptives alive at the beginning of each phase of forced migration.

Sources: Young Ship Log; McCalla Journal; reel 177B, folder Letters Rec'd "Liberated Africans," ACSR; Letters Received from John Seys, reel 10, RSI; John Seys, Certificate of Receipt of Liberated Africans, reel 3, RSI; Howard, *American Slavers and the Federal Law*, 223–54.

efforts of her companions to pull her back. The distraught young woman, noted Young, had been "punished for some misdemeanor" and had become "violently excited." Nor was hers an isolated act, for Young recorded "two or three others" who also attempted to jump overboard.[90] On the *Star of the Union*, one man, described by Grymes as "partially insane," jumped into the sea overnight.[91] Others died a slower death. Refusal to eat, vacant stares, "listlessness and apathy"—signs of what biomedical diagnoses might now characterize as deep depression, malnutrition, or even dehydration—took hold of some of the passengers. Some deaths occurred even in cases when Grymes could detect "few signs of disease." He sadly concluded, "Never did I see a race of people have so little hold on life—they did not fear death."[92] In the face of his own inability to intervene, Grymes fell back on his worldview of racial difference, attributing death to an apparent inherent African fatalism. Seen from the perspective of some recaptive forced migrants, however, the Liberian voyages may have carried them further into a world too exhausting and disorienting to be endured.[93]

Death punctuated the rhythms of daily life on recaptive Liberian passages. However calculated, the losses were appalling. With 34 percent mortality—the highest of all four Liberian voyages—the *South Shore* lost more than a third of its young passengers on the journey from Key West. The *Niagara* and *Castilian* shipmates both lost approximately a quarter of their company. Even *Star of the Union* shipmates, who arrived at Key West in better health than other recaptives, suffered 12 percent mortality before reaching Liberia (see Tables 2 and 3). On all four journeys, the daily mortality rate rose when

TABLE 4 Daily Mortality Rates by Phase of Voyages

Name of Slave Ship/ U.S. Ship to Liberia	Middle Passage to U.S. Camps	In U.S. Camps	Voyage to Liberia
Echo/Ft. Sumter/*Niagara*	6.04 (53)	5.20 (22)	5.46 (48)
Wildfire/Ft. Taylor/*Castilian*	4.15 (53)	3.25 (57)	3.97 (58)
William/Ft. Taylor/*South Shore*	4.63 (67)	5.56 (60)	6.48 (53)
Bogota/Ft. Taylor/*Star of the Union*	0.32 (52)	1.36 (50)	2.50 (48)

Mortality rate = (deaths per number embarked/voyage length in days) × 1000

Note: Length in days is given in parentheses.

Sources: Young Ship Log; McCalla Journal; reel 177B, folder Letters Rec'd "Liberated Africans," ACSR; Letters Received from John Seys, reel 10, RSI; John Seys, Certificate of Receipt of Liberated Africans, reel 3, RSI; Howard, *American Slavers and the Federal Law*, 223–54.

recaptives moved from federal camps on land to the second sea voyage (see Table 4). As Young worried in his private journal, "If we do not soon reach Cape Mount there will be but few left to deliver to the resident Agent at that place."[94] Acknowledging this devastating mortality deepens our awareness of the resourcefulness and resilience required by recaptive children and adults to struggle for survival and social connection. In the face of severe obstacles, social relations continued to evolve, influenced by the age and gender distribution as well as the diverse origins of distinct shipmate groups.

The "Politics of Survival" in Adult and Child Recaptive Journeys

Given the dire nature of recaptive journeys, Vincent Brown's concept of a "politics of survival" directs our attention to the ways in which slave ship captives sought to "withstand the encroachment of oblivion and to make social meaning from the threat of anomie."[95] Separated from the crew and government agents by a gulf of language and racial ideology and confronting daily sea burials of their companions, slave ship survivors built an interior world of relationships within the ships' confines. To do this required several acts of reclamation, beginning with reclaiming the meaning of death and continuing on to reclaiming the spaces of the ship and even the bodies of surviving recaptives. More so than children who had not yet come of age before their transatlantic enslavement, adults possessed a greater repertoire of social knowledge and cultural practices with which to engage in these acts of reclamation. Yet even adults had to improvise from the immediate environment, sometimes repurposing ship stores in the effort to make survival mean more than avoiding death. Without any attempt to minimize the traumatic consequences of death and repeated displacement, the remainder of this chapter turns to the reconstitution of social life for children and adult recaptives under the tight constraints of the Liberia passages of 1858 and 1860.

DEATH AND MOURNING

The crisis of alienated death and burial followed recaptive shipmates from government camps to Liberian transports. Recaptives had little control over conditions of burial at sea. On the sixth night after weighing anchor from Key West, for example, McCalla watched as crewmembers bound a woman's body in white muslin weighted with coal and threw the body into the sea. The white bundle bobbed for some time on the moonlit swell, then the ship surged forward and left the corpse behind.[96] On the *Niagara*, the *Echo* shipmates' dead received formal naval rites before being tipped off a plank through one of the ship's gun ports. In fact, *Frank Leslie's* illustrations of such burial scenes, drawn by a correspondent on board, depict no recaptive companions in attendance, only uniformed officers and sailors.[97] Although Anglo-American sea burials had their own protocol and protective rituals, they offered little comfort to recaptive shipmates.[98] Some burials on the Liberian transports lacked any sense of ceremony. When recaptives died while the *Niagara* stopped to refuel with coal in the Cape Verde Islands, crewmembers rowed a small boat out to deeper waters before heaving a dead body overboard.[99] Far from ancestral soil and horrifically oblivious to the imperatives of the deceased, these unmarked interments at sea threatened an irreparable spiritual breach for recaptive survivors clinging to an ever diminishing shipmate community.[100]

In the face of great odds, however, some managed to fashion observances that transcended the perfunctory ritual of sea burial. A week into the *Castilian*'s voyage, a sixteen-year-old girl was found dead at the bottom of the steps leading down from the forehatch. Only thirty minutes before the discovery, she had been on deck in good health with her companions. In the face of this sudden and unexplained tragedy, Young noted, "some of the other women appeared much distressed by her death, tho' the majority were—as they have been in every other instance—entirely unmoved." He then recorded how the headwoman Bomba "dressed the body of this woman in the clothes she had on," reserving one piece of her clothing to tear into thin strips. "All who could obtain pieces rolled them into cords and tied them about their wrists," continued Young. After the brief ceremony, "a gloom rested upon the women during the remainder of the evening, and they did not indulge their usual songs."[101] In one sense, the women's ceremony hints at how recaptive transport passages differed from the tight control and oversight on slave ships, for few such records of African funerary practices on the middle passage exist.[102] Even more importantly, however, the women's collective response illuminates how recaptives' politics of survival began by confronting the meaning of death itself. The recaptive women's collective act reclaimed their companion from an anonymous death at sea by recognizing her relationship to the West Central African world of ancestors.

Under Bomba's leadership, the women transformed the calico clothing donated by a Key West women's benevolent society into the materials for rites of recognition and protection. On the surface, the cords fashioned from the perished woman's clothing might be read as an act of remembrance in the Anglo-American tradition of keepsakes from the deceased.[103] If the young woman's recaptive companions merely sought to keep their sister shipmate's memory alive, that in itself powerfully refuted the anonymity of saltwater burial. Yet the collective knotting of wrist cords resonated more deeply with West Central African ideas about the potency of the passage from the world of the living to the mirrored "otherworld" of the dead.[104] A bad death in already terrible circumstances, the young woman's unexpected demise may have required the kind of protection that came from ritual mourning. Central African scholar Wyatt MacGaffey describes twentieth-century Congolese funerary rites in which relatives of the deceased "wear white headbands to protect them from unwelcome visitations, such as seeing the dead in dreams."[105] Furthermore, MacGaffey, Suzanne Blier, and other scholars of West and West Central Africa have unpacked the dense network of associations between the tying of cord and the binding, containment, and activation of powerful interventions by ancestors and nature spirits.[106] Without more specific evidence of Bomba's origins and intentions, such associations remain only suggestive. Yet Bomba's preparation of the girl's body and the tearing and tying of wrist cords clearly had shared meaning to shipmates assembled on the *Castilian*'s deck. Situated within a long history of African bodies tossed anonymously into the Atlantic, the women's actions acquire enormous significance as an example of how recaptives improvised from available materials to insist upon a shared understanding of death.

Bomba's leadership in moments of crisis also raises the question of how certain adult recaptives acquired authority within shipmate age and gender hierarchies. Bomba's shipmate, the 22-year-old Francisco, parlayed his linguistic skills and exposure to Luandan colonial society into a position as "headman" that continued from the Key West Depot on to the *Castilian*'s voyage. In contrast, Bomba, an adult woman—perhaps one of the few women

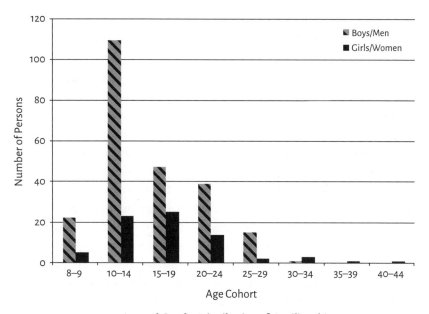

FIGURE 5.2 Age and Gender Distribution of *Castilian* Shipmates.
Source: American Colonization Society Records, Series 1.E.

between ages 30 and 40 aboard—became visible in Young's journal as a leader among female recaptives.[107] A detailed roster from the *Castilian* revealed that close to 52 percent of surviving recaptives had estimated ages of 14 years or younger (see fig. 5.2). Male recaptives especially skewed toward the very young; a quarter of all males were 10 years or younger, compared with only 16 percent of all females. Boys and young men would thus have dominated the passenger deck of the *Castilian*, with women and girls comprising roughly a quarter of all recaptives. Put differently, women and young people 14 years and younger comprised two-thirds of the *Castilian*'s survivors. It is possible that beyond the authority of her age as an adult woman, the deference shown to Bomba may have derived from ritual initiation that invested her with knowledge in preparing the bodies of the dead and attending pregnant women in distress.[108] Historian James Sweet has argued that enslaved Africans torn from their homes and kin gravitated toward those with "specialized knowledge that was situationally useful," thus crafting new forms of belonging.[109] Bomba's authority at the thresholds between life and death suggests how adult women traveling among recaptive youth could become valuable figures of mediation and protection.[110]

Though it may seem at first counterintuitive, recaptives also asserted social identities and forged shipmate relations through negotiation and disputes over food, berths, and sexual partners. In the zero-sum world of the transport ship, the young and the sick proved most vulnerable. Noticing the animated bartering that followed each meal, William Young observed, "Everyone tried to overreach his neighbor, and the strong generally fare the best."[111] Fights also broke out among recaptive passengers jammed into tight sleeping quarters.[112] Two weeks into the journey, for example, one of the older adult men (said by his shipmates to have also killed others on the *Wildfire*'s middle passage) choked a younger man to death.[113] To impose better order, the *Castilian*'s crew built a wooden bulkhead to divide the berths of adult men from the space designated for women, girls, and boys. "Great confusion ensued in the selection of berths," Young noted.[114] On the *Niagara*, hundreds of young recaptives without adult protection created their own alliances for security. A *Frank Leslie's* correspondent noted divisions among the shipmates, observing "the boys, in particular, forming themselves into parties for mutual protection and defence [sic]."[115] Groups of recaptive children fought over food supplies and blankets but also spent time playing during the long days at sea.[116] While language and geographic origin probably contributed to the boundaries of these competing "parties" of recaptive youth, expressions of ethnic identity did not seem to be the primary means by which child recaptives formed bonds with one another.[117] Rather, in the gender-segregated spaces of the *Niagara*, male youth turned to each other to secure the most basic resources for bodily survival.

In contrast to the *Niagara*, among the older cohort of West African passengers on the *Star of the Union*, geography and homeland played a larger part in structuring shipmate relations. Evidence collected from government agents reflects the European perception of African "tribal" organization yet also suggests how recaptives' political and linguistic affiliations shaped the nature of shipboard conflicts. For example, surgeon Grymes attributed "bitter hostilities" among the Ouidah-embarked shipmates to divisions between "three different tribes." Exacerbated by constant proximity in tight ship spaces, differences of West African language, religion, status, and routes into enslavement could not easily be bridged. As previously discussed, survivors of the *Bogota* included Yoruba speakers captured by Dahomean soldiers but also some Fon speakers from Dahomey and Hausa as well.[118] Discord and threats elicited discipline from several layers of shipboard authority, according to Grymes's report. Quarrels over theft, noise, and "disregard of the hygienic regulations," for instance, resulted in "a sound flogging with a rope's end, by one of the headmen of their own tribe." And when shipmates threatened fellow shipmates with murder, the captain ordered the aggressors put in irons and fed a diet of bread and water.[119] Such divisions, while disrupting the peace of the voyage, nevertheless called upon social and political affiliations from the recaptives' previous lives and drew men and women into new alliances for protection and survival. As Grymes also noted, "Many of them were related & they showed, many marks of interest and affection when any weal or woe, happened to one of their respective relatives or friends."[120] Presumably, older recaptives who had been fully initiated into their home societies as adults would have felt a greater stake in such identifications and thus sought to draw on affiliations of town, lineage, and other group identities. Such hostilities, while clearly posing individual dangers, revealed not an alienated, atomized group of captives but a vitally contesting gathering of shipmates whose members drew on past social identities to gain protection and confront enemies in the effort to survive their second ocean crossing.

Rare evidence hints at hostility generated by contested sexual partnerships as a specific category of conflict among adults and maturing youth during the Liberian passages. For example, one evening when darkness had fallen over their ship, McCalla and Grymes heard "screams and loud language" below deck prompted by a fight between a woman called Princess (who traveled with her young child) and two men. The secondhand nature of its accounting obscures much of the meaning of the quarrel. However, McCalla wrote that in a subsequent hearing on deck, the contesting parties and witnesses pinned the outburst on one of the men, who had threatened to kill the woman and her child "because she wanted to spread her blanket near him."[121] Grymes, also on the *Star of the Union*, wrote that many of the "squabbles" among recaptives revolved around the "ladies" and violations of the gender-designated sleeping spaces.[122] Regulation of sexual mores may have been what Captain Gorham had in mind when he officiated at the marriage of twenty-four shipmate couples in the third week of the *Star of the Union*'s voyage. Through the interpreter, the captain explained to each couple the principles of permanent and monogamous union to which the wedding ceremony bound them. To be sure, the captain's stateroom ceremonies reflected prevailing Anglo-American notions of marriage as a civilizing institution, yet the weddings also signified an important social bond that would continue to play a part in shipmate networks in Liberia.[123]

Throughout their journeys, shipmates of all ages also acted together to secure resources for themselves and shape the ship's environment to their own ends. As McCalla's discussion of Princess revealed, men and women crossed the boundaries of areas officially designated as gender-segregated spaces of the *Star of the Union*. The boys or young men punished for stealing bread on the *Castilian* used the cover of night to slip through the ship's forward hatch and into the lower hold where provisions were stored.[124] As earlier mentioned, Bomba disregarded the male nurse George by removing the young woman who had miscarried from the *Castilian*'s "hospital" area to the women's quarters. In the first days of the *Star of the Union*'s voyage, men and women literally reshaped their physical surroundings by convincing James Grymes to jettison hundreds of pine-board berths and uncomfortable straw mattresses that added to the crowded and airless conditions between decks.[125] From the empty cotton mattress ticks, recaptive shipmates then created clothing to replace or supplement the motley assortment of donated American clothing items, eliciting admiration from Grymes on the variety and "ingenuity" of their improvised designs.[126] In these and other small daily acts, recaptive men and women collectively pushed back against the coercive constraints of transport ships. Their actions illuminated creativity and appropriation in the midst of scarcity as another element of recaptive politics of survival.

SOOTHING, HEALING, AND SORCERY

Through acts of appropriation and improvisation, recaptives sought to relieve their aching, itching, and malnourished bodies. Some of the most basic methods of relief could be practiced widely and without specialized skills. The same protracted deprivation under crowded and exposed conditions that led to blindness, edema, and dysentery also wreaked havoc on people's skin. Fleas, chiggers, and lice tormented recaptives of all ages, who tended to one another's scalps and skin to soothe their persistent itching.[127] Dehydration cracked open dry lips, and malnutrition led to the ulceration of common sores.[128] Something as simple as fat or oil brought relief by calming and softening the skin. Rather than drinking all their ration of castor oil, Grymes observed, African men and women reserved a portion for rubbing into their skin. One group of shipmates went so far as to dip into the cook's "slush" barrel—a reservoir for meat fats and pork drippings—for use as an emollient.[129] Such measures of physical relief could be shared widely across recaptive communities, but other afflictions had more specialized origins requiring greater expertise.

Although forced voyages across the Atlantic cut off enslaved captives from familiar therapies and practitioners, some adult recaptives had apparently been trained and initiated as healers. Given the wide geographic regions represented by the four shipmate groups in this study, fragments of evidence revealing healing among recaptives can only be interpreted in general terms. Yet the evident desire of slave trade refugees to seek out healers among fellow shipmates illuminates the material and spatial politics of survival, as does the innovation required by ritual specialists to practice in exile. The government appointed white doctors who designated a ship hospital, but in truth, recaptive ships revealed an environment of medical pluralism that transcended designated medical spaces.[130] On the *Castilian*, for example, Young observed a woman "making *gashes* with a razor on the swollen feet of a scurvy patient."[131] To an American doctor trained in humoral therapies of bleeding and purging, the opening of "anasarcous" (fluid-filled) limbs to relieve swelling seemed rational. Furthermore, Young correctly assumed this to be an "accustomed" remedy among the *Castilian*'s West Central African shipmates. In fact, Lower Congo *nsamba* (medicated incisions) reaching back at least to the nineteenth century, if not earlier, represented only part of a larger regional therapeutic intervention that involved an initiated practitioner (*nganga nkisi*) slicing shallow cuts into the skin, cupping the incisions with a horn, and inserting herbal medicines into the cutaneous openings.[132] Equally important during such treatments, as anthropologist John Janzen has argued for twentieth-century Zaire (Democratic Republic of Congo), the sufferer expected to be surrounded with kin who provided advice and practical support during treatment.[133] Bomba and other recaptive women exercised a similar role in the case of their companion's miscarriage. Ship doctors' accounts of this and other medical crises expose the stark spaces in which recaptive healers and sufferers existed. Yet they also vividly show that interactions surrounding health and healing served as important sites for building shipmate social relations.

Shipmate groups with a larger proportion of adults improved the likelihood that ritual specialists might be present to contribute to the healing resources of the shipmate community. The ethnic diversity of captives sold to the *Bogota* captain in Ouidah, for example, meant that *Bogota* shipmates could potentially include several different kinds of therapeutic practitioners. Among West African adult captives sold to nineteenth-century transatlantic slavers—and thus possibly in recaptive communities—could be found Yoruba *babalowe*, Fon- and Gbe-speaking initiates of particular vodun, Hausa bonesetters, and Muslim clerics specializing in protective amulets.[134] On the

Bogota, for example, McCalla recorded his observations of a "charm doctor" working over an ailing woman: "The man sat down beside the young woman rubbing the palms of his hands together and with his mouth close to them, he would mutter some cabalistic words—he would then blow and spit in his hands and put them around the woman's body, drawing them tightly beginning at the backbone and bringing them around to the breasts and then make a gesture as if he had gathered a handful of 'evil spirit' which he threw away to one side."[135] Despite the biases of McCalla's language, we can observe the improvised space in which the healer worked without access to necessary ritual family, materials, and dedicated spaces. As James Sweet's study of the eighteenth-century healer Domingos Álvares shows, enslaved and exiled West African healers spent years struggling to re-create the "ritual symbolism and practice" of their homelands.[136] McCalla's observation offers a glimpse of a fragile and early example of such ritual reconstitution, in which the healer used his knowledge, hands, and breath to address the sufferer's pain and sense of disorder.

Other afflicted recaptives, however, remained cut off from specialists who could counter the threat of illness and wasting bodies. The two women mentioned previously as having been put in irons on the *Niagara* had come to blows over the question of a young child's affliction. As the *Frank Leslie's* correspondent put it, "The mother accused another woman of bewitching it; and using the arts of sorcery to destroy its life." In the Loango and Kongo regions from which many of the *Niagara*'s passengers had been enslaved, witchcraft constituted the central framework for understanding maldistribution of resources, acquisition of wealth at the expense of others, and malevolent consumption of life. Witchcraft, Ralph Austen argues, served as "the immediate idiom" that best expressed the exploitive nature of transatlantic enslavement.[137] Given the perils and misfortune of displacement from the *Echo* to Fort Sumter to the *Niagara*, it is entirely comprehensible that a recaptive West Central African mother would charge her fellow shipmate with witchcraft as her child's life ebbed away. The point here, however, is that traveling among many boys and youth, these women most likely had no kin group and little chance of finding a ritual specialist who could mediate their disagreement, determine the source of the affliction, and offer a remedy. Although the *Niagara*'s records suggest that the baby did indeed reach Liberia alive, the ritual impoverishment of the naval steamer's environment gave the unnamed mother few means by which to meaningfully address the social crisis of her child's illness.[138] By confronting her shipmate on the shared terrain of witchcraft accusation, this woman invoked a juridical system that would have been familiar to many of her shipmates, thus creating an improvised West Central African social world aboard the *Niagara*.

BEAUTIFICATION AND BODY AESTHETICS

While many recaptives waged their struggle for existence at the very threshold of death, the politics of survival also had an aesthetic dimension, where slave ship survivors reasserted corporate belonging through artistic creation. A compelling example appears in McCalla's observation of a West African woman inscribing a new "tattoo" on her shipmate's arms.

> I saw one of the women tattooing another one to-day. The performer took a razor and made incisions about three quarters of an inch long— and about the twelfth of an inch deep—at regular and fanciful intervals along the fore-arm of the other woman—who—though she bled a good deal did not wince or appear to suffer the least pain. After the cutting was finished—common grease or slush was rubbed freely over the arm—this was wiped off—then lemon juice applied and in a few minutes wiped off—and finally powdered charcoal—was rubbed over the arm and permitted to dry there. These substances so applied produce a slight irritation and a singularly raised and glossy scar is the result. All of the negroes are marked in some design to show their tribe and country. Some of them have the most elaborate designs over their backs, faces— arms, breasts—abdomen and legs—representing—leaves—vines— diamonds—squares, etc.[139]

By stepping back to consider the broader significance of West African scarification, we can see that what McCalla perceived as a static sign of "tribe and country" is best understood as a significant act of political and social reclamation through bodily aesthetics.

Across West Africa, cicatrization of the face and body communicated a dense network of social significance. Taken together, the location of the patterns, the quality of the work, the age at which a person acquired various marks, and the specificity of design indicated multiple kinds of corporate identification. Specific facial and body markings signified, among other meanings, nobility, social status, age class, subgroup identity, or political allegiance. As "citizenship symbols," facial cicatrices distinguished stranger from resident, protected against enslavement, and sometimes gave evidence of a person having undergone specific curative rituals. Through scarification, one manifested one's history and identity. Loss of a loved one, stages of betrothal, and signs of initiation could all be read in artistically modified surfaces of the skin.[140] So nuanced were the meanings embedded through facial patterns, in particular, that Yoruba speakers used different verbs to designate different ways of being marked.[141]

Using McCalla's description in combination with a careful reading of contemporary anthropological writing on Yoruba scarification, one possible interpretation of what McCalla saw is the application of aesthetic marks known in contemporary Yoruba as *kóló*, a series of "closely spaced hatch marks" made primarily (but not exclusively) for women on many parts of the body, including the upper and lower arms.[142] In observations by anthropologist Henry John Drewal among Ohori and Egbado Yoruba during the 1970s, the body artist achieved the distinct "cicatrice designs" of *kóló* in much the same manner observed by McCalla, though inserting a "colorant (usually charcoal or lampblack)" into the cuts.[143] According to Drewal, "The emphasis [of *kóló*] is clearly on the visible display of the enhanced and beautified human body."[144] Furthermore, such acts of beautification should not be considered mere surface indulgences, for *kóló* carried with it moral and transformative implications as well. The raised patterns visually confirmed a woman's strength in the face of pain, and the rippled surface offered sensual pleasure to the touch of a lover.[145] Although we cannot, of course, be certain of the meanings for these recaptive women, further consideration of *kóló* within the tradition of Yoruba scarification can unfold the profound significance of recaptive body artistry.[146]

If, indeed, McCalla witnessed the creation of *kóló* marks, he unwittingly documented the duality of continuity and innovation among recaptive artistic practice in forced migration. Because of the specialized iron instruments used in scarification, Yoruba body art had close associations with the orisha Ogún. The specially initiated Yoruba practitioners described by Drewal used a ritually consecrated, delicate Y-shaped iron blade to carve the fine lines of *kóló* into the skin.[147] No such precisely crafted tools existed on the *Star of the Union*, however. Instead, McCalla described how the practitioner used a simple straight razor to make her marks. McCalla's co-physician, James Grymes, added that recaptives used "the blade of a razor, knife, a shell or any sharp instrument" to make their marks.[148] Charcoal, lemon, and grease would presumably have been obtained from the ship's galley, possibly suggesting exchange with the crew or appropriation of supplies, as with the cook's slush barrel for skin ointment. The improvisation may have extended as far as the female gender of the practitioner. Due to its connection to Ogún,

Yoruba-speaking societies reserved body artistry with few exceptions to male practitioners (*oloola*).[149]

Although it is impossible to confirm absolutely the making of *kóló* on the *Star of the Union*, the creation of artistic marks intended to be seen and understood by others nevertheless signified an act of imagination in the midst of severe deprivation. Samuël Coghe's work on recaptured Africans adjudicated by the Luandan mixed-commission court shows how officials "shaped" recaptive bodies through coerced vaccination, branding, and regulation of punishments.[150] One could similarly argue that recaptives in U.S. custody continued to be regulated, disciplined, and physically shaped well after leaving the confinement of illegal slave ships. Yet in the hours it took for one recaptive woman to painfully beautify another, these women asserted themselves as more than branded cargo and isolated bodies. Although sources are not clear about whether the enslaved captives of the *Bogota* had been branded at the coast, other Ouidah records indicate branding continued in the illegal trading period, for the purpose of distinguishing the claims of multiple clandestine investors.[151] In this moment recorded by McCalla, however, aesthetic expression reasserted social connection within a cultural context understood by the unnamed woman's shipmate. More than the marking of an individual body, the act of creation and a mutual understanding of the marks' significance crucially asserted corporate membership within the alien space of the transport vessel.

—

In terms of racial hierarchies and the prevalence of death, U.S. transports to Liberia sailed directly in the wake of illegal slavers and gave urgency to the politics of survival. Survival had a politics because, for recaptives, pursuit of life drew them into a contest for resources, meaning, and connection. The ubiquitous threat of isolation, violence, and death lent urgency to the efforts of recaptives to survive their ordeal not just individually but in shipmate collectives. In the face of death, groups of recaptives strengthened their shipmate relations, as evidenced by young women's improvised rites of mourning led by the headwoman Bomba. On these four U.S. recaptive voyages, shipmate collaboration manifested not in ship revolt, but in daily reclamations of knowledge, ship spaces, material provisions, and socially embedded bodies.

As this chapter has shown, shipmates came to know one another in the course of their journeys enough to cooperate in accessing the locked-away food stores, gathering around the sick and dying, interceding with ship physicians, and navigating conflicts among their shipmates. Shipmate networks gained depth through the accretion of memories gathered from their shared ordeal on two transatlantic passages. While traveling on the *Castilian*, for example, the former captives of the *Wildfire* mourned the death of a man they had called Warrior.[152] When a woman Young called Fancy went into convulsions, the headman Francisco remembered she had suffered six other seizures "on the passage from Africa."[153] Through such memories, shipmates recognized and reclaimed one another as people with specific histories and losses. The politics of survival was also an embodied politics, expressed in healing, mourning, and bodily aesthetics. Staying alive was indeed important for most recaptives, but survival went beyond that, joining shipmates together in shared understandings of affliction, health, sociability, and beauty.

At the same time, the nature of shipmates' survival politics and the cultural resources available for this work of reclamation depended greatly on age and experience. Three of the four groups of recaptives considered here carried a majority of young people from West Central Africa, children and adolescents who would never come of age in their own societies. Benjamin Lawrance's argument that the "orphans" of the *Amistad* lived under the shadow of a "permanent state of childhood" is highly relevant to the children of this study as well.[154] Many child recaptives from the *Echo*, *Wildfire*, and *William* had been enslaved and on the move for most, if not all, of their known lives, exposed to an excess of death and violence. The American sailor Lucius Vermilyea, for example, observed child captives embarked from the Congo River on the *Montauk* in 1860: "So used were they to death, that little girls would point at and laugh at a corpse lying near them."[155] Like the boys who grouped together for self-defense on the *Niagara*, large numbers of children and youth aboard illegal slavers and recaptive transports experienced extreme vulnerability and exposure. Compared with the few children scattered among the *Bogota* adult shipmates, hundreds of West Central African children, many of whom were already sick when they embarked from Key West, had far less access to healing skills and ritual expertise. Evidence from U.S. recaptive transports thus sheds light on how the age profile of particular shipmate groups offered varying resources for survival and social relations.

To a large extent, recaptive shipmates in transit were left to their own devices by crew and agents who demonstrated little of the colonizing or civilizing zeal that officials would direct at recaptives upon their arrival in Liberia. Only Grymes's report to the ACS and McCalla's journal comments on the marriage services performed aboard the *Star of the Union* expressed any sense that recaptive voyages might serve some didactic purpose for acculturating African recaptives to Protestant, Anglo-American mores.[156] In the vacant spaces created by language barriers and American racial disdain, recaptive forced migrants built upon the experience of middle passage trauma to further develop shipmate affiliations that covered the spectrum from conflict to collaboration. Those who survived to disembark in Liberia encountered a more extended phase of exile, where discrete groups of shipmates would be governed by the system of Liberian apprenticeship and incorporated into a larger "Congo" recaptive identity.

6

Becoming Liberian "Congoes"

Jah-Jah! The children crying in the wilderness.
Send us a prophet, to warn the nation.
All the children in this creation,
All the people that you see
Will be the children of the Most High.

—"Children Crying" lyrics, The Congos,
Heart of the Congos album, 1977

MARRIED.—On Thursday, the 17th inst. (March,) at the
Colonization Receptacle in Monrovia, by the Rev. John Seys, KABENDAH,
alias JAMES BUCHANAN, to KANDAH, alias ANN LIBERIA JEFFS,
both liberated Africans of the company by the US Ship Niagara.

—*African Repository* quoting *Liberia Christian Advocate*, 1859

Four months after their arrival in Monrovia, Kandah and Kabendah, former recaptives of the *Echo*, were married by the U.S. agent for recaptured Africans John Seys. Everything about the ceremony revealed the tenuous nature of the couple's new lives in Liberia. The wedding took place among fellow shipmates in the designated quarters ("Receptacle") for newly arrived recaptives. According to a Liberian newspaper, Methodist clergyman Seys officiated, "in as nearly a civilized and christian style as their own rude and barbarous state would admit of."[1] Considering the transatlantic ordeal Kandah and Kabendah had survived together, their union powerfully illustrates how new social bonds could be built upon existing ties between shipmates. Indeed, as we shall see, just two weeks before this marriage ceremony, *Echo* recaptives had forcefully exerted themselves on behalf of a fellow shipmate—a fact that went unmentioned in the *African Repository* announcement. At the same time, however, the language of the announcement conveys how Liberian colonial interests shaped the pathways by which West Central African recaptives slowly became Liberian "Congoes." Having passed through stormy U.S. debates over slavery and race, slave trade refugees like Kandah and Kabendah would now be claimed by a Liberian civilizing mission premised upon the wary incorporation of recaptives into African American emigrant households. Owing to the influx of an unprecedented wave of West Central African recaptives in the years immediately following their arrival, Kandah and Kabendah would become known not only by newly assigned English names but also by the broad ethnonym "Congoes."[2]

Kandah and Kabendah's story reveals in microcosm how recaptives removed to Liberia by U.S. mandate continued to confront death, dislocation, and dependency. African passengers had disembarked from the *Niagara*'s long voyage only to experience the death of ten more of their shipmates from illness and exhaustion. During the early months of 1859, American Colonization Society (ACS) and Liberian officials divided surviving shipmates into smaller contingents and distributed them throughout the settler population. A group of ailing recaptives remained behind in the Monrovian receptacles, but Liberian authorities and the U.S. agent sent approximately thirty people each to the smaller settlements of Robertsport in Grand Cape Mount, Grand Bassa, Sinoe, and Cape Palmas (see fig. 6.1).[3] Protestant missions took in some of the children, while others remained in temporary housing until they could be apprenticed to Liberian families.[4] As the ship's company fragmented, Kandah remained behind in Monrovia, while Kabendah, according to the *Liberian Christian Advocate*, sailed unwillingly south to Grand Bassa, where he grieved for Kandah until authorities decided the two should be reunited. Although details of the pair's relationship are sparse, we should look beyond the obvious sentimentalization of the *Christian Advocate* story to grasp the couple's resolve not to be separated by administrative decision. Recaptive children, men, and women sought to build on and protect the social bonds they had forged throughout their voyages. Their initial years under Liberian apprenticeship, however, revealed the limitations of enacting emancipation within the constraints of a colonial society.

In contrast to the American policy of deportation, Liberian recaptive policy aimed to incorporate and assimilate slave trade refugees like Kandah and Kabendah, albeit as a subordinate population. From its inception by the ACS, Liberia's founding mission connected the suppression of the slave trade to the spreading of "civilization, commerce, and Christianity."[5] By midcentury, thousands of free and manumitted African American emigrants had built a

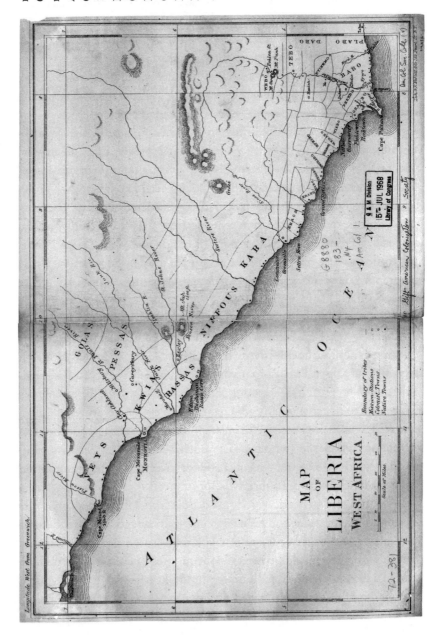

FIGURE 6.1 American Colonization Society map of Liberia, West Africa. G. F. Nesbitt & Company, *Map of Liberia, West Africa* (New York: Lith. G. F. Nesbitt & Co., 183?). Courtesy of Library of Congress, Geography and Map Division, Washington, D.C., https://www.loc.gov/item/9668498з.

settler society in Liberia around an Americo-Liberian identity reflected in Westernized institutions of church, school, and family. The double naming of bride and groom in the wedding announcement thus conveyed the expectation that Kandah and Kabendah would be transformed into Ann Liberia Jeffs and James Buchanan, with the attendant acculturation these names implied.[6] Received as "savages" into Liberian households, recaptives in Liberia were nevertheless valued by the settler population as potential laborers, converts, and allies in the young republic's future growth.[7] As a result, apprenticeships, agricultural and industrial labor, militia service, and Christian proselytization exposed recaptives to new forms of exploitation even as they offered opportunities for building collective affiliations with a larger "Congo" population.

The emergence of recaptives under the Liberian term "Congoes" provides an instructive case study of how Atlantic World processes of "political upheaval and violence" generated new forms of identification.[8] In recent years, scholars have vigorously interrogated the historical processes of ethnogenesis in the African diaspora. Ethnic signifiers such as "Igbo" and "Yoruba," once treated as relatively fixed, now appear as complex, malleable categories shaped by forced migration, social rupture, and political turmoil. Both identification from within and imposition from without played a role in the formation of new recaptive, or "liberated African," communities throughout the Atlantic World.[9] In Liberia, an examination of the historical emergence of the "Congoes" label suggests how recaptives were grouped under the term to serve missionary and Liberian state interests. Ironically, by the mid-twentieth century, the term "Congo" had come to mean not only the descendants of recaptives but also those of black American migrants, in contrast to the indigenous "country" population.[10] In the nineteenth century, however, both white ACS authorities and Liberian colonists used "Congo" to denote a specific recaptive population distinguished from both the migrant black American and the indigenous populations.[11] To some extent, West Central African recaptives actively pursued affiliations with earlier generations of recaptives on the basis of geographic origin and forced migration experiences. Yet, as we have seen, children made up large portions of the recaptive population. As these young people sought protection and security in the wake of slave ship terrors, they experienced continued danger and vulnerability. Age thus played a large role in the degree of control that recaptives had over their Liberian environment. As a result, the "Congo" ethnonym emerged largely in the context of struggle with dependency and subordination in Liberian colonial society.

Recaptives in Liberian Colonial Strategy, 1820s–1840s

Shipmates of the *Echo, Wildfire, William*, and *Bogota* found themselves transported to a small West African republic where the demographic category of "recaptured African" had already played a sustained role in colonial development. Although many studies of Liberia understandably focus on the ACS's colonization of free and manumitted African Americans, the suppression of the transatlantic slave trade and the resettlement of Africans seized on illegal slavers also figured significantly in Liberia's history.[12] As we saw earlier, ACS success in lobbying for U.S. federal appropriations in 1819 rested heavily on the society's promise to secure a West African outpost where recaptives could be resettled "beyond the limits of the United States."[13] Claims that Liberia's existence contributed to slave trade suppression and provided a refuge for the victims of illegal slavers appeared prominently in ACS appeals for private donations and federal funding.[14] From the early years of colonization in the 1820s, ACS agents in Liberia also frequently doubled as U.S. government agents for recaptured Africans.[15] Furthermore, slave trade suppression objectives underwrote the deployment of U.S. naval resources along the coast of a colony not even officially claimed by the American government.[16] Finally, the right of the ACS to continue to settle recaptives with American financial support after Liberian independence in 1847 constituted one of the key issues in post-independence negotiations.[17] In short, the entanglement of U.S., ACS, and Liberian slave trade suppression politics strongly limited the conditions under which recaptives could establish a new life in the wake of their transatlantic voyages.[18]

Liberia's colonizers also expected slave trade recaptives to play a strategic role in the balance of power between colonists and indigenous groups. The small but growing population of African American migrants nurtured by the ACS at Cape Mesurado displaced and disrupted many existing polities already residing in the region of the Grain Coast.[19] Indigenes including Bassa, Grebo, Dei, Vai, Kpelle, and Gola often resisted Liberian emigrants' efforts to claim permanent title to land. Others, such as the residents of coastal Kru towns, proved far more interested in potential commercial opportunities than appeals to Christian conversion.[20] Vai traders long established near the region colonists called Grand Cape Mount fought both colonists and other contending indigenous groups for access to trade relations with Europeans that included the slave trade.[21] In this unstable colonial borderland, the ACS and African American emigrants looked to recaptives as an alternative labor source and a population buffer between settlers and indigenes.[22] Meanwhile, missionaries anticipated that orphaned and destitute recaptives would prove better candidates than indigenous societies for Christian conversion. Publicly, both Liberian leaders and missionaries spoke of recaptives as a providential population who promised in theory to become "a blessing to Africa" as they merged with the Liberian emigrant population.[23]

In actuality, the recaptive population was neither as numerous nor as tractable as colonizationist rhetoric anticipated. Compared with the steady arrival of nearly 99,000 people registered as liberated Africans in the adjacent British colony of Sierra Leone, limited U.S. slave trade suppression efforts yielded only three unevenly sized generations of recaptives arriving in Liberia during the nineteenth century.[24] ACS records show that the U.S. transported 286 recaptives to Liberia in the colonial period up to the 1843 census. As recounted in Chapter 1, African captives from the captured vessels *Antelope* and *Fenix*, along with the shipwrecked slaver *Guerrero*, constituted a significant portion of the early recaptive population.[25] Survivors from these ships arrived at Cape Mesurado after years of legal limbo in Florida, Savannah, and New Orleans. In addition, colonists in Liberia seized another 150 captives from nearby Spanish coastal slaving operations during the 1820s and settled them within the new colony's boundaries.[26] By the 1830s, a recaptive community described as both "Congo" and "Eboe" (Igbo) grew up in New Georgia, roughly five miles north of Monrovia on Stockton Creek.[27] A few eventually made their way to Sierra Leone or blended into the indigenous population, but most recaptives in New Georgia formed families, farmed crops, and cut timber for the Monrovia markets, living alongside a handful of African American colonists.[28] Missionaries and ACS agents emphasized the assimilation of the New Georgians, citing school attendance, church membership, and even the exemplary rise of one recaptive "citizen" to legislative office.[29] Yet, historian Claude Clegg reminds us, recaptives in Liberian society remained "a people between two worlds," living with a legacy of displacement from their homelands while forging a new existence between indigenes and colonists.[30] That intermediate status meant that future groups of recaptives would face colonial administrators who perceived them as both a national resource and a disorderly presence.[31]

Ambivalent Liberian views of recaptives intensified with the arrival of the second generation of recaptives. In December 1845, the American barque *Pons* appeared at Cape Mesurado carrying 756 young West Central Africans in an extreme state of trauma. Having been seized just three days out from Cabinda, the *Pons* took another sixteen days to reach Monrovia, during which time 150 recaptives perished. Horrified eyewitnesses who boarded the ship described how, in the absence of even a rough wooden slave deck, hundreds of boys and young men had been "piled almost in bulk, on the water casks" in the stench of the closed and darkened hold. Meanwhile, 47 girls and women crowded into a portion of the roundhouse cabin in close proximity to the captain's and mates' berths.[32] Like the other slavers embarking from West Central Africa in this study, the *Pons* held a majority of young people between the ages of ten and twenty who had clearly experienced successive phases of violence and loss before being forced aboard a foreign vessel.[33] Coming ashore in Monrovia, young people of the *Pons* more than tripled the colony's recaptive population and placed heavy demands on local resources.[34] Their arrival presented Liberian colonists with a humanitarian crisis of unprecedented proportions that would become all too familiar in later years.

Even as officials struggled to feed, clothe, and medically care for almost 800 young people in desperate condition, portions of Liberian colonial society saw these young refugees as a blessing in disguise for their nascent republic. The *Pons* recaptives arrived in the midst of debates over the question of Liberia's capacity to function as an independent state.[35] Both symbolically and practically, young shipmates of the *Pons* represented future labor and an expanded colonial population for those invested in Liberian autonomy. James Washington Lugenbeel, a white North Carolina ACS agent who became the U.S. agent for recaptives in this period, reported the eagerness with which colonists sought to take recaptives into their households, some out of benevolent sympathy, others happy to avail themselves of apprenticed labor in homes, businesses, and fields. Lugenbeel doled out recaptives to colonists he deemed able to care for them, requiring a signature of agreement to return in two months for formal apprenticeship proceedings.[36] In a significant exception to this pattern, he placed seventeen "headmen" of the *Pons* shipmates in New Georgia "under the care of some of their countrymen," thus connecting first and second generations of West Central African recaptives.[37] The vast majority of recaptives, however, entered colonial households for seven years under apprenticeship laws written primarily for indigenous youth. It was this arrangement in the homes of better-off Monrovian colonists that Samuel S. Ball, a Colored Baptist Association elder who traveled from Illinois to Liberia in 1848, described as a starkly subordinate form of labor. According to Ball, "About their houses, these natives [including *Pons* apprentices] do all the menial service; such as packing wood and water and cooking and waiting about the house." Most egregious in Ball's view was the inability of apprenticed children to attend school as equals of Liberian youth.[38]

Liberian and ACS officials assumed that the apprenticing of recaptives into settler households would result in their assimilation into Liberian, Christian social institutions.[39] In this regard, child recaptives of the *Pons*, especially malleable in their orphaned state, generated special empathy and interest among resident missionaries. Methodist Episcopal clergy eagerly accepted 100 *Pons* children—80 boys and 20 girls—from the Monrovian receptacle. Caring for these orphans far from their homes, white Methodist clergyman John B. Benham hoped, would cultivate their "gratitude and fidelity," thus leading to Christian conversion and future church membership. In a promotional letter designed for U.S. home audiences, Benham depicted the arrival of recaptive youth as a providential opportunity for "obtaining children for our mission schools, who will, in all probability, be permanently connected with them until they shall have arrived at adult age."[40] His statement conveyed the general missionary perception that slave trade suppression beneficially produced, in historian Benjamin Lawrance's words, a "repository of vulnerable, kinless individuals."[41] Recaptive girls in particular represented "a great acquisition." As missionary Susan Benham claimed in a letter to American church members, indigenous families resisted sending their daughters to mission schools, and thus even a small number of recaptive girls improved the gender balance among their charges.[42] Missionary evangelists thus placed high hopes in the female portion of the *Pons* children, depending on the girls for the transmission of "civilization" through marriage and the reproduction of Christian converts. Ann Wilkins, a white long-term Methodist missionary, promised U.S. donors a personal stake in the civilizing mission by offering them the privilege of renaming recaptive girls at her boarding school in Millsburg.[43] As many Liberian missionaries at the time viewed it, the "great evil" of the slave trade promised to "bring good" to Liberia in the form of pliable recaptive children.[44]

Yet some Liberian emigrants remained skeptical, seeing more threat than promise. Many African Americans, free and recently manumitted, came to Liberia with expectations shaped by Western civilization discourse, but they also subsequently developed a "siege mentality" as the result of contentious relations with indigenous neighbors.[45] Fears of disorder deepened when large numbers of young *Pons* recaptives apparently escaped the homes of their Liberian guardians. The immediate cause of their flight lay in the inability of the ACS and the U.S. government to adequately subsidize the support of almost 800 destitute children and young adults. In addition, their escape may have been prompted not only from hunger but also from fear of further enslavement; a few may have nurtured misinformed hopes of reaching their faraway West Central African homelands.[46] As we shall see with later recaptive groups, attempted escape from apprenticeship was not an uncommon response. Between late 1846 and early 1847, newspaper reports of "fugitive savages" hidden in the forests and seeking to "plunder from the colonists" turned preconception to fear.[47] Matilda Lomax, a Virginia-born African American woman who emigrated to Monrovia as a girl, described the *Pons* "Congoes" as "the most Savage, & blud thirsty people I ever saw or ever wishes to see."[48] Views of recaptives as untamed and violent existed among Liberian colonists in uneasy tension with hopes for their future acculturation.

Colonists' anxieties quieted, however, as some young *Pons* recaptives found life on the margins of settlements untenable. Governor Joseph J. Roberts reassured the ACS in October 1846 that many runaways had returned and been bound out to "suitable homes."[49] Beyond the valuable labor they represented for Liberian farming and timbering, recaptives were, the *Liberia Herald* reported, "becoming of value to their guardians" through their impact on Liberian relations with indigenous groups. One Grand Bassa colonist in 1847 described recaptives as shifting the balance of tensions between their small settlement and nearby towns: "Our Congoes have really turned out manly; they have thrown more dread upon the Fishmen, (our former antagonists,) and the surrounding tribes, than I have ever known exerted upon them before."[50] Two years later, in the same area, twenty-five "Congoes" from the *Pons* participated in an armed attack on slave trader operations at New Cess.[51] The emphasis on the militancy of "Congo" men in these examples diverges from most Liberian accounts of *Pons* survivors as abject and uncivilized. Both versions, however, defined recaptives as a distinct population whose arrival would shape Liberia's future for better or worse. By the 1860s, when the largest and final generation of recaptives arrived, Liberians were describing surviving *Pons* shipmates as "docile, industrious, and worthy," in other words—like their New Georgian predecessors—symbols of Liberia's civilizing influence and national potential.[52]

Overall, the Liberian response to *Pons* recaptives established the terms under which a much larger, third generation of recaptives would end their forced Atlantic travels. First, young survivors of the *Pons* became a bridging generation for later recaptives. Having been brought to Liberia as children and teenagers, many *Pons* recaptives served as interpreters and supervisors when the *Echo* shipmates arrived on the *Niagara* twelve years later. Second, the economic imperatives of a small and newly independent black republic after 1847 would continue to shape a resettlement policy that apprenticed recaptives with Liberian families. The young age of many recaptives, of course, also led to their placement as dependents within settler households and shaped external perceptions of them as a permanently dependent class.[53] At the same time, future recaptives, like some of the *Pons* shipmates, resisted their apprenticeships through escapes and other forms of protest. Third and finally, the embarkation of *Pons* shipmates from Cabinda reinforced the broad umbrella term of "Congo" for the West Central African recaptive population.[54] The term had first been applied, in Liberia within missionary and ACS lexicons, to the New Georgia settlement. By 1860, with the mass entrance of thousands of recaptives, "Congoes" became an ethnic designation that merged a generalized geographic origin with a historically specific experience of Atlantic displacement.[55]

The 1860s "Congo Question" and Recaptive Apprenticeship

In May 1861, the ACS periodical *African Repository* remarked, "The 'Congo question,' as the Liberians term the introduction of recaptured Africans, has caused no little excitement. All, however, is quiet now on that score."[56] Despite the ACS's attempt at reassurance, the arrival of the third generation of recaptives caused a long-term social, cultural, and economic transformation of Liberian society.[57] And, in turn, Liberian political and economic imperatives shaped and constrained the worlds recaptives built on the foundation of their shipmate bonds. Between 1858 and 1861, the final wave of forced immigrants arrived in Liberia, numbering a total of 4,675 recaptives on nine different ships (see Table 5). At the time, the settler population of the tiny republic numbered less than 10,000, mostly concentrated in Monrovia and in colonial settlements along the St. Paul River.[58] The emigration of hundreds of impoverished former slaves from the United States during this same period compounded the human costs of what Claude Clegg terms Liberia's "era of despair."[59] Such conditions set the stage for potential friction, if not outright exploitation, between Liberian immigrants and hundreds of recaptives produced by the heightened efforts of U.S. naval patrols.

Shipmates of the slaver *Echo*, the first of a third wave of slave trade refugees, arrived from Charleston on the USS *Niagara* in early November 1858. Conflict followed quickly, as recaptive men, women, and children spent months confined to the receptacle in Monrovia under the supervision of ACS agent Henry Dennis and U.S. agent for recaptured Africans John Seys. In March 1859, tensions over conditions and treatment in the receptacle ignited when the husband of Mrs. Freeman, one of the women employed to serve as nurse and "matron" to recaptive children, beat a recaptive youth for failing to perform an order. Significantly, Mr. Freeman did not play any official role in the receptacle but simply lived with his employed wife. In Seys's opinion at least, Mr. Freeman had wrongly attempted to use recaptive labor for his personal benefit. An angry crowd immediately left the receptacle with the injured young man, searching for Seys at the U.S. consulate office. Their march to the consulate building suggests that for recaptives, survival strategies included acquiring knowledge about the terrain of local authority in their new environment. However, failing to find an interpreter who could help them express their indignation over the young recaptive's bleeding eye and welted back, a growing crowd turned their anger on Mr. Freeman, who had hidden in a nearby home. The ensuing rare description of recaptive armed resistance suggested a sense of cohesion among *Echo* shipmates forged across their extended journey.[60]

Retaliation by recaptives on behalf of an injured shipmate reflected both an ethos of collective protection and a refusal to accept arbitrary violence as a condition of their new lives. According to John Seys, "The whole congoe fraternity rallied around their injured brother." He went on to describe the growing "mob" of "men—women—boys—girls—all uniting and all armed with stones, clubs, and some with cutlasses," as they attacked the home where Freeman had sought refuge. During the dispute, Liberians fired muskets upon the angry "Echoites," and a young recaptive woman received a gunshot wound before the protest was finally put down by local authorities. After the magistrate court imposed a fine on Freeman and had the leaders of the protest "soundly thrashed," U.S. agent John Seys held a mass meeting, asking recaptives to bring future grievances to him and other agents, who would "see them redressed."[61] At the same time, ACS agent Dennis quickly mobilized to remove "unruly" recaptives from Monrovia and contract them as apprentices throughout Liberia's rural districts.[62] Though quickly suppressed, the *Echo* shipmates' rebellion illuminates both shipmate solidarity and Liberian supervisors' concerns with controlling potential unrest.

Compared with *Echo* shipmates, recaptives of the three chartered vessels sailing from Key West less than two years later entered Liberia in much different circumstances alongside a swelling tide of recaptives newly seized off the West Central African coast. In August 1860, U.S. Navy prize crews brought two slavers, the *Storm King* and the *Erie*, into Monrovia, carrying a total of nearly 1,500 young recaptives embarked from the Congo River barracoons.[63] Within the next half year, the U.S. Africa Squadron intercepted three additional American-built slavers near the African coast (*Cora, Bonito,*

TABLE 5 Recaptive Arrivals in Liberia, 1858–1861

Ship	Date Arrived Liberia	Disembarkation Point	Persons Disembarked
Niagara from Charleston (*Echo* shipmates)	8 November 1858	Monrovia	200
Storm King (embarked from Congo River and seized at sea)	21 August 1860	Monrovia	616
Erie (embarked from Congo River and seized at sea)	22 August 1860	Monrovia	867
Castilian from Key West (*Wildfire* shipmates)	27 August 1860	Robertsport, Cape Mount	308
Star of the Union from Key West (*Bogota* shipmates)	5 September 1860	Sinoe	337
South Shore from Key West (*William* shipmates)	6 September 1860	Grand Bassa	233
Cora (embarked from Congo River and seized at sea)	16 October 1860	Monrovia	694
Bonito (embarked from WCA coast and seized at sea)	29 October 1860	Monrovia	616
Nightingale (embarked from Cabinda and seized at sea)	13 May 1861	Monrovia	801
TOTAL			4,675*

*Including 3 recaptive boys from the *Wm. R. Kibby*, arrived in *M.C. Stevens*, 15 December 1860.
  Source: Letters Received from John Seys, reel 10, RSI.

and *Nightingale*), bringing another 2,100 young people to Liberia's doorstep.[64] The majority of recaptives sailing from Key West thus entered Liberia with thousands of other slave trade refugees, considered by Liberian officials to be their "countrymen" and fellow "Congoes."[65]

Overwhelmed with *Storm King* and *Erie* shipmates at the Monrovia receptacles, the U.S. agent sent each of the three Key West groups to a different peripheral settlement along the Liberian coast. In each location, recaptives from Key West joined a smaller group of *Echo* shipmates. For example, *Wildfire* shipmates, including Francisco and Bomba, disembarked at Cape Mount near Liberia's northern border. The *William's* sick and emaciated young passengers came ashore at the small settlement of Bassa Cove roughly 60 miles southeast of Monrovia, where the previously mentioned Kabendah had been transported before his return to Monrovia. Finally, the *Bogota's* shipmates from the Bight of Benin arrived at Greenville, Sinoe, a small settlement about 150 miles southeast of Monrovia. Sinoe had been colonized initially as Mississippi in Africa but merged with Liberia in 1841.[66] As we shall see, the Bight of Benin shipmates remained an anomaly within the larger West Central African recaptive population, first for their distinct origins primarily in Yoruba towns and, second, for their more adult company. Geography and language influenced their exclusion from the broad "Congo" ethnonym, while age and experience offered adults additional resources for asserting greater autonomy and control over their futures.

Given the crisis conditions under which recaptives arrived in Liberia in 1860, the "Congo question" actually posed several different simultaneous problems. Liberian leaders President Stephen Benson and Secretary of State John N. Lewis wondered how to access promised American funding for recaptive support while defending the integrity of the young nation's sovereignty. U.S. and Liberian agents and physicians on the front lines of recaptive reception asked how to feed, clothe, and shelter thousands of recaptives. Liberian intellectuals such as Alexander Crummell worked to assuage concerns about how Liberia could assimilate so many "Congo" newcomers into the "settler standard" of Christianity and republicanism without endangering the dream of Liberia as a beacon of African civilization.[67] And through it all, young shipmates all too familiar with separation, violence, and forced migration searched for security and belonging through reinvented social connections of kinship and community.

Liberia's tangled relationship with the ACS and U.S. slave trade suppression increased political tensions resulting from the third wave of slave ship recaptives. Since 1819, the ACS had received occasional U.S. congressional appropriations for the support of recaptured Africans and the U.S. Agency for Recaptured Africans stationed at Monrovia.[68] After Liberia declared independence on 26 July 1847, it drew up a legal agreement outlining its political and financial relationship to the ACS. Article 1 of this agreement secured the receptacles as ACS property, while Article 4 agreed that recaptives would continue to be allowed to enter Liberia with support from the U.S. government.[69] Despite these provisions, however, U.S. presidents continually refused to grant diplomatic recognition to Liberia. Given these circumstances, the U.S. intent to settle thousands of recaptives in Liberia aroused Liberian leaders' understandable concern. If the United States expected Liberia to admit thousands of recaptives, President Benson demanded, contracts should be drawn up with Liberia, not the ACS, and U.S. funds should flow directly to Liberian treasuries. Until funding issues could be resolved, the Liberian government insisted that recaptives remain in the receptacle areas owned by the ACS.[70]

Furthermore, the Liberian government swiftly declined U.S. agent John Seys's request to print his own promissory notes for paying recaptive expenses.[71]

As negotiations proceeded, Liberian secretary of state John Lewis pled for direct U.S. funding as the only means by which Liberia could mitigate the moral threat posed to the "civilized" emigrant population by "wild heathens from various tribes." Lewis, like many other Liberian emigrants, clearly supported the idea of a black republic taking a leading role in the suppression of the slave trade.[72] Yet his arguments also reflected concern over the risks posed by incorporating recaptives into the Liberian settler population.[73] President Benson proposed to the ACS a plan whereby large groups of recaptives could be settled on Liberian land under long-term support and supervision that included manual labor training. Notably Benson's plan would have removed recaptives from ACS-controlled receptacles once U.S. funding had been received, thus offering a second option for recaptive residence alongside apprenticeship.[74] After a drawn-out negotiation, the ACS agreed to turn over U.S. funds to the Liberian treasury beginning in 1861. However, agent John Seys, with his own long and controversial history in Liberian politics, would remain in place to sign off on Liberian compliance before the United States fully subsidized recaptive expenses.[75] The administrative imperative to account to the U.S. government for recaptive numbers provided a structure for oversight of recaptive apprentice treatment. Yet it also contributed to the surveillance and constrained geographic mobility experienced by recaptives during their first year in Liberia.

Recaptives spent their first days and weeks in Liberian receptacles where imposed confinement and the politics of survival shifted from ship to shore. Built by the ACS to accommodate new emigrants and recaptives in their transition to more permanent settlement, the simple brick or wood-frame receptacles located in Monrovia and other emigrant settlements served as sites of shelter and provision as well as medical care, schooling, and Christian proselytization.[76] For newly arrived slave trade refugees, however, the spare rooms of the receptacles may have appeared as simply another carceral space, like the Cabinda barracoons, Fort Sumter, or the Key West Depot. Added to the prevalence of illness and death, receptacles were often overcrowded and chaotic. Recall how, in 1859, *Echo* shipmates protested the violence of daily life in the receptacles. By 1860, officials scrambled to find room for the flood of new arrivals. In Monrovia, for example, Seys had to place some of the *Storm King* shipmates in several unoccupied houses after the receptacle overflowed. Once the *Storm King* and *Erie* recaptives disembarked together, it was difficult for agents to distinguish between the two groups of shipmates.[77]

The beleaguered agent spent considerable energy and cash simply finding sufficient stores of rice, country cloth, calico, and denim to feed and clothe 1,500 children and young adults.[78]

For most recaptives gathered in Liberian receptacles, the future must have seemed tenuous at best. Many survived their Atlantic voyages only to expire shortly thereafter.[79] *Star of the Union* recaptives, for example, arrived in the Sinoe receptacle stunned by their most recent loss of nine men and one woman who had drowned in the roiling surf of the sandbar as Kru mariners ferried the ship's small boats ashore. James Grymes, the white physician who crossed with them, noted with distress the men and women, recently jubilant with the end of their journey, now "wailing over the dead bodies, washed upon the beach—(scarcely cold)."[80] Thirty-one of the *Castilian*'s passengers perished in the Robertsport receptacles within the first five months of arrival.[81] One man from the *Storm King* or *Erie*, according to Seys, hung himself "in a fit of mental despondency," and two individuals from the later-arriving slaver *Bonito* died after apparently refusing all nourishment.[82] Such reports testify to the physical and existential crisis of recaptivity caused by both slave ship journeys and their aftermath.

Amidst the confusion and stark human need, singular moments of recognition occurred. As had happened at least once in Key West, a few recaptives found their countrymen or -women among the crowds. Seys reported the elated reunion of siblings and spouses who had been parted at some point before or in the Congo River barracoons and, once joined together again, pleaded "not to be separated."[83] Such rare encounters happened only where more than one ship arrived together and were thus not possible, at least immediately, to recaptives from Charleston and Key West, who were diverted to separate ports. Overall, however, the concentration of West Central African recaptives in Liberia produced circumstances in which slave trade refugees might find commonalities of language, homeland, and even kinship among fellow recaptives.

In these chaotic first days at the receptacles, newly arrived shipmates also encountered people from former recaptive generations with whom they made their first connections to a Liberian "Congo" identity. A "Congo man," from Monrovia, for example, lived with a small group of the *Echo* shipmates in their first months of resettlement at Cape Palmas.[84] During the flood of slave trade refugees into Monrovia in 1860, Seys employed seasoned "Congoes from the *Pons* and *Echo*" as interpreters and overseers to assist him with the boys and young men of the *Storm King* and *Erie*.[85] Benjamin Stryker and John James, for example, earned 50 cents per day for interpreting and general domestic work in the Monrovia receptacle during October 1860.[86] Nathaniel Freeman, quite possibly the instigator of the 1859 *Echo* shipmates' protests, worked as a cook and interpreter along with his wife, Julie C. Freeman, who provided nursing care and domestic service for recaptives in Monrovia.[87] No further details exist of daily interactions between newcomers and the receptacle workers, nor should we assume that these two generations of recaptives identified immediately with one another. Yet we can say that, for many of the disoriented 1860 recaptives, someone in their new surroundings spoke a familiar language and could provide information about their prospects. These early receptacle encounters spun the first threads out of which a more sturdy social fabric could be woven.

Liberia's distinctive context for recaptive community formation becomes clearer by comparison with the evolution of Sierra Leone's liberated African policies. Sierra Leone began in the 1780s as a British abolitionist "Province of Freedom," colonized by a first generation of black loyalist migrants in the wake of the American Revolution.[88] Quickly, however, Sierra Leone became the destination for recaptives of illegal slave ships—at least 440 captured slave ships with their human cargo arrived at Freetown during the period of British slave trade suppression.[89] Recaptive Africans in British custody who disembarked at Freetown entered the walled-off compound called the King's Yard to await a verdict on their seized slave ship.[90] The yard, like the Liberian receptacles, also employed former recaptive interpreters and overseers to orient newcomers and embraced a similar imperial mission that viewed recaptives as dependent and uncivilized.[91] Yet with its encampment of thousands of newly arrived recaptives from multiple regions of West and West Central Africa, the Freetown yard operated on a much larger scale than the Liberian receptacles. Thus, as soon as they arrived in the King's Yard, liberated African men and women could join shipmate mutual aid clubs as well as more culturally and religiously specific associations.[92]

Significantly, British policy in Sierra Leone also diverged from Liberian practices in the establishment of communities for liberated Africans. Immediately after the 1807 ban, the colonial government attempted several forms of local recaptive apprenticeship. Some younger children were also sent to Church Missionary Society schools.[93] By the 1820s, however, policies had shifted toward direct settlement of recaptives in one of several villages of liberated Africans on the peninsula near Freetown or in the surrounding mountains. (Not all recaptives took this route, for some young men were forcibly recruited into the West Indian military, and thousands of other recaptives were sent as indentured laborers to Caribbean plantations.)[94] Within Sierra

Leone's villages of liberated Africans, residents organized by broad linguistic, religious, and regional affiliations and generated new political and cultural institutions.[95] Though subject to colonial rule like other settlements for liberated Africans in the Caribbean, Sierra Leone's liberated African villages nevertheless afforded survivors of the transatlantic trade a semiautonomous space for rebuilding political, social, and economic life.[96] The recognition of these communities by Sierra Leone's colonial administration represented a crucial difference between Liberian and Sierra Leone recaptive policy, although this difference would not have been felt by many young children who continued to be placed in Sierra Leone missionary schools and apprenticeships.[97]

Rather than rebuilding life in villages under the wing of earlier arrivals, almost all Liberian recaptives spent their first years in the country apprenticed to black American emigrant households or to missionary stations.[98] According to U.S. agent John Seys, committees of "respectable citizens" distributed thousands of young people from the third wave of recaptives across 600 Liberian households and businesses in placements ranging from single individuals to as many as forty recaptives at a time.[99] During the colonial period, Liberia had passed apprenticeship laws mainly designed for the sons and daughters of indigenes, with some features closely resembling local systems of pawnship.[100] The arrival of the *Pons* prompted a new 1846 law directed at both adults and children, crafted to incorporate recaptives as well as indigenous youth. That law allowed the binding of recaptives to Liberian households for seven years or until age twenty-one for males and eighteen for females. Households, in turn, owed recaptives clothing, provisions, decent treatment, and instruction in "civilized life."[101] During the first six months to one year of the apprenticeship (depending on specific contracts) the United States agreed to subsidize the apprenticing household heads.[102] Although many Liberian colonists remained wary of recaptives as a potentially disorderly population, the apprenticeship policy served the interests of the Liberian economy. Some liberated African men enlisted in recaptive militias that defended settler communities, and others worked as porters on trading expeditions inland.[103] Timber businesses on the Liberian frontier and planters on the St. Paul River north of Monrovia welcomed the infusion of a dependent labor source to cultivate sugar and coffee crops.[104] In fact, historians generally attribute Liberia's mid-nineteenth-century expansion of commodity exports to the mass arrival of recaptive laborers.[105]

Liberian intellectual Alexander Crummell clearly articulated this convergence of Liberian national interest and recaptive policy during a U.S. speaking tour in 1861. Crummell, whose own Temne father had been sold to slave traders as a child in West Africa, believed that "the Congo inundation" (as he later called it) would contribute to Liberia's larger mission of African redemption.[106] "The Congoes," he claimed, "are remarkably pliant and industrious, and peculiarly proud and ambitious of being called 'Americans.'"[107] Already they manifested their industry in the "hundreds of acres being cleared for sugar farms." Here Crummell used "American" to indicate acculturation to Liberian settler society and its attendant institutions of church, school, English language, and commercial capitalism. Praising these "American" aspirations, Crummell envisioned incoming slave trade refugees as a counterweight to indigenous groups who greatly outnumbered Liberian colonists. As he put it in an 1861 letter to a Philadelphia paper: "The Congo additions to our force already staggers and confuses the natives at all our settlements." Indeed, Crummell predicted that the arrival of recaptives would realign relations between settlers and indigenes and end all "native wars."[108] Furthermore, Crummell argued that an "excess of females" among Liberian emigrants conveniently matched the predominantly male population of recaptive Africans and augured well for future intermarriages. This last suggestion indicated Crummell's distinct vision of a common future that Liberian colonists would build with native Africans under the mantle of civilization.[109]

Although other Liberians proved more wary than Crummell of intermarriage, many viewed the apprenticeship of recaptives in their households as an act of Christian benevolence and a boon to their own future prosperity. For example, William C. Burke, who emigrated from Virginia in 1853 after he and his family were manumitted by Robert E. Lee, worked on the committee that divided the shipmates of the *Storm King* and the *Erie* among hundreds of Liberian emigrant households. Together the Presbyterian minister William and his wife, Rosabella, took twelve "men, women & boys" into the Clay Ashland farm they christened Mount Rest. Burke's expressed motivation for sheltering young "Africans of the Congo tribe" was explicitly to "Civilize and Christianize" them. His letters to the ACS reflect a sense of personal calling to redeem African children traumatized by the "horrors of the slave trade" through a reciprocal arrangement in which the young recaptives could be "a blessing to us and we a blessing to them."[110] In terms of the language of Christian benevolence, his paternalistic viewpoint may not have differed greatly from that expressed by James Pennington in his New York–based advocacy. At the same time, Burke was a household head benefiting from recaptive labor, and his assumption of mutually shared interests bespoke an inability to fully comprehend the terrors precipitated by placement in settler and missionary households.

These fears weighed hard on young recaptives intimately familiar with processes of inspection, selection, and distribution that characterized market sites along the Atlantic's slaving routes. Shipmates of the *Storm King* and the *Erie*, for example, revealed deep concern about separation and reenslavement when faced with Liberians interested in apprenticing them.[111] Agent John Seys's wife, Ann, wrote of her experience with the Monrovia receptacle in a letter of appeal to American Christian women. She noted, "I have watched their intense anxiety not to be separated—those of the same family—when they were to be distributed among the citizens of Liberia."[112] A white Lutheran minister's arrival at the receptacle stirred similar terrors. Speaking through an interpreter, Rev. Morris Officer attempted to communicate his plan for choosing a group of recaptive children for the mission. After promises of food and good treatment, he recounted, "I then began to pick out such as I wanted." When the clergyman approached the girls, they ran and hid from him in the nearby bushes, leading Officer to send his "hired man" to coax them back. The sight of the canoe intended to transport the children to the mission prompted tears and anxiety about a new ocean passage until an interpreter could again explain the intent of the upriver voyage.[113] Eventually, twenty boys and twenty girls traveled with Officer back to the new Lutheran mission at Muhlenberg, where a "Congo" man—most likely a *Pons* survivor—worked as their interpreter. Separated from many of their shipmates, these recaptive children joined a motley community including white missionaries, Kru canoe men, and the older recaptive interpreter, presumed by Officer to be one of their "countrymen."[114]

Along with the label "Congo," recaptives also acquired new personal names. Like the shipmates Kandah and Kabendah, all recaptive arrivals to Liberia were assigned English names, either by U.S. agents at the receptacle or in the households to which they had been sent. For this reason, it is difficult to identify *Wildfire* shipmates such as Francisco, Constantia, and Bomba on the ACS's list of survivors, where recaptives now bore names such as John Dorsey, Abraham Goods, and Eliza Holland.[115] Like the earlier *Pons* children named by church missionary donors, most 1860 recaptives had virtually no choice in the renaming process. Lutheran minister Morris Officer described how he gathered his missionary household together to brainstorm "American" names for the forty recaptive boys and girls selected from the Monrovia receptacles. He and his assistants hung paper cards on strings around the necks of their new charges, in many cases assigning the names of American Lutheran luminaries. One young boy, for instance, received the name Samuel S. Schmucker, an homage to the revered founder of Pennsylvania's Gettysburg College.

In his journal, Officer described how missionaries then attempted to teach the children how to say their new names, adding, "Many of them readily remembered them but others could not."[116] The assignment of these new names also indirectly contributed to externally imposed ethnogenesis, for with English-language names now indistinguishable from those of Liberian emigrants, recaptives were often designated in Liberian records by their personal English names and the umbrella term "Congo."[117] Individual renaming thus reflected Liberia's assimilationist policies, while the emergence of the "Congo" ethnonym maintained the recaptives as a distinct and largely subordinate collective.

While it is likely that some traumatized young recaptives found a measure of security and an end to repetitive displacement in their apprenticeships, others entered new forms of servitude and abuse. Just months after the initial distribution of apprentices, Seys reported that in a few instances "some have been ill used and I have had to take them away and put them in other and better hands."[118] Recaptives, including young boys and girls, were put to a variety of agricultural and domestic work even as they continued to experience health problems from their previous enslavement. For some, illness and accidents ended their short existence in Liberia. In September 1860, coroner Thomas Travis had to be called to examine the body of a recaptive boy who died in the home of Liberian emigrant Walker Wright.[119] The persistence of commodification that accompanied his apprenticeship surfaced in the coroner's description of the boy as having been "possessed by" Wright. Travis found his skills called for once again in November when the death of a "Congoe boy" at Officer's Lutheran mission compelled him to assemble twelve men for an inquest.[120] The young boy renamed Samuel S. Schmucker had drowned in the river while bathing with a group of recaptive youth. He was buried near the Muhlenberg mission, far from where he had been born.[121] These two recorded deaths call attention to the many other slave trade refugees whose short lives ended anonymously and without ceremony soon after they arrived in Liberia.

A good number of Liberia's apprentices took advantage of the relatively relaxed oversight (compared with receptacles and barracoons) and struck out beyond the boundaries of their assigned households.[122] The pattern of group escapes suggests that shipmate relations, such as the tight-knit groups of young men and boys mentioned previously on the *Niagara*, formed the social bonds on which "runaway" recaptives relied. From Monrovia, Seys reported, "A number of our recaptives have wandered away under the idea of returning to their own country." The apprehension of twenty-five of these recaptives in a single day implies the scale of cooperation among West Central African shipmates.[123] From Cape Mount, a missionary reported that twenty-four of the *Wildfire* company, "enticed away by the natives," had left the receptacle.[124] At the Muhlenberg mission, eleven of twenty *Erie* and *Storm King* shipmates, ranging from young to older boys, determined they would leave the mission after learning that recaptive apprentices at the nearby Outland farm had already made their escape. The fact that the recaptive youth learned this information upon being sent to the area to cut grass indicates both communication between apprentices on nearby farms and the labor regimes that some recaptives sought to escape. (Both boys and girls regularly worked clearing and then cultivating the new mission's twenty acres.)[125] The runaways left the mission several days later with their grass-cutting knives, gathering cassava and a canoe as they tracked the sun to the southeast. In response to a passerby who asked, they reported that they "were on their way to the Congo country" aiming to navigate their way home by the position of the sun.[126]

The paradox of Liberian apprenticeship status appears starkly in the efforts and expense devoted to recapturing the recaptives. Without living recaptives under his supervision, Seys could not file for the U.S. government reimbursement, which was calculated per person. With no hint of irony, Seys paid Solomon S. Winkey, a formerly enslaved emigrant from Kentucky, for "Arresting and Delivering 4 fugitive Liberated Congoes."[127] Nor did efforts to capture runaways abate as the months wore on. In April and May 1861 alone, Seys recorded fifty-six recaptives "brought in" either by "commissioners" in charge of apprentices or by others paid to find escapees.[128] Missionary Morris Officer reported that the eleven youth who set out from the Muhlenberg mission to find their homes encountered a violent "battle" while passing through a Kuwaa town, where some of the younger runaways were reportedly taken as slaves. At least four were injured badly in the fight, and after their leader's final attempt to hide in a nearby swamp, Kru workers retrieved them all.[129] After the boys' return and punishment, Careysburg doctor Daniel Laing operated on and treated four of the most gravely wounded.[130]

Officer's subsequent interviews with the boys provide crucial glimpses of social bonds among apprenticed youth and deep antipathy to apprenticeship status shaped by former identities. The carefully planned exodus was led by Menzamba, an older youth who asserted that neither he nor his father were slaves, and thus, in Officer's words, "good or noble blood flowed in his veins."[131] These sentiments, conveyed through an interpreter to Morris Officer, suggest that Menzamba and perhaps other of his companions perceived their apprenticeship to be a form of enslavement. Menzamba cited his personal lineage to reject his subordinate status in Officer's missionary household. Furthermore, the older boys sought to protect the younger ones in the last battle that led to their recapture. Finally, Officer's frequent use of the boys' "country names" (Zinga, Loangu, and Kualla, for instance) indicates that, at least in their first weeks of apprenticeship, young recaptives continued to assert their West Central African names, despite their involuntary renaming in Liberia.

In contrast to the efforts of younger West Central African recaptives to resist their apprenticeships, the shipmates of the *Bogota* drew upon their experiences of war and displacement to oppose their planned dispersal to Greenville's settler households. The diverse assembly of West Africans included a large group of Yoruba speakers comprised of less than 10 percent children.[132] As previously related, at least forty-eight men and women underwent a Christian marriage ceremony on the voyage from Key West and thus arrived in Liberia joined by a domestic institution at least theoretically recognized within Liberian settler society. All these factors together made the *Bogota* shipmates more likely to expect a certain amount of self-determination in their Liberian resettlement, and indeed, Liberians called them "recaptives from Whydah" or even "Dahomeans" to distinguished them from young "Congoes."[133] While still under joint U.S. and ACS supervision, the roughly 300 shipmates had resided together in "thatched houses" near the entrance to Greenville in Sinoe County.[134] Henry Stewart, a Congregational minister who immigrated to Greenville with his family after their manumission from a Georgia slaveowner, recounted what happened next. "They were told Shortly after Landing that they were to be taken in a body to the falls," he wrote. "Their was no Dissatisfaction with them in that arrangement."[135] The *Bogota* company's response reflected the sentiments of recaptive shipmates from Rio de Janeiro to St. Helena who weathered daunting displacements while resisting further separation.[136]

Understandable alarm ensued, therefore, when in early 1861, the Liberian government took responsibility for recaptive oversight and attempted to apprentice a portion of the group. Liberian colonists in Sinoe, who struggled continually to attract emigrants to their sparsely populated town, must have viewed these mature, majority-male recaptives as a valuable infusion of agricultural labor.[137] As Stewart reported, "When this Change was made and they were informed that they were to be sepperated, they immediately question the Sincerity of our motive in Doing them Good." Apprenticeship placements directly threatened social bonds forged in two ocean crossings. Furthermore, the broken promise raised fears of reenslavement and subordination within

Liberian settler households. Described throughout their Atlantic journeys as "fierce and intractable," physically imposing, and "men of resolute and determined spirit," the *Bogota* shipmates actively resisted apprenticeship.[138] Militia members mustered to suppress the "troubles," and President Benson had to visit the town twice to reassure apprehensive recaptives.[139] In the ensuing conflict, Stewart reported, "Some have been Shot and others got Drowned in makein[g] their escape."[140] In the end, Greenville emigrant families prevailed in forcibly separating the tight-knit group by apprenticing more than forty recaptives, yet an older portion of the shipmates persisted in moving together to the new settlement of Ashmun at Sinoe River Falls, twelve miles from Greenville.[141] Over time, Ashmun built the kind of symbiotic economic relationship with Greenville seen earlier between New Georgia and Monrovia.[142]

The episode at Greenville, in addition to highlighting the importance of shipmate bonds in Atlantic displacement, may also show how recaptives struggled to translate homegrown ideals of political organization into a tenuous Liberian future. The expectations of Yoruba-speaking men and women who comprised a large subgroup among the *Bogota* shipmates had been shaped by decades of civil war and Dahomean raids that followed the decline of Oyo. Although by the 1850s many towns in the southwestern regions of Yorubaland were composed of displaced war refugees, residents nevertheless held on to the basic Yoruba political unit of the *ilu*, or town, which contrasted starkly with the rural isolation of apprenticeship on Liberian farms. In war-torn Yorubaland, displaced people regrouped within towns, re-creating neighborhood compounds governed by councils of elders.[143] As a dominant force within the *Bogota* company, Yoruba-speaking shipmates most likely sought to retain some of this ideal in their Liberian exile both in their separate settlement near the entrance to Greenville and then in their relocated residence at Sinoe Falls. As people well versed in various forms of servitude and dependence even in West Africa, they fought to maintain their collective, semiautonomous status in Liberia.[144] In addition, recaptive men and boys may also have translated martial skills and military organization into Liberian militias. Ibadan, an emerging power center in the mid-nineteenth century, for example, drew much of its administrative structure from a hierarchical "chain" of military titles through which warriors might ascend to authority.[145] It is likely that Yoruba-speaking recaptives in Greenville had been taken prisoners of war in towns west of Ibadan, but similar martial backgrounds most likely prevailed among them. In 1863, Henry Stewart remarked on the "imposing sight" of eighty recaptive men from the Ashmun settlement drilling with the Greenville militia company. "Their deportment and orderly behavior won the respect of all," he concluded with satisfaction.[146]

Overall, although adult *Bogota* shipmates could not fully control the circumstances of their resettlement, their deeper reservoirs of knowledge, training, and memory enabled them to defend their community against the threat of division. In comparison, West African children had less control over their immediate circumstances, and most entered a period of Liberian apprenticeship subject to more direct pressure for acculturation and demands for their labor. Yet, as historian William Allen argues, we should not assume assimilation was all one-way, as Liberians adapted many aspects of West African indigenous foodways, architecture, and farming technology, and it would not be surprising to find they were influenced by thousands of West Central African youth taken into their households.[147] Nevertheless, having escaped from chattel enslavement in the Americas, recaptives made their new lives in a Liberian colonial context shaped by the crucible of American slavery. Doubly dependent as young strangers, many recaptives entered subordinate roles in Liberian society as domestic servants and menial laborers. In the Liberian colonial borderlands, building the bonds of a larger community would prove to be a crucial dimension of freedom.

From Shipmates to "Congoes"

Beginning in the crucible of the receptacles, West Central African shipmates came to be known collectively in Liberia as "Congoes."[148] The word came first from the historical Kongo Kingdom, stretching back to the early fifteenth century and dispersed around the Atlantic, beginning with the Portuguese slave trade. "Congoes" had been present in Liberia since the founding of New Georgia decades earlier. The successive waves of recaptives, and in particular the massive third generation, cemented its usage as a term that encompassed West Central African origins, linguistic commonalities, and a historical experience of slave trade exile. To a large degree, missionaries and Liberian settler elites imposed the term "Congoes" as a "tribal" designation, using it alongside other indigenous labels like Kru, Dei, and Vai. The partial nature of existing evidence makes it difficult to determine how actively recaptives embraced this term as a way of identifying with one another in the aftermath of their arrival.[149] What is clear, however, is the progression of social connections from shipmate bonds to broader ties fostered by institutions of marriage, church, and village.

Compared with their counterparts in Sierra Leone and the Caribbean,

Liberia's recaptive population was more heavily West Central African.[150] Apart from the unique case of the *Bogota* shipmates, the only other recaptives embarking from any other region arrived very early in the colony's history. In the 1830s, for example, Igbo-speaking captives from the Bight of Benin lived with "Congo" neighbors along two opposite sides of New Georgia's main street.[151] Every slave ship the U.S. Navy intercepted after 1840, except for the *Bogota*, embarked from either Cabinda or Congo River barracoons. Of course, West Central Africa is a vast region, and recaptives arrived from multiple polities. Yet their origins from Lower Kongo and northern Angola homelands reinforced the Liberian idea of a "Congo tribe."[152] The presence of West Central African interpreters and overseers from one generation to the next strengthened the association between recaptive status and shared "Congo" origins. The sheer size of the third wave of recaptive arrivals increased the likelihood that young slave trade refugees would find other newcomers who shared mutually intelligible languages and the same desire for security, protection, and belonging.

Among men and women deemed old enough to begin families of their own, marriage represented a socially acceptable step toward adulthood recognized by both recaptives and Liberian officials. Through marriage, recaptives could transition out of their placement in settler households.[153] Historian Benjamin Lawrance has argued that many child recaptives, like those of the *Amistad*, faced a form of permanent dependency as a result of being stripped from their kin and age sets before they could undergo crucial coming-of-age rituals.[154] In the case of Liberian recaptives, the chance to reintegrate with homeland communities was never an option, which might have made new marriage practices possible even in the absence of required initiations. Over the years, many younger recaptives who married and established families did so within the framework of Liberian Christian mores, such as the emphasis on monogamy. Thus, in comparison with the "social exclusion" of *Amistad* orphans never circumcised and never married, young West Central African men and women had recourse to socially recognized adulthood, but only through the colonial institutions of Liberian society.[155]

Some of the first recorded marriages occurred within shipmate groups or across two different companies of West Central African shipmates. The earlier-mentioned matrimonial ceremony between Kandah and Kabendah joined together two *Echo* shipmates who had known each other at least since the barracoons of Cabinda. With 93 percent of the third wave of recaptives embarking from Congo River and Cabinda sites, marriages also occurred across shipmate groups within the West Central African population.[156] A man from the *Echo* sent in 1858 to Grand Cape Mount, for example, married a woman from the *Erie*'s company soon after her arrival in Monrovia.[157] A young woman from the *Storm King* married a shoemaker who had come to Liberia on the *Pons* as a small boy.[158] While the couple might have shared a more specific home region, it was just as likely that their mutual recaptive experiences and broader linguistic and geographic commonalities drew them together. Even so, during the initial period of oversight, recaptive couples had to apply to Seys for permission to marry officially, another sign of their subordinate position in Liberia.

As Alexander Crummell had anticipated and recommended, the heavily male recaptive population also looked for wives among Liberian African American emigrants. In New Georgia during the 1830s, recaptive men coming from several years of detention in Georgia had married women from among the less elite class of African American emigrants.[159] Although some critics, such as William Nesbit, looked down on such unions as a mark of colonists' "degradation," others like Crummell viewed marriage between Liberian emigrants and native Africans as a bridge to a more unified Liberian future.[160] According to Seys, two men among the *Echo* shipmates found African American wives.[161] Given their varying experiences of enslavement and migration, neither recaptives nor Liberian settlers would have brought extended kin networks or many material resources to their partnerships. Nevertheless, marriage offered recaptives some measure of economic stability, recognition of adulthood, and, of crucial importance, the hope of future generations who could maintain the relationship between the worlds of the living and the dead.

The collective "Congo" identity was fostered as well in religious communities and missions. As missionaries anticipated, both the vulnerability of youth and distance from home opened doors for sustained Protestant proselytization, although it is equally important to remember that some West Central African recaptives, such as Francisco and Constantia of the *Wildfire*, had experiences with Christianity that pre-dated their terrible Atlantic journeys. Drawing on studies of Yoruba identity in Sierra Leone, historian David Northrup suggests that the Christian gospel offered "spiritual consolation" to traumatized slave trade refugees.[162] Recaptive converts in Liberia's churches may have viewed their new communities in the nuanced terms expressed by Samuel Ajayi Crowther, the West African Anglican bishop. Crowther described his journey out of enslavement as guided by Providence "to a place where His Gospel is preached." Nonetheless, he never forgot that his spiritual journey began with being "violently turned out of my father's house, and separated from relations."[163] The theft of old communities and the birth of new ones remained joined in Crowther's memory.

Although there is a lack of sources on Liberian recaptives' own responses to proselytization, mission schools and churches in Liberia clearly offered new forms of belonging that bridged past ruptures and addressed the crisis of isolation. Daniel Bacon's story of conversion and ordination serves as a case in point. Brought to Liberia as a nine-year-old on the *Pons*, Bacon grew up in the household of Methodist Episcopal preacher J. W. Roberts.[164] In 1861, the Methodist Episcopal Church licensed Bacon as an "exhorter." Bacon's 1863 report for a short three-month period placed him at recaptive congregations scattered in at least seven different settlements on both banks of the St. Paul River, where a large number of recent recaptives had been apprenticed.[165] His work bridged generations of recaptives and connected apprenticed youth who could not yet travel as freely as he did.

With the heavy emphasis on recaptive church membership and conversion, existing sources only hint at culturally specific practices carried to Liberia from the lower Congo River region. The *Liberia Herald* relayed one such instance of an encounter in 1847 between two New Georgia boys with a lingering illness and a recaptive healer from the *Pons*, who informed the boys' caretakers, "I go make da witch come up" from the afflicted children.[166] Although the *Herald* recounted the anecdote as an exposé of a devious and fraudulent African "conjurer," the practitioner's ritual cutting of the boys, herbal applications, and suction over the site of affliction correspond closely to Kongo therapeutic practices of *nsamba*.[167] After the massive 1860 "Congo inundation," missionaries and Liberian officials preferred to emphasize reports of church membership and newly acquired literacy.[168] Yet the interaction of New Georgians with a trained ritual specialist suggests an initiated adult enslaved with the *Pons*'s many youths. It reveals not only the culturally specific practices of a West Central African healer living in an established recaptive community but also the disdain with which Liberian emigrant society greeted such open practices. Prevailing silences on continuities of Kongo tradition in Liberian written sources should not be taken as proof of their absence in recaptive communities.

In addition to the slowly growing recaptive church networks, recaptive residential patterns also signified continued "Congo" affinities. Although we need to know more about how West Central African notions of status, lineage, and leadership were negotiated over time, the presence of these residential centers is clear. As recaptives ended their apprenticeships, married, and acquired plots of land, West Central African settlements prolifer-

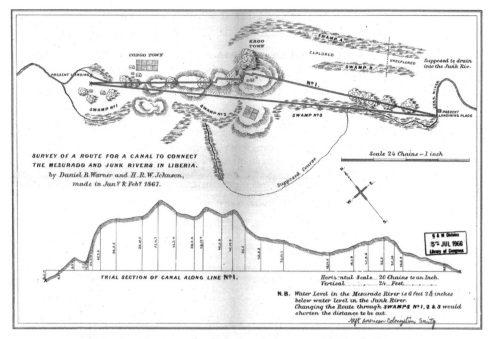

FIGURE 6.2 An 1867 survey clearly depicts the houses and fields of a Congo Town between the Mesurado and Junk Rivers in Liberia. Captn. Kelly, *St. Pauls River, Liberia at its mouth* (New York: Endicott & Co. Lith, 1867), map detail. Courtesy of Library of Congress, Geography and Map Division, Washington, D.C., https://www.loc.gov/item/96684981.

ated on Liberian maps. For example, one such Congo Town appeared on the south bank of the Junk River north of Marshall, another Congo Town emerged along a Mesurado River tributary that was christened Congo Creek, and another similar settlement appeared in the backcountry to the east of Louisiana on the St. Paul River. Just southeast of Robertsport, on the beach where the *Castilian* shipmates had disembarked, yet another Congo Town took shape.[169] Although many of these towns sprang up in proximity to older colonial settlements, some Liberian emigrants opposed the mobility and autonomy that such settlements implied. Petitions from Bassa County, for example, sought legislative prohibitions against centers of Congo residence not approved in advance by the Liberian government. Other Liberian citizens unsuccessfully sought to limit the free movement of recaptives across county lines and between settlements.[170] Regardless of settler opposition, persistence of Liberian Congo Towns suggests affinities between recaptives that reached beyond individual shipmate bonds to the formation of broader communities (see fig. 6.2).

The term "Congoes" in Liberia signified only one form of collective identification created by West Central Africans around the Atlantic World. From Cuba's Kongo *cabildos* to Liberia's Congo Towns, the varying meanings of Congo/Kongo trace a history of vast dislocation and remarkable reinvention developed over more than 300 years.[171] To borrow from Alexander Byrd's discussion of enslaved "Igbos," Liberian "Congoes" were a "people *in the making*," a group forged by "centripetal exigencies of violence and suffering."[172] The forces that flung enslaved West Central Africans together did not cease with their interception by U.S. Navy warships or with their arrival in Liberia. Instead, recaptives found themselves confronting a new set of expectations for labor and compliance with Liberian institutions, all under the umbrella of slave trade suppression and African "civilization."

—

Despite John Seys's praise for the policy that rescued enslaved Africans "from endless bondage and sent them here to be free and happy," the agent's own records reveal a more troubled and complicated Liberian story.[173] The U.S. policy of recaptive removal, it is true, spared thousands of child and adult recaptives from the brutal regime of Cuban sugar production. Yet the alternative of Liberian apprenticeship incorporated slave trade refugees into a Liberian colonial order birthed by U.S. second slavery politics. In particular, Liberian responses to the *Pons* recaptives in 1845 laid the groundwork for practices of U.S. subsidy and oversight, missionary recruitment of children, and use of Liberia's native apprenticeship laws. By 1860, all the interested parties in Liberia believed that recaptives, if supervised and subordinated, could strengthen the young republic. The incorporation of recaptive "Congoes" into Liberian society promised needed agricultural labor, young pupils for mission schools, and ultimately, a buffer population between emigrants and indigenes. This endeavor was no cynical ploy but, rather, an illustration of how antislavery benevolence, however sincerely embraced, nevertheless constrained recaptive futures and furthered the colonization of West Africa.[174]

The degrees of freedom that recaptives could find within Liberian apprenticeships depended heavily on health and age. In particular, the experience of young recaptives challenges what Benjamin Lawrance calls the "myth of blanket freedom," which in its most simplistic form views all captive Africans liberated by law from enslavement to be "free."[175] Even in their existence outside legal enslavement, recaptive children remained doubly dependent, both as apprenticed minors and as "uncivilized" subjects. Their youth and malleability carried the dual promise of valuable labor and cultural adaptability, to be realized through incorporation as dependents in mission compounds and emigrant households. The civilizing agenda of apprenticeships placed recaptives in a heavily regulated position, which some clearly resisted, as in the attempted escape from Officer's Lutheran mission. For some vulnerable dependents suffering the total exposure of capture and forced migrations, however, a certain degree of protection and safety found in mission schools or settler households may have mattered more than an autonomous "free" existence they could not meaningfully claim.[176]

Although most scholars note at least briefly the role of recaptives in the formation of Liberia, this chapter has attempted instead to examine Liberia's role in shaping recaptive experience. In the aftermath of barracoons, slave ships, and detention camps, recaptives around the Atlantic shared similar traumas of medical crisis as well as social and spiritual alienation. Liberia's origins as an ACS colony for African American emigrants and slave trade refugees created a distinctive context for recaptive responses to that trauma. It is important to acknowledge death as one of these responses. Not all recaptives survived the transition to Liberian society. Of those who did, some violently protested abuse in their new surroundings, while others tried unsuccessfully to escape and travel home. *Bogota* recaptives fought, with mixed results, to stay together and resist dependency and servitude in their Sinoe County settlement. Many young West Central Africans slowly rebuilt collective affiliations of family, church, and neighborhood under the label of "Congoes." In light of their class subordination within Liberian society, freedom became meaningful largely through these social institutions of recaptive life. Christian converts like Daniel Bacon found status and community within church circles. Individual recaptive men and women sought mates either within their shipmate networks, with those from other recaptive ships, and less frequently, among Liberian colonists. And by the late 1860s, Congo Towns cropped up across the Liberian landscape, evidence of continued co-residence and of recaptives' distinct sense of origin and history within the Liberian population. In no way should these Congo Towns be considered, as some U.S. agents liked to think, a recaptive homecoming. Rather, we might think of these small settlements as outposts in the uneven Atlantic geography of slavery and emancipation, testaments to the intertwined nature of recaptive loss and innovation.

Conclusion

⁓

In recent decades, Atlantic World historians have challenged the simplistic idea of the nineteenth century as an age of emancipation. Rather, as historian Rebecca Scott maintains, freedom was often "paper thin," lost and won and lost again by people of African descent as they moved across the boundaries of conflicting legal zones. In the wake of the Haitian Revolution, for example, free people of color actively used the Cuban, Jamaican, and American courts to battle the property interests of would-be owners who sought to exploit the "latent 'property-ness'" adhering to black bodies.[1] Latent "property-ness" manifested itself fiercely in the second slavery society of the United States, where free people of color experienced an increasing threat of kidnapping and fugitive slaves who "stole themselves" faced rendition and retaliation from slaveowners. Simply put, black mobility raised suspicions and posed a potential threat to property interests throughout nineteenth-century slave societies.[2] The emergence of free-soil spaces across the Atlantic raised the hopes of slavery's opponents, but it also heightened the prevailing suspicion of black movement and spawned alternative forms of coerced labor that would outlast the old regimes of chattel slavery.

Against this shifting geography of nineteenth-century slavery and abolition, recaptivity is best understood as a liminal category in the borderlands between enslavement and emancipation.[3] As one overview of the status of Africans seized on illegal slavers around the Atlantic concludes, "Liberated Africans were to be found in every category that historians have defined as falling between full chattel slavery at one end of the spectrum and a wage-free full personal freedom at the other."[4] Regardless of the flag under which they were seized, all recaptives shared conditions of isolation, trauma, stark dependence, and exploitability. Stateless people in an era of nation-building became, to use historian Linda Kerber's phrase, the "Citizen's Other," occupying a position of "extreme otherness and extreme danger."[5] Displaced, dispossessed, and often unable to speak the language of their captors, newly arrived recaptives entered their capturing societies as the "extreme other." In the case of the United States, attempts by a predatory group of planters to kidnap African youth from the Key West Depot reveal one dimension of recaptive vulnerability. On the second Atlantic passage to Liberia, the high recaptive death toll, including suicides, indicates another form of existential danger.

As a liminal and hence unstable and potentially threatening category, Atlantic recaptivity also provoked political controversy. The degree to which these controversies invoked the latent "property-ness" of African recaptives depended heavily on the slavery politics of the custodial nation and empire. For example, British officials applied diplomatic pressure to bring *africanos livres* and *emancipados* in Brazil and Cuba under the mantle of emancipation and free labor practices. During the operation of the mixed-commission courts, Brazil, Spain, and Portugal all fought with British officials over the question of how recaptives would be resettled and who would take custody of them.[6] Moreover, Brazil's legislature wrestled internally with the question of whether to incorporate or "reexport" *africanos livres*. Finally, critics in second slavery societies were quick to point out the contradictions between British moral rhetoric and the self-interested (often coercive) recruitment of "liberated Africans" as apprentices for British West Indian plantations. Captives of illegal slavers thus often disembarked slave ships only to face new uncertainties produced by international tensions surrounding slave trade suppression.

Political firestorms likewise swirled around African recaptives in U.S. custody. A central goal of this book has been to make recaptives and the condition of recaptivity more visible within studies of nineteenth-century U.S. slavery. The historical narrative of a divided nation has made familiar the salient categories of enslaved, free black, and fugitive life—and to a lesser extent the condition of marronage.[7] The recaptive is a much less familiar figure that complicates the American domestic geography of slavery and forces antebellum U.S. history into Atlantic perspective. The very existence of recaptives under U.S. custody highlighted the contradiction between the rapid internal expansion of U.S. second slavery and the enforcement of federal slave trade suppression laws abroad. Furthermore, the American-built origins of the intercepted *Echo*, *Wildfire*, and *William*, from which almost 1,500 recaptives were seized, exposed American complicity in illegal slave trafficking despite accelerated naval efforts to intercept such ships. Finally, the question of what to do with recaptives on U.S. soil tapped older debates about the acceptable disposition of recaptive Africans released from illegal slavers. The continued U.S. reliance on Liberia to receive African recaptives "removed" from Charleston and Key West sparked a contentious discussion in American newspapers over black labor and black citizenship across the Atlantic. In short, the history of U.S. responses to recaptives of the illegal slave trade recasts our understanding of late-antebellum slavery politics, revealing a transatlantic geography full of symbolic import for contending forces of abolition, colonization, and proslavery imperialism.

The illegal slave trade and its suppression furthermore played an important part in congealing American racial thought in the 1850s. We have seen how the state-sponsored "recapturing" of trafficked Africans, perceived as permanent, uncivilized strangers, produced an alchemic conversion of human suffering to racial spectacle. In this sense, the representation of slave ship recaptives in antebellum illustrated newspapers demonstrates how popular print culture disseminated the hardening racial ideology of the 1850s. As this study has shown, the timing of the U.S. Navy's peak slave trade suppression efforts beginning in the late 1850s contributed to the racial objectification of recaptive Africans in word and image. The popularization of racial ethnography, the rise of the illustrated press, and the cultural phenomenon of displaying exoticized racial subjects created a perfect storm of voyeuristic interest in slave trade recaptives. In Charleston, proslavery ethnography in service to slave trade revival strongly influenced elite discussion of recaptives, while entrepreneurs sought to exploit recaptive bodies for public exhibition. Two years later, the well-known *Harper's Weekly* engravings of *Wildfire* shipmates promoted the image of national benevolence and African exoticism. The spectacles generated in periodicals and newspapers can be seen as progenitors of late nineteenth-century racial exhibitions and even the modern phenomenon of today's disaster tourism.[8] Although journalists did cover the controversial political status of recaptives, the sensational emphasis on "wild Africans" overshadowed any nuanced discussion of redress and remedies for young people caught in an illegal traffic.

At its heart, then, the history of recaptive Africans in U.S. custody constitutes an important chapter in the longer history of nineteenth-century human rights struggles. Viewed by observers primarily as either pitiable savages or potential property, recaptured Africans had very few advocates who could see their condition in terms of rights or justice. Notable exceptions to the prevailing racialization of recaptives include the little-known activism of James W. C. Pennington and the piercing condemnation of the *Anglo-African* press, both of which furthered a black diasporic vision of human rights. In word and deed, they challenged the biological essentialism of polygenists and critiqued U.S. legal hypocrisy at home and abroad, linking the predicament of fugitives and recaptives. Pennington's long experience with fugitive slaves and the shipmates of the *Amistad* shaped his plea for humane conditions and protection for recaptives in Key West and for three West Central African boys in New York's Eldridge Street jail. Seen in this light, Pennington's advocacy on recaptive issues transcended a narrow antislavery position and evoked a broader human rights claim.

Regardless of debates that circled around them, recaptive Africans were forced to look internally, within shipmate networks, for means of survival and modes of social belonging. Recaptive journeys from slave ships to Liberian apprenticeships demand that we ask, rather than assume, what freedom in limited degrees meant for shipmate communities. For some, death and isolation overwhelmed the struggle to assert new forms of social identity. Recall that especially among young West Central African recaptives, the exit from slave ships did not mean an end to dependence and vulnerability. Particularly for children and youth, as historian Benjamin Lawrance has argued, it is likely that abstract concepts of legal freedom paled in the face of continued subordination as orphaned minors.[9] Interrupted initiations and unfinished educations in home societies stranded young recaptives, setting barriers to adulthood and mature social identities. Such assertions of permanent alienation and dependence exist in creative tension with the arguments of other historians about the imperatives of re-creation and social "resurrection" acted upon throughout the diaspora of African enslavement and displacement.[10] Scholars who insist on the ability of enslaved Africans to reject social death and painstakingly rebuild new associations may overlook the realities of isolation, poor health, linguistic barriers, young age, and numerous other factors. On the other hand, scholars who emphasize the heavy shadow of death, debility, and permanent exile may underestimate the ability of shipmate bonds and resourceful innovation to facilitate the reconstruction of shattered worlds.

Throughout this book, I have sought to show that a comprehensive understanding of the liminal status of slave trade recaptives incorporates the perspectives of both the threat of social death and the hope of social resurrection. The Atlantic voyages of recaptive men, women, and children bound for Liberia vividly illustrate the ways in which age informed recaptives' survival politics and social resources.[11] Perhaps because this study involves recaptive adults traveling alongside children, I have argued for the twinned nature of trauma and collective resilience rather than choosing one side of the debate over the other. Life and death inextricably wove together in the elemental world of recaptive voyaging. In this history of survival strategies, we cannot lose sight of how many died along the way. Fully half of those embarking on four illegal slave ships from Ouidah and the Congo River region lost their lives in transit. Others did not last even through the first months in Liberia. As we have seen, surviving adults and children drew on reserves of knowledge and memory, at first to forge shipmate bonds and later to build more enduring networks of family and neighborhood in Liberia. The *Bogota* shipmates and West Central African adults, like the *Wildfire* headwoman Bomba, demonstrated their deeper repertoire of life experiences in acts of healing, leadership, and group opposition to Liberian apprenticeship. At the same time, the willingness of young recaptives to oppose abuse, risk escapes, and gradually build new forms of belonging in Liberian Congo communities testifies to the resourcefulness and adaptability of children and youth in forced Atlantic migration.

The story of *Echo, Wildfire, William,* and *Bogota* shipmates who made double Atlantic crossings directs our attention to the responses of African recaptives to the immediate aftermath of the catastrophe of saltwater enslavement. Many times in the course of writing this book, I have longed for richer records of recaptive testimony, of words that revealed more clearly individual perceptions, motivations, and the forever-lost moments that occurred outside the view of mostly white observers. In the absence of those records, I have taken as guide Joseph Miller's call to find "plausible, even probable answers . . . not by attempting to 'read the lips' of those silenced" in written sources, "but by watching what those who expressed themselves in deed, not words, did, based on an informed sense of what values they brought with them from Africa that their experience of enslavement most threatened."[12] Evidence of the deeds of silenced recaptives is often fragmentary and flawed, embedded in more copious accounts of slave ships and slave traders. Today, exciting new studies continue to emerge on the slaver networks, financial institutions, and international politics that set both illegal slave ships and slave trade suppression in motion across the Atlantic Basin.[13] However, this book has examined instead the experience and treatment of Africans forced together as shipmates by the flawed and contradictory attempt of the United States to end the largest forced migration in human history. Only by putting recaptive experience at the center of inquiry can we fully grasp the human consequences of a transatlantic slave trade suppression policy carried out by the American slaveholding republic.

As a coda to the mid-nineteenth-century journeys of African shipmates, it is also instructive to consider the global transformations of colonized labor that took place within the lifetimes of the last generation of slave trade recaptives. Just as the figure of the recaptive complicates the concept of an age of emancipation, so, too, do new forced voyages in the wake of the last known slave ships complicate the idea of the end of the middle passage. Throughout this account, we have seen hints of the arrangements of indenture and apprenticeship emerging to take the place of a system of chattel slavery in the Americas. French recruitment of "indentured" African laborers and the mass transportation of Chinese and South Asian workers in the "coolie" trade are just two of the primary examples of the shifting character of forced migration in the wake of the American hemispheric emancipations.[14] As with the illegal slave trade, children in forced migration continued to supply global labor markets. Child captives, for example, comprised more than 60 percent of the Central African captives transshipped from East Africa across the Atlantic and Indian Oceans to destinations as far away as the Persian Gulf and India.[15] The sobering truth is that we should see the young recaptives in this study not as some of the last among millions but as an early generation of an ongoing traffic in young people that extended beyond the Atlantic and continues today in the form of modern-day slavery.[16]

Furthermore, the global movement to suppress the banned slave trade combined with the expansion of consumer markets in European countries to produce a new wave of colonization in Africa. Many of the colonial practices of mission schooling, waged and apprenticed labor, and military enlistment first devised for recaptives in Liberia and Sierra Leone now extended into new regions and new populations across the African continent. European powers moved inland from the coast, imposing colonial administrations and marshaling new forms of coerced labor and commodity extraction. These late nineteenth-century developments opened up new routes of "return" previously closed to former recaptives. Once again, certain groups of recaptives occupied a liminal position, between the powers of colonization and newly targeted indigenous populations.

Two anecdotes involving recaptive "Congo" communities in the Bahamas and Liberia illustrate continued migration (or aspirations of migration) set in motion by late nineteenth-century colonial developments. By 1885, Leopold II of Belgium had claimed direct rights to a vast holding in Central Africa that he called the Congo Free State. Compelled by Belgium's humanitarian rhetoric of "civilization" and "free labor," former recaptive "Congoes" began to explore the prospects of migration, ironically to the very sites of former slaver trading along the lower banks of the Congo River. Historian Rosanne Adderley depicts how, long after their seizure from a Spanish slaver by the British, liberated Africans in the Bahamas joined together in the Congo No. 1 mutual aid society. In 1888 they petitioned Leopold for funds to migrate to the Congo Free State, staking their claim of natal belonging with the opening declaration, "We were born in the Congo Land beside the Great River."[17] As a diasporic community acculturated to British West Indian society, these exiled "Natives of the Congo" saw in the Belgian takeover an opportunity for repatriation to a region they already figuratively claimed as home. At the same time, their construction of a return, as Adderley points out, was premised on "transplanting" many of the norms of West Indian colonial society.[18] The petition reached the Belgian archives but does not seem to have resulted in the desired migration.

On the opposite side of the Atlantic, Liberian "Congoes" made their move to the Congo Free State in an exodus that illustrated the complicated dynamics of return. In 1889, a twenty-six-year-old Belgian agent named Dragutin Lerman visited Liberia.[19] He had heard that two Congo families had recently moved their coffee-farming operations from Liberia to "their old homes," near Boma, along the lower Congo River near the West Central African coast. The commissioned civil servant for King Leopold sought to capitalize on the acculturation and language skills of Liberian Congoes. Within just a few months, Lerman had relocated six additional families of former recaptives to Boma, where he hoped they would "continue the life of Christianity and be a good example to their savage brethren."[20] Given the date and the presence of children, these migrant families would have been not only returnees from enslavement thirty years earlier but also the children of those recaptives born in Liberia. The 1889 migration of former West Central African recaptives from Liberia takes us full cycle. Child captives, possibly sold from Boma, the headquarters for slave trade barracoons in 1860, could now find themselves migrating back to Boma, the leading edge of Leopold's devastating colonial reign.

The Boma migrations serve as reminders of the elusive nature of "home" for recaptives in diaspora and the efforts of recaptive shipmates to create collective identities in spite of imposed exile.[21] Recaptives could not help but be transformed by their experiences of forced migration and struggles to survive U.S. camps, transport ships, and Liberian apprenticeships. Their arrival in Boma as "civilized" recruits of Belgian agents and farmers of colonial export commodities positioned them in a new kind of liminal zone between the colonial administration and the current inhabitants of their "old homes." No longer propertyless and having built precious family and church community ties, recaptives nevertheless still inhabited a world of "betweens." Stories of subsequent migration to the Congo Free State remind us once more of the many ways in which recaptives sought to ensure survival and enact freedom while confronting the complex legacies of both transatlantic slavery and its suppression.

NOTES

Abbreviations

ACSR   American Colonization Society Records, Library of Congress, Washington, D.C.

Courier   *Charleston Daily Courier*

Eason Journal Henry Eason, "Journal, 1858–September 1860," Log 902, G. W. Blunt White Library, Mystic Seaport Museum Inc., on-line document, http://library.mysticseaport.org/initiative/PageImage.cfm?BibID =32915 (accessed 12 January 2016)

Frank Leslie's *Frank Leslie's Illustrated Newspaper*

Grymes Report J. W. Grymes, "Report of Doctr Grymes of Wash. City, D.C.," 10 December 1860, Series 1.E, Miscellaneous Incoming Correspondence, folder 1860 "Liberated Slaves," ACSR

Harper's   *Harper's Weekly*

Herald   *New York Herald*

LNS   Logs of US Naval Ships, 1801–1915, Logs of Ships and Stations, 1801–1946, Record Group 24: Records of the Bureau of Naval Personnel, NARA

McCalla Journal John Moore McCalla Journal, 1860–61, John M. McCalla Papers, David M. Rubenstein Rare Book and Manuscript Library, Duke University, Durham, North Carolina

Mercury   *Charleston Mercury*

NARA   National Archives and Records Administration, Washington, D.C., and College Park, Maryland

NYT   *New York Times*

Officer Diary Morris Officer Diary, Lutheran Historical Society, Lutheran Theological Seminary, Gettysburg, Pennsylvania

RSI   Records of the Office of the Secretary of the Interior Relating to the Suppression of the African Slave Trade and Negro Colonization, 1854–1872, NARA

SCHS   Folder Correspondence, 1855–1858, Grimball, John, 1840–1922, John Grimball Family Papers, 1804–1893 (bulk 1858–1885) (0426), South Carolina Historical Society, Charleston

Young Ship Log William Proby Young, "Ship Log, New York to Liberia, 1860," Mss 5:1 Y876:1, Virginia Historical Society, Richmond

Introduction

1. Calculated from 1836, when a transatlantic slaving ban was passed for Portuguese territories in Africa; see *Voyages Estimates* search 1836–1866, http://www.slavevoyages.org/estimates/Oy8At2u2 (accessed 23 February 2016). See also table 1.7 in Eltis and Richardson, "New Assessment of the Transatlantic Slave Trade."

2. Douglass, "Freedom in the West Indies," 218.

3. Domingues da Silva, Eltis, Misevich, and Ojo, "Diaspora of Africans," 349.

4. Hawthorne, "'Being Now, as It Were, One Family'"; Cole, "Liberated Slaves and Islam"; Fyle, "Yoruba Diaspora in Sierra Leone's Krio Society"; Jones, "Recaptive Nations"; Mamigonian, "In the Name of Freedom"; Sundiata, *From Slaving to Neoslavery*, 7–8; Schuler, *Alas! Alas! Kongo*; Schuler, *Liberated Africans in Nineteenth Century Guyana*; Adderley, *"New Negroes from Africa"*; Fernández, "Havana Anglo-Spanish Mixed Commission"; Conrad, "Neither Slave nor Free"; Asiegbu, *Slavery and the Politics of Liberation*; Pearson, *Distant Freedom*.

5. Du Bois, *Suppression of the African Slave-Trade*, 95–96, 108–9; Finkelman, "Regulating the Slave Trade"; Mason, "Slavery Overshadowed"; Burin, "Slave Trade Act of 1819," 6.

6. *An Act to Prohibit the Importation of Slaves*, 428.

7. *An Act in Addition to the Acts*, 532–34.

8. Younger, "Liberia and the Last Slave Ships," 427; Burin, "Slave Trade Act of 1819."

9. Finkelman, "Regulating the Slave Trade," 403.

10. Du Bois, *Suppression of the African Slave-Trade*, 136–41; Bryant, *Dark Places*, 35–38.

11. See Foote, *Africa and the American Flag*, and Mayer, *Captain Canot*, both discussed in Chapter 1.

12. Douglass, "Slavery and the Limits of Nonintervention," 282.

13. Curtis, "Native Africans in the Bay," *Courier*, 30 August 1858.

14. Kaplan, "'Left Alone with America.'"

15. For a similar administrative viewpoint on St. Helena, see Pearson, Jeffs, Witkin, and MacQuarrie, *Infernal Traffic*, 148.

16. Law, "Yoruba Liberated Slaves"; Northrup, "Becoming African"; Conrad, "Neither Slave nor Free"; Fernández, "Havana Anglo-Spanish Mixed Commission."

17. Smallwood, *Saltwater Slavery*.

18. Miller, *Way of Death*; Byrd, *Captives and Voyagers*; Larson, "Horrid Journeying."

19. Miller, "Retention, Reinvention, and Remembering."

20. Kunz, "Refugee in Flight"; Chan and Loveridge, "Refugees 'in Transit.'" Adderley introduces the term "slave trade refugees" in *"New Negroes from Africa,"* 2, 3.

21. Percentages based on weighted mean ratios in Eltis and Engerman, "Fluctuations in Sex and Age Ratios," table 1, 310.

22. Wright, *Strategies of Slaves and Women*, 26, 67. Lawrance contributes the analytical category of "orphan" in *Amistad's Orphans*, 15–21, 28–39.

23. Lawrance, *Amistad's Orphans*; Lovejoy, "Children of Slavery," 198–99; Campbell, Miers, and Miller, *Child Slaves in the Modern World*.

24. The importance of shipmate relationships as foundational for enslaved Africans in the Black Atlantic has been well established in several decades of historical scholarship. See Mintz and Price, *Birth of African-American Culture*, 43–44; Morgan, *Slave Counterpoint*, 448–49; Brown, *Reaper's Garden*, 45–46; Adderley, *"New Negroes from Africa,"* 67, 88; Rediker, *Slave Ship*, 305–7; Slenes, "'Malungu, Ngoma's Coming!,'" 222; Hawthorne, "'Being Now,

as It Were, One Family'"; Lindsay, "'To Return to the Bosom of Their Fatherland,'" 28; Northrup, "Becoming African," 12; and Borucki, *From Shipmates to Soldiers*, 57–83.

25. Hawthorne, "'Being Now, as It Were, One Family,'" 59, 56.

26. Domingues da Silva, Eltis, Misevich, and Ojo, "Diaspora of Africans," 361.

27. Zeuske, *Amistad*, 18.

28. Northrup, "Becoming African," 4, 9, 17.

29. Brown, "Social Death and Political Life," 1248.

30. Patterson, *Slavery and Social Death*, 13 (emphasis in original).

31. Mason, *Social Death and Resurrection*; Hawthorne, "'Being Now, as It Were, One Family'"; Sweet, "Defying Social Death"; Candido, *African Slaving Port*, 18, 120, 219; Lawrance, *Amistad's Orphans*, 18–21.

32. Sinha, *Counterrevolution of Slavery*, 155–56; Johnson, *River of Dark Dreams*, 407, 414–15; Takaki, *Pro-Slavery Crusade*, 212–24.

33. Spratt, *Speech Upon the Foreign Slave Trade*, 9 (emphasis in original); Spratt, *Foreign Slave Trade the Source of Political Power*, 17–22.

34. Rothman, *Slave Country*; Beckert, "Emancipation and Empire," 405–38.

35. Brown, *Reaper's Garden*, 234; Rugemer, *Problem of Emancipation*; White, *Encountering Revolution*, 124–65; Schoeppner, "Status across Borders," 47.

36. Cottrol, *Long, Lingering Shadow*, 48–50.

37. Johnson, *River of Dark Dreams*, 14.

38. Tomich, "'Second Slavery.'"

39. Horne, *Deepest South*, 117; Johnson, *River of Dark Dreams*, 303–94.

40. Johnson, *River of Dark Dreams*, 8.

41. Curtin, *Image of Africa*, 289–317.

42. DeLombard, *In the Shadow of the Gallows*, 6–10.

43. Van Evrie, *Negroes and Negro Slavery*; Luse, "Slavery's Champions Stood at Odds."

44. On the transatlantic orientation of nineteenth-century American abolitionist ideology, lecture circuits, and funding networks, see Blackett, *Building an Antislavery Wall*; Rice and Crawford, *Liberating Sojourn*; and Sinha, *Slave's Cause*, 339–80.

45. Akpan, "Black Imperialism"; Clegg, *Price of Liberty*; Everill, *Abolition and Empire*.

Chapter 1

1. Du Bois, *Suppression of the African Slave-Trade*, 199.

2. Du Bois, "Apologia," 327–29.

3. Gould, "Entangled Histories, Entangled Worlds."

4. Tomich, "'Second Slavery,'" 104; Zeuske and Lavina, *Second Slavery*; Kaye, "Second Slavery."

5. Domingues da Silva, Eltis, Misevich, and Ojo, "Diaspora of Africans," 349.

6. I use "ethnography" as a term that best differentiates the racialized "customs and manners" popular literature from racial science ethnology publications by scientists in the same period. Antebellum writers, however, often used "ethnology" and "ethnography" interchangeably in the absence of clear distinctions between professional and popular domains. See Stocking, *Victorian Anthropology*; Poignant, "Surveying the Field of View"; and Erickson, "American School of Anthropology."

7. Foote, *Africa and the American Flag*; Mayer, *Captain Canot*.

8. On the ahistorical nature of European ethnological discussions of non-Western societies, see Wolf, *Europe and the People*, and Trouillot, *Global Transformations*.

9. Tomich, "'Second Slavery,'" 115.

10. Marques, "Contraband Slave Trade," 1; Zeuske, *Amistad*, 82–94.

11. Mouser, "Baltimore/Pongo Connection"; Brooks, *West Africa and Cabo Verde*; Zeuske, *Amistad*, 193–202.

12. Tomich, "'Second Slavery,'" 109.

13. Eltis, *Economic Growth*, 83.

14. Bridge, *Journal of an African Cruiser*, 112. The wry phrasing is most likely from Nathaniel Hawthorne, who edited Bridge's "journal" heavily. See Brancaccio, "Black Man's Paradise."

15. Brooks, "Samuel Hodges, Jr."; Brooks, *West Africa and Cabo Verde*; Law, *From Slave Trade to "Legitimate" Commerce*; Lovejoy, *Transformations in Slavery*.

16. Law, *Ouidah*, 203–14, 222–30; O'Hear, "Enslavement of Yoruba," 65–66.

17. Heywood, "Slavery and Forced Labor," 417–18; Gordon, "Abolition of the Slave Trade," 920, 928.

18. Harms, "Sustaining the System"; Broadhead, "Slave Wives, Free Sisters," 174–79; Lovejoy, *Transformations in Slavery*, 237–38.

19. Lovejoy, *Transformations in Slavery*, 237–38.

20. Miller, "Atlantic Ambiguities"; Lovejoy, *Transformations in Slavery*, 141; Eltis, *Economic Growth*, 225–26.

21. Marques, "United States and the Transatlantic Slave Trade," 189–91; Zeuske, *Amistad*.

22. This arrangement helped slave traders evade seizure by British patrols under the 1835 equipment provisions of international treaties that criminalized the possession of equipment associated with the slave trade. By refusing to enter such treaties, the United States was able to carry slaving equipment and trading supplies on the outbound leg of many slaving voyages that returned from Africa under a different flag. See Marques, "Contraband Slave Trade," 18–19. Marques provides a nuanced analysis of how U.S. participation in the transatlantic slave trade varied over time from 1776 to 1867. See also Graden, *Disease, Resistance, and Lies*, 12–39.

23. Harris, "New York Merchants and the Illegal Slave Trade"; Marques, "Contraband Slave Trade," 26–28.

24. See for example, Park, *Travels in the Interior Districts of Africa*, and Equiano, *Interesting Narrative*. Equiano argued that the end of the slave trade would create new sources of cotton and indigo and a huge African consumer market: "It opens a most immense, glorious, and happy prospect—the clothing, &c. of a continent ten thousand miles in circumference, and immensely rich in productions of every denomination in return for manufactures" (253–54). See also Brown, "British Government and the Slave Trade."

25. Curtin, *Image of Africa*, 289–317; Temperley, *White Dreams, Black Africa*.

26. Mann, *Slavery and the Birth of an African City*, 87–91, quote on 91. For economic destabilization and political upheaval due to coastal factories and missions along the equatorial coast region, see Vansina, *Paths in the Rainforest*, 210–11, 230–35.

27. Eltis, *Economic Growth*, 88–89, 224–32; Law, "Abolition and Imperialism"; Howard, "Nineteenth-Century Coastal Slave Trading."

28. Eltis, *Economic Growth*, 81–101; Mann, *Slavery and the Birth of an African City*, 87; Asiegbu, *Slavery and the Politics of Liberation*.

29. Du Bois, *Suppression of the African Slave-Trade*, 136–48. In 1836, Portugal had banned

the slave trade in the South Atlantic but resisted signing a treaty with Britain that would allow rights of mutual search. Capitulation to British search rights in 1839 occurred in the context of British coercion. See Fehrenbacher, *Slaveholding Republic*, 161–62, and Law, *Ouidah*, 155–60.

30. Eltis, *Economic Growth*, 88–89.

31. Foote, *Africa and the American Flag*, 253; Du Bois, *Suppression of the African Slave-Trade*, 192.

32. Brooks, "Samuel Hodges, Jr.," 103.

33. John Quincy Adams, *Memoirs of John Quincy Adams*, 6:35–37, quoted in Mason, "Keeping Up Appearances," 821–22. See also Mason, "Battle of the Slaveholding Liberators," and Tucker, "Lieutenant Andrew H. Foote," 32–33. Only in 1862 did Secretary of State William Henry Seward, under the Lincoln administration, negotiate a treaty establishing mutual search rights with British and U.S. participation in courts of mixed commission.

34. Foote, *Africa and the American Flag*, 300–301. This chapter makes an argument about the cultural impact of naval memoirs and thus focuses on the text of *Africa and the American Flag*. Some evidence from private journals and published letters suggests that Foote's own personal views were more critical of U.S. slave trade suppression policy and more egalitarian in terms of racial equality than he expressed in the published narrative. See Tucker, "Lieutenant Andrew H. Foote," 34–35, 38, 39.

35. "Webster-Ashburton Treaty," 9 August 1842, Avalon Law Project, http://avalon.law .yale.edu/19th_century/br-1842.asp (accessed 28 May 2015).

36. In fact, in 1855 (the year following the publication of *Africa and the American Flag*), the United States exported $1.3 million worth of goods to ports along the African coast, an amount comparable to its shipments to Holland. See Canney, *Africa Squadron*, 39, 56–57; Brooks, "Samuel Hodges, Jr.," 101–15; and Harmon, "Suppress and Protect."

37. MacMaster, "United States Navy and African Exploration."

38. Canney, *Africa Squadron*, 57.

39. France also resisted signing treaties with Britain, while Britain refused to pass anti–slave trade measures that would obstruct the flow of private capital into the banned trade. See Marques, "Contraband Slave Trade," 33.

40. Eltis and Richardson, "New Assessment of the Transatlantic Slave Trade," 28.

41. Douglass, "Freedom in the West Indies," 218. See also Foote, *Africa and the American Flag*, 157.

42. Drake and Shufeldt, "Secret History of the Slave Trade," 223.

43. In comparison, Britain sent twenty-two warships to the African coast in 1844. See Canney, *Africa Squadron*, 63, 226–27.

44. John Laurence Fox to Elizabeth Amory (Morris) Fox, 22 February 1848, BF box 3: F–Fox, folder 18, Papers of Edward Griffin Beckwith and John Laurence Fox, 1805–1909, Huntington Library, San Marino, California.

45. "The Slave-Trade—the Actual Character of the Traffic," *NYT*, 17 March 1860.

46. The increased U.S. naval deployment on the African coast resulted in the seizure of several slavers with thousands of recaptives who were transported on the slavers directly to Liberia. For a discussion of recaptives from the *Storm King*, *Erie*, *Cora*, *Bonito*, and *Nightingale*, see Chapter 6. The U.S. Navy's procurement of five steamers in the summer of 1859 developed out of their earlier leasing by the United States for use against Paraguay, thus demonstrating linkages between U.S. slave trade suppression and other early uses of U.S. naval force abroad. See Canney, *Africa Squadron*, 202–3.

47. *H.R. Ex. Doc. No. 7*, 107–10; Fehrenbacher, *Slaveholding Republic*, 184–85; Younger, "Liberia and the Last Slave Ships," 430–32; Johnson, *River of Dark Dreams*, 304–14, 363–65, 405–6.

48. *H.R. Ex. Doc. No. 7*, 605–20; Canney, *Africa Squadron*, 221.

49. The ten vessels were *Echo*, *Wildfire*, *William*, *Bogota*, *William R. Kibby*, *Storm King*, *Erie*, *Bonito*, *Cora*, and *Nightingale*. The number of recaptives on these ships represented 73.9 percent of all recaptives taken under the U.S. flag (6,346). See Domingues da Silva, Eltis, Misevich, and Ojo, "Diaspora of Africans," 350.

50. Historiographic debates on U.S. slave trade suppression include Du Bois's condemnation of inaction as moral wrong, *Suppression of the African Slave-Trade*; Howard's emphasis on the systemic failure of U.S. courts and lawmakers rather than the performance of the navy, *American Slavers and the Federal Law*, 206–10; and Canney's defense of the navy's performance given its limited resources, *Africa Squadron*, 227. In contrast to most historians who argue that the vast majority of U.S. involvement occurred in the banned transatlantic trade to the Caribbean and Latin America, Obadele-Starks, in *Freebooters and Smugglers*, emphasizes the failure of the United States to curtail slave smuggling into the Gulf states. For a careful critique of Du Bois's *Suppression* legacy, a caution against overemphasizing the U.S. role in the contraband trade, and an argument for better Atlantic framing of the U.S. role, see Marques, "United States and the Transatlantic Slave Trade," 18–19. Younger, "Liberia and the Last Slave Ships," emphasizes the need to include recaptives in U.S. histories of slave trade suppression.

51. Domingues da Silva, Eltis, Misevich, and Ojo, "Diaspora of Africans," 349.

52. For arguments on the political importance of the category of recaptive in Brazilian history, see Mamigonian, "To Be a Liberated African in Brazil," 4, 31.

53. Shaw, "British, Persecuted Foreigners, and the Emergence of the Refugee Category."

54. Finkelman, "Regulating the Slave Trade," 401–2; Du Bois, *Suppression of the African Slave-Trade*, 96–102; *An Act to Prohibit the Importation of Slaves*, 426–30.

55. Bidwell, Cook, and others, *Annals of Cong.*, 9th Cong., 2nd Sess., p. 201, quoted in Du Bois, *Suppression of the African Slave-Trade*, 97.

56. Du Bois, *Suppression of the African Slave-Trade*, 109.

57. Batterson, "Horde of Foreign Freebooters," 13.

58. Page, "Case of Opportunity." Georgian authorities auctioned off over 100 *Tentativa* captives to local slaveowners under the guise of bonding them out for expenses. In the months just prior to the arrival of the *Antelope*, Richard Habersham attempted unsuccessfully to regain federal custody of the bonded Africans. See Bryant, *Dark Places*, 92–94.

59. Batterson, "Horde of Foreign Freebooters," 12; Landers, *Black Society in Spanish Florida*, 180–81.

60. Gould, *Among the Powers of the Earth*, 157–77.

61. *An Act in Addition to the Acts*, 532–34. Rather than paying prizes through the resale of illegally trafficked Africans, the 1819 law established a U.S. government payout of $25 per recaptive to the prize crews (distributed according to rank) and a $50-per-recaptive incentive to informers.

62. DeLombard, *In the Shadow of the Gallows*; Dain, *Hideous Monster of the Mind*.

63. Jefferson, *Notes on the State of Virginia*, 144.

64. Mason, *Slavery and Politics in the Early American Republic*, 106–29; Rael, *Black Identity and Black Protest*, 54–117.

65. Rothman, *Slave Country*, 83–84.

66. Staudenraus, *African Colonization Movement*; Burin, *Slavery and the Peculiar Solution*; Tomek, *Colonization and Its Discontents*; Lapansky-Werner and Bacon, *Back to Africa*; Everill, *Abolition and Empire*.

67. Melish, *Disowning Slavery*; Horsman, *Race and Manifest Destiny*.

68. Burin, "Slave Trade Act of 1819," 6.

69. Ibid., 7.

70. Sidbury, *Becoming African in America*, 173, 185; Clegg, *Price of Liberty*, 37.

71. Staudenraus, *African Colonization Movement*, 67. See also Burin, *Slavery and the Peculiar Solution*.

72. "Table of Emigrants," *African Repository* 27, no. 5 (May 1851): 149–50.

73. "Table of Emigrants," *African Repository* 33, no. 5 (May 1857): 152–55; Clegg, *Price of Liberty*, 198–99.

74. Scott, "Paper Thin," 1086–87.

75. The complicated legal dispute over the *Antelope* recaptives is narrated in detail in Bryant, *Dark Places*, and Noonan, *Antelope*. The Portuguese claim stemmed from the privateer's capture of enslaved Africans on a different Portuguese vessel at the same time that the privateer seized the *Antelope*. See Noonan, *Antelope*, 13–30.

76. Bryant, *Dark Places*, 104–5, 127, 161–64, 172; Noonan, *Antelope*, 45–46, 123–24, 127. While Morel justified these actions to his superior as helping to keep costs down, he profited doubly—once from recaptives' labor on his estate and once from federal government reimbursements for recaptive provisions and shelter.

77. Bryant, *Dark Places*, 148–52. This last part of the ruling pertained to Africans captured by the privateer from an illegal U.S. slaver, the *Exchange*, whose captives merged with the *Antelope* shipmates.

78. Bryant, *Dark Places*, 159–60; Noonan, *Antelope*, 65–66.

79. Bryant, *Dark Places*, 218–39, 257–63.

80. Ibid., 263–67. Arriving in 1830 and also settled in New Georgia were Africans seized aboard the slave ship *Guerrero*. The *Guerrero* ran onto a reef off Key Largo during a pursuit by the British ship *Nimble*. Rescued by salvagers, African captives of the *Guerrero* stayed in Key West for seventy-five days before the U.S. marshal sent them to St. Augustine. Because they came into U.S. hands through a shipwreck, they too did not qualify under the 1819 provision for intentionally trafficked Africans. While in Florida, they were rented out to planters, such as Zephaniah Kingsley, who held thirty-six of the captives as laborers. A special appropriation from Congress funded their transport to Liberia in March 1830 on the ACS ship *Heroine*. See Swanson, *Slave Ship Guerrero*, and Bryant, *Dark Places*, 287–88.

81. "Intelligence. Recaptured Africans," *African Repository and Colonial Journal* 3, no. 5 (July 1827): 154; Noonan, *Antelope*, 133–48. The flagrant corruption and cronyism that allowed Georgia congressman Richard Henry Wilde to gain ownership of the group allotted to the Spanish party is detailed in Noonan, *Antelope*, 139–44.

82. As Swanson suggests for the *Guerrero* shipmates, some of the *Antelope* recaptives carried to Liberia the surnames of elite U.S. slaveholders who "leased" them while legal proceedings were under way. See Swanson, *Slave Ship Guerrero*, 77, 120. Census data on the *Antelope* survivors arriving by the *Norfolk* appears in *Senate Ex. Doc. No. 150*, 175–79.

83. British reports identified the "Phoenix" as formerly the *Trimmer* of New Orleans. See George Salkeld to W. S. Macleay, 23 July 1840, in "Correspondence with the British Commissioners, Havana, No. 99." Although sources do not discuss the origins of the *Fenix*'s African captives, a comparison of names of the *Fenix* shipmates recorded in 1835 in Liberia

with the *African Origins* database suggests West African origins, including Igbo-language and Muslim (Arabic) names. See *Senate Ex. Doc. No. 150*, 261–63.

84. "On the Capture, by a United States Vessel, of the Spanish Ship Fenix," in box 4, U.S. v. Schooner Fenix, Sept. 1831, Record Group 60: Supreme Court Case Papers, 1809–1870, General Records of the Department of Justice, NARA. The little-known history of the *Fenix* and its West African recaptives in New Orleans during several years of litigation calls for further exploration.

85. The reprinted congressional document names "Alfred Heuner, Esq." as the lawyer submitting the habeus corpus claim. No such name appears among New Orleans records, but Alfred Hennen was a leading lawyer and known colonizationist in the city. Born in Maryland in 1786, Hennen moved to New Orleans during the territorial years and was widely known as a jurist and church leader. Like most southern colonizationists, he was also a slaveowner, having acquired a plantation in St. Tammany Parish in 1822, where by 1838 he kept twenty to thirty enslaved laborers. See Reilly, "Louisiana Colonization Society"; Reilly, "Conscience of a Colonizationist," 425; and Curry, *Reports of Cases Argued and Determined*, 192.

86. "On the Capture, by a United States Vessel, of the Spanish Ship Fenix," in box 4, U.S. v. Schooner Fenix, Sept. 1831, Record Group 60: Supreme Court Case Papers, 1809–1870, General Records of the Department of Justice, NARA, 871.

87. Ibid. Appropriations reported in *Newbern Sentinel*, 31 August 1831, 1.

88. "Report of the Managers to the American Colonization Society, at Its Nineteenth Annual Meeting," *African Repository and Colonial Journal* 12, no. 1 (January 1836): 16.

89. Apparently, the privateer had intercepted a slave ship outbound from Cape Mesurado in West Africa. After delivering the captives for bounty to authorities in the British West Indies, Chase then signed on a small group of men and boys as crew members before departing for Baltimore. See Mouser, "Baltimore/Pongo Connection," 316. This ship had previously been named the *General Peace* and was owned by George DeWolf of the DeWolf family of slave traders in Bristol, Rhode Island; see Marques, "United States and the Transatlantic Slave Trade," 114, 134.

90. Notably, the district attorney for Georgia, Richard Habersham, had filed the *Antelope* case with the Supreme Court just seven months before. However, both the *Antelope* case and a decision on the status of the *General Páez* African captives stalled out with little direction from the Monroe administration and a less-than-promising prospect for the struggling ACS venture in West Africa. See Noonan, *Antelope*, 74.

91. Bruce Mouser has detailed the legal twists and turns of this case as well as the trade connections between Baltimore and the Windward Coast. See Mouser, "Baltimore's African Experiment."

92. Ibid., 117.

93. Ibid., 120.

94. "Sixth Annual Report," 71; also excerpted in "Liberated Africans," *Religious Intelligencer*, 31 January 1824, 549–51. The *African Origins* database shows several men and boys named Doree or some variations of this name, identified as a Mende-language name. They had embarked from the Gallinas region. See African IDs 21076, 20923, and 108008.

95. Lawrance, *Amistad's Orphans*, 228–38.

96. Out of the original fourteen Africans, three young men remain unaccounted for in Baltimore's extant records. See Mouser, "Baltimore's African Experiment," 120, 125 (n. 28), and Southard, "Documents," 280.

97. See Mouser's argument that the *General Páez* case depicts the U.S. government shifting from repatriation to deportation of illegally trafficked Africans. When courts ruled that the African men in question could not be transported under section 2 of the 1819 act, both the attorney general and the secretary of the navy explored the possibility of whether Monroe could issue a presidential order for deportation to authorize their removal. See Mouser, "Baltimore's African Experiment," 118, 120.

98. Samuel H. Harper, "United States vs. 62 Africans arrived in Schooner Fenix," in box 4, U.S. v. Schooner Fenix, Sept. 1831, Record Group 60: Supreme Court Case Papers, 1809–1870, General Records of the Department of Justice, NARA, 3 March 1831.

99. Lawrance, *Amistad's Orphans*, 219–65.

100. Mouser, "Baltimore/Pongo Connection," 313–33; Rediker, *Amistad Rebellion*, 213–15; Lawrance, *Amistad's Orphans*, 221–28.

101. "Capture of the Slaver *Pons*," *Boston Daily Atlas*, 19 March 1846; Charles H. Bell, "The Captured Slave Ships," *African Repository and Colonial Journal* 22, no. 4 (April 1846): 115–16.

102. Gilliland, *Voyage to a Thousand Cares*, 196–97, 271–85, 294–99. The crew of the USS *Yorktown* divided $18,900 of prize money, distributed through all ranks, from captain to Kru mariners. The crew of the *Pons* could not be prosecuted because they were not U.S. citizens.

103. Curtin, *Image of Africa*; Brantlinger, *Rule of Darkness*; Lively, *Masks*; Lee, *Slavery and the Romantic Imagination*; White, *Dark Continent of Our Bodies*.

104. Livingstone, *Missionary Travels and Researches*; Pettitt, *Dr. Livingstone, I Presume?*

105. See Chapter 2.

106. The 1820 designation of slaving as piracy in U.S. law further amplified the appeal of slaver narratives like Canot's by associating them with romantic sea ventures of bygone pirate ships. See DeLombard, *In the Shadow of the Gallows*, 254. On the *Wanderer*, see *Voyages*, ID #4974; Sinha, *Counterrevolution of Slavery*, 153–86; Calonius, *Wanderer*, 186–220, 229–38; Wells, *Slave Ship Wanderer*; and Soodalter, *Hanging Captain Gordon*, 9–10.

107. "The Slave Trade in New York," *National Era*, 21 December 1854, 201; "The Slave Trade in New York," *De Bow's Review* 18, no. 2 (1855): 223–28. Both of these papers republished an original interview with James Smith from the New York paper *The Evangelist*.

108. DeLombard, *In the Shadow of the Gallows*, 254–55.

109. "The Wanderer's Cargo," *Mercury*, 17 December 1858; Howard, *American Slavers and the Federal Law*, 145–46.

110. Sinha, *Counterrevolution of Slavery*, 163–64, 169–72.

111. "Grand Democratic Musical Festival and Breakdown," *Weekly Anglo-African*, 12 May 1860.

112. Diouf, *Dreams of Africa*, 92–94; Davis, "Buchanian Espionage," 271–78; Davis, "James Buchanan," 446–59.

113. "The Slave Trade in Alabama," *Daily Evening Bulletin*, 7 August 1860; Diouf, *Dreams of Africa*, 87–88.

114. "'More Africans,'" *Courier*, 11 July 1860.

115. Bridge, *Journal of an African Cruiser*, v.

116. See also Bridge, *Journal of an African Cruiser*, and Thomas, *Adventures*. Thomas was an English-born Methodist clergyman from Georgia who served as chaplain for the Africa Squadron on the *Jamestown* between 1855 and 1857. He first published his account of African travels in serialized chapters in 1858 in the *Southern Christian Advocate*.

117. Miller, "Atlantic Ambiguities," 686, see also 678–79. Also on early decades of American empire, see Streeby, "American Sensations." Slave trade suppression provides an excel-

lent case study for Amy Kaplan's suggestion that insight is gained from understanding "United States nation-building and empire-building as historically coterminous and mutually defining" (Kaplan, "'Left Alone with America,'" 17).

118. Renda, *Taking Haiti*, 17–18. Curtin, *Image of Africa*, 322, identifies naval memoirs of slave trade suppression as a subset of British exploration literature on Africa. Other than biographical articles or "fact checking" approaches, almost no literary or historical criticism exists on the genre of U.S. slaver narratives. One exception is DeLombard, *In the Shadow of the Gallows*, 252–94.

119. Foote's generally optimistic assessment relied heavily on ACS agent J. W. Lugenbeel's positive report *Sketches of Liberia*.

120. "Africa and the American Flag," *African Repository* 30, no. 7 (July 1854): 213; D. Appleton advertisements in *Christian Review* 19, no. 77 (July 1854): 491, and "Captain Foote's Africa and the American Flag," *National Era*, 14 September 1854, 147; "Book Trade—2. *Africa and the American Flag.*"

121. Blum, *View from the Masthead*, 4–10. For other slaver narratives in this genre, see Drake and West, *Revelations of a Slave Smuggler*; Manning, *Six Months on a Slaver*; Thomes, *Slaver's Adventure*; and Vermilyea, *Slaver, the War, and around the World*.

122. Mouser, "Théophilus Conneau," 98.

123. Holsoe, "Theodore Canot at Cape Mount"; Mouser, "Théophilus Conneau," 99; Canney, *Africa Squadron*, 92–93; B., "Cape Mount," 63.

124. Mouser, "Théophilus Conneau," 97. Hall first met Canot in 1836–37 in West Africa; see Jones, "Théophile Conneau," 90. In 1976, Prentice Hall published the manuscript of Theophilus Conneau, allegedly found in editor Brantz Mayer's papers, as *A Slaver's Log Book*. Because this chapter is concerned with the publicly marketed version of Canot's life, I have used the 1854 New York publication of *Captain Canot* as primary source and have referenced Conneau's manuscript only to gain a sense of Mayer's editorial contributions. Because literary representation is the focus of this section, I refer to "Canot" to designate Conneau's literary persona.

125. Jones, "Théophile Conneau," 89–90. Mayer's experiences with early imperial ventures of the U.S. government actually linked him more directly with Foote than Canot; see New-England Historic Genealogical Society, *Memorial Biographies*, 321. Other titles by Mayer include *Mexico: Aztec, Spanish, and Republican* and *History of the War between Mexico and the United States*. In another link to important antebellum slavery literature, Mayer dedicated *Captain Canot* to "N.P. Willis of Idlewild." Nathaniel Parker Willis was a well-known American writer and employer of the fugitive author Harriet Jacobs. See Jacobs, *Incidents in the Life of a Slave Girl*, xvi.

126. See, for example, "Captain Canot," *North American Review*; "Captain Canot; or Twenty Years of an African Slaver," *National Era*, 26 October 1854, 170; "The African Slave Trade," *De Bow's Review* 18, nos. 1 & 3 (January & March 1855): 16–20, 297–305; "Capt. Canot," *African Repository* 30, no. 11 (November 1854): 327–30.

127. Equiano, *Interesting Narrative*, 223.

128. On the gothic turn and body horror, see Halttunen, *Murder Most Foul*, 47–57, and Lively, *Masks*, 64–85.

129. Foote, *Africa and the American Flag*, 228–29. The description, quoted in British parliamentary papers, came from Walsh, *Notices of Brazil*, 479–88.

130. Foote, *Africa and the American Flag*, 243–46, 247.

131. Mayer, *Captain Canot*, 74 (emphasis in original).

132. Ibid., 104.

133. Ibid., 105.

134. Drake and West, *Revelations of a Slave Smuggler*, 21–22, 88–89.

135. Mayer, *Captain Canot*, 408.

136. Ibid., 228–29.

137. Ibid., 126, 128, 387.

138. See, for example, Dalzel, *Kingdom of Dahomey*.

139. Mayer, *Captain Canot*, 126, 128. For this figure, Mayer cites Lugenbeel, *Sketches of Liberia*, 45. The circularity between Canot's and Lugenbeel's texts continued when Lugenbeel publicly endorsed the authenticity of Canot's account. See Lugenbeel, "Authenticity of Captain Canot," 2.

140. "Captain Canot," *North American Review*, 153–54.

141. Foote, *Africa and the American Flag*, 180.

142. For historical analysis of slavery in Africa, see Miller, *Problem of Slavery as History*; Lovejoy, *Transformations in Slavery*; Manning, *Slavery and African Life*; and Robertson and Klein, *Women and Slavery in Africa*.

143. Foote, *Africa and the American Flag*, 51–52.

144. Ibid., 207. Foote later contradicted his earlier generalizations about the ubiquity of African cruelty when he explained that "natives" at the mouth of the Congo River had grown "treacherous and cruel" through association with the slave trade, but that "interior" groups untouched by the slave trade were "civil and inoffensive" (ibid., 347).

145. Equiano, *Interesting Narrative*, 218–19.

146. Eason Journal, 14 May 1858.

147. Thomas Aloysius Dornin, 8 March 1861, Journal & Remarks on Board the U. States Frigate San Jacinto, Huntington Library, San Marino, California.

148. "Capt. Canot," *African Repository* 30, no. 11 (November 1854): 329.

149. Mayer, *Captain Canot*, 184–89. For other accounts of rescue of enslaved Africans by Canot, see 391, 443, 425. Foote excerpts British officer Frederick Forbes's account of rescuing several war captives on the verge of their deaths in a Dahomean ceremony. Quoted in Foote, *Africa and the American Flag*, 88–89. See Forbes, *Dahomey and the Dahomans*, 2:49–51, 206. Horatio Bridge's naval memoir remarked on the desire to intervene in a ceremony of "human sacrifice": "We are all anxious to go on shore to see the ceremonies, and try to save the destined victim" (Bridge, *Journal of an African Cruiser*, 127).

150. The perception of Africans as metaphorical children has been discussed in Campbell, Miers, and Miller, "Children in European Systems of Slavery," 175, and King, *Stolen Childhood*, xvii. Bianca Premo adds the important insight that processes of colonization "transformed the status of the minor into a multivalent legal category based only partially on age," thereby subsuming a large number of colonized subjects into a state of legal minority; see Premo, *Children of the Father King*, 19–20.

151. Mayer, *Captain Canot*, iv–v.

152. Tucker, "Lieutenant Andrew H. Foote," 34, 42.

153. Foote, *Africa and the American Flag*, 180.

154. Ibid., 205, 195.

155. Ibid., 389–90.

156. "Africa and the American Flag," *African Repository* 30, no. 7 (July 1854): 213.

157. "The Recaptured Africans," *African Repository* 34, no. 10 (October 1858): 298–300.

158. Mudimbe, *Invention of Africa*, 2.

159. Johnson, *River of Dark Dreams*, 395–97; Sinha, "Judicial Nullification."

160. Johnson, *River of Dark Dreams*, 11–12.

161. "The Sentiment of the State," *Courier*, 7 September 1858.

162. Edmund Ruffin, "African Colonization Unveiled," *De Bow's Review* 29, no. 5 (November 1860): 642.

163. DeLombard, *In the Shadow of the Gallows*, 252–53.

164. "Remarks of Frederick Douglass at Zion Church on Sunday 28, of Dec.," *Douglass' Monthly*, January 1863, 770.

165. Deyle, "Irony of Liberty."

166. Henry Wheaton, *The Antelope*, 10 Wheaton 66, 70–14, quoted in Noonan, *Antelope*, 100.

Chapter 2

1. "The Slaver and Cargo," *Mercury*, 1 September 1858; A Charlestonian, "The Africans in the Bay," *Mercury*, 2 September 1858.

2. Miller, "Retention, Reinvention, and Remembering"; Bailey, *African Voices of the Atlantic Slave Trade*; Smallwood, *Saltwater Slavery*; Mustakeem, *Slavery at Sea*; Larson, "Horrid Journeying"; Sweet, *Domingos Álvares*, esp. 39–42; Rediker, *Slave Ship*.

3. Younger, "Liberia and the Last Slave Ships." This chapter adds a cultural argument to Manisha Sinha's political analysis of the *Echo* and slave trade revival in South Carolina and geographically extends Walter Johnson's discussion of proslavery imperialism beyond the Lower Mississippi Valley to South Carolina. See Sinha, *Counterrevolution of Slavery*, 125–52, and Johnson, *River of Dark Dreams*, 395–422.

4. "Civil incapacity" comes from DeLombard, *In the Shadow of the Gallows*, 40, 62, 64.

5. Mudimbe, *Invention of Africa*, 22.

6. *Voyages Estimates*, http://www.slavevoyages.org/estimates/aFfJm47f (accessed 24 February 2016); Zeuske, *Amistad*. In the last decade of Atlantic World scholarship, a focus on the Brazilian and Cuban slave trades has helped to correct the overly heavy emphasis, at least in English-language publications, on the North Atlantic. See Eltis and Richardson, "New Assessment of the Transatlantic Slave Trade."

7. "History of the Captured Slaver," *Mercury*, 3 September 1858; *Voyages*, ID #4284. The best synthesis of the *Echo*'s itinerary, ownership, and funding appears in Harris, "Voyage of the *Echo*."

8. *Voyages Estimates*, http://www.slavevoyages.org/estimates/bjtbcSP8 (accessed 24 February 2016).

9. My thinking about recaptivity as a condition of existential crisis borrows from Vincent Brown's powerful discussion of enslavement as "social and spiritual crisis," in *Reaper's Garden*, 44.

10. Patterson, *Slavery and Social Death*; Penningroth, *Claims of Kinfolk*, 8, 22–27; Smallwood, *Saltwater Slavery*, 60–61.

11. MacGaffey, "Economic and Social Dimensions of Kongo Slavery."

12. Miller, "Retention, Reinvention, and Remembering," 83; Miller, *Problem of Slavery as History*, 134–35 and table 4.3, 172.

13. "From Liberia—Return of the Niagara," *African Repository* 35, no. 1 (January 1859): 2.

14. Moráguez, "African Origins of Slaves Arriving in Cuba," table 6.3, 185. On Central Africans' influence in shaping slave societies of the Americas, see Miller, "Central Africa during the Era of the Slave Trade," 23–35, and Vansina foreword, xi.

15. Ferreira, "Suppression of the Slave Trade," 325–28; Broadhead, "Slave Wives, Free Sisters," 160–81; Hilton, *Kingdom of Kongo*, 221; Martin, "Cabinda and Cabindans"; Herlin, "Brazil and the Commercialization of Kongo," 262–67; Vos, "'Without the Slave Trade.'"

16. Eason Journal, 29 March 1859.

17. The term "Miquombas" aligns most closely with "Muchicongo" and thus, according to Jelmer Vos, signifies someone originating in or near the capital of the old Kongo Kingdom, Mbanza Kongo; see Vos, "'Without the Slave Trade,'" 52. See also "Muchicongo" or "Mexicongo" in Karasch, *Slave Life in Rio De Janeiro*, 374, and Harris, "The *Echo* Captives," in Harris, "Voyage of the *Echo*," http://ldhi.library.cofc.edu/exhibits/show/voyage-of-the-echo-the-trials/the-echo-captives (accessed 31 January 2016).

18. Miller, "Central Africa during the Era of the Slave Trade," 41; Eltis, *Economic Growth*, 174; Moráguez, "African Origins of Slaves Arriving in Cuba," 189, 192–93; Martin, *External Trade of the Loango Coast*. Linda Heywood notes that increasing chaos of the disintegrating Kongo kingdom led by the eighteenth century to Kongo subjects being traded through Vili networks to Loango. See Heywood, "Slavery and Its Transformation," 20–21. As discussed in Chapter 3, captives in the late slave trade from the Congo River region also included those enslaved from coastal areas and shipped up the coast from Luanda.

19. Lovejoy, "Pawnship, Debt, and 'Freedom,'" 55–78; Miller, *Way of Death*, 94–103; Gordon, "Abolition of the Slave Trade," 925; Vansina, *Paths in the Rainforest*, 207–37; Heywood, "Slavery and Forced Labor," 417–19.

20. Vansina, "Ambaca Society," 10, 11, 13, 16. For the concept of collective responsibility applied in the early history of the Kongo Kingdom, see Heywood, "Slavery and Its Transformation," 15. Gordon, "Abolition of the Slave Trade," 931, notes that in Chibembe, the language of the interior regions targeted by slave and ivory raiders that fed into Luanda, *musha* meant "debt," and a *mushapôle* indicated "a female slave without relatives able to reclaim her." The process by which a person was enslaved or "disappear[ed] into slavery" through debt was expressed in the phrase *lobelela mu musha*. See also Curto, "Experiences of Enslavement in West Central Africa," and Miller, *Way of Death*, 48–53.

21. Vansina, "Ambaca Society," 18–19.

22. Koelle, *Polyglotta Africana*, 15; Curtin and Vansina, "Sources of the Nineteenth Century Slave Trade," 199, 204.

23. For two recaptive narratives of raid and abduction, see Hoyt, *Land of Hope*, 80.

24. "The Slaver, Her Crew and Cargo," *Mercury*, 30 August 1858; Candido, *African Slaving Port*, 191–236.

25. Candido, "African Freedom Suits," 450–54. Authorities in Portuguese "enclaves" viewed Africans who professed Catholicism or claimed to be a subject of the Portuguese Crown as protected from enslavement by the principle of "original freedom." Candido shows that the concept was not consistently applied, however. See Candido, *African Slaving Port*, 204, 221.

26. "The Slaver and Cargo," *Mercury*, 1 September 1858.

27. Martin, "Cabinda and Cabindans," 80–96; Eltis, *Economic Growth*, 176–77.

28. Coquery-Vidrovitch, "African Slaves and the Atlantic," 7.

29. Hawthorne, *From Africa to Brazil*; Candido, *African Slaving Port*; Adderley, *"New Negroes from Africa"*; Ferreira, *Cross-Cultural Exchange*.

30. Slenes, "'Malungu, Ngoma's Coming!,'" 222–23.

31. "The Captured Slaver," *Daily Ohio Statesman*, 17 September 1858; "Capture of a Slaver," *Farmer's Cabinet*, 8 September 1858; "A Precedent," *Pittsfield Sun*, 30 September 1858. Accord-

ing to newspapers, adults of the *Echo* ranged from ages twenty to thirty-four. For observations on height, see A Charlestonian, "The Africans in the Bay," *Mercury*, 2 September 1858.

32. Eltis and Engerman, "Was the Slave Trade Dominated by Men?," 241, 256; Lawrance, *Amistad's Orphans*, 27–46. On varying definitions of childhood, see Campbell, Miers, and Miller, *Children in Slavery through the Ages*, 3; Campbell, Miers, and Miller, *Child Slaves in the Modern World*, location 22–28, Kindle version; Richardson, "Shipboard Revolts," 85 (n. 57); and Lawrance, *Amistad's Orphans*, 28–30.

33. Eltis and Engerman, "Fluctuations in Sex and Age Ratios," 310.

34. Candido, *African Slaving Port*, 209–10; Klein, "African Women in the Atlantic Slave Trade," 30–32; Harms, "Sustaining the System," 95–110; Nwokeji, "African Conceptions of Gender," 55–56. See also Miller, *Way of Death*, 40–70, and Guyer, "Wealth in People, Wealth in Things," 83–90. The proportion of children in the East African slave trade reached even higher; see Morton, "Small Change."

35. Lawrance, *Amistad's Orphans*, 36–37, emphasizes the demands of slavers. For evidence of the Angolan slave trade trend toward a majority of young boys as a result of drought and war in the late eighteenth century, see Miller, "Slave Prices in the Portuguese Southern Atlantic," 57–59, 61–62. See also Manning, *Slavery and African Life*, 99; Lovejoy, "Children of Slavery"; Miller, *Way of Death*, 245–83; and Harms, *River of Wealth, River of Sorrow*, 3–5.

36. Miller, "Retention, Reinvention, and Remembering," 83; Sweet, "Defying Social Death," 254–57.

37. Wright, *Strategies of Slaves and Women*, 1–2, 9, 21.

38. Martin, *External Trade of the Loango Coast*, 142–45.

39. "The Captured Africans," *Courier*, 30 August 1858; A Charlestonian, "The Africans in the Bay," *Mercury*, 2 September 1858.

40. Candido, *African Slaving Port*, 211.

41. Crowther, "Narrative of Samuel Ajayi Crowther," 310.

42. Woodruff, *Report of the Trials*, 100. In general, the high numbers of children and youth may also have contributed to the declining occurrence of uprisings on nineteenth-century slave ships. See Richardson, "Shipboard Revolts," 78, 92.

43. "Statement of the Captain of the Slave Brig," *Mercury*, 10 September 1858; Levien, *Case of the Slaver Echo*, 8; "The Recaptured Africans," *African Repository* 34, no. 10 (October 1858): 289–300.

44. Woodruff, *Report of the Trials*, 8. Lieutenant Carpenter, who boarded the *Echo* at the time of naval seizure, described the size of the brands in his Boston testimony against accused captain Townsend. See "Boston, Sept. 28," *Mercury*, 1 October 1858, and "Examination of the Slaver Captain," *Mercury*, 2 October 1858.

45. "Captured Slave Brig," *Daily Ohio Statesman*, 3 September 1858; "Captain of the Slaver," *Georgia Telegraph*, 14 September 1858. The accused captain of the slaver said that the captives' diet included beans, rice, pork, whiskey, and tobacco. See Woodruff, *Report of the Trials*, 9.

46. Woodruff, *Report of the Trials*, 8. On conditions at time of capture based on a naval officer's eyewitness account, see "The Cruise of the Dolphin," *Courier*, 31 August 1858.

47. Thornton, "Religious and Ceremonial Life"; MacGaffey, *Religion and Society in Central Africa*, 42–62. For a discussion of how the Lemba ritual sought to curtail the disorder caused by the impact of the European slave trade on Kongo regional trade, see Janzen, *Lemba*.

48. Schuler, "Liberated Central Africans," 325–26.

49. Ferreira, *Cross-Cultural Exchange*, 71–77.

50. For the deeper history of the connection between witchcraft and the transatlantic slave trade, see Thornton, "Cannibals, Witches, and Slave Traders"; Austen, "Moral Economy of Witchcraft"; MacGaffey, *Religion and Society in Central Africa*, 62; and Sweet, *Recreating Africa*, 162–64. Monica Schuler argues for the lasting association between enslavement and witchcraft in liberated African ritual and memories. See Schuler, "Enslavement, the Slave Voyage, and Astral and Aquatic Journeys," 186–89.

51. Law, *Ouidah*, 148–49.

52. For an example of the focus on American and slaver agency, see Howard, *American Slavers and the Federal Law*, 71–84.

53. Martin, "Cabinda and Cabindans," 86–87. Martin details the important role of Cabinda mariners in deflecting the suspicions of British patrols with false papers that identified enslaved captives as "passengers."

54. Hurston, "Cudjo's Own Story," 658; Diouf, *Dreams of Africa*, 69.

55. Wright, "Joseph Wright of the Egba," 331.

56. "The Slave Trade in New York," *National Era*, 21 December 1854, 201.

57. Law and Lovejoy, *Biography of Mahommah Gardo Baquaqua*, 156.

58. "Capture of the Slave Vessels and Their Cargoes," *Frank Leslie's*, 23 June 1860, 65–66. Foote, *Africa and the American Flag*, 244, notes eighteen died and one jumped overboard during the *Pons*'s lockdown while trying to evade detection (hovering near shore overnight).

59. Forbes, *Six Months' Service in the African Blockade*, 99. See Pentangelo, "Sailors and Slaves," 10 ("nothing to eat or drink for 30 hours"), and Wright, "Joseph Wright of the Egba," 332 ("Many of the slaves had died for want of water, and many men died for crowdedness"). See also Mayer, *Captain Canot*, 207.

60. L.T., "Capture of a Slave Brig, with over Three Hundred Africans," *NYT*, 30 August 1858; Burroughs, "Eyes on the Prize," 104; Saunders, "Liberated Africans in Cape Colony," 224. Several of the *Echo* captives may have had a better view of the USS *Dolphin*; some accounts indicate captive Africans visible on the deck before the slaver was seized. See "Statement of the Captain of the Slave Brig," *Mercury*, 10 September 1858. In some cases, it was the naval crew instead who cheered in anticipation of prize money when they opened the hatches and discovered a human cargo. See "A Capture and Its Consequences," *NYT*, 30 August 1858.

61. Crowther, "Narrative of Samuel Ajayi Crowther," 312. Monica Schuler found that, similar to descriptions from slave ship embarkation, recaptives in 1843 disembarking in Trinidad feared being eaten by Europeans. See Schuler, "Enslavement, the Slave Voyage, and Astral and Aquatic Journeys," 188.

62. See Chapter 1 for an overview of U.S. transatlantic slave trade abolition legislation.

63. Walsh, *Notices of Brazil*, 488. In one account of illegal slaving on the Indian Ocean, captives quickly let British boarding officers know their enslaved status, indicating their understanding of the British role in suppression. See Alpers, "Other Middle Passage," 29. Caroline Emily Shaw notes that the joy of recaptives upon seizure became a narrative element in British press coverage on naval suppression; see Shaw, "British, Persecuted Foreigners, and the Emergence of the Refugee Category," 248. For accounts of joyous greetings of U.S. and British "liberators," see *Illustrated London News*, 28 April 1860, 410; Foote, *Africa and the American Flag*, 224, 226; "Capture of a Slaver," *Illustrated London News*, 19 September 1857, 283–84; and "Slave Trade," *African Repository and Colonial Journal* 1, no. 2 (April 1825): 64.

64. Burroughs, "Eyes on the Prize," 104.

65. Crowther, "Narrative of Samuel Ajayi Crowther," 313, 314.

66. "The Dolphin at Key West—Her Stern-Chase after a Slaver," *NYT*, 1 September 1858; L.T., "Capture of a Slave Brig, with over Three Hundred Africans," *NYT*, 30 August 1858.

67. "Capture of a Slaver," *Illustrated London News*, 20 June 1857, 596, for *Zeldina* recaptives who "tore everything to pieces on board in search of food."

68. "The Slaver Prize in Our Port," *Courier*, 2 September 1858; also reported in "The Slave Brig," *Mercury*, 2 September 1858.

69. All evidence from "The Slaver, Her Crew and Cargo," *Mercury*, 30 August 1858.

70. This paragraph is based on descriptions in "The Slaver Prize in Our Port," *Courier*, 2 September 1858. For the fears of slave ship contagion in nineteenth-century Cuba, see Graden, *Disease, Resistance, and Lies*, 51–61. On yellow fever in Charleston and the debate over whether or not quarantine was necessary, see "The Yellow Fever Epidemic in Charleston," *Mercury*, 25 August 1858; "Yellow Fever in the City," *Mercury*, 9 September 1858; "Abatement of the Fever," *Mercury*, 27 September 1858; and Morgan, *Slave Counterpoint*, 73–79, 444–46.

71. "The African Negroes—Correspondence between the Sheriff of Charleston District and the U.S. Marshal," *Mercury*, 1 September 1858.

72. See photograph "Interior View of Fort Sumter," 14 April 1861, Record Group 121: Series, Photographs of Federal and Other Buildings in the United States, 1857–1942, NARA. My description of Fort Sumter as a space for recaptive detention is also drawn from a National Parks tour, 6 June 2009, conducted by Ranger Nate Johnson.

73. A Charlestonian, "The Africans in the Bay," *Mercury*, 2 September 1858.

74. Levien, *Case of the Slaver Echo*, 6.

75. Woodruff, *Report of the Trials*, 10.

76. Sweet, "Quiet Violence of Ethnogenesis."

77. Smallwood, *Saltwater Slavery*, 43–52.

78. See, for example, the conditions of *Pons* recaptives described in Charles H. Bell, "The Captured Slave Ships," *African Repository and Colonial Journal* 22, no. 4 (April 1846): 115–16.

79. Adderley, *"New Negroes from Africa,"* 52.

80. Krauss, "In the Ghost Forest," 96.

81. "The Slaver and Cargo," *Mercury*, 1 September 1858; Hawthorne, "Gorge."

82. Martin, *External Trade of the Loango Coast*, 167–68.

83. Mariana Candido makes a similar point about the implicit "violence of the law" in her discussion of late eighteenth-century Benguela uses of the concept of "original freedom." See Candido, *African Slaving Port*, 207, 218, 224.

84. A Charlestonian, "The Africans in the Bay," *Mercury*, 2 September 1858.

85. For the importance of drumming, music, and dance in Freetown's Liberated African Yard, see Peterson, *Province of Freedom*, 185–86. Marcus Rediker writes about the potential for communication and creation of social connection in the face of slave ship commodification; see his *Slave Ship*, 282–84.

86. Howard, "A Slaver in Our Port," *Mercury*, 28 August 1858. This was not the only comparison between *Echo* recaptives and other news sensations. One newspaper account exclaimed that Charlestonians reacted to the slave ship as New Yorkers would to the "advent of Jenny Lind [a Swedish opera singer celebrity], the funeral of Bill Poole [New York boxer and political leader who died of a gunshot in 1855], or the news of a successful cable" ("The Congo Fever in Charleston," *Milwaukee Daily Sentinel*, 8 September 1858).

87. Immediately after the *Echo*'s capture, Maffitt had attempted to turn over the *Echo*

to Key West authorities; but district court judge William Marvin was absent, and federal marshal Fernando Moreno would not accept the ship without the judge's warrant. Lieutenant Maffitt apparently based his decision to send the *Echo* to Charleston rather than the closer harbor of Key West on practical considerations of the available telegraph line, water supply, health conditions in Key West, readiness of the Charleston U.S. district court, and even prevailing winds. Maffitt had been ordered to Boston for his next assignment, and he later said that he would even have sent the *Echo* to Boston but, given the medical condition of the captives, feared the longer journey would result in more loss of life. See "Washington, September 22," *Mercury*, 27 September 1858, and "Examination of the Slaver Captain," *Mercury*, 29 September 1858. For a northern Republican view, see the editorial in the *New-York Daily Tribune*, 10 September 1858. Another factor may have been reported yellow fever and quarantine in Key West; see "Cuban Intelligence," *Courier*, 31 August 1858. Yellow fever was also present in Charleston, and one of the *Echo* crewmembers was even reported to have contracted yellow fever; but the location of Africans at Fort Sumter would have prevented contact between most Charleston residents and the shipmates. See E. B. Grimball to John Grimball, 1 September 1858, SCHS; *Mercury*, 22 September 1858; and "The Cargo of Negroes," *Mercury*, 27 September 1858. By May 1861, Maffitt had resigned his duties in the U.S. Navy and assumed command as a Confederate officer; see Maffitt, *Life and Services of John Newland Maffitt*, 219.

88. Du Bois, *Suppression of the African Slave-Trade*, 168–78; Takaki, *Pro-Slavery Crusade*.

89. Sinha, *Counterrevolution of Slavery*, 126–35.

90. House Special Committee on Slavery and the Slave Trade, *Report of Special Committee* and *Report of the Minority*.

91. Sinha, *Counterrevolution of Slavery*, 171.

92. Ibid., 153–72; Wells, *Slave Ship Wanderer*, 51. Rhode Island–born Captain Edward Townsend also later walked free from a Key West courtroom.

93. Sinha, *Counterrevolution of Slavery*, 170; Woodruff, *Report of the Trials*, 69.

94. Sinha, *Counterrevolution of Slavery*, 170–71.

95. "The African Negroes—Correspondence between the Sheriff of Charleston District and the U.S. Marshal," *Mercury*, 1 September 1858; Levien, *Case of the Slaver Echo*, 7.

96. Levien, *Case of the Slaver Echo*, 56–58; Sinha, *Counterrevolution of Slavery*, 156; Fett, "Middle Passages and Forced Migrations," 79–80.

97. "The Rescued African Negroes," *Courier*, 8 September 1858.

98. J. Fraser Mathewes, "For the Mercury," *Mercury*, 31 August 1858. Mathewes also wrote to South Carolina congressman William Porcher Miles attempting to make apprenticeship arrangements for the *Echo* recaptives. Interior Secretary Jacob Thompson denied Mathewes's request, explaining that recaptives were to be removed to West Africa. See Jacob Thompson to William P. Miles, 6 June 1860, reel 1, RSI.

99. Sinha, *Counterrevolution of Slavery*, 156.

100. "The Slave Trade," *Courier*, 31 August 1858. "U.S. hotel" made sarcastic reference to the initial detention of recaptives under federal guard in Castle Pinckney on the small island of Shute's Folly.

101. See Sinha, *Counterrevolution of Slavery*, for a far-reaching analysis of the legal and political significance of the *Echo* and *Wanderer* trials.

102. Holt, "Marking." For treatments of antebellum racial ideology argued within national and sectional frameworks, see Horsman, *Race and Manifest Destiny*, 139–57, and Bay, *White Image in the Black Mind*.

103. Fowler, "Phrenological Developments of Joseph Cinquez," 136–38; Rediker, *Amistad Rebellion*, 128–31.

104. "The Mendian Exhibition," *American and Foreign Anti-Slavery Reporter*, 1 July 1840, quoted in Rediker, *Amistad Rebellion*, 196–208, quote on 205. According to Rediker, *Amistad* committee member Joshua Leavitt defended the moral purpose of these public exhibitions: "It was no part of the design to *show off* these Mendians for the purpose of indulging mere curiosity" (204, emphasis in original).

105. For an example of racial arguments for lesser intellectual capacity among Africans from an ACS officer at the time of the *Amistad* case, see Lindsly, "Differences in the Intellectual Character of the Several Varieties of the Human Race."

106. Stanton, *Leopard's Spots*, 25–35; Gould, *Mismeasure of Man*, 30–72; Bay, *White Image in the Black Mind*, 42–44. Pre-Adamic and polygenist theories have roots in early modern philosophy. See Smith, *Nature, Human Nature, and Human Difference*, 92–113.

107. Morton, *Crania Americana*, 5, table on p. 65; Carson, *Measure of Merit*, 4, 81–97; Fabian, *Skull Collectors*.

108. Luse, "Slavery's Champions Stood at Odds"; Stephens, *Science, Race, and Religion*, 165–66; Will, "American School of Ethnology." South Carolina's J. H. Guenebault played a role in the rise of American ethnology with his translation of French polygenist work in 1837. See Drescher, "Ending of the Slave Trade," 375.

109. McCord, "Diversity of the Races," 399.

110. Nott and Gliddon, *Types of Mankind*, 550. Dedicated to Samuel Morton, *Types of Mankind* excerpted Morton's publications and included writing by other leading scientific voices, such as Louis Agassiz.

111. Horsman, *Josiah Nott of Mobile*; Weiner with Hough, *Sex, Sickness, and Slavery*, 17–19.

112. Stephens, *Science, Race, and Religion*, 165–217.

113. Agassiz, "The Diversity of Origin of the Human Races," *Christian Examiner and Religious Miscellany* 49 (July 1850): 125, quoted in Rogers, *Delia's Tears*, 218.

114. Rogers, "Slave Daguerreotypes of the Peabody Museum," 39–41, 51. See also Stephens, *Science, Race, and Religion*, 174; Wallis, "Black Bodies, White Science," 45–54; and Reichlin, "Faces of Slavery."

115. Bowen, *Central Africa*, 331, 350, 113.

116. Ibid., 160. Leonidas Spratt, in his defense of the *Echo* crew, cited Bowen, Livingstone, and *Captain Canot*, among others, to claim that the slavers could not have robbed their captives of freedom (i.e., committed piracy) because most Africans were already slaves. See Woodruff, *Report of the Trials*, 69. Although Bowen did discuss forms of slavery in West Africa, in truth *Central Africa* argued that societies in the interior did not participate in slavery to the extent that coastal peoples did. In contrast to Spratt's citation of *Captain Canot* to assert that "five-sixths" of Africans were slaves, Bowen emphatically claimed of Yoruba society, "At least *four fifths* of the people are free" (320).

117. Meyer, "T. J. Bowen and Central Africa," 247–60; MacMaster, "United States Navy and African Exploration." Bowen received praise from both the *Liberator* and Liberian president Stephen Benson for his portrayals of wealth and civilization in Africa. See "Learned and Wealthy Africans," *Liberator*, 29 July 1859, 119, and Guannu, *Inaugural Addresses of the Presidents of Liberia*, 32.

118. P.A.F., "The Law of Piracy," *Mercury*, 15 October 1858. Several months after the departure of the *Echo* shipmates, a Charleston writer accused Bowen of "making a *show* of science"

to support his colonization schemes. See Ductor Dubitantium, "For the Mercury—the Rev. T. J. Bowen," *Mercury*, 9 November 1858.

119. Stephens, *Science, Race, and Religion*, 166, 197–206, 216. Bachman criticized the methods used by Agassiz to contrast "Mandingo" and "Guinea" as distinct African racial types.

120. First-person archival discussions of this event remain elusive. All evidence on the 31 August encounter at Fort Sumter comes from "The Slaver and Cargo," *Mercury*, 1 September 1858. The *Mercury*'s account of the 31 August event circulated nationally. See "The Slaver Echo and Her Cargo at Charleston," *NYT*, 6 September 1858.

121. Nott and Gliddon, *Types of Mankind*, 185, 180, 416. Bowen, despite his defense of the civilizable "interior tribes," described the people of Congo as "short, stubby, silly fellows" (*Central Africa*, 94).

122. Maffitt, *Life and Services of John Newland Maffitt*, 206; Hunt, *Negro's Place in Nature*, 18; "Correspondence of the Mercury, Washington, D.C., Aug 31," *Mercury*, 3 September 1858; "Highly Interesting from the Gulf," *Chicago Press and Tribune*, 8 June 1860; "The Africans of the Slave Bark 'Wildfire,'" *Harper's*, 2 June 1860, 345.

123. Gomez, *Exchanging Our Country Marks*, 135–37; Hall, *Slavery and African Ethnicities*, 159–60; Young, *Rituals of Resistance*; Thornton, "African Dimensions of the Stono Rebellion."

124. A Charlestonian, "The Africans in the Bay," *Mercury*, 2 September 1858.

125. Burmeister, *Black Man*, 1. Indicating his popular audience, Burmeister's piece was published in the *New York Evening Post* as well as in separate book form. Burmeister took a monogenist position that "the negro is like the European, a man," but he also viewed white supremacy as a biological fact and believed the slave trade to be ineradicable for centuries to come due to human tendencies for the strong to dominate the weak. On the "discovery" of "Bantu" by European scientists studying African languages in Brazil, see Slenes, "'Malungu, Ngoma's Coming!,'" 221.

126. A Charlestonian, "The Africans in the Bay," *Mercury*, 2 September 1858.

127. Stephanie M. H. Camp, "Race and Visual Culture before the Twentieth Century" (unpublished manuscript shared by Camp with author in July 2012), forthcoming in *Oxford Handbook of the History of Race*, ed. Matthew Pratt Guterl.

128. Rogers, *Delia's Tears*, 221.

129. Recaptive images in illustrated newspapers are discussed in Chapter 3.

130. P.A.F., "For the Mercury—the Law of Piracy," *Mercury*, 14 October 1858.

131. Ibid., 20 October 1858.

132. Thurs, *Science Talk*, 22–52; Pandora, "Popular Science in National and Transnational Perspective."

133. Willie Lightheart, "Correspondence of Carolina Spartan," *Carolina Spartan*, 16 September 1858, 2. A reprinted *New York Herald* correspondent, referencing a milk scandal in New York that received much coverage in the illustrated press, wrote, "If an artist of one of the illustrated papers could only have taken a sketch to this group of black animals, it would have beaten all the swill milk illustrations extant" ("The Niagara and the Negros," *Mercury*, 28 September 1858, originally in *Herald*, 21 September 1858).

134. Wallis, "Black Bodies, White Science," 41; Fausto-Sterling, "Gender, Race, and Nation"; Crais and Scully, *Sara Baartman and the Hottentot Venus*.

135. Poole, *Vision, Race, and Modernity*, 9–17.

136. Reiss, *Showman and the Slave*.

137. Pearson, "'Infantile Specimens,'" 342.

138. "The African Negroes—Correspondence between the Sheriff of Charleston District and the U.S. Marshal," *Mercury*, 1 September 1858.

139. Bridge, *Journal of an African Cruiser*, 84.

140. Eason Journal, 1 April 1859.

141. "The Ketch Brothers," *Mercury*, 11 November 1858. These gifts linked the U.S. Navy to Charleston's naturalist circles. Africa Squadron lieutenant C. M. Morris sent the tusk in care of Lieutenant Edward Stone of the *Brothers*'s prize crew to Gabriel Manigault. Manigault was one of Charleston's naturalists, who knew ichthyologist and medical professor John E. Holbrook, with whom Agassiz stayed in South Carolina in 1850. See Stephens, *Science, Race, and Religion*, 98, and Ravenel, *Charleston*, 476.

142. "The Slaver and Cargo," *Mercury*, 1 September 1858.

143. "Extracts from Letters Respecting the Capture of the Slave Ship 'Pons,'" [1845?]. The history of abolitionist display of slave ships begins, of course, with the famous *Brooks* image. See Rediker, *Slave Ship*, 308–42, and Wood, *Blind Memory*, 14–68, 295–301.

144. Willie Lightheart, "Correspondence of Carolina Spartan," *Carolina Spartan*, 16 September 1858.

145. Halttunen, "Humanitarianism and the Pornography of Pain," 303–34; Hartman, *Scenes of Subjection*; Wood, *Slavery, Empathy, and Pornography*.

146. Curtis, "Native Africans in the Bay," *Courier*, 30 August 1858; "The Slaver, Her Crew and Cargo," *Mercury*, 30 August 1858. In accordance with Charleston's quarantine laws, the ship had to remain in quarantine until cleared by the port physician, Dr. W. C. Ravenel. See Levien, *Case of the Slaver Echo*, 5, and "The Slaver, Her Crew and Cargo," *Mercury*, 30 August 1858. The navy's acquiescence to South Carolina quarantine regulations would later become an issue in jurisdiction debates as South Carolina states' rights men argued that if state law prevailed over naval ship movements in the harbor, state law should also prevail over recaptives brought to the harbor by the navy.

147. F.A.P., "Who Are the Pirates?," *Mercury*, 18 September 1858.

148. Berkley Grimball to John Grimball, 27 September 1858, SCHS. The same excursion is recalled in Charles Manigault to Louis Manigault, Charleston, 28 February 1861, in Clifton, *Life and Labor on Argyle Island*, 316. Thanks to Kevin Dawson for this citation.

149. "For Mulberry and Cooper River," *Mercury*, 31 August 1858; "The Rice Harvest," *Mercury*, 10 September 1858.

150. "Excursion to Fort Sumter," *Mercury*, 7, 8 September 1858; "Excursion to Fort Sumter," *Courier*, 8 September 1858.

151. "Fort Sumter," *Mercury*, 7 September 1858.

152. "Excursion to Fort Sumter," *Courier*, 9 September 1858; "Excursion to Fort Sumter, Via Sullivan's Island," *Mercury*, 9 September 1858.

153. Several newspaper articles indignantly refuted expectations that Charleston slaveholders might try to defy federal authority and abduct recaptives from Fort Sumter. They condemned the charge as dishonorable to Charleston and the state of South Carolina. For example, see "When Was It Made?," *Courier*, 8 September 1858.

154. "The Excursions to Fort Sumter," *Mercury*, 9 September 1858. Excursion agent H. L. P. McCormick defended his reputation, insisting that the intention of the outing had never included a tour of the fort's interior and that the language of the advertisement had been accurate. See H. P. McCormick, "To the Public," *Mercury*, 13 September 1858.

155. F.A.P., "Who Are the Pirates? No. IV," *Mercury*, 18 September 1858.

156. "Meeting on Board Steamer Gen. Clinch," *Courier*, 9 September 1858 (this article

claims there were 500 passengers aboard the *General Clinch* on the thwarted trip). See also F. A. Porcher, *Mercury*, 13 September 1858, and McCormick, "To the Public," *Mercury*, 13 September 1858.

157. The *Niagara*'s voyage to Liberia is discussed in Chapter 5.

158. Bowen, *Central Africa*, 331 (see also 330, 333); Livingstone, *Missionary Travels and Researches*, 92, 437, 675–767.

159. Spratt, *Speech Upon the Foreign Slave Trade*.

160. Johnson, "White Lies," 239–41.

161. Mamigonian, "In the Name of Freedom," 43.

162. Merrill, "Exhibiting Race," 322; Samuels, "Examining Millie and Christine McKoy"; Edwards, *Anthropology and Photography*; Crais and Scully, *Sara Baartman and the Hottentot Venus*; Poignant, *Professional Savages*.

Chapter 3

1. Fernando Moreno to Jacob Thompson, 28 May 1860, reel 6, RSI.

2. See Toucey's order to bring recaptives to Boston or Portsmouth, N.H., and Craven's explanation for deviating from it. Toucey accepted Craven's rationale and altered his orders by July 1860. See *H.R. Ex. Doc. No. 7*, 615–20.

3. See Chapter 2 discussion of Lieutenant Maffitt and the *Echo*.

4. Peterson, *Province of Freedom*, 181–88; Pearson, *Distant Freedom*, 106–53; Northrup, "Becoming African"; Mamigonian, "To Be a Liberated African in Brazil," 30–47.

5. "The Captured Slaver. Reception of the Negroes at Key West—How They Fare," *NYT*, 21 June 1860.

6. Thompson to D. H. Hamilton, 16 July 1860, and to President Buchanan, 21 May 1860, reel 1, RSI.

7. Browne, *Key West*, 166.

8. "The Captured Slaver. Reception of the Negroes at Key West—How They Fare," *NYT*, 21 June 1860.

9. *The Mountaineer*, 16 June 1860, 2, and 23 June 1860, 5, 6. In "The Raw Darkies," the *Manitowoc Herald*, 21 June 1860, announced, "There are now at Key West seventeen hundred Africans rescued from slavers. They are a lot of dusky, greasy cannibals, eat raw beef, and some of them occasionally gnaw away at a dead nigger."

10. *H.R. Ex. Doc. No. 7*, 615–16 (*Wildfire*) and 616–17 (*William*).

11. Ibid., 614. John Maffitt, lieutenant commander of the *Crusader*, learned from the *Bogota*'s "supercargo" (slaver in disguise as passenger) that New York investors owned two-thirds of the vessel (ibid., 621).

12. For details on attempted prosecution and foreign immunity, see Malcom, "Key West and the Slave Ships of 1860," 5. Admiralty courts in Key West condemned both ships and ordered the sale of the ships and their goods. After court expenses, the *Wildfire* netted $6,088; the *William*, $4,344. See "The United States vs. Bark Wildfire & Cargo" and "The United States vs. Bark William & Cargo," in Admiralty Final Record Books of the U.S. District Court for the Southern District of Florida (Key West), 1829–1911, vol. 6: July 1857–Dec. 1860, 500–501, 503–7, NARA.

13. Miller, "Central Africa during the Era of the Slave Trade," 57, 58, 66. In table B, p. 66, compare 95,000 estimated captives sold from the Zaire River and north to 15,300 sold from

Ambriz, Luanda, and Benguela in 1851–60. See also Eltis, *Economic Growth*, 173–77, and Ferreira, "Suppression of the Slave Trade," 314–15.

14. Vos, "'Without the Slave Trade,'" table 2.1, 47.

15. "The African Slave Trade," *Herald*, 11 October 1860; Hilton, *Kingdom of Kongo*, 221; Herlin, "Brazil and the Commercialization of Kongo," 262–67; Harris, "New York Merchants and the Illegal Slave Trade."

16. Curto, "Experiences of Enslavement in West Central Africa," 383.

17. Lindsly, "Dreadful Sufferings Caused by the Slave Trade," 108; Webster Lindsly to William McLain, 3 September 1860, reel 10, RSI.

18. "The Africans of the Slave Bark 'Wildfire,'" *Harper's*, 2 June 1860, 344; "The Capture of the Slave Bark Wildfire," *New-York Daily Tribune*, 15 May 1860. In this paragraph, unless otherwise noted, the information on *Wildfire* shipmates comes from the *Harper's* article.

19. Candido, *African Slaving Port*, 229–32, 237–12; Heywood, "Slavery and Its Transformation"; Gordon, "Abolition of the Slave Trade"; Hilton, *Kingdom of Kongo*, 221–23.

20. Candido, "Tracing Benguela Identity to the Homeland."

21. Vos, "'Without the Slave Trade,'" 51–53.

22. "The Returning Africans. Letter from the Ship Castilian," *NYT*, 17 October 1860. Candido, *African Slaving Port*, 210, documents "endemic raiding" and upheaval in the Angolan hinterland well into the 1850s.

23. Candido, *African Slaving Port*, 196–97.

24. Miller, "Central Africa during the Era of the Slave Trade," fig. 1.6, 57.

25. Vos, "Kongo, North America, and the Slave Trade," 45.

26. "The Returning Africans. Letter from the Ship Castilian," *NYT*, 17 October 1860.

27. Vermilyea, *Slaver, the War, and around the World*, 7.

28. On the lack of initiation among some *Clotilda* survivors, see Diouf, *Dreams of Africa*, 118, and Lawrance, *Amistad's Orphans*, 30–31, 248–64.

29. "The Africans of the Slave Bark 'Wildfire,'" *Harper's*, 2 June 1860, 344–45.

30. Pearson, Jeffs, Witkin, and MacQuarrie, *Infernal Traffic*, table 4.7 and 59, 63–72, 152, 153. Archaeological digs at the cemetery in Rupert's Valley, St. Helena (a receiving point of many West Central African recaptives), showed 115 of 303 skeletons with cultural modifications of teeth, which appeared primarily among adolescents through adults, but only in about 10 percent of older children. Art history scholarship provides a sense of the social meanings attached to dental modification in regions of West Central Africa. For example, African art historian Ezio Bassani identified a series of *nkonde* figures from the Chiloango River region of western Congo bordering Cabinda. Each of these powerful figures, carved by a sculptor and activated by an *nganga*, possessed pointed, filed teeth. See Bassani, "Kongo Nail Fetishes," 38, 40. Chokwe aesthetics (far to the southeast of the Congo River) prized pointed teeth as an attribute of beauty and womanhood. See Bastin, "Arts of the Angolan Peoples," 40–47, 60–64. For significance of tooth filing and removal as a male rite of passage in twentieth-century West Africa (Dahomey), see Sweet, *Domingos Álvares*, 22. On body modification among recaptives on Liberian transports, see Chapter 6.

31. Thornton, *Africa and Africans*, 235–36; Sweet, *Domingos Álvares*.

32. Heywood, "Slavery and Its Transformation," 15–16.

33. Heywood, "Slavery and Its Transformation"; Martin, "Cabinda and Cabindans," 167–68. In the *African Origins* database, two women of "Congo" origin named Madia are listed in Havana Mixed Commission records as liberated from the slaver *Matilde* in 1837, which embarked from Ambriz. See African IDs 79504 and 79505.

34. On Luso-African creolization in coastal Angolan ports, see Heywood, "Portuguese into African"; Hawthorne, *From Africa to Brazil*; and Candido, *African Slaving Port*, 115, 193–98, 212, 288–89.

35. In the Portuguese slave trade, the significance of baptism for enslaved West Central Africans varied from an extended relationship with the church to a perfunctory rite required to certify captives as legitimately sold to foreign slave traders. See Candido, *African Slaving Port*, 215–16, and Miller, *Way of Death*, 402–5.

36. For slaving frontier, see Miller, *Way of Death*, 140–46. For revision, see Candido, *African Slaving Port*, 193–98, 288–89; Candido, "African Freedom Suits"; Ferreira, "Suppression of the Slave Trade," 321; Ferreira, *Cross-Cultural Exchange*, 52–87; and Hawthorne, *From Africa to Brazil*, 63–63.

37. Candido, *African Slaving Port*, 112.

38. Ferreira, *Cross-Cultural Exchange*, 52–125. For similar dangers of enslavement in the Portuguese colonial port of Benguela, see Candido, *African Slaving Port*, 191–236.

39. An 1854 Lisbon publication, quoted in Ferreira, *Cross-Cultural Exchange*, 98.

40. Ferreira, "Suppression of the Slave Trade," 314–17, 321–28. Ferreira (p. 328) mentions the role of "seasoned Cabindan sailors" who facilitated coastal trade between Ambriz and Cabinda. On the extension of Luso-Brazilians from Luanda to Cabinda and other northern ports, see Herlin, "Brazil and the Commercialization of Kongo," 263, 272.

41. "The Africans of the Slave Bark 'Wildfire,'" *Harper's*, 2 June 1860, 345; Heywood, "Slavery and Its Transformation"; Curto, "Experiences of Enslavement in West Central Africa."

42. On "orphanhood claims" as "a social praxis of resistance to slavery by children for whom freedom is illusory, unimaginable or unknown," see Lawrance, *Amistad's Orphans*, 16.

43. "The Africans of the Slave Bark 'Wildfire,'" *Harper's*, 2 June 1860, 345.

44. Young Ship Log, 1 July 1860.

45. Log of United States Steamer *Crusader*, 23 May 1860, LNS; "Key West and the African Strangers," *Courier*, 4 June 1860. The *Bogota's* identity remained obscured in the days after its seizure, and thus the ship was often referred to as "name unknown." The French origins of the ship and French trading posts in the Bight of Benin may help to explain the ship's trade with Ouidah, rather than the Congo River area. The captain, thought to be French with possible ties to New Orleans, denied all nationality in hopes of escaping prosecution. See "Our Key West Correspondence," *Herald*, 22 July [written from Key West 8 July] 1860, 2. Indeed, he was not retained for prosecution by the U.S. Navy but was dropped as "supercargo" in Havana; see *H.R. Ex. Doc. No. 7*, 621. The crew was reported to be Spanish; see "Key West and the African Stranger," *Courier*, 4 June 1860, 2. The *Bogota* ("Name Unknown") was confiscated and sold for $4,572 in the Key West Admiralty Court. See "The United States Vs. Bark Name Unknown & Cargo," in Admiralty Final Record Books of the U.S. District Court for the Southern District of Florida (Key West), 1829–1911, 28 May 1860, NARA.

46. Fernando Moreno to Jacob Thompson, 28 May 1860, reel 6, RSI.

47. Ibid., 10 June 1860.

48. Diouf, *Dreams of Africa*, 30–54. Further indication of Yoruba speakers making up at least a portion of the *Bogota* shipmates comes from a list of Yoruba words recorded by McCalla on the Liberia crossing. See "African Words for Parts of the Body," included in John Moore McCalla Papers, West Virginia and Regional History Center, West Virginia University Libraries, Morgantown.

49. On nineteenth-century history of upheaval in West Africa, particularly present-day

Benin and western Nigeria, see Peel, *Religious Encounter*, 50; Eltis, "Diaspora of Yoruba Speakers"; and O'Hear, "Enslavement of Yoruba."

50. Law, *Ouidah*, 50–58.

51. Diouf, *Dreams of Africa*, 45–46; Law, *Ouidah*, 235. For reports of the *Bogota* recaptives as prisoners of the Dahomean king, see the *Liberator*, 29 June 1860, 101, and Grymes Report, 31. The *New Orleans Delta* correspondent aboard the USS *Crusader* characterized the recaptives as having been "selected" from the Dahomey king's recently captured prisoners of war. See *Delta* article reprinted in "Highly Interesting from the Gulf," *Chicago Press and Tribune*, 8 June 1860.

52. Bay, *Wives of the Leopard*, 192, 230; Law, *Ouidah*, 233; Diouf, *Dreams of Africa*, 34. Frederick E. Forbes noted that annual wars and "slave hunts" began in November or December and ended in January; see his *Dahomey and the Dahomans*, 1:15.

53. Law, *Ouidah*, 111; Diouf, *Dreams of Africa*, 49–50. Given the lack of evidence, it is difficult to ascertain exactly how many of those sold to the *Bogota* slavers were officially royal slaves. Although U.S. contemporary reports maintained the *Bogota* shipmates had been selected from the king's war captives, the exposure of U.S. readers to Western accounts of the Dahomean king may have distorted their understanding of the Ouidah trade. European and American traders at Ouidah were required to buy a portion of the king's captives first, but they also engaged in a vigorous trade with private merchants in captives. However, because trade at Ouidah was supervised by royal officials (who also traded privately themselves at times), the impression in the American press may have been that those sold to the *Bogota*'s captain were all prisoners of war. See Law, *Ouidah*, 111–19, and Bay, *Wives of the Leopard*, 105.

54. *Voyages*, http://www.slavevoyages.org/voyages/7vAXZCtG (accessed 27 February 2016). On the history of Ouidah, particularly during the years of Atlantic slave trade suppression, see Law, *Ouidah*, 18, 31–41, 160–88, 194–203, 232–37. The connection between internal Dahomean political tensions and the shift in policy to pursue the slave trade again is not entirely clear. According to Law, missionary and diplomatic evidence indicates "divisions over commercial policy." Some of King Gezo's advisors and his son Glele were unhappy with the shift toward palm oil, regarding it as a decline in Dahomey's autonomy and traditional economy. Gezo had already lost power to this group of advisors, which secured its aims further when Glele came to power.

55. Diouf, *Dreams of Africa*, 151–81. Lewis, then a young man of about nineteen years, embarked from Ouidah in May 1860 in the hold of the *Clotilda*, the last recorded slave ship to enter the United States. Emancipated after the Civil War, Lewis and other *Clotilda* shipmates formed a community of West Africans in Alabama known as African Town. Sylviane Diouf's research on the origins of the *Clotilda* shipmates provides excellent background as well for those enslaved on the *Bogota*. Both groups of captives included a large number of Yoruba prisoners of war who were sold through Ouidah within just a few months of one another.

56. Diouf, *Dreams of Africa*, 47. Zora Neale Hurston published Lewis's story first in 1927, but she borrowed heavily from Emma Langdon Roche's 1914 account. In 1928, however, Hurston interviewed Lewis more extensively and wrote an unpublished manuscript called "Barracoon." See Hurston, "Cudjo's Own Story."

57. Describing *Bogota* shipmates in Liberia in 1861, C. C. Hoffman wrote, "There are Annagoes, Argis, Mobis, Barabas, and Housas" ("From Rev. C. C. Hoffman," *African Repository* 37, no. 5 [May 1861]: 132). My appreciation to Henry Lovejoy for help with "Mobis" (email

correspondence, 27 March 2015). For similar origins among *Clotilda* captives, see Diouf, *Dreams of Africa*, 35–36.

58. Grymes Report, 31.

59. Law, *Ouidah*, 20, 124; Diouf, *Dreams of Africa*, 35–36; Bay *Wives of the Leopard*, 48, 120.

60. Grymes Report, 31.

61. Diouf, *Dreams of Africa*, 56, 51–53; Crowther, "Narrative of Samuel Ajayi Crowther," 310–11. Crowther described the bruising and choking of young boys at night that occurred when large strong men pulled on their own neck chains in anger or in order to sleep more comfortably. The young were also punished with the entire group of captives when adults fought in the holding pens in Lagos. He reported the boys' relief when they were finally unchained and confined separately from the men.

62. Grymes Report, 31.

63. Law, *Ouidah*, 141–42.

64. Law and Lovejoy, *Biography of Mahommah Gardo Baquaqua*, 149, 150. Available sources do not specifically mention the branding of *Bogota* shipmates.

65. Law, *Ouidah*, 138–44, 157–58, 191–92; Diouf, *Dreams of Africa*, 60; Bay *Wives of the Leopard*, 47.

66. Hurston, "Cudjo's Own Story," 657. On the humiliation of public exposure, see Diouf, *Dreams of Africa*, 60–61.

67. List of crew and passengers onboard the *Star of the Union*, John Moore McCalla Diary typescript, John Moore McCalla Papers, West Virginia and Regional History Center, West Virginia University Libraries, Morgantown. The total of 383 is confirmed by Grymes in Grymes Report, 7, and John Moore McCalla to Jacob Thompson, 10 December 1860, Series 1.E, Miscellaneous Incoming Correspondence, folder 1860 "Liberated Slaves," ACSR. McCalla's age estimates are rough because he failed to designate the ages used to define "children." However, the assessment comports with other scholarly estimates of the percentages of child captives in the late Bight of Benin slave trade. According to Diouf, between 1851 and 1867, captives below the age of fifteen comprised 19 percent of all enslaved captives embarked from the Bight of Benin; see Diouf, *Dreams of Africa*, 65.

68. Johnson, *History of the Yorubas*, 109–10; Afolayan, "Kingdoms of West Africa," 161. Age-grades were also important to some societies of West Central Africa, although they were replaced by other institutions in other polities. See Vansina, *Paths in the Rainforest*, 79–80, 116–17, 278.

69. Grymes Report, 12–13; McCalla Journal, 7 August 1860; Handler, "Middle Passage and the Material Culture." My arguments on the significance of age for recaptives' survival strategies and perceptions of slavery and freedom have been reinforced and clarified by Lawrance, *Amistad's Orphans*.

70. Pearson, *Distant Freedom*, 123.

71. Kunz, "Refugee in Flight," 126, 135, 140; Chan and Loveridge, "Refugees 'in Transit.'"

72. Warner, "Social Support and Distress," 197–98.

73. Chan and Loveridge, "Refugees 'in Transit,'" 756.

74. Federal marshal Fernando Moreno, perhaps in emulation of Fort Sumter's similar usage in 1858, had unsuccessfully requested Fort Taylor, also still under construction, as a site for holding Africans seized in the course of slave trade suppression. See Fernando Moreno to Jacob Thompson, 13 May 1860, reel 6, RSI. Although President Buchanan refused Moreno's request to use the fort itself, the temporary shelter built at Whitehead Point near Fort Taylor remained under federal military guard and physically separated from the free

and enslaved residents of Key West. Marshal Moreno in fact sought to recoup the cost of renting a horse to travel three to four times daily from downtown Key West to the African Depot, a distance of approximately three-quarters of a mile. See Fernando Moreno to Jacob Thompson, 21 October 1860, reel 6, RSI. On slavery in Key West, see Smith, "Engineering Slavery," 498–500.

75. Fernando Moreno to Jacob Thompson, 10 May 1860, reel 6, RSI; McCalla Journal, 17 July 1860.

76. Fernando Moreno to Jacob Thompson, 10 May 1860, reel 6, RSI. Conditions on the island by mid-July were parched; see *Key of the Gulf*, 14 July 1860.

77. Fernando Moreno to Jacob Thompson, 13 May 1860, reel 6, RSI.

78. The nine-room shelter was reported to have a total of 9,460 square feet. Taking daily mortality into account, a peak population of about 1,329 recaptives in the depot would have occurred when the *Bogota* shipmates landed on 2 June. Even if 180 people had been in the 2,675-square-foot hospital building, as reported by a Key West newspaper on 19 May (reprinted in the *New York Times*, below), the main depot rooms, though described as "spacious and well ventilated," would have been quite crowded at about 8.2 square feet per person (roughly 1 foot 4 inches by 6 feet per person). See "Africans at Key West. Affecting Scenes among the Negroes," *NYT*, 2 June 1860.

79. "Full Particulars of the Capture of the Slaver *Wildfire*," *Herald*, 14 May 1860; Fernando Moreno to Jacob Thompson, 10 May 1860, reel 6, RSI. The USS *Wyandotte* sent a marine guard on shore to Key West with six weeks of rations. See Log of United States Steamer *Wyandott* [*sic*], 17 May 1860, LNS, and "African Depot," *Courier*, 29 May 1860.

80. Log of United States Steamer *Wyandott* [*sic*], 17 May 1860, LNS; Fernando Moreno to Jacob Thompson, 10 May 1860, reel 6, RSI. Fort Taylor's civil engineer James Clapp also lent Moreno advice and materials for the construction of the temporary camp. Moreno's letters indicate his unfulfilled expectation that Key West would become a receiving point for more recaptive Africans and would require a permanent set of buildings for that purpose.

81. Scarlet, "The Africans at Key West. The Barracoons Empty—the Rumored Attempt at a Rescue," *NYT*, 8 August 1860, 3; Young Ship Log, 1 July 1860; Fernando Moreno to Jacob Thompson, 25 July 1860, reel 6, RSI. For rumors that Key West graves stood empty to mask recaptives sold in New Orleans, see Diouf, *Dreams of Africa*, 77–78. For rumors of intended raiding of recaptured Africans as they embarked for Liberia from Fort Sumter, see "The Steam Ship *Niagara*," *Courier*, 8 September 1858.

82. Young Ship Log, 1 July 1860. The planters lodged with the U.S. agent William Young at the Russell House in Key West. Young recorded his conversation with Morrison in detail in his daily journal. In 1860, R[ichard] T. Morrison was a planter in Christ Church Parish, Charleston County. The 1850 Slave Schedule shows he owned twenty-three enslaved men and women. Since Morrison also had a son named R. T., Young may have spoken with either the son or the father. See U.S. Federal Slave schedule, R. T. Morrison in Christ Church Parish, Charleston County, September 1850, and U.S. Federal Census, *St. James Santee, Charleston, South Carolina*, 1860, *Ancestry Library* database. British spy correspondence from Havana also indicates rumors of the kidnapping and sale of more than 200 Key West recaptives to Havana. Thank you to John Harris for generously sharing this information with me (Sanchez to British Consul, 24 July 1860, FO84/1111, Foreign Office: Slave Trade Department, National Archives, London). After combing through the U.S. government records on Key West and consulting with other researchers in Key West, I have found no supporting evidence for a mass abduction from the Key West Depot. Pursuing the rumor into Cuban

archives lies beyond the scope of this book, and I leave this unresolved trail for future researchers. An abduction of this scale would have been very difficult to conceal, given all of the U.S. government departments tracking the Key West recaptives. However, if the British intelligence report of kidnapping was true, even in smaller numbers, it would further demonstrate the persisting insecurity and commodification of slave trade recaptives.

83. Camp, *Closer to Freedom*, 12–34, quotes on 12.

84. Scarlet, "The Africans at Key West. The Barracoons Empty," *NYT*, 8 August 1860; "The Africans of the Slave Bark 'Wildfire,'" *Harper's*, 2 June 1860, 344–46; "Africans at Key West. Affecting Scenes among the Negroes," *NYT*, 2 June 1860.

85. Fernando Moreno to Jacob Thompson, 2, 6, 10 May 1860, reel 6, RSI. Crew and captain on illegal slavers frequently claimed to be passengers to avoid indictment.

86. Ibid., 28 May 1860.

87. Young Ship Log, 1 July 1860.

88. "The Africans of the Slave Bark 'Wildfire,'" *Harper's*, 2 June 1860, 345.

89. Vermilyea also reports the same arrangement of captive children on the exposed deck of the *Montauk*. See *Slaver, the War, and around the World*, 7–8.

90. Young Ship Log, 1 July 1860.

91. McCalla Journal, 17 July 1860. One paper even reported that Moreno had procured "a band of music for their amusement" ("Later from Havana—Important from Key West and Mexico—Capture of the Slaver Wildfire," *Courier*, 14 May 1860).

92. Fabre, "Slave Ship Dance."

93. Camp, *Closer to Freedom*, 62, 68.

94. McCalla Journal, 17 July 1860.

95. "Africans at Key West. Affecting Scenes Among the Negroes," *NYT*, 2 June 1860, 8; "Still Another Slaver Captured," *Florida Peninsular*, 2 June 1860. In Freetown, with its more permanent liberated African yard and numerous arrivals of captured slavers, reunions were even more likely. See Peterson, *Province of Freedom*, 186–87.

96. On possibilities of relatives being sold together onto slave ships after initial capture as prisoners of war, see Rediker, *Slave Ship*, 304. For a rare eighteenth-century account of sisters reunited in the hold of a slave ship after being sold to the same European slaver, see Lovejoy, "Children of Slavery," 210.

97. Sweet, "Defying Social Death," 251–72. On the need for better language to represent non-nuclear African family forms, see Sweet, "Teaching the Modern African Diaspora," 109. On U.S. antebellum inability to recognize the plurality of various African family forms, see Lawrance, *Amistad's Orphans*, 228–38.

98. In a letter submitted to the U.S. press after his Liberian voyage, William Young referred to two of the younger women as "nieces" rather than daughters of the older woman. See "The Returning Africans. Letter from the Ship Castilian, of the Colonization Society's Expedition," *NYT*, 17 October 1860.

99. Brown, *Reaper's Garden*, 29–59.

100. Letters from T. M. Craven to Isaac Toucey, *H.R. Ex. Doc. No. 7*, 619; Young Ship Log, 1 July 1860; "The Slave Bark William," *Courier*, 23 May 1860; Fernando Moreno to Jacob Thompson, 10, 24 May 1860, reel 6, RSI; Webster Lindsly to William McLain, 3 September 1860, reel 10, RSI. For an excellent discussion of recaptive debility and disease in the aftermath of the middle passage, see Pearson, *Distant Freedom*, 154–200.

101. "Capture of the Slave Vessels and Their Cargoes," *Frank Leslie's*, 23 June 1860, 65–66; Lindsly, "Dreadful Sufferings Caused by the Slave Trade," 108–10.

102. Rosanne Adderley identifies health care as one of the major administrative challenges for British officials charged with the reception of liberated Africans in the Bahamas and Trinidad; see *"New Negroes from Africa,"* 31–32, 52.

103. Whitehurst and Skrine are reported as the two physicians in "Africans of the Slave Bark 'Wildfire,'" *Harper's*, 2 June 1860, 344. Hamilton Weedon, the Key West port physician, may have joined the effort after more recaptives arrived. Whitehurst had served in the 1830s as ACS employee and later government agent overseeing resettlement of recaptive Africans in Liberia. He married Henrietta Weedon Williams Whitehurst and was thus Weedon's brother-in-law. See Weedon and Whitehurst Papers Finding Aids, Southern Historical Collection, Wilson Special Collections Library, University of North Carolina, Chapel Hill, http://www2.lib.unc.edu/mss/inv/w/Weedon_and_Whitehurst_Family.html (accessed 17 January 2016), and 1860 Federal Census, Key West, Monroe, Florida, roll M653 108, p. 387, image 387, Family History Library Film 803108, *Ancestry Library* database.

104. Fernando Moreno to Jacob Thompson, 10 June, 25 July (emphasis in original) 1860, reel 6, RSI.

105. Pearson, *Distant Freedom*, 198.

106. Figures in this and the next paragraph are based on analysis of the death statements, arranged by date and gender, submitted by Fernando Moreno to Secretary of the Interior Jacob Thompson on 26 July 1860, reel 6, RSI: "No. 1. Statement of the Number of Births and Deaths Which Occurred at Key West, among the African Negroes Recaptured on Board of the Bark *Wildfire*"; "No. 2. Statement Showing the Number of Deaths Which Occurred at Key West, among the African Negroes Recaptured on Board of the Bark *William*"; and "No. 3. Statement Showing the Number of Deaths Which Occurred at Key West, among the African Negroes Recaptured on Board of the Bark Name Unknown [*Bogota*]." See also tables 2, 3, and 4 in this book for aggregate figures.

107. Malcom and Conyers, "Evidence for the African Cemetery at Higgs Beach," 1, 8; Swanson, "African Cemetery," 24–28.

108. Brown, "Social Death and Political Life," 1241.

109. Handler, "Prone Burial from a Plantation Slave Cemetery"; Brown, *Reaper's Garden*, 63–74; Reis, *Death Is a Festival*; Jamieson, "Material Culture and Social Death"; Frohne, *African Burial Ground in New York City*.

110. Smallwood, *Saltwater Slavery*, 60–61, 139–41, 152. Smallwood discusses Akan funerary rites that would not have been practiced by recaptives at Key West. However, her discussion concerning death outside a meaningful social and cultural context provides important insights into recaptives' social crisis.

111. Johnson, *History of the Yorubas*, 137–40.

112. Malcom and Conyers, "Evidence for the African Cemetery at Higgs Beach."

113. MacGaffey, *Religion and Society in Central Africa*, 72, 45, 55–56, 64–73. MacGaffey describes bodies buried "with their heads toward the rising sun" (45) so that when the deceased arose as ghosts in the land of the dead, they could continue a counterclockwise journey.

114. Ibid., 54. For a description of another ritual (*lufwalakazi*, from *lufwa* [death]) observed by a bereaved wife or husband with his or her relatives to "remove the curse of widowhood," see Bentley, *Appendix to the Dictionary and Grammar*, 862.

115. Ferreira, *Cross-Cultural Exchange*, 181–82, 186–87; Candido, *African Slaving Port*, 128.

116. Smallwood, *Saltwater Slavery*, 137–39. My discussion of Key West death reports is heavily influenced by Stephanie Smallwood's approach to slave ship mortality records,

which examines the daily social impact of mortality in light of the "temporal and spatial realities" of captive Africans (137).

117. "The Africans of the Slave Bark 'Wildfire,'" *Harper's*, 2 June 1860. The only birth at Key West occurred on 28 May, after this infant died.

118. Malcom, "Cemeteries at South Beach," figs. 4 and 5. The African Cemetery at Higgs Beach in Key West is now an official site on the National Register of Historic Places and has been commemorated with a public memorial.

119. The 19 May 1860 *Key of the Gulf* article was reprinted by several papers, including "The African Depot," *Courier*, 29 May 1860; "Africans at Key West. Affecting Scenes among the Negroes," *NYT*, 2 June 1860; and "Still Another Slaver Captured," *Florida Peninsular*, 2 June 1860. See Browne, *Key West*, 17.

120. Similar evidence for combined European and African burial practices appears in several infant coffin burials in the Rupert's Valley cemetery, St. Helena. See Pearson, Jeffs, Witkin, and MacQuarrie, *Infernal Traffic*, 108, 159–60.

121. Secretary of the Interior Thompson, for example, calculated his reimbursable expenses for housing the recaptives at Key West at 37 cents per person per day. More importantly, the U.S. government had contracted to pay the American Colonization Society a fixed amount of money per person for one year of support in Liberia. See Thompson to McLain, 13 August 1860, reel 1, RSI. Thompson made his remarks in the context of the ACS's failure to meet contractual obligations to remove recaptured Africans from Key West by a certain date. See also Younger, "Liberia and the Last Slave Ships," 433.

122. Examples of the naval capture genre of engraving include "Capture of a Brazilian Slaver by 'H.M.S. Rattler' off Lagos," *Illustrated London News*, 29 December 1849, 440; "H. M. Gun-boat 'Teaser,' Capturing the Slaver," *Illustrated London News*, 19 September 1857, 284; and Foote, *Africa and the American Flag*, 286.

123. "The Africans of the Slave Bark 'Wildfire,'" *Harper's*, 2 June 1860, 344 (emphasis added).

124. Stephanie M. H. Camp, "Race and Visual Culture before the Twentieth Century" (unpublished manuscript shared by Camp with author in July 2012), forthcoming in *Oxford Handbook of the History of Race*, ed. Matthew Pratt Guterl.

125. Coghe, "Problem of Freedom," 485; Anderson et al., "Using African Names," 167; Adderley, *"New Negroes from Africa,"* 95; Mamigonian, "To Be a Liberated African in Brazil," 54.

126. Register of the *Águila*, FO84/128 version, *Liberated Africans Project*, http://www .liberatedafricans.org/hstc/ships/18_aguila/08_aguila_fo84_la_rigister.pdf (accessed 24 February 2016).

127. Mamigonian, "To Be a Liberated African in Brazil," 44, 51; Nwokeji and Eltis, "Roots of the African Diaspora," 371–73.

128. The most well known of these are the photographs of East African recaptives on a dhow seized by the HMS *Daphne* on 1 November 1868, FO84/1310, National Archives, London.

129. The exception is the *Castilian* roll of names discussed in Chapters 5 and 6. However, this list contained no other descriptions beyond gender, age, and newly assigned English-language names.

130. "The Africans of the Slave Bark 'Wildfire,'" *Harper's*, 2 June 1860, 344.

131. "Full Particulars of the Capture of the Slaver *Wildfire*," *Herald*, 14 May 1860.

132. The 1860 census listed Key West's population at 2,832, of which 15 percent (435) were enslaved. See Langley and Langley, *Key West*, 19.

133. "The Africans of the Slave Bark 'Wildfire,'" *Harper's*, 2 June 1860, 344–45.

134. "The Captured Africans—the Necessity of Doing Something," *Herald*, 4 June 1860.

135. Stebbins, *City of Intrigue*; Langley and Langley, *Key West*, 12–17.

136. Swanson, *Slave Ship Guerrero*, 33–45.

137. Some U.S. publications also experimented with illustrated news soon after 1842 but struggled to find the market and the technology that would make their endeavors profitable. In 1855, however, an English-born engraver and former employee at the *Illustrated London News*, Henry Carter (under the pseudonym Frank Leslie), hatched *Frank Leslie's Illustrated News*, which revolutionized U.S. newspaper illustration. The Harper Brothers publishing house joined the competition in 1857 by marketing the new *Harper's Weekly* to a more genteel, middle-class readership whose sensibilities were not completely attuned to *Frank Leslie's* hard-hitting urban exposés. See Brown, *Beyond the Lines*, 4, 12–14, 25–31, 41; Zboray, "Antebellum Reading," 76; Pearson, "*Frank Leslie's*"; Lehuu, *Carnival on the Page*; and Sinnema, *Dynamics of the Pictured Page*, 61–65.

138. "Capture of a Slaver," *Illustrated London News*, 19 September 1857, 283–84. See also "Capture of a Slaver" from "A young officer of HMS *Antelope*," *Illustrated London News*, 17 October 1857, 393; "Chase and Capture of a Slaver," *Illustrated London News*, 1 May 1858, 435–36; and "The Slaver 'Sunny South,' Alias 'Emanuela,'" *Illustrated London News*, 8 December 1860, 546, 530. Editors' references to the submitted photographs or sketches served to authenticate the newspapers' engravings. Sinnema, *Dynamics of the Printed Page*, 63–71, discusses the *Illustrated London News* "artist as reporter (Special Artist)," the local commissioned artist, and the in-house artist who drew images based on newspaper reporting; however, Sinnema does not discuss the sketches and photographs submitted to the press by interested observers.

139. "Capture of a Slaver," *Illustrated London News*, 20 June 1857, 595–96; *Voyages*, ID #4229, *Zeldina*, beginning in New York and embarking 500 African captives at Cabinda.

140. "Capture of a Slaver," *Illustrated London News*, 20 June 1857, 595.

141. Bender, *Antislavery Debate*; Eltis, *Economic Growth*; Davis, *Inhuman Bondage*, 231–49.

142. "Capture of a Slaver," *Illustrated London News*, 20 June 1857, 595.

143. See Anderson et al., "Using African Names," 181.

144. Adderley confirms the self-congratulatory tenor of Colonial Office officials charged with overseeing liberated Africans in the British West Indies; see *"New Negroes from Africa,"* 43, 48. For comparison, see the analysis of mainstream French antislavery framing of lithographs depicting Brazilian slavery, in Slenes, "African Abrahams."

145. Zboray, "Antebellum Reading," 77. Although *Frank Leslie's* and *Harper's* took Unionist positions after the outbreak of civil war, during the 1860 summer months, they still sought to maintain sectional neutrality. See Brown, *Beyond the Lines*, 46–47; Pearson, "*Frank Leslie's*," 88, 92; and Mason, "Keeping Up Appearances," 809–32.

146. *Harper's* opened its story on Key West similarly with an account of naval capture. Both papers used familiar devices to establish authenticity by noting the origins of the images: "From a Daguerreotype," in the case of *Harper's*, and, in *Frank Leslie's*, from the camera of Newburgh, New York, photographist David Lawrence. See "Capture of the Slave Vessels and Their Cargoes," *Frank Leslie's*, 23 June 1860, 65–66. David T. Lawrence is listed under "Daguerreotypists, Ambrotypists and Photographists" in the 1859 New York State Business Directory, 383, and as a maker of "Lockets and Miniatures" in the IRS Tax Assessment Lists for New York, District 11, November 1864, *Ancestry Library* database.

147. "Capture of the Slave Vessels and Their Cargoes," *Frank Leslie's*, 23 June 1860, 65–66.

148. "The Africans of the Slave Bark 'Wildfire,'" *Harper's*, 2 June 1860, 345.

149. See Rediker, *Slave Ship*, 143.

150. Fernando Moreno to Jacob Thompson, 10 May 1860, reel 6, RSI. Mel Fisher Maritime Museum archaeologist Corey Malcom showed me the probable location of the *Wildfire* on the wharf near Fort Taylor during a tour of Key West, 10 February 2009.

151. Diouf, *Dreams of Africa*, 61.

152. Wallis, "Black Bodies, White Science," 46–56. See also Stepan, *Picturing Tropical Nature*, 97–98.

153. Wallis, "Black Bodies, White Science," 49.

154. For a discussion of both academic and popular uses of ethnographic photography, see Edwards introduction and Poignant, "Surveying the Field of View," 42–73.

155. "Chiefs of the Soudan, Etc. Africa," *Illustrated London News*, 24 April 1858, 417.

156. "Death of John McNevin: A Man Who Sketched Battle Pictures in Two Wars," *Brooklyn Daily Eagle*, 1 March 1894; *The Brooklyn City Directory for the Year Ending May 1, 1862* (Brooklyn: J. Lain & Co.), 295, http://www.bklynlibrary.org/citydir/ (accessed 10 June 2015). McNevin signed the *Wildfire* illustration "M'N." My survey of McNevin's varying signatures in other *Harper's* issues in 1859–61 led me to the conclusion that this illustration is McNevin's work. To my knowledge, the artist of this well-known *Wildfire* image has not been previously identified.

157. 1860 Manuscript Census, Brooklyn Ward 13, District 2, Kings, New York, roll M653 772, p. 997, image 359, Family History Library Film 803772, *Ancestry Library* database; Voorsanger and Howat, *Art and the Empire City*, 255.

158. Sometime between 1853 and 1860, John McNevin immigrated to the United States. There is a small chance he was working at the *Illustrated London News* when it published the *Zeldina* images, for which the artist is unknown.

159. Descriptions of women's shaved heads illustrate how the ethnographic lens obscured the experience of commodification in the slave trade, for captives routinely had their heads shaved before embarking from African slaving ports. See Diouf, *Dreams of Africa*, 57.

160. "The Africans of the Slave Bark 'Wildfire,'" *Harper's*, 2 June 1860, 345.

161. On "image-text collaboration" and the generation of meaning through interaction between words and pictures in illustrated weeklies, see Sinnema, *Dynamics of the Pictured Page*, 2–3, 30–48, 30.

162. Sinnema makes a similar point regarding the function of illustrated travel literature in Victorian England; see ibid., 45.

163. Wallis, "Black Bodies, White Science," 55; Foreman, "Who's Your Mama?," 517.

164. See, for example, "Stowing the Cargo of a Slaver at Night," in Howe, *Life and Death on the Ocean*, facing p. 537, and "Blacks in the Ship's Hold," by J. M. Rugendas, as discussed in Slenes, "African Abrahams," 150, 160.

165. Morgan, *Laboring Women*, 12–49.

166. For similar open-blouse images in illustrated news, see "Women of the Ouled-Riah Tribe," in "Modern Algiers," *Harper's*, 4 December 1858, 772–73. See also the central female figure in "New Blacks," by J. M. Rugendas, as discussed in Slenes, "African Abrahams," 156–57.

167. Thank you to Gabrielle Foreman for important insights on the analysis of nineteenth-century domestic portraiture in this image.

168. Williams, *Alchemy of Race and Rights*.

169. Thompson to McLain, 9 June 1860 (suggestions originally made by the ACS leader McLain and approved by Thompson), reel 1, RSI.

170. Young Ship Log, 1 July 1860.

171. Grymes Report, 31; Webster Lindsly to McLain, 3 September 1860, reel 10, RSI.

172. Webster Lindsly to McLain, 3 September 1860, reel 10, RSI.

Chapter 4

1. "The Three African Boys—Further Efforts to Converse with Them," *NYT*, 30 August 1860. On conditions in the jail, see "Eldridge-Street Jail" and "The Black Hole on Eldridge-Street," *NYT*, 25 May 1857.

2. "The Slavers in Port—Visit to the Three Captive Africans in Eldridge-Street Jail," *NYT*, 17 August 1860. The Eldridge Street jail was, in fact, the same jail where Mahommah Gardo Baquaqua had been confined for several weeks after he sought his freedom from a Brazilian ship captain who had sailed to New York City in 1847. See Law and Lovejoy, *Biography of Mahommah Gardo Baquaqua*, 45–46.

3. The egalitarian concept of "human rights" discussed here extends beyond African American abolitionists to both white and black activists who embraced immediate abolition. See Stauffer, *Black Hearts of Men*, 98. However, this chapter emphasizes the stake that black abolitionists in particular had in asserting their human rights during the 1840s and 1850s in the face of the polygenist argument.

4. Rael, "Common Nature, a United Destiny," 197; Bay, *White Image in the Black Mind*, 38–74. See also Melish, "'Condition' Debate and Racial Discourse," and Sinha, "Coming of Age," 27–28.

5. Curry, *Free Black*, table A-7, 250. In absolute terms, New York's African American population fell from its peak 16,358 in 1840 to 12,472 in 1860. Leslie Harris attributes the decline to economic hard times, political discrimination, the threat of slave catchers, and outmigration to Brooklyn and rural areas to the north and west; see Harris, *In the Shadow of Slavery*, 275. Key studies of African Americans in New York include Hodges, *Root and Branch*; Harris, *In the Shadow of Slavery*; Alexander, *African or American?*; Wilder, *In the Company of Black Men*; and Hodges, *David Ruggles*.

6. Sinha, "Black Abolitionism," 241; Wilder, *In the Company of Black Men*, 36–53.

7. Harris, *In the Shadow of Slavery*, 212; Hodges, *David Ruggles*, 4 (practical abolition), 97–98, 131.

8. Law and Lovejoy, *Biography of Mahommah Gardo Baquaqua*, 45–46, 195–212. This rescue is also discussed (with some inaccuracies) in 1860 in relation to the *William R. Kibby* boys in "The Slavers in Port—Visit to the Three Captive Africans in Eldridge-Street Jail," *NYT*, 17 August 1860.

9. "The Slave Trade of New York," *World*, 29 June 1860.

10. Howard, *American Slavers and the Federal Law*, 32–39, 53–55; Fish, "War on the Slave Trade," 156–57; Vinson, "Law as Lawbreaker."

11. Foner, *Business and Slavery*; Quigley, "Southern Slavery in a Free City."

12. "The Slave-Trade—the Actual Character of the Traffic," *NYT*, 17 March 1860; Howard, *American Slavers and the Federal Law*, 49; Davis, "James Buchanan," 448.

13. Many of the remaining twenty-two voyages began in Cuba but often utilized American-built ships, the U.S. flag, and American financial backing. See *Voyages*, http://slavevoyages.org/voyages/EyV7qP9t (accessed 27 February 2016).

14. *Voyages*, ID #4362, for New York origins of *Wildfire* 1860 voyage; Drake and Shufeldt, "Secret History of the Slave Trade," 221.

15. Vermilyea, *Slaver, the War, and around the World*, 5.

16. "Is the Plan of the American Union under the Constitution Anti-Slavery or Not?," 160.

17. Harris, *In the Shadow of Slavery*, 170–216; Hodges, *Root and Branch*, 187–226, 256–61; White, *Stories of Freedom*; McHenry, *Forgotten Readers*, 84–140; Wilder, *In the Company of Black Men*, 101–80.

18. On the increasingly dire situation of northern African American communities, see Harris, *In the Shadow of Slavery*, 264–78; Rael, *Black Identity and Black Protest*, 237–78; Swift, *Black Prophets of Justice*, 244–316; and Stauffer, "Fighting the Devil with His Own Fire," 74–77.

19. On the political and cultural significance of the *Anglo-African Magazine* and the *Weekly*, see Ball, *To Live an Antislavery Life*, 109–31, and Jackson, "'Cultural Stronghold.'"

20. "The Revival of an Old Branch of Commerce," *Weekly Anglo-African*, 23 June 1860.

21. Fish, "War on the Slave Trade," 155.

22. Vinson, "Law as Lawbreaker," 37–42.

23. Howard, *American Slavers and the Federal Law*, 194–96.

24. "The Revival of an Old Branch of Commerce," *Weekly Anglo-African*, 23 June 1860.

25. "More Slave-Hunting in New York," *Weekly Anglo-African*, 5 May 1860.

26. Anbinder, "Isaiah Rynders," 46.

27. For proslavery imperialism, see Johnson, *River of Dark Dreams*, 14–15, 303–29.

28. Harris, *In the Shadow of Slavery*, 243, notes that William J. Wilson wrote in the mid-1850s for Douglass's newspaper *The North Star* under the pseudonym "Ethiop." See also Rael, *Black Identity and Black Protest*, 238, and Bay, *White Image in the Black Mind*, 75.

29. Sinha, *Counterrevolution of Slavery*, 157–72.

30. Ethiop, "The Anglo-African and the African Slave Trade," 285–86. Ethiop's point here was that a reopened slave trade would have unintended consequences for whites: "When the final day does come, as come it must, and should it be a hand-to-hand struggle, it may then be with the Anglo-African a question of numbers on this continent." For similar sharp satirical analysis, see Ethiop, "What Shall We Do with the White People?"

31. "That Oyster Bed," *Weekly Anglo-African*, 7 October 1859. On African American critiques of liberty rhetoric in the revolutionary and early national period, see Sinha, "Alternative Tradition of Radicalism."

32. For titles available from Thomas Hamilton at 48 Beekman St., the *Anglo-African* office, see *Weekly Anglo-African*, 24 November 1860.

33. Delany, *Blake*, 3, xi. On the political significance of Delany's novel, see Stauffer, *Black Hearts of Men*, 182, and Sundquist, *To Wake the Nations*, 182–85.

34. "The Horrors of the Slave Trade, A Narrative of Thrilling Interest," *Weekly Anglo-African*, 24 November 1860; Drake and West, *Revelations of a Slave Smuggler*.

35. On the significance of African American reading rooms and connections to the black press, see McHenry, *Forgotten Readers*, 84–140. McHenry notes (135) that the *Anglo-African* reading room opened in November 1859 and was located at 178 Prince Street.

36. "The Re-Opening of the Slave Trade," *Anglo-African Magazine* 1, no. 9 (September 1859): 301. Anti–slave trade activism can be understood as part of the *Anglo-African Magazine*'s revolutionary transnational ideology. See Ball, *To Live an Antislavery Life*, 117–24. On the idea of a "redeemer race," see Bay, *White Image in the Black Mind*, 38–74.

37. "'The Rev. J. W. C. Pennington,'" *Anti-Slavery Reporter*, 28 June 1843.

38. Blyden, "Chapter in the History of the African Slave Trade," 184. On French recruitment of African apprenticed labor, see Vos, "'Without the Slave Trade.'"

39. In addition to the New York scholarship on this point, cited previously, see the recent study of the problem of northern slavery in the early republic period by Gigantino, *Ragged Road to Abolition*, and Sinha, *Slave's Cause*, 65–96.

40. Walker, "Walker's Appeal"; Quarles, *Black Abolitionists*, 3–22; Sidbury, *Becoming African in America*, 169, 190; Blackett, *Building an Antislavery Wall*, 47–78; Rael, *Black Identity and Black Protest*, 39, 90, 160, 163–64, 181; Hodges, *David Ruggles*, 39–41.

41. "Colonization Society" and "For the Freedom's Journal," *Freedom's Journal*, 7 September 1827.

42. Blackett, *Building an Antislavery Wall*, 47–78; Cornish and Wright, *Colonization Scheme*.

43. Pennington, *Fugitive Blacksmith*, 54; Blackett, *Building an Antislavery Wall*, 175–78. In addition to opposing the ACS, Pennington almost always opposed emigration to Africa, although at certain points in his career he explored Jamaica as a possible destination for black emigrants from the United States. See Alexander, *African or American?*, 222, and Blackett, *Beating against the Barriers*, 75.

44. Blackett, *Beating against the Barriers*, 55; Hodges, *David Ruggles*, 199; Harris, *In the Shadow of Slavery*, 272.

45. On African American debates over the colonization movement, see Moses, *Liberian Dreams*; Power-Green, *Against Wind and Tide*; and Everill, "'Destiny Seems to Point Me to That Country.'"

46. Canney, *Africa Squadron*, 99, 106, 123–24, 149.

47. Fanning, *Caribbean Crossing*.

48. Blackett, *Building an Antislavery Wall*, 175–78; Swift, *Black Prophets of Justice*, 286–99; Blackett, "Martin R. Delany and Robert Campbell"; Fairhead, Geysbeek, Holsoe, and Leach, *African-American Exploration in West Africa*.

49. Blackett, *Building an Antislavery Wall*, 162–94; Swift, *Black Prophets of Justice*, 252–53, 285, 286, 292–93.

50. "Great Meeting in New York," *Weekly Anglo-African*, 28 April 1860; "The Colored Citizens of New York and the African Civilization Society," *Liberator*, 4 May 1860, 72; J. W. C. Pennington, "Rev. J. Sella Martin and the African Civilization Society," *Weekly Anglo-African*, 12 May 1860; "Meeting of the African Civilization Society," *Weekly Anglo-African*, 17 March 1860; Alexander, *African or American?*, 141–49.

51. "The Colored Citizens of New York and the African Civilization Society," *Weekly Anglo-African*, 21 April 1860.

52. Blackett, *Beating against the Barriers*, 75; Swift, *Black Prophets of Justice*, 297. For details, see William Herries, "The African Civilization Society," *Frederick Douglass' Paper*, 8 July 1859, in which Herries lists Pennington on the side of African Civilization Society supporters, and "The Deceptive African Civilization Society," *Frederick Douglass' Paper*, 22 July 1859, in which George Downing notes Pennington's disavowal of the society.

53. Douglass, *Claims of the Negro*, 10; Pennington, *Text Book*; Garnet, *Past and the Present Condition*, 12.

54. Bay, *White Image in the Black Mind*, 8, 15, 19, 36–74.

55. Pennington, *Text Book*, 54. On Pennington as "steadfastly egalitarian," see Bay, *White Image in the Black Mind*, 51. See also Sinha, "Coming of Age," 27–28.

56. Garnet, *Past and the Present Condition*, 6. See also Sinha, "Coming of Age," 27–28.

57. Douglass, *Claims of the Negro*, 9–10.

58. Frederick Douglass, "Postmaster General Blair and Frederick Douglass," *Douglass' Monthly*, October 1862, 726.

59. Rael, "Common Nature, a United Destiny," 185; Rael, *Black Identity and Black Protest*, 237–78; Melish, "'Condition' Debate and Racial Discourse"; Bay, *White Image in the Black Mind*, 18, 41, 219–22.

60. Bay, *White Image in the Black Mind*, 58–63; McCune Smith and Stauffer, *Works of James McCune Smith*, xxix–xxxiv.

61. McCune Smith, "Civilization"; Bay, *White Image in the Black Mind*, 61.

62. "Annual Meeting of the Coloured Orphan Asylum," *National Anti-Slavery Standard*, 22 February 1849.

63. Concession, one of five tropes of engagement with racial science that Rael identifies, acknowledged the degradation of a black subject in order to position "African Americans as a group requiring redemption from injustice" (Rael, "Common Nature, a United Destiny," 188).

64. "Annual Meeting of the Coloured Orphan Asylum," *National Anti-Slavery Standard*, 22 February 1849.

65. Douglass, *Claims of the Negro*, 34.

66. Sinha, *Counterrevolution of Slavery*, 125–54.

67. *The World* began publishing its daily paper in June 1860. It aimed to promote middle-class values of Christianity and self-improvement in a secular newspaper. See editorial statement of purpose, *The World*, 14 June 1860. The *Liberator* would not have been a likely choice for Pennington in any case, since he had been at odds with the Garrisonians for at least a decade due to his affiliation with the Presbyterian denomination as well as rumors of irregularities in his fundraising activities. See Blackett, *Beating against the Barriers*, 48–50.

68. Blackett, *Beating against the Barriers*, 20–22. On black millennial thought, see Rael, *Black Identity and Black Protest*, 266–78; Blight, *Frederick Douglass' Civil War*, 8–10; and Swift, *Black Prophets of Justice*, 249–51.

69. Pennington, "Great Conflict Requires Great Faith," 344–45.

70. Pennington, *Fugitive Blacksmith*, 1–11.

71. Hodges, *David Ruggles*, 34. Hodges refers to a specific New York cohort, but the term "Freedom Generation" first appears in Berlin, *Generations of Captivity*, 8, 245–71.

72. 1855 New York Census and 1860 Federal Census, *Ancestry Library* database. Thomas H. Pennington was born in 1844, when Pennington was married to Harriet Pennington.

73. This biographical summary draws from Pennington's narrative as well as Blackett, *Beating against the Barriers*, 6–70; Swift, *Black Prophets of Justice*, 204–43; and Webber, *American to the Backbone*.

74. See Chapter 1 for a discussion of the period of "second slavery."

75. Pennington, "American Slave in England."

76. Pennington, "Review of Slavery and the Slave Trade." A comparative discussion of slavery as an institution not born in Africa but "an institution of the *dark age!*" appears in Pennington, *Text Book*, 43 (emphasis in original).

77. Moses, *Classical Black Nationalism*; Moses, *Golden Age of Black Nationalism*, 33–55. For eighteenth-century African American thought on African redemption and the nineteenth-century shifts in that thinking on African Americans' relationship to Africa, see Sidbury, *Becoming African in America*.

78. Pennington, "Intelligence from Jamaica."

79. Pennington, "Self-Redeeming Power of the Colored Races of the World," 315, 314.

80. Pennington, "Instructions of the Executive Committee," 66.

81. Blackett, *Beating against the Barriers*, 22–25.

82. Ibid., 27.

83. Swift, *Black Prophets of Justice*, 204, 237, 245, also makes this point in reference to Pennington and Henry Highland Garnet. See "benighted" in "Instructions of the Executive Committee," 65, and Pennington, "Letter from Rev. Dr. Pennington." See also "Anti-Slavery Fair," *Frederick Douglass' Paper*, 11 December 1851, and "The Late Fugitive Slave Case," *Frederick Douglass' Paper*, 9 June 1854. In the appendix of his narrative, Pennington also refers to "the native Africans" owned by Frisby Tilghman, who would stand alongside the slaveholder before the judgment seat after his death; see Pennington, *Fugitive Blacksmith*, 82. "Mandingo," used as an ethnonym in North American sources, usually referred to Mande-speaking people (often Muslim) from Senegambia and Sierra Leone. See Gomez, *Exchanging Our Country Marks*, 39–40, 68, and Hall, *Slavery and African Ethnicities*, 48, 54, 99–100.

84. "'The Rev. J. W. C. Pennington,'" *Anti-Slavery Reporter*, 28 June 1843.

85. Pennington, "Report on Colonization," 47.

86. Pennington, "Review of Slavery and the Slave Trade," 93. In *Text Book*, 42–43, Pennington uses de las Casas's metaphor of a devouring lion to describe the Spanish colonization of the Americas. However, Pennington did not address the recommendation, which de las Casas later regretted, that Spain consider Africans as an alternative source of enslaved labor. See Clayton, *Bartolomé de las Casas*, 103, 135–39. Earlier black abolitionist anticolonial arguments appear in Cornish and Wright, *Colonization Scheme*, 12–14.

87. Pennington, "Report on Colonization," 56. Pennington characterized the right of African Americans to "remain where they are, and eventually occupy the lands which they have watered with their sweat and tears," as "distributive justice" (Pennington, introduction to *Narrative of the Events from the Life of J. H. Banks*, 5).

88. *National Anti-Slavery Standard*, 25 June 1846, 15; Blackett, *Beating against the Barriers*, 40.

89. Blackett, *Beating against the Barriers*, 32–43.

90. Rev. Dr. Pennington, "Successful Purchase of a D.D.," *National Anti-Slavery Standard*, 19 June 1851, and "The Purchaser of Dr. Pennington," *National Anti-Slavery Standard*, 23 August 1856.

91. Blackett, *Beating against the Barriers*, 57; Swift, *Black Prophets of Justice*, 263. On the vigilance committee, see Harris, *In the Shadow of Slavery*, 206–14, and Hodges, *David Ruggles*, 1, 5, 89–101, 127, 133.

92. "Escape and Capture of Stephen Pembroke, Related by Himself," *New-York Daily Tribune*, 18 July 1854; Blackett, *Beating against the Barriers*, 57–59; Foner, *Gateway to Freedom*, 169–71; Webber, *American to the Backbone*, 404–7, 410–12; Swift, *Black Prophets of Justice*, 264.

93. Still, *Underground Railroad*, 172–74.

94. The allegation that Pennington had become a "confirmed drunkard" comes from Lewis Tappan's letterbook report of an 1854 meeting with Samuel Cornish. Although it is evident that the mid- to late 1850s constituted a crisis period for Pennington personally and professionally, the degree of Pennington's use of alcohol in the crisis is less clear. Pennington's biographers have taken the drinking charge seriously, but at least one scholar questions the motives and meaning of Tappan's phrasing. Blackett interprets Tappan's report as confirmation that Pennington "had lapsed into alcoholism" (*Beating against the Barriers*, 72). Swift uses the presbytery hearing minutes to conclude that the church's disciplinary proceedings indicated the "occasional or regular consumption of alcohol" (*Black Prophets of Justice*, 269–70). Webber is more defensive of Pennington, pointing out Cornish's anger at the Presbyterian Church's position on slavery, the condemnation of temperance societies of even limited alcohol consumption, and the "gossipy" nature of Tappan's remarks against

Pennington; see *American to the Backbone*, 408–10. If Pennington was indeed consuming alcohol on a regular basis, it would have violated his own temperance position. In one of his sermons Pennington drew a parallel between the slaveholder, the lottery dealer, and the rum seller; see Pennington, *Two Years' Absence*, 25.

95. Blackett, *Beating against the Barriers*, 71, 79. "His problems with alcoholism," writes historian R. J. M. Blackett, "which seem to have lasted until 1858, temporarily destroyed Pennington's self-esteem." In the last decade of his life, he never returned to his previous national leadership status.

96. Pennington to Gerrit Smith, 5 September 1859, Gerrit Smith Papers, Syracuse University, Black Abolitionist Papers, *Proquest*, http://gateway.proquest.com/openurl?url_ver =Z39.88–2004&res_dat=xri:bap:&rft_dat=xri:bap:rec:bap:10171 (accessed 17 January 2016). Pennington asked John Jay for a $5 loan, noting that his Newtown teaching and preaching garnered only a small annual salary of $200. See J. W. C. Pennington to John Jay, 12, 17 December 1859, Columbia University, John Jay Papers, Black Abolitionist Papers, *Proquest*, http://o-gateway.proquest.com.oasys.lib.oxy.edu/openurl?url_ver=Z39.88–2004&res_dat =xri:bap:&rft_dat=xri:bap:rec:bap:00279 (accessed 17 January 2016). See also Blackett, *Beating against the Barriers*, 39, 73.

97. "Lecture by Dr. Pennington," *Weekly Anglo-African*, 15 October 1859; Pennington to Gerrit Smith, 5 September 1859, Gerrit Smith Papers, Syracuse University, Black Abolitionist Papers, *Proquest*, http://gateway.proquest.com/openurl?url_ver=Z39.88–2004&res_dat =xri:bap:&rft_dat=xri:bap:rec:bap:10171 (accessed 17 January 2016); "Free Suffrage Convention," *Weekly Anglo-African*, 19 May 1860.

98. Pennington, "Slave Trade—Wildfire" (emphasis in original).

99. On Foote's *Africa and the American Flag*, see Chapter 1.

100. Pennington, "Slave Trade—Wildfire."

101. Pennington, "Why the Guilty Slavers Are Never Punished."

102. "A Thought by the Way," *Colored American*, 17 April 1841.

103. "'A Thought by the Way,'" *Colored American*, 24 April 1841.

104. "The Captured Africans," *World*, 14 July 1860.

105. J. L. D., "Africa for the Africans," *World*, 16 July 1860.

106. "What Shall Be Done with the Recaptured Africans?," *World*, 16 July 1860. On African American legal challenges to segregated streetcars and the development of "minority-rights advocacy" (133), see Volk, *Moral Minorities*, 132–66.

107. "The Captured Africans," *World*, 14 July 1860.

108. "What Shall Be Done with the Darkies?," *Liberator*, 31 August 1860, 138.

109. J. L. D., "Africa for the Africans," *World*, 16 July 1860.

110. *Voyages*, ID #4356. The *William R. Kibby* embarked 724 African captives and disembarked only 600. Other newspaper reports indicated 400 disembarked in Cuba but did not mention the original number of captives.

111. Log of United States Steamer *Crusader*, Commanded by Lieut J. N. Maffitt, 23 July–30 July 1860, LNS; "The Slaver Kibby and Her Captain," *Times-Picayune*, 8 August 1860.

112. Jacob Thompson to Isaiah Rynders, 24 August, 3, 17 September, 17 October 1860, reel 1, RSI. Thompson mistakenly calls Rynders "Josiah."

113. "The Slave-Trade," *NYT*, 16 August 1860; "The Slavers in Port—Visit to the Three Captive Africans in Eldridge-Street Jail," *NYT*, 17 August 1860; "The Three African Boys—Further Efforts to Converse with Them," *NYT*, 30 August 1860.

114. In addition to Pennington, *Fugitive Blacksmith*, 9–11, 21–22, see also the attention

given to the space of the jail as a "place of punishment," rather than a "place of detention," in Pennington, *Narrative of the Events from the Life of J. H. Banks*, 81. I use "carceral spaces" here to mean formal jails and prisons, but Pennington's experiences would have alerted him to the broader "remaking of space as discipline" discussed by Walter Johnson in his analysis of the Lower Mississippi's "carceral landscape," in *River of Dark Dreams*, 209–43.

115. Rediker, *Amistad Rebellion*, 122–51. Rediker places the *Amistad* shipmates' jailing within a broader context of the "transatlantic chain of incarceration" that accompanied the slave trade. See also Christopher, Pybus, and Rediker, *Many Middle Passages*, 2. My work shows the relevance of this "chain of incarceration" to recaptive experience. See Fett, "Middle Passages and Forced Migrations."

116. Dudley (alias James Snowden) had been found a fugitive slave and given a two-year sentence in New York for theft. Jay and Pennington secured a pardon twenty-four hours before slaveowner Allen Thomas returned to claim Dudley as a fugitive at the end of his sentence. For details, see "Escape of a Slave," *Liberator*, 18 May 1852; "Gov. Hunt and the Fugitive Slave Nicholas Dudley," *Liberator*, 28 May 1852, 1–2; "Slave Case," *North Star*, 13 June 1850; "James P. Snowden," *Anti-Slavery Standard*, 3 June 1852; and Henry Bibb, "Slave Hunters Baffled," *Voice of the Fugitive*, 17 June 1852. See also Foner, *Gateway to Freedom*, 138.

117. "The Slavers in Port—Visit to the Three Captive Africans in Eldridge-Street Jail," *NYT*, 17 August 1860. Beyond probabilities known from the West Central African slaving routes at this time, the boys' words for cardinal numerals 1 through 10 reprinted in the *New York Times* align closely with Kikongo dictionaries. See Laman, *Grammar of the Kongo Language*.

118. "The Three African Boys—Further Efforts to Converse with Them," *NYT*, 30 August 1860. The 1850 U.S. Federal Census lists Henry Carter, born in Africa, a fifty-two-year-old whitewasher who lived in the First Ward of New York; see *Ancestry Library* database. Carter brought a "paper of candy" to give the boys.

119. The *William R. Kibby* was condemned by the Southern District of New York Court and sold as a prize ship, but it is not clear whether the boys ever served as witnesses in these proceedings. See Howard, *Americans Slavers and the Federal Law*, 221.

120. Advocacy on behalf of children of color in New York reached back to the 1830s, when Elizur Wright Jr., Arthur Tappan, William Goodell, and a group of black New York residents worked on behalf of black children kidnapped from New York's streets and condemned to southern enslavement. See Hodges's discussion of the 1834 Henry Scott case, *David Ruggles*, 61–62.

121. Jacob Thompson to Josiah [Isaiah] Rynders, 24 August, 17 September, 17 October 1860, reel 1, RSI.

122. On Rynders's political career, see Anbinder, "Isaiah Rynders," 31–53, quote on 32.

123. New York courts later dismissed Tappan's charges of assault against Rynders. See "The Three Negroes and Marshal Rynders. Beauty, Philanthropy and Ruffianism" and "A Question Answered," *Anti-Slavery Bugle*, 10 November 1860.

124. C. C. Hoffman, "From the Rev. C. C. Hoffman," *African Repository* 37, no. 5 (May 1861): 132–34.

125. Blackett, *Beating against the Barriers*, 78, 79, 84; Webber, *American to the Backbone*, 505–57.

126. Pennington, "Self-Redeeming Power of the Colored Races of the World," 314.

127. Hodges mentions increasing illegal slave trade activity from New York as one of

the factors motivating David Ruggles in the direction of a more confrontational politics; see *David Ruggles*, 4.

128. Sinha, "Coming of Age."

129. Equiano, *Interesting Narrative*.

130. "Edward Jordan," *Weekly Anglo-African*, 24 November 1860 (emphasis added).

Chapter 5

1. Young Ship Log, 17 August 1860. If the woman were six or seven months pregnant, as Young guessed, she would have conceived before embarking on the *Wildfire* from the Congo/northern Angola region.

2. Brown, "Social Death and Political Life," 1246.

3. Benjamin Lawrance discusses the tensions between scholarship that emphasizes "recreation" of Africa and his own focus on "the mechanics of survival in the context of trauma and distress" (*Amistad's Orphans*, 30).

4. Miller, "Retention, Reinvention, and Remembering."

5. Hawthorne, "'Being Now, as It Were, One Family,'" 63.

6. Lawrance, *Amistad's Orphans*, 6, 34.

7. Young Ship Log, 17 June 1860. On the back of the sketch Young wrote, "This red plaid shirt was sent to the wash at Cape Mount, Liberia, and never returned. Nigger stole it." Interestingly, *Captain Canot* mentioned that Canot's "well-known cruising dress" included a red flannel shirt. Another depiction of a plaid shirt as a hallmark of the tropical explorer is featured in Henry Walter Bates, *The Naturalist on the River Amazons* (1863), in Stepan, *Picturing Tropical Nature*, 22.

8. "The Returning Africans. Letter from the Ship Castilian, of the Colonization Society's Expedition," *NYT*, 17 October 1860; "The Captured Negroes Homeward Bound," *Herald*, 24 November 1860.

9. McCalla Journal, 1 August 1860. On the idea of tropicality in the Western imagination, see Stepan, *Picturing Tropical Nature*.

10. J. M. Grymes to Col. B. A. Payne, 18 December 1860, Series 1.E, Miscellaneous Incoming Correspondence, folder 1860 "Liberated Slaves," ACSR.

11. Domingues da Silva, Eltis, Misevich, and Ojo, "Diaspora of Africans," 352–53; Adderley, *"New Negroes from Africa,"* 23–91; Schuler, *Alas! Alas! Kongo*, 17–52; Asiegbu, *Slavery and the Politics of Liberation*.

12. Burroughs, "Eyes on the Prize," 103–9.

13. Peterson, *Province of Freedom*, 182–84; Burroughs, "Eyes on the Prize," 101.

14. Pearson, *Distant Freedom*, 14–17, 32.

15. John Seys to Isaac Toucey, 24 August 1860, Series 1.E, Miscellaneous Incoming Correspondence, folder 1860 "Liberated Slaves," ACSR; Howard, *American Slavers and the Federal Law*, 137–38; Younger, "Liberia and the Last Slave Ships," 424, 442.

16. "Despatches from Liberia," *African Repository and Colonial Journal* 22, no. 4 (April 1846): 112.

17. Mamigonian, "To Be a Liberated African in Brazil," 33–34.

18. On second slavery and the emergence of multilateral slave trade suppression treaties, see Chapter 1.

19. Adderley, *"New Negroes from Africa,"* 89; Mamigonian, "In the Name of Freedom," 43. Robert Burroughs shows how political opposition forces in Britain applied middle passage

rhetoric to recaptive experiences to undercut the moral claims of British suppression policies; see Burroughs, "Eyes on the Prize."

20. Mamigonian, "In the Name of Freedom," 43. For a triple Atlantic crossing by recaptives caught in a case of contested jurisdiction, see the 1833 voyage of the *Maria de Gloria*, in which only 150 of 430 in the original group of captives survived; see Burroughs, "Eyes on the Prize," 110.

21. Asiegbu, *Slavery and the Politics of Liberation*; Schuler, *Alas! Alas! Kongo*; Schuler, "Recruitment of African Indentured Labourers"; Pearson, *Distant Freedom*.

22. Asiegbu, *Slavery and the Politics of Liberation*, 31–32; Schuler, *Alas! Alas! Kongo*, 25.

23. Adderley, *"New Negroes from Africa,"* 73–82.

24. Ibid. 19, 68, 73–75.

25. Pearson, *Distant Freedom*, chap. 6; Schuler, *Alas! Alas! Kongo*, 17–28. Adderley, *"New Negroes from Africa,"* 66–69, notes that liberated Africans brought to the Bahamas arrived in entire shipmate groups, whereas liberated Africans brought to Trinidad as migrant laborers had been separated into gender-balanced groups that disrupted some, but not all, shipmate bonds. Schuler also discusses the role of fearful rumors in building resistance to labor recruiters among recaptives; see Schuler, "Enslavement, the Slave Voyage, and Astral and Aquatic Journeys," 187, 202.

26. After Brazilian independence and during the 1831 senate and assembly debates over slave trade abolition, both Brazilian legislative bodies approved a "re-exportation" law that would send recaptives from Brazil to Africa. This law was never implemented, however. See Mamigonian, "To Be a Liberated African in Brazil," 21–22.

27. "What Is to Be Done with the Negro," *Mercury*, 4 October 1858. Interestingly, this article was attributed originally to the *Liverpool Post*, a sign of the international interest in the Charleston story and of British postemancipation racial discourse on black labor.

28. A sampling of public opinion on the issue includes the following: "What's to Be Done?," *Courier*, 2 September 1858; "What to Do with Them," *Courier*, 1 September 1858; "What Shall Be Done with the Recaptured Africans?," *World*, 16 July 1860; A.F.R., "What Shall Be Done with the Darkies?," *Liberator*, 31 August 1860, 138; "The *Echo*'s Cargo—What Shall Be Done with It?," *National Era*, 9 September 1858. One of the valid objections to simply disembarking recaptives anywhere in West Africa was the risk of reenslavement, especially for unprotected children. See Lawrance, *Amistad's Orphans*, 36.

29. Younger, "Liberia and the Last Slave Ships," 426–29, 438–41. Lawyers for the Charleston sheriff Carew argued that state regulatory laws should allow South Carolina to take possession of *Echo* recaptives to prevent the "discontent and disturbance" caused among Carolina's enslaved population by the presence of free people of color. See Levien, *Case of the Slaver Echo*, 11; Burin, "Slave Trade Act of 1819"; and Finkelman, "Regulating the Slave Trade," 403–5.

30. Rediker, *Amistad Rebellion*, 215–17, Kinna's letter to Tappan quoted on 216.

31. C. C. Hoffman, "From Rev. C. C. Hoffman," *African Repository* 37, no. 5 (May 1861): 132.

32. Jacob Thompson to Daniel H. Hamilton, 10 September 1858, M160, reel 1, RSI. On the USS *Niagara*, see Canney, *Old Steam Navy*, 52–58.

33. "The Frigate Niagara and Her New Mission," *NYT*, 8 September 1858. For contrasting, hostile responses to the *Niagara*, see F.A.P., "Who Are the Pirates?," *Mercury*, 21, 23 September 1858, and "The Exportation of the Africans," *Mercury*, 20 September 1858. In the same article, the *Mercury* praised U.S. agent Thomas Rainey for supplying the newspaper with information on the *Niagara* after *Mercury* editor Rhett had been denied a tour. The

restriction of the public from the *Niagara* in Charleston may have stung all the more because when the *Niagara* had been docked at the navy yard in New York, "thousands" of sightseers had been allowed to tour the interior of the ship recently returned from its Atlantic cable mission. See "The Frigate Niagara and Her New Mission," *NYT*, 8 September 1858.

34. "From Liberia—Return of the Niagara," *African Repository* 35, no. 1 (January 1859): 2.

35. "The Recaptured Africans," *Mercury*, 4 October 1858.

36. "Personal," *Mercury*, 15 September 1858; "The African Agent," *Courier*, 13 September 1858; Rainey, *Ocean Steam Navigation*. Rainey studied medicine in Missouri but never graduated from medical school. In his later life in New York, he became known as an avid promoter of the Queensborough Bridge. See "Dr. Rainey, 'Father of Bridge,' Glad Life-Work Is Completed," *Brooklyn Daily Eagle*, 12 June 1909, 38.

37. A detailed list of sailors by rank appears in Log of United States Naval Ship *Niagara*, 10–12 September 1858, LNS. See also "The Exportation of the Africans," *Mercury*, 20 September 1858.

38. Jacob Thompson to President Buchanan, 16 [May], 21 May 1860, and to Isaac Toucey, 30 May 1860, reel 1, RSI. A 7 June 1860 letter from Thompson to Commander Bruse in the New York Navy Yards, reel 1, RSI, rejects the *South Side* as an "A2" vessel not meeting the "A1" criteria. However, a certificate from Marine Inspector E. Davis in Boston gives the *South Shore* his "full confidence" to ship to "any part of the navigable world" (5 June 1860, Series 1.E, Miscellaneous Incoming Correspondence, folder 1860 "Liberated Slaves," ACSR). If both records refer to the same ship, there may have been disagreement over the quality of the *South Shore* before it was accepted for the Liberian voyage.

39. Letters of appointment from Jacob Thompson, 4 June 1860 (Young and Lindsly), 8 June 1860 (McCalla), in reel 1, RSI. Both McCalla and Grymes belonged to the District of Columbia Medical Society. Grymes had been born in Norfolk, Virginia, and received his M.D. in 1853 from Georgetown Medical School. McCalla was born in Lexington, Kentucky, and received his M.D. in 1853 from Columbia Medical School. See Nichols, *History of the Medical Society*, 253. John Moore McCalla Sr. supported the ACS, and some former McCalla slaves had emigrated to Liberia in the 1830s. See John M. McCalla Papers, David M. Rubenstein Rare Book and Manuscript Library, Duke University, Durham, North Carolina.

40. J. M. Grymes to B. A. Payne, 18 September 1860, Series 1.E, Miscellaneous Incoming Correspondence, folder 1860 "Liberated Slaves," ACSR; J. M. Grymes to Rev. Wm. McLain, 18 December 1860, reel 10, RSI. Illegal slavers were built small and fast to avoid patrolling warships. Each of the four slaving vessels, listed by tonnage in the *Voyages* database, registered around 300 tons. Each chartered vessel for Key West recaptives registered at around 1,000 tons (*Castilian*, 1,000; *South Shore*, 941; *Star of the Union*, 1,057). Tonnage of the charter ships appears in "Forty-Fourth Annual Report of the American Colonization Society," *African Repository* 37, no. 3 (March 1861): 70.

41. Christopher, Pybus, and Rediker, *Many Middle Passages*, 1–19, quote on 2.

42. "What Is to Be Done with the Africans?," *Courier*, 6 September 1858; "For Africa Direct," *Courier*, 22 September 1858. Examples of proslavery advocates claiming that recaptives wanted to remain with U.S. slaveowners include "Later from Havana," *Courier*, 14 May 1860, and Edmund Ruffin, "African Colonization Unveiled," *De Bow's Review* 29, no. 5 (November 1860): 644.

43. Fernando Moreno to Jacob Thompson, 25 June 1860, reel 6, RSI.

44. "The Key West Africans," *Constitution*, 17 July 1860, 83; Scarlet, "Key West Marine Correspondence," *Courier*, 18 July 1860.

45. "Later from Havana and Key West," *Courier*, 18 July 1860.

46. Eason Journal, 5 August 1860.

47. "The Exportation of the Africans," *Mercury*, 20 September 1858; Log of United States Naval Ship *Niagara*, 19 September 1858, LNS; also described in Berkley Grimball to John Grimball, 27 September 1858, SCHS. While the *Mercury*'s racialized construction of recaptive Africans as cargo is indisputable, it was a common maritime practice to move individual passengers between vessels in rough seas using similar devices such as a "bos'ns chair" or "basket-chair," known in the twentieth century as a "navy high-line." Thank you to H-Maritime members Penelope Hardy and John Rusk for this information provided via email, 10 April 2015.

48. Webster Lindsly to William McLain, 3 September 1860, reel 10, RSI.

49. For Young's reference to "shipping our cargo," see Young Ship Log, 1 July 1860, and "Shipping the Recaptured Africans on Board the U.S. Steam Frigate Niagara, at Charleston, S.C.," *Frank Leslie's*, 9 October 1858, 298.

50. On rumors and confusion regarding recaptive migrant labor transport to Trinidad, see Adderley, "*New Negroes from Africa*," 77–80. For temporal and spatial disorientation in transatlantic slave passages, see Smallwood, *Saltwater Slavery*, 122.

51. Jacob Thompson to James Conner, 12 October 1859, and to John Y. Bryant, 29 October 1859, reel 1, RSI; "The Dolphin's Crew," *Mercury*, 29 September 1858; "Return of the Captured Negroes to Africa, on Board the U.S. Steamship Niagara," *Frank Leslie's*, 8 January 1859, 86–87.

52. "The Slaver Echo and Her Cargo at Charleston," *NYT*, 6 September 1858; "The Africans of the Slave Bark 'Wildfire,'" *Harper's*, 2 June 1860, 345.

53. McCalla Journal, 1, 27 July, 14 August 1860.

54. On the acquisition of new languages over the course of enslaved captives' journeys to the African coast, see Slenes, "'Malungu, Ngoma's Coming!,'" 221.

55. Young Ship Log, 17 August 1860. "Picanini" has Portuguese, Spanish, and English usage and would have been familiar in most Atlantic ports of trade.

56. Young Ship Log, 21 July 1860.

57. Grymes Report, 7.

58. Webster Lindsly to William McLain, 3 September 1860, reel 10, RSI. Lindsly reported that he was unable to provide the ACS with the requested roster of names, ages, sexes, and origins because of his inability to communicate with recaptives aboard the *South Shore*.

59. "The Cargo of Negros," *Mercury*, 27 September 1858; "The Niagara," *Mercury*, 14 September 1858. A contemporary account describes the unusually "clear and unobstructed space" of the *Niagara*'s spar deck. See Mullaly, *Laying of the Cable*, 77.

60. Young Ship Log, 1 July 1860. On *Echo* slave ship conditions, see Woodruff, *Report of the Trials*, 8.

61. Grymes Report, 16.

62. "From Liberia—Return of the Niagara," *African Repository* 35, no. 1 (January 1859): 2. On the *Castilian*, Young reported seventeen deaths within the first week, primarily from diarrhea, which he attributed to the impact of the slave ship voyage and the "difference in water and food at Key West" (Young Ship Log, 8 July 1860).

63. See, for example, Hu-DeHart, "La Trata Amarilla." On nineteenth-century technologies of mass, forced sea transport, see also Foxhall, "From Convicts to Colonists."

64. McCalla Journal, 26 July 1860. An ACS emigrant ship used a similar tag system to organize passenger meals; see Cowan, *Liberia, as I Found It*, 9–10.

65. Grymes Report, 9.

66. Ibid., 3–4, 7–9. For examples of slave ship mess routines, see Vermilyea, *Slaver, the War, and around the World*, 7; Byrd, *Captives and Voyagers*, 33–34; and Rediker, *Slave Ship*, 237–38. Grymes stressed the healthfulness of these arrangements. In his professional view, to have fed weakened recaptive passengers "luxuriantly" on the ship's stores of coffee, tea, sugar, and molasses would have imperiled their survival. He reported to the ACS that he left these stores untouched and transferred them to Liberian officials for recaptives' enjoyment "in their own native and happy land." Grymes's ideas reflected common antebellum assumptions about the necessity of a mild, nonstimulating diet for invalids.

67. Grymes Report, 4. After the *Star of the Union*'s Liberian voyage, the *William*'s boiler was transferred to the recaptive reception yard at Sinoe.

68. Webster Lindsly to William McLain, 3 September 1860, reel 10, RSI. See also Malcom, "Transporting African Refugees." Young's description aligns with the host of illnesses and disabilities seen among survivors of the transatlantic passage in Brazil, though fortunately, there were no cases of smallpox. See Karasch, *Slave Life in Rio de Janeiro*, 151.

69. Webster Lindsly to Harvey Lindsly, 28 August 1860, Series 1.B, Incoming Correspondence, Letters from Liberia, 1 March 1859–22 October 1860, ACSR.

70. Webster Lindsly to William McLain, 3 September 1860, reel 10, RSI; Young Ship Log, 5 Aug 1860. Malcom notes contrary evidence that marshal Moreno did supply provisions high in vitamin C at Key West; see "Transporting African Refugees," 6 n. 6.

71. Rainey's report, in contrast to Grymes's, blamed the previous middle passage entirely. See "From Liberia—Return of the Niagara," *African Repository* 35, no. 1 (January 1859): 1–7.

72. Grymes Report, 21.

73. R. R. Gurley to John Moore McCalla, 8 June 1860, John Moore McCalla Papers, West Virginia and Regional History Center, West Virginia University Libraries, Morgantown. See also Letters of appointment from Jacob Thompson, 4 June 1860 (Young and Lindsly), 8 June 1860 (McCalla), in reel 1, RSI.

74. On white southern doctors' views of black patients, see Fett, *Working Cures*, 142–92.

75. Young Ship Log, 1, 21 July, 7 August 1860.

76. McCalla Journal, 19 August 1860. As later discussed, the headman, Gooser, may have married his wife on the *Star of the Union*. It is also remotely possible that Gooser and his wife, already married, were enslaved in Dahomean military raids and sold from Ouidah together. Two males with the name Goosee appear in the *African Origins* website, embarking from Lagos and an unspecified Bight of Benin location; see African IDs 176004, 180795.

77. Young Ship Log, 28 July 1860. Young wrote this passage with a degree of sympathy and noted that the girl "gained courage when she found that the pain was not severe."

78. See Log of United States Naval Ship *Niagara*, 25, 27 September, 2, 3, 7, 13, 16, 30 October, and 4 November 1858, LNS.

79. Ibid., 4 November 1858.

80. Young Ship Log, 14 July 1860 (emphasis in original).

81. Ibid., 12 July 1860.

82. Ibid., 12, 15 July 1860. Young made several references to the stealing of food. On 8 July 1860, he reported that one male recaptive was found with two dozen ship's biscuits hidden in his blanket, which Young said he had stolen overnight. It is reasonable to ask whether prior periods of deprivation resulted in attempts to hoard food on the *Castilian*. Further references to flogging of recaptives as punishment for fighting appear in Grymes Report, 10–11.

83. Young Ship Log, 29 July 1860.

84. Ibid., 2 August 1860.

85. McCalla Journal, 23, 28 July 1860.

86. Young Ship Log, 15, 2 August 1860.

87. Ibid., 2 August 1860.

88. Quotes from Grymes Report, 11, 12. Similar descriptions of racial traits appear in Webster Lindsly to Harvey Lindsly, 28 August 1860, Series 1.B, Incoming Correspondence, Letters from Liberia, 1 March 1859–22 October 1860, ACSR.

89. Rediker, *Slave Ship*, 10. Although sailors on the Liberian voyages were not involved in the production of enslaved captives, as were slave ship crew members, their daily relations with recaptive Africans reflected some similar patterns of abuse and callousness. See Christopher, *Slave Ship Sailors*, 163–94.

90. Young Ship Log, 31 July 1860.

91. J. M. Grymes to William McLain, 4 September 1860, reel 10, RSI; Grymes Report, 24.

92. Grymes Report, 20–22.

93. Schuler, "Enslavement, the Slave Voyage, and Astral and Aquatic Journeys," 186; Snyder, *Power to Die*, 23–45.

94. Young Ship Log, 13 August 1860.

95. Brown, "Social Death and Political Life," 1232. Alexander Byrd describes the impact of serial dislocation as "the slow recession of former social ties and the domestication of new ones" (*Captives and Voyagers*, 26).

96. McCalla Journal, 24 July 1860.

97. "Return of the Captured Negroes to Africa, on Board the U.S. Steamship Niagara," *Frank Leslie's*, 8 January 1859, 86–87.

98. Stewart, "Burial at Sea." Stewart (280–81) discusses the "nasal stitch," a practice lasting into the nineteenth century of sewing the last stitch of a burial shroud through the corpse's nose, said to assure the peaceful rest of the dead spirit and perhaps guard against accidental live burial.

99. Log of United States Naval Ship *Niagara*, 21, 24, 26 October 1858, LNS. The *Niagara* log regularly noted burials at sea, accompanied by the reading of the "Naval Service."

100. For two of the most perceptive and eloquent discussions of alienated death in enslaved ocean passages, see Smallwood, *Saltwater Slavery*, 140–41, and Brown, *Reaper's Garden*, 38–48.

101. Young Ship Log, 6 July 1860.

102. For sailor William Butterworth's description of an enslaved woman's improvised funeral on the 1786 voyage of the *Hudibras*, see Brown, "Social Death and Political Life," 1231–32.

103. Jalland, *Death in the Victorian Family*, 284–99.

104. MacGaffey, *Religion and Society in Central Africa*, 74, 42–89 passim.

105. Ibid., 53.

106. Ibid., 63. Suzanne Blier's extensive discussion of cord and binding pertains to a specific category of West African art produced far from the *Wildfire* shipmates' West Central African origins. I cite it here not to identify a specific ethnic practice engaged by Bomba but to signal the potential depth and complexity of the collective action Young observed. See Blier, *African Vodun*, 242–49, 293–95.

107. "Roll of Names of Recaptives Landed at Robertsport per Ship Castilian in August

1860," Series 1.E, Miscellaneous Incoming Correspondence, folder June–December 1860, ACSR.

108. Names related to the phonetic "Bomba" appear several times in the *African Origins* database. Several women listed as "Bombah" appear in the liberated African registers in Freetown. *African Origins* connects this name to the Kongo language group. For examples, see African IDs 29627, 50076, and 50210. Finally, there is the possibility that Bomba's name had a link to the *Mbumba Nkisi / N'kisi Bomba* nature spirit centered in Vili and Yombe regions north of the Congo River. *Mbumba* is associated with the rainbow, snakes, and dual forces of construction and destruction. See Hersak, "There Are Many Congo Worlds," and Janzen, *Lemba*, 53. Janzen (254) discusses the mid-nineteenth-century *minkisi* cult Pfemba (Phemba), related to women and midwifery.

109. Sweet, "Defying Social Death," 257.

110. Wright, *Strategies of Slaves and Women*, 1–2, 9.

111. Young Ship Log, 8 July 1860.

112. Rediker, *Slave Ship*, 270–72; Byrd, *Captives and Voyagers*, 44–46.

113. Young Ship Log, 11, 12 July 1860.

114. Ibid., 23 July 1860. Young's log does not indicate how the steerage space was divided between men and women, and children and adults, prior to this point.

115. "Return of the Captured Negroes to Africa, on Board the U.S. Steamship Niagara," *Frank Leslie's*, 8 January 1859, 86.

116. For children's circle dance, see McCalla Journal, 3 August 1860.

117. Lawrance, *Amistad's Orphans*, 6–7, 87, 239.

118. Grymes Report, 10; C. C. Hoffman, "From Rev. C. C. Hoffman," *African Repository* 37, no. 5 (May 1861): 132–34. For discussion of *Bogota* captive origins, see Chapter 3.

119. Grymes Report, 10–11.

120. Ibid., 17.

121. The phrasing here is ambiguous but seems to imply that one man objected to the woman coming into the men's quarters at night; see McCalla Journal, 14 August 1860. Apart from this incident, evidence from the Liberian voyages is silent on the whole range of interactions related to sexual relationships and sexual violence that might have arisen on such an ocean voyage. The conflict may also have involved some violation of acknowledged status, since the "Princess" could have come from a Fon noble family, as occasionally happened when high-ranking free persons in Dahomey were either convicted of a crime or exiled for political reasons. See Diouf, *Dreams of Africa*, 33.

122. Grymes Report, 14.

123. McCalla Journal, 5 August 1860. These weddings provide intriguing counterevidence for historians who have claimed the taboo nature of sexual relations between shipmates. See Sweet, "Defying Social Death," 271. Diouf, *Dreams of Africa*, 112, 271 n. 71, traces this unattributed idea of a proscription back to Patterson, *Sociology of Slavery*, 150. She found that *Clotilda* shipmates followed endogamous marriage patterns, though not exclusively so. Marriage files in late eighteenth-century Montevideo show the significance of shipmate ties and common origins in slaving ports in building social networks between grooms and their male witnesses. See Borucki, *From Shipmates to Soldiers*, 57–83. See also Chapter 6 for a discussion of marriage between West Central African shipmates in Liberia.

124. Young Ship Log, 14 July 1860.

125. Grymes Report, 6. Grymes wrote that he at first refused their request, thinking that

the presence of "bed and bunk" would serve as instruction "of the comforts of civilization," but eventually he conceded for reasons of health.

126. Ibid., 14, 6–7. Grymes especially noted how the mattress bedding was cut up, fringed, and fit "for use and comfort."

127. Young Ship Log, 13 July 1860. On the terrible itching of what English speakers called "scabies" and other skin diseases afflicting enslaved Africans in Rio in the nineteenth century, see Karasch, *Slave Life in Rio de Janeiro*, 163–66.

128. Grymes Report, 23, lists scabies, scurvy, wounds, and ulcers as the skin conditions that distressed recaptives on the *Star of the Union*.

129. Grymes Report, 25. Because slush was considered the "perquisite" of the galley cook, who would sell it to others on the ship for such purposes as the making of candles, this was a significant appropriation of ship supplies. See "Slush" in the on-line version of *Oxford Companion to Ships and the Sea* (Oxford University Press, 2007) (accessed 26 March 2015). The use of oils for skin may have had an aesthetic component as well, given the exposure to sea and salt and the rationed water supplies. On the aesthetics and philosophical connotations of oiled and glowing skin in mid-twentieth-century Nigeria's Benue Valley, see Bohannan, "Beauty and Scarification," 77–78.

130. For scholarship on medical pluralism in precolonial Africa, see Janzen, "Ideologies and Institutions," and Westerlund, "Pluralism and Change."

131. Young Ship Log, 23 August 1860.

132. Janzen, *Quest for Therapy*, 106, plate 15; MacGaffey, *Religion and Society in Central Africa*, 222–24. Although Janzen and MacGaffey researched Congo therapies in the twentieth century, both anchor descriptions of the contemporary healing they observed in nineteenth-century practices. Of course, West Central African healing practices did not remain static over the convulsive years of colonialism and independence, and thus anthropological studies are only suggestive of therapeutic principles with which the *Wildfire* recaptive shipmates would have been familiar. Contemporary anthropologists also discuss the tradition of therapeutic and empowering incisions among Yoruba specialists. See Drewal and Mason, "Ogun Mind/Body Potentiality," 336–37.

133. Janzen, *Quest for Therapy*, 77–79, 132–33, 225. Janzen and other medical anthropologists have called this attending group of kin the "therapy management group."

134. Alanamu, "Indigenous Medical Practices," 23; Sweet, *Domingos Álvares*, 9–26; Johnson, *History of the Yorubas*, 123.

135. McCalla Journal, 8 August 1860.

136. Sweet, *Domingos Álvares*, 123–45, quote on 123.

137. Austen, "Slave Trade as History and Memory," 238; MacGaffey, *Religion and Society in Central Africa*, 38, 160–65; Janzen, *Lemba*, 53–55. For twentieth-century anthropological studies, see Hersak, "There Are Many Congo Worlds," 628, and Petridis, "Of Mothers and Sorcerers."

138. Log of United States Naval Ship *Niagara*, 19 September, 9 November 1858, LNS. Two infants boarded the ship in Charleston and two disembarked in Liberia. No deaths or births of infants were reported, so the child most likely survived.

139. McCalla Journal, 7 August 1860.

140. Drewal, "Beauty and Being"; Berns, "Ga'anda Scarification."

141. Lovejoy, "Scarification and the Loss of History," 104–10; "citizenship symbols" in Ojo, "Beyond Diversity," 367–68; Reis and Mamigonian, "Nagô and Mina," 82–83; Johnson,

History of the Yorubas, 104–10, verbs on p. 109. On linguistic terminology, see also Drewal, "Beauty and Being," 84–85.

142. Drewal, "Art or Accident," 247–51, quote on 247.

143. Ibid., 247; fieldwork described in Drewal, "Being and Beauty," 96 n. 1.

144. Drewal, "Art or Accident," 248.

145. Drewal and Mason, "Ogun Mind/Body Potentiality," 332–35.

146. With appreciation to Henry Drewal for confirming the plausibility of this historical application of his contemporary work in an email exchange, 6 April 2015.

147. Drewal, "Art or Accident," 252–53.

148. Grymes Report, 12–13.

149. Drewal, "Art or Accident," 258 n. 6. However, it is important to note that since neither practitioner nor recipient was specifically identified by group origins, they may have come from other West African groups where older women practiced body artistry as well. See, for example, Berns, "Ga'anda Scarification," 58. Although recaptive passengers on the *Star of the Union* were not likely to have come from the region of present-day Nigeria identified by Berns as Ga'anda, Berns does provide an example of female body artists in West Africa.

150. Coghe, "Problem of Freedom," 485–89.

151. Law, *Ouidah*, 141–42; Law and Lovejoy, *Biography of Mahommah Gardo Baquaqua*, 149, 150.

152. Young Ship Log, 23 August 1860.

153. Ibid., 29 July 1860.

154. Lawrance, *Amistad's Orphans*, 23.

155. Vermilyea, *Slaver, the War, and around the World*, 7.

156. Grymes Report, 6; McCalla Journal, 5 August 1860.

Chapter 6

1. "Intelligence from Liberia," *African Repository* 35, no. 9 (September 1859): 277–78. The *Christian Advocate*'s notice of the marriage appeared in the American Colonization Society journal *African Repository* as well as in the *Weekly Anglo-African*.

2. The term "Liberian" in this chapter refers to the colonial population of African American emigrants and their families, who often called themselves Americo-Liberians to indicate their Westernized, American origins.

3. John Seys to Jacob Thompson, 31 October 1860, reel 10, RSI; John Seys, "From the Rev. John Seys, Government Agent for Recaptured Africans," *African Repository* 35, no. 6 (June 1859): 163; Crummell, "Address of Rev. Alexander Crummell"; see also Sawyer, *Emergence of Autocracy*, 102. Tensions between the Liberian government and the ACS over control of recaptive funding and distribution of recaptives was apparent by the spring of 1859. See John Seys to William McLain, 10 March 1859, Series 1.B, Incoming Correspondence, Letters from Liberia, 1 March 1859–22 October 1860, ACSR.

4. The Presbyterian Board of Missions in Monrovia adopted eight "youth" from the *Niagara*'s company. See "Recaptured Africans of the 'Echo,'" in *Forty-Second Annual Report of the American Colonization Society*, 19. Plans for these adoptions were also reported in the *Courier*, 18 September 1858.

5. Everill, *Abolition and Empire*, 10; Clegg, *Price of Liberty*, 4, 180; Younger, "Liberia and

the Last Slave Ships," 428. Clegg notes that Liberia's function as a haven for African recaptives proved rhetorically useful in fending off abolitionist charges against the proslavery leanings of the colonization movement.

6. The *African Repository*, which reprinted the notice, used both the names Kalendah and Kabendah for the man, and Kandah and Kandah-Kabendah for the woman. Because the *Echo* embarked from Cabinda, it is entirely possibly that none of these names reflects a name of birth but, rather, names imposed at embarkation or some point in their enslavement. See "Intelligence from Liberia," *African Repository* 35, no. 9 (September 1859): 277–78.

7. Akpan, "Black Imperialism."

8. Sweet, "Quiet Violence of Ethnogenesis," 210.

9. Northrup, "Becoming African," 17; Byrd, *Captives and Voyagers*, 20, 27, 29, 32; Peel, *Religious Encounter*, 283–88; Sidbury and Cañizares-Esguerra, "Mapping Ethnogenesis"; Burroughs, "'True Sailors of Western Africa.'" For challenges or modifications to Peel's arguments on the ethnogenesis of "Yoruba," see Ojo, "Beyond Diversity"; Apter, "Yoruba Ethnogenesis from Within"; and Law, "Yoruba Liberated Slaves."

10. Cooper, *House at Sugar Beach*, 6, 10, 15.

11. Clegg, *Price of Liberty*, 110–11.

12. Staudenraus, *African Colonization Movement*; Tyler-McGraw, *African Republic*. More analytic focus is given to recaptives in Clegg, *Price of Liberty*, 92–94, 245–46; Akingbade, "Liberian Settlers and the Campaign"; Younger, "Liberia and the Last Slave Ships"; and Lindsay, "Boundaries of Slavery."

13. Staudenraus, *African Colonization Movement*, 148–58; Burin, "Slave Trade Act of 1819," 6–9.

14. "United States Agency for Recaptured Africans," *African Repository and Colonial Journal* 22, no. 6 (June 1846): 176–80; "Liberia a Means of Abolishing the Slave Trade," *African Repository and Colonial Journal* 3, no. 5 (July 1827): 129–36. Other examples of the efficacy of colonization for ending the slave trade appear in "'The Pons,'" *African Repository and Colonial Journal* 22, no. 5 (May 1846): 137–40, and "Thirtieth Annual Report of the American Colonization Society," *African Repository and Colonial Journal* 23, no. 3 (March 1847): 78.

15. Clegg, *Price of Liberty*, 57; Staudenraus, *African Colonization Movement*, 56–57; Mouser, "Baltimore's African Experiment," 116–17.

16. Canney, *Africa Squadron*, 15–18, 135–36; P. F. Voorhees to Levi Woodbury, "Letter from Captain Voorhees of the United States Navy," *African Repository and Colonial Journal* 10, no. 1 (March 1834): 20–22.

17. "Articles of Agreement between the Republic of Liberia and the American Colonization Society," 23 March 1849, Series 1.E, Miscellaneous Incoming Correspondence, ACSR; Younger, "Liberia and the Last Slave Ships," 436.

18. Younger, "Liberia and the Last Slave Ships," 427.

19. Lindsay, "Boundaries of Slavery," 261–62; Lindsay, "Atlantic Bonds"; Tyler-McGraw, *African Republic*, 130; Akpan, "Black Imperialism," 227 n. 66; Everill, *Abolition and Empire*, 28–29, 58–59, 63–78.

20. Clegg, *Price of Liberty*, 94–95, 102–12, 214–17.

21. Ibid., 201–2.

22. Lindsay, "Boundaries of Slavery"; Clegg, *Price of Liberty*, 112; Younger, "Liberia and the Last Slave Ships," 438–41. On recaptives as a buffer population on a colonial "middle ground," see Clegg, *Price of Liberty*, 92–95. An early articulation of this distinction between "native" and "recaptured Africans" from African American physician Robert McDowell

appears in "Latest from Liberia," *African Repository and Colonial Journal* 11, no. 2 (February 1836): 41–47.

23. "Meeting Called on the Arrival of the 'Pons,'" *African Repository and Colonial Journal* 22, no. 5 (May 1846): 145–46; John Seys, "The Recaptured Africans in Liberia," *African Repository* 41, no. 1 (January 1865): 15–18; Crummell, "Rev. Mr. Crummell on the Congo Recaptives."

24. Domingues da Silva, Eltis, Misevich, and Ojo, "Diaspora of Africans," 253 and 369, table A.3. On Sierra Leone numbers, see Anderson et al., "Using African Names," 167. On Liberia and slave trade suppression in the 1820s and '30s, see Tyler-McGraw, *African Republic*, 160–64.

25. *Senate Ex. Doc. No. 150*, 175–79, 198–201, 261–63.

26. Clegg, *Price of Liberty*, 93. In 1822, the first group of fifteen young African men declared free by federal circuit court *Antelope* decision arrived at Cape Mesurado with early U.S. colonists on the ACS brig *Strong*. See Chapter 1 for discussion of *Antelope* legal decisions. See also Bryant, *Dark Places*, 187–92.

27. The designation of "Eboe" (Igbo) identifies Igbo-language speakers embarked from the Bight of Biafra among the first recaptive generation. The most likely origin for this group was the *Guerrero*, which wrecked near Key West in 1827, but some captives from the Bight of Biafra were also seized with the *Fenix* in 1830. Approximately 90 recaptives arrived on the ACS ship *Heroine* in March 1830. See Swanson, *Slave Ship Guerrero*, and Cowan, *Liberia, as I Found It*, 48. See also J. Mechlin to Rev. R. R. Gurley, *African Repository and Colonial Journal* 8, no. 7 (September 1832): 200–201; "Intelligence from Liberia," *African Repository and Colonial Journal* 11, no. 3 (March 1835): 81–89; and "Kentucky State Colonization Society," *African Repository and Colonial Journal* 10, no. 7 (September 1834): 209–10. On the process of "Igboization," see Nwokeji, *Slave Trade and Culture*, 5–6, 105, 125.

28. "The Recaptured Africans," *African Repository and Colonial Journal* 10, no. 3 (May 1834): 90; Tyler-McGraw, *African Republic*, 134 ; Sawyer, *Emergence of Autocracy*, 100.

29. "United States Agency for Recaptured Africans," *African Repository and Colonial Journal* 22, no. 6 (June 1846): 180; "Condition and Expense of the United States Agency for Recaptured Africans," 146.

30. Clegg, *Price of Liberty*, 93.

31. Shick, *Behold the Promised Land*, 72.

32. "Capture of the Slaver Pons," *Boston Daily Atlas*, 19 March 1846; J. W. Lugenbeel to Wm. McLain, 29 December 1845, "Despatches from Liberia," *African Repository and Colonial Journal* 22, no. 4 (April 1846): 112–13.

33. J. W. Lugenbeel, "Communications. Letter from Dr. Lugenbeel," *African Repository and Colonial Journal* 22, no. 5 (May 1846): 143.

34. "Table of Emigrants," *African Repository* 27, no. 5 (May 1851): 149–50. According to ACS records, the ACS laid out provisions for *Pons* recaptives for which they were later compensated $37,800 by the U.S. government. See McLain to O. H. Browning, 14 April 1868, reel 10, RSI.

35. Burrowes, *Power and Press Freedom*, 46–49, 59–62.

36. J. W. Lugenbeel, "Despatches from Liberia," *African Repository and Colonial Journal* 22, no. 4 (April 1846): 112–13.

37. J. W. Lugenbeel, "Despatches from Liberia," *African Repository and Colonial Journal* 22, no. 5 (May 1846): 154.

38. Ball, *Report on the Condition and Prospect*, 10–11. William Nesbit, an African American traveler sponsored by the ACS, wrote an even stronger denunciation of Liberian colonists'

labor system in 1853; see Nesbit, "Four Months in Liberia," 102–4. Writing in 1857, black American missionary Samuel Williams defended the Liberian apprenticeships, arguing that although individual abuses might occur, it was a system regulated by the courts that applied only to a temporary period of a young apprentice's life. See Williams, "Four Years in Liberia," 172.

39. Tyler-McGraw, *African Republic*, 168.

40. J. B. Benham, "Communication from the Rev. J. B. Benham," *African Repository and Colonial Journal* 22, no. 5 (May 1846): 146, 149. In March 1848, John and Susan Benham returned to Baltimore traveling with a "Congo girl." See *Twenty-Ninth Annual Report of the Mission Society of the Methodist Church*, 17.

41. Lawrance, *Amistad's Orphans*, 190.

42. Susan H. Benham, "Letter from Mrs. Benham," *African Repository and Colonial Journal* 22, no. 5 (May 1846): 149–50; "Meeting Called on the Arrival of the 'Pons.'" *African Repository and Colonial Journal* 22, no. 5 (May 1846): 145–46. As Susan Benham saw it, indigenous family heads resisted sending daughters to the mission due to fears that "enlightened" young women would no longer submit to "all the drudgery imposed by their domineering lords" ("Letter from Mrs. Benham," 150).

43. A. Wilkins, "Letter from Mrs. Ann Wilkins," *African Repository and Colonial Journal* 22, no. 5 (May 1846): 151–52. The naming opportunities described by Ann Wilkins resembled Church Mission Society practices in Sierra Leone, discontinued after 1819, where donors could rename a recaptive child. See Fyfe, "A. B. C. Sibthorpe," 328, and Jones, "New Light on the Liberated Africans."

44. On missionary involvement with recaptives in Liberia, see also Younger, "Liberia and the Last Slave Ships," 439; W. B. Hoyt, "Extract of a Letter," *African Repository and Colonial Journal* 22, no. 5 (May 1846): 143–45; J. W. Lugenbeel, "Religion among the Congoes by the Pons," *African Repository and Colonial Journal* 24, no. 2 (February 1848): 37–39; Hoyt, *Land of Hope*, 100; and Wm. C., "Methodist Episcopal Missions in Liberia," *African Repository and Colonial Journal* 24, no. 10 (October 1848): 295.

45. Clegg, *Price of Liberty*, 110–11, 241. James Sidbury argues that many black American emigrants over the course of the nineteenth century turned away from a diasporic label of "African" in favor of developing an "American" identity in Liberian colonial society. The third and largest generation of recaptives arrived in Liberia in the third quarter of the nineteenth century when this divide between black American emigrants and Liberian native groups had matured and intensified. See Sidbury, *Becoming African in America*, 183–202.

46. Younger, "Liberia and the Last Slave Ships," 440.

47. "Those Congoes," *African Repository and Colonial Journal* 23, no. 1 (January 1847): 25; J. J. Roberts, "The Recaptured Africans," *African Repository and Colonial Journal* 22, no. 10 (October 1846): 301–2; "Thirtieth Annual Report of the American Colonization Society," *African Repository and Colonial Journal* 23, no. 3 (March 1847): 77; "Letter from Dr. Lugenbeel," *African Repository and Colonial Journal* 23, no. 5 (May 1847): 142.

48. Wiley, *Slaves No More*, 67. Matilda Skipwith was manumitted for emigration from Virginia in 1834. By 1848, she had married Samuel B. Lomax, a cooper. See Emigrants table on *Virginia Emigrants to Liberia* website, http://www.vcdh.virginia.edu/liberia/focus.php ?id=1102 (accessed 2 July 2015).

49. J. J. Roberts to A.G. Phelps, *African Repository and Colonial Journal* 23, no. 2 (February 1847): 61.

50. "The Africans by the 'Pons,'" *African Repository and Colonial Journal* 23, no. 6 (June 1847): 188–89.

51. One Congo man was shot during this conflict. See Solomon S. Page to Charles W. Andrews, Edina, 1849, in Wiley, *Slaves No More*, 107–8, 323 n. 2.

52. John Seys to Isaac Toucey, 24 August 1860, reel 3, RSI; "Letter of Rev. J. Rambo," *African Repository* 29, no. 9 (September 1853): 261; "From Liberia," *African Repository* 37, no. 11 (November 1861): 349–51; William C. Burke to Ralph R. Gurley, 23 September 1861, in Wiley, *Slaves No More*, 211–12.

53. Lawrance, *Amistad's Orphans*, 226–28.

54. For "umbrella terms" as opposed to more precise ethnonyms, see Borucki, *From Shipmates to Soldiers*, 45, 82–83.

55. Examples of the term "Congo" used for *Pons* recaptives include Ball, *Report on the Condition and Prospect*, 10; J. W. Lugenbeel, "Religion among the Congoes by the Pons," *African Repository and Colonial Journal* 24, no. 2 (February 1848): 37–39; and "Letter of Kong Koba," *African Repository and Colonial Journal* 23, no. 8 (August 1847): 244.

56. "Return of the Stevens," *African Repository* 37, no. 5 (May 1861): 130.

57. Clegg, *Price of Liberty*, 245.

58. Younger, "Liberia and the Last Slave Ships," 442. The Liberian colonist population in the 1858–61 period is difficult to determine. The 1843 census showed a total colonist population of 2,388, with 912 individuals residing in Monrovia. See Shick, *Behold the Promised Land*, 34, table 5. From 1844 to 1856, ACS records show 5,251 emigrants arriving, but mortality figures were high. See "Table of Emigrants," *African Repository* 33, no. 5 (May 1857): 152–55. Burrowes, *Power and Press Freedom*, 72–73, places Monrovia's population at 5,000 in 1856 and 12,000 in 1861, indicating both Monrovia's economic growth and large numbers of recaptives who arrived during that period of time. Kentucky State Colonization Society agent Alexander Cowan estimated Liberia's colonist population in 1858 at 7,621; see *Liberia, as I Found It*, 166. On St. Paul River settlements, see Shick, *Behold the Promised Land*, 73–87.

59. Clegg, *Price of Liberty*, 199.

60. See John Seys to William McLain, 10 March 1859, Series 1.B, Incoming Correspondence, Letters from Liberia, 1 March 1859–22 October 1860, ACSR. Because, as discussed later, a Nathaniel Freeman shows up in Seys's 1860 receipts as an interpreter for recaptives of the *Bonito*, it is possible that "Mr. Freeman" himself was a former recaptive, perhaps of the *Pons*, and that the conflict had more specific political dynamics understood only by Freeman and the *Echo* shipmates.

61. See ibid.

62. See H. W. Dennis to William McLain, 14 May 1859, and John Seys to William McLain, 19 March 1859, Series 1.B, Incoming Correspondence, Letters from Liberia, 1 March 1859–22 October 1860, ACSR.

63. *Voyages*, IDs #4393, #4653; William Inman to Isaac Toucey, 14 August 1860, Letters received by the Secretary of the Navy, RG45, reel 11, NARA. On the capture of the *Storm King*, see Dornin to Judge of the U.S. District Court of the Eastern District of Virginia, 9 August 1860, Letterbook of Thomas Aloysius Dornin, Huntington Library, San Marino, California.

64. *Voyages*, IDs #4655, #4656, #4955. On the capture of the *Bonito*, see Dornin to Judge of the U.S. District Court of the Eastern District of Virginia, 17 October 1860, Letterbook of Thomas Aloysius Dornin, Huntington Library, San Marino, California.

65. Due to the similarities in recaptive experiences of Liberian resettlement as well as

an abundance of Monrovia-generated records, this chapter draws on evidence for the entire pool of the third generation of recaptives in Liberia, including not only shipmates of the *Echo*, *Wildfire*, *William*, and *Bogota*, but also the *Erie*, *Storm King*, *Cora*, *Bonito*, and *Nightingale*. The latter group were transported directly to Liberia after naval interception near the West Central African coast.

66. Tyler-McGraw, *African Republic*, 139, 159.

67. Shick, *Behold the Promised Land*, 42–63 passim, uses "settler standard" to describe the U.S.-influenced culture of Liberian settler society, with its emphasis on propriety, piety, self-sufficiency, benevolence, and respectability.

68. Sawyer, *Emergence of Autocracy*, 73.

69. "Articles of Agreement between the Republic of Liberia and the American Coloniza-tion Society," 23 March 1849, Series 1.E, Miscellaneous Incoming Correspondence, ACSR.

70. John Seys to Jacob Thompson, 31 October 1860, reel 10, RSI.

71. John Seys to Isaac Toucey, 28 December 1860, reel 10, RSI; Boyd, "Negro Colonization in the National Crisis," 68–71; Younger, "Liberia and the Last Slave Ships," 435–37.

72. Lindsay, "Atlantic Bonds," 13–16.

73. John Lewis to John Seys, 22 August 1860, and John Seys to John Lewis, 23 August 1860, Series 1.E, Miscellaneous Incoming Correspondence, folder 1860 "Liberated Slaves," ACSR.

74. "Meeting of the Board of Directors," *African Repository* 36, no. 12 (December 1860): 355–58. For the Liberian government's objection to recaptives being held "under the aus-pices of foreign bodies," see "From the Liberia Herald of September 19," *African Repository* 37, no. 1 (January 1861): 28.

75. "Articles of Agreement Respecting Recaptured Africans Entered into in the City of Monrovia," 21 December 1860, Series 1.E, Miscellaneous Incoming Correspondence, folder 1860 "Liberated Slaves," ACSR. Born in St. Croix, West Indies, to Danish slaveholding parents, John Seys (1799–1872) became a Wesleyan Methodist minister in 1829. He spent many years in Liberia in a variety of roles, including superintendent of Methodist Episco-pal missions of West Africa and U.S. agent for recaptured Africans (whom he frequently called "liberated Africans," following British terminology). Seys was a controversial figure in Liberian politics in the 1830s and '40s, an opponent of the ACS administration prior to independence, in alliance with less elite colonists and merchants. See Park, *"White" Americans in "Black" Africa*, 132–37; Sawyer, *Emergence of Autocracy*, 119; Burrowes, *Power and Press Freedom*, 46–49, 59–62; and Boyd, "American Colonization Society and the Slave Recaptives," 117.

76. Several receptacles, including one in Monrovia and one farther up the St. Paul River near Virginia, were built in response to the arrival of the *Pons* shipmates. See "The Slaves Liberated from the 'Pons,'" *African Repository and Colonial Journal* 22, no. 4 (April 1846): 130–31. Positive descriptions of Liberia praised the receptacles as signs of Liberia's readi-ness for emigrants, while the more critical literature on Liberia in the 1850s criticized the receptacles as squalid and decayed. See Cowan, *Liberia, as I Found It*, 65–66; Nesbit, "Four Months in Liberia," 90; and Washington, "Liberia As It Is, 1854," 206.

77. John Seys to Isaac Toucey, 24 August 1860, reel 3, RSI.

78. Seys receipts, reel 10, RSI: Seys to B. R. Wilson, $280.15, August and September 1860; Seys to Mary Anderson, $31.35, September 1860; Seys to Thomas Cooper, $66.28, Septem-ber 1860; Seys to S. Washington, "country cloths for Congoes," December 1860. See also John Seys to Morris Officer, 31 December 1860, and to Isaac Toucey, 16 October 1860, reel 3, RSI.

79. John Seys to Isaac Toucey, 24 August, 16 October 1860, reel 3, RSI; John Seys, "U.S. Agency for Liberated Africans, Monrovia," 17 October 1860, Series 1.E, Miscellaneous Incoming Correspondence, folder June–December 1860, ACSR; Young Ship Log, 29 August 1860.

80. Grymes Report, 29.

81. "Roll of Names of Recaptives Landed at Robertsport Per Ship Castilian in August 1860," Series 1.E, Miscellaneous Incoming Correspondence, folder June–December 1860, ACSR.

82. John Seys to Isaac Toucey, 16, 31 October 1860, reel 3, RSI.

83. John Seys to Isaac Toucey, 26 October, 1860, reel 3, RSI. See also another, but probably less reliable, account of the reunion of *Pons* survivor Daniel Bacon with a brother on the *Echo*: [Seys], S. "A Leaf from 'Reminiscences of Liberia,'" *African Repository* 41, no. 5 (May 1865): 149–51. This account bears similarities to the romance of reunion employed in press representations of the *Amistad* recaptives, in which reunion helped to reinforce a stark line between slavery and freedom and placed antislavery personnel in a heroic light. See Lawrance, *Amistad's Orphans*, 221–38.

84. C. C. Hoffman, "The Recaptured Africans Returned by the Niagara," *African Repository* 36, no. 6 (June 1860): 172; "From Liberia," *World*, 7 July 1860.

85. John Seys to Isaac Toucey, 24 August 1860, reel 3, RSI.

86. See receipts for services paid, John Seys, 1860, reel 10, RSI. The list of interpreters named in John Seys's records (and billed for support of particular shipmate groups) includes John James (*Cora* shipmates), Benjamin Stryker (*Cora*), Adam Morris, Nathaniel Freeman, John Benson (*Bonito*), John Miner, and Thomas David (*Bonito*).

87. Ibid.

88. Pybus, *Epic Journeys of Freedom*; Sanneh, *Abolitionists Abroad*, 22–65; Byrd, *Captives and Voyagers*, 122–243.

89. *Voyages*, http://slavevoyages.org/tast/database/search.faces?yearFrom=1808&yearTo =1866&fate3=3&sla1port=60200 (accessed 6 July 2015). The distribution of embarkation regions for the 446 voyages seized under the British flag and disembarking in Sierra Leone between 1808 and 1866 demonstrates the ethnic diversity of Sierra Leone's recaptive population: 149 ships embarked captives from Bight of Benin; 136, from Bight of Biafra and Gulf of Guinea Islands; 70, from Sierra Leone; 29, from West Central Africa and St. Helena; 22, from Windward Coast; 19, from other unnamed African regions; 10, from Gold Coast; 10, from Senegambia; 1, from Southeast Africa and Indian Ocean. See http://www.slavevoyages .org/voyages/sglhUfeg (accessed 4 March 2016).

90. Lawrance, *Amistad's Orphans*, 194–98.

91. Peterson, *Province of Freedom*, 184–87; Everill, *Abolition and Empire*, 17–32.

92. Northrup, "Becoming African," 11–12; Cole, "Liberated Slaves and Islam," 383–403; Fyle, "Yoruba Diaspora in Sierra Leone's Krio Society," 366–80; Everill, *Abolition and Empire*, 21, 39, 47, 49.

93. Lawrance, *Amistad's Orphans*, 186–89, 190–91. Lawrance notes the exploitative and abusive nature of these apprenticeships, often resulting in virtual enslavement but also kidnapping and literal reenslavement.

94. Domingues da Silva, Eltis, Misevich, and Ojo, "Diaspora of Africans," 359–62; Peterson, *Province of Freedom*, 163.

95. Peterson, *Province of Freedom*, 150–73.

96. Domingues da Silva, Eltis, Misevich, and Ojo, "Diaspora of Africans," argues that

Sierra Leone was the place where recaptive Africans had, in relative terms, the most control to shape their lives after slave ship interception. See also Peterson, *Province of Freedom*, 189–271. On liberated African villages in the Americas, see Schuler, *Alas! Alas! Kongo*, 65–84, and Adderley, *"New Negroes from Africa,"* 92–248 passim.

97. After undergoing court proceedings to condemn captured vessels, adult male recaptives in Freetown received six months of per diem support, adult women received only three months, and children "above a certain age" were apprenticed. See Lawrance, *Amistad's Orphans*, 197, and Domingues da Silva, Eltis, Misevich, and Ojo, "Diaspora of Africans," 362.

98. Younger, "Liberia and the Last Slave Ships," 437–38.

99. John Seys to Isaac Toucey, 28 November 1860, reel 10, RSI; John Seys, "Report of Recaptured Africans, Liberia," 31 March 1861, Series 1.E, Miscellaneous Incoming Correspondence, folder Correspondence, January–June 1861, ACSR. See also receipt from John Seys to Tobias Outland for services on the "committee in giving out congoes" at Monrovia, 2 January 1861, reel 10, RSI.

100. Lindsay, "Boundaries of Slavery," 268–69.

101. Sawyer, *Emergence of Autocracy*, 185–88; Cowan, *Liberia, as I Found It*, 66.

102. President Buchanan asked Congress for $45,000 for expenses related to transport and support of *Echo* recaptives for one year. See James Buchanan to William McLain, 7 September 1858, Series 1.E, Miscellaneous Incoming Correspondence, folder Letters Rec'd 1856–1859, ACSR. In addition to a separate agreement made for *Echo* recaptives, in 1860–61, the United States signed four separate contracts with the ACS for support of roughly 4,500 recaptives on 20 July 1860, 22 October 1860, 2 March 1861, and 29 July 1861. See "Contracts with the U.S.," 4 March [n.d.], Series 1.E, Miscellaneous Incoming Correspondence, folder June–December 1860, ACSR. The paperwork and reporting of these expenses posed enormous logistical challenges, leading to contestation of Seys's reports by the U.S. Congress. See John Seys to Isaac Toucey, 16 October 1860, reel 3, RSI. The argument over U.S. reimbursement to Liberia based on John Seys's reports continued through 1865. In the end, the United States paid only a partial amount of the contracted support, thus leaving the small republic of Liberia to subsidize U.S. recaptive policy. See Younger, "Liberia and the Last Slave Ships," 427–34.

103. Clegg, *Price of Liberty*, 94, 107, 245–46; Younger, "Liberia and the Last Slave Ships," 438; Akpan, "Black Imperialism," 227; Sawyer, *Emergence of Autocracy*, 115.

104. "Letter from Rev. John Seys," *African Repository* 37, no. 2 (February 1861): 62; *Forty-Seventh Annual Report of the American Colonization Society*, 11; Clegg, *Price of Liberty*, 245.

105. Clegg, *Price of Liberty*, 246; Sawyer, *Emergence of Autocracy*, 114, 187.

106. Crummell, "Regenerating Policy of Liberia," 232.

107. Crummell, "Rev. Mr. Crummell on the Congo Recaptives," 313.

108. Ibid.

109. Moses, *Creative Conflict in African American Thought*, 82–138.

110. William C. Burke to Ralph R. Gurley, 31 August 1860, 23 September 1861, in Wiley, *Slaves No More*, 210–12. On the migration of Burke and his family, see *Virginia Emigrants to Liberia* database, http://www.vcdh.virginia.edu/liberia/focus.php?id=211 (accessed 2 July 2015).

111. The Protestant Episcopal Mission at Cape Palmas adopted ten children from the *Echo*'s company, but little other evidence is available for the apprenticeship or mission experiences of *Wildfire* and *William* shipmates. See "Recaptured Africans of the 'Echo,'" in *Forty-Second Annual Report of the American Colonization Society*, 9.

112. Ann Seys, "Appeal for the Congoes by Mrs. Seys," *African Repository* 37, no. 4 (April 1861): 113.

113. Imhoff, *Life of Rev. Morris Officer*, 237–39. In this account, Imhoff quoted from Officer's correspondence. Officer's journal entry discusses his visit to the receptacle but does not mention responses of recaptive children to being transported to the mission; see Officer Diary, 25 September 1860. Officer, a Lutheran clergyman who had also traveled to the Mendi mission in Sierra Leone, arrived in Liberia around April 1860 and had newly established the Muhlenberg school when the third wave of recaptives arrived in Liberia. See "Lutheran Mission Institute," *African Repository* 36, no. 11 (November 1860): 350–51.

114. Imhoff, *Life of Rev. Morris Officer*, 240–43.

115. "Roll of Names of Recaptives Landed at Robertsport Per Ship Castilian in August 1860," Series 1.E, Miscellaneous Incoming Correspondence, folder June–December 1860, ACSR. No "Frank" appears on the roster, only Francis and Franklin listed at nine and eleven years old, respectively. The rupturing act of forced renaming makes it extremely difficult to follow Francisco's story further into Liberia. Given the close attention Young paid to Francisco in his journal, he would almost certainly have mentioned it if Francisco had died aboard ship. Therefore, I conclude that Francisco lived to disembark at Cape Mount. The ship's roster of disembarking recaptives offers only one admittedly speculative clue to Francisco's existence. The first name ("No. 1") on the list was a twenty-two-year-old man, christened Steven Benson (also the name of the then-current Liberian president). Such a description generally matches Young's identification of Francisco's age in a newspaper article as twenty-two as well as *Harper's* description of Francisco as a "young man." For comparative purposes, see renaming process in Brazil in Mamigonian, "To Be a Liberated African in Brazil," 39–46.

116. Officer Diary, 15 September 1860; Imhoff, *Life of Rev. Morris Officer*, 243–44.

117. Consider, for example, an ACS announcement about several Liberian students studying at Lincoln University in Pennsylvania. The young men included Thomas Roberts (Vey nation), John Johns (Congo), Samuel Sevier (Bassa), Calvin Wright, and Robert King. See "Preparing for Liberia," *African Repository* 56, no. 10 (April 1880): 63.

118. John Seys to Isaac Toucey, 26 October 1860, reel 3, and 28 November 1860, reel 10, RSI.

119. John Seys to Thomas Travis, Coroner, 28 September 1860, reel 10, RSI.

120. John Seys to Thomas Travis, Dr., 6 December 1860, reel 10, RSI.

121. Officer Diary, 16 November 1860; Imhoff, *Life of Rev. Morris Officer*, 258.

122. In his 23 September 1861 letter to Gurley, Burke notes that "churches and Sabbath schools are every Sabbath crowded" with recaptives in Clay Ashland. See Wiley, *Slaves No More*, 212.

123. Seys to Toucey, 16 October 1860, reel 3, RSI.

124. "From Rev. C. C. Hoffman," *African Repository* 37, no. 5 (May 1861): 132.

125. Officer Diary, 24, 29 September 1860. On 10 September 1860, Officer notes, "Congo boys rebellious while I was absent would not get wood for cooking," concluding that he expected to examine and punish the boys. On 6 October 1860, Officer mentions twenty "Congo boys" sent to cut rice in the fields of Jolla Billa, a "native chief." See also Imhoff, *Life of Rev. Morris Officer*, 304–5.

126. Officer Diary, 24 September 1860; Imhoff, *Life of Rev. Morris Office*, 245–49.

127. Seys receipt to S. S. Winkey, 23 October 1860, and receipt for Burt Colbert's "Apprehending two Africans," 26 November 1860, reel 10, RSI. For Solomon Winkey's emigration in 1839, see "The Sixteenth Annual Report of the American Society for the Colonizing of

the Free People of Colour of the United States," *African Repository and Colonial Journal* 16, no. 3 (March 1840): 25.

128. United States Agency for Liberated Africans, 30 September 1861, reel 10. RSI.

129. Officer Diary, 28 September 1860.

130. Seys to Laing, for medical attendance on Recaptives at Careysburg from 30 August 1860 to 7 January 1861, and Seys to M. Officer for bill paid to Dr. Laing, 25 January 1861, reel 10, RSI. Daniel Laing, along with Martin Delany, first attempted to train at Harvard but completed his medical degree at Dartmouth under the sponsorship of the Massachusetts Colonization Society after being ejected from Harvard due to white student protest. For Laing's arrival in Liberia, see "More Immigrants Than Could Be Accommodated," *African Repository* 30, no. 7 (July 1854): 194.

131. Officer Diary, 29 September 1860. All references to the escape in this paragraph come from this day's diary entry.

132. See Chapter 3 for origins of *Bogota* shipmates.

133. "Letter from Pres. Stephen A. Benson," *African Repository*, 37, no. 1 (January 1861): 30; "From Rev. C. C. Hoffman," *African Repository* 37, no. 5 (May 1861): 134; Crummell, "'Africa and Her People,'" 66.

134. C. C. Hoffman, "From Rev. C. C. Hoffman," *African Repository* 37, no. 5 (May 1861): 134.

135. Henry B. Stewart to Ralph R. Gurley, Greenville, 16 March 1861, quoted as spelled in Wiley, *Slaves No More*, 303.

136. Hawthorne, "'Being Now, as It Were, One Family'"; Watson, "'Prize Negroes' and the Development of Racial Attitudes," 161.

137. Established in the mid-1830s, first as Mississippi in Africa by the Mississippi Colonization Society, Sinoe consistently had the smallest population of colonists. The 1843 census recorded only seventy-nine emigrants. See Clegg, *Price of Liberty*, 146–47.

138. Fernando Moreno to Jacob Thompson, 28 May, 10 June 1860, reel 6, RSI; "From Liberia," *African Repository* 37, no. 6 (June 1861): 161–62; C. C. Hoffman, "From Rev. C. C. Hoffman," *African Repository* 37, no. 5 (May 1861): 134. For a similar comparison of "fierce" Yoruba with tractable "Congo" in Trinidad, see Adderley, *"New Negroes from Africa,"* 111.

139. "From Liberia," *African Repository* 37, no. 6 (June 1861): 161–62.

140. Perhaps indicating his disagreement with their treatment, Stewart portrayed the shipmates' defiance as a predictable "native" reaction against the broken word of colonial supervisors, adding, "Whatever may be Said of these People of being Lawless or Rebellious I have not Seen it" (Henry B. Stewart to Ralph R. Gurley, Greenville, 16 March 1861, quoted as spelled in Wiley, *Slaves No More*, 302).

141. "Dr. Hall, and the Sinou River Falls," *African Repository* 37, no. 5 (May 1861): 147; "From Liberia," *African Repository* 37, no. 6 (June 1861): 161–62.

142. "From Liberia," *African Repository* 37, no. 6 (June 1861): 162. Henry Stewart in 1863 remarked on the "industry" of recaptives at Ashmun, noting that they "in a great measure supplied the town of Greenville with the products of their industry" (Stewart to Gurley, 18 September 1863, in Wiley, *Slaves No More*, 303–4). In 1865, John Seys noted Sinoe recaptives' cultivation of "plantains, bannanas, eddoes, yams, peanuts, capavas, sweet potatoes, and various kinds of fruit that they carry daily into Greenville for sale to the Liberians." Recaptives freed Greenville emigrants from food production, Seys argued, thus allowing American-born Liberians to focus on commerce and export commodities of coffee, sugar, cotton, and cocoa. See John Seys, "The Recaptured Africans in Liberia," *African Repository* 41, no. 1 (January 1865): 16.

143. Peel, *Religious Encounter*, 28–30, 37–38. Peel argues that Yoruba speakers in the Oyo Kingdom established the "basic social forms" of the "nucleated settlement," lineages structured along agnatic descent, "cultic" and occupational associations, and status conferred through title. However, even in what would come to be known as Yorubaland, war, refugee movements, and economic instability prevented these forms from being realized in their ideal; see ibid., 30–31. Thus, we can understand the *Bogota* shipmates as facing an extreme version of the challenges to social cohesion already under way in their home areas.

144. Thank you to Lisa Lindsay for this insight. See O'Hear, "Enslavement of Yoruba," and Lovejoy, "Yoruba Factor."

145. Peel, *Religious Encounter*, 36–37.

146. Stewart to Gurley, 18 September 1863, in Wiley, *Slaves No More*, 303–4.

147. Allen, "Liberia and the Atlantic World," 27–28.

148. Sawyer, *Emergence of Autocracy*, 115–16.

149. Clegg, *Price of Liberty*, 98, eloquently discusses the transition of recaptives through multiple identities over the course of their captivity, enslavement, and recaptivity. For an excellent discussion of the relationship between external imposition and internal identification, see Borucki, *From Shipmates to Soldiers*, 218–23.

150. Curtin and Vansina, "Sources of the Nineteenth Century Slave Trade," map 6, 203; Domingues da Silva, Eltis, Misevich, and Ojo, "Diaspora of Africans," 347–69. See *Voyages* search discussed in n. 89 above.

151. "Kentucky State Colonization Society," *African Repository and Colonial Journal* 10, no. 7 (September 1834): 209–10; J. Mechlin to Rev. R. R. Gurley, *African Repository and Colonial Journal* 8, no. 7 (September 1832): 200–201.

152. Some of the more knowledgeable Liberians, perhaps attuned to missionary ethnographies produced in Sierra Leone, demonstrated awareness of diverse origins among West Central African recaptives. In Sierra Leone, the liberated African and Anglican bishop Samuel Crowther had applied the term "Yoruba" (in use by Hausa speakers to designate members of the Oyo Empire) to all Yoruba speakers. However, Crowther also used the term "Yoruba proper," giving primacy to residents of Oyo over Egba and other Yoruba speakers. See Peel, *Religious Encounter*, 284–85. Perhaps drawing on Crowther's distinction, a *Liberian Herald* editor in 1862 sought to sift the nuanced linguistic and geographic distinctions between the various groups of West Central Africans embarking from the Congo River. Thus, the editor praised the rapid assimilation of "the CONGO (Congo proper) people, and such other tribes as come from the country adjacent to Congo" ("From Liberia," *African Repository* 38, no. 12 [December 1862]: 377).

153. For an anecdote about a Liberian emigrant woman who demanded her husband live with her and not in his household of apprenticeship, see Crummell, "Address of Rev. Alexander Crummell," 277.

154. Lawrance, *Amistad's Orphans*, 219–65.

155. Ibid., 262, 263.

156. See Table 5 in this chapter.

157. John Seys to Jacob Thompson, 31 October 1860, reel 10, RSI.

158. John Seys, "The Recaptured Africans in Liberia," *African Repository* 41, no. 1 (January 1865): 16.

159. "Kentucky State Colonization Society," *African Repository and Colonial Journal* 10, no. 7 (September 1834): 209; "The Recaptured Africans," *African Repository and Colonial Journal* 10, no. 3 (May 1834): 90.

160. Nesbit, "Four Months in Liberia," 107; Crummell, "Address of Rev. Alexander Crummell," 277; Crummell, "Rev. Mr. Crummell on the Congo Recaptives"; "Kentucky State Colonization Society," *African Repository and Colonial Journal* 10 no. 7 (September 1834): 209–10. Elder Samuel Ball concluded that "amalgamation" between colonists and natives very rarely took place due to the "prejudice existing between them" (Ball, *Report on the Condition and Prospect*, 11). William E. Allen discusses intermarriage and intergroup sexual unions but focuses largely on relations between elite Americo-Liberian men and indigenous women; see Allen, "Liberia and the Atlantic World," 39–41.

161. John Seys to Jacob Thompson, 31 October 1860, reel 10, RSI.

162. Northrup, "Becoming African," 6.

163. Crowther, "Narrative of Samuel Ajayi Crowther," 299.

164. "African Missions," *African Repository* 37, no. 10 (October 1861): 317.

165. "Report of the Preacher to Recaptive Africans," *African Repository* 39, no. 10 (October 1863): 294–95.

166. "A Conjurer and Conjuration," *African Repository and Colonial Journal* 23, no. 1 (January 1847): 20–21.

167. See discussion of medicated incisions (*nsamba*) in Chapter 5.

168. For a conversion narrative relayed in first person from a *Pons* youth for a missionary audience, see J. W. Lugenbeel, "Religion among the Congoes by the Pons," *African Repository and Colonial Journal* 24, no. 2 (February 1848): 37–39. Other missionary descriptions of apprenticed recaptives include M. A. Ricks, "Letters from Liberia," *African Repository* 39, no. 1 (January 1863): 29–30; J. L. Mackey, "Intelligence," *African Repository* 38, no. 1 (January 1862): 24; and Washington McDonogh, "Scholars at Settra Kroo—Progress since 1843," *African Repository* 38, no. 3 (March 1862): 92.

169. Map titled "North west Part of Montserrado County, Liberia: in ten square miles," http://hdl.loc.gov/loc.gmd/g8883m.lm000018 (accessed 19 February 2016). The Muhlenberg Mission, built in 1860, provides a rough date for this undated map. More such Congo Town settlements may have existed in the southern counties not included on the map. The Congo Town located near Congo Creek appears on the map "St. Pauls River, Liberia at its mouth," http://hdl.loc.gov/loc.gmd/g8882s.lm000005 (accessed 15 May 2015). Both maps are from Maps of Liberia, 1830–1870, Library of Congress, Geography and Map Division. See also Sawyer, *Emergence of Autocracy*, 188. Numerous references to Congo Towns and Congo settlements in Liberia appear in the *African Repository* well into the 1880s. One of these near Caldwell was called by the 1880s Gardnerville.

170. Shick, *Behold the Promised Land*, 71.

171. On Congo/Kongo in diaspora, see Young, *Rituals of Resistance*; Childs, *1812 Aponte Rebellion*, 98, 101, 109–15; and Borucki, *From Shipmates to Soldiers*, 161–68. Vos, "'Without the Slave Trade,'" 59, notes that among twentieth-century Sundi of Central Africa, people with enslaved ancestors were known as Kongo, a reflection of their origins through internal slave trade networks from the south. See also "Congo" as surname in Mamigonian, "To Be a Liberated African in Brazil," 80–133 and passim; Peterson, *Province of Freedom*, 62, 254; Adderley, *"New Negroes from Africa,"* 123, 203–10; Heywood, *Central Africans and Cultural Transformations*; and Cooksey, Poynor, and Vanhee, *Kongo across the Waters*.

172. Byrd, *Captives and Voyagers*, 32 (emphasis in original).

173. John Seys to Jacob Thompson, 31 October 1860, reel 10, RSI.

174. Everill, *Abolition and Empire*, 13. For a scathing critique of "Congos" as agents of Americo-Liberian imperialism, see Akingbade, "Liberian Settlers and the Campaign," 366–68.

175. Lawrance, *Amistad's Orphans*, 180–93.

176. Wright, *Strategies of Slaves and Women*, 1–2, 9, 21; Miller, "Retention, Reinvention, and Remembering," 88–91.

Conclusion

1. Scott, "Paper Thin," 1086; Scott, *Was Freedom Portable?*

2. Camp, *Closer to Freedom*; Wong, *Neither Fugitive nor Free*.

3. The concept of liminality appears in several discussions of recaptivity. See DeLombard, *In the Shadow of the Gallows*, 304–5; Conrad, "Neither Slave nor Free"; Mamigonian, "To Be a Liberated African in Brazil," 4–5; and Fernández, "Havana Anglo-Spanish Mixed Commission," 214.

4. Domingues da Silva, Eltis, Misevich, and Ojo, "Diaspora of Africans," 366.

5. Kerber, "The Stateless as the Citizen's Other," 14.

6. Mamigonian, "In the Name of Freedom"; Adderley, *"New Negroes from Africa,"* 45–52; Coghe, "Problem of Freedom," 482–83; Fernández, "Havana Anglo-Spanish Mixed Commission."

7. Diouf, *Slavery's Exiles*; Roberts, *Freedom as Marronage*.

8. Poignant, *Professional Savages*; Blanchard et al., *Human Zoos*; Sharpley and Stone, *Darker Side of Travel*; Lennon and Foley, *Dark Tourism*; Hartnell, "Katrina Tourism."

9. Lawrance, *Amistad's Orphans*, 6, 268, 271.

10. Sweet, "Defying Social Death"; Mason, *Social Death and Resurrection*; Hawthorne, "'Being Now, as It Were, One Family.'"

11. Lawrance, *Amistad's Orphans*, 34.

12. Miller, "Retention, Reinvention, and Remembering," 81.

13. Harris, "New York Merchants and the Illegal Slave Trade"; Zeuske, *Amistad*; Marques, "United States and the Transatlantic Slave Trade."

14. Vos, "'Without the Slave Trade'"; Yun, *Coolie Speaks*; Lai, *Indentured Labor*; Hoefte, *In Place of Slavery*; Sundiata, *From Slaving to Neoslavery*.

15. Lovejoy, "Children of Slavery," table 2, 201; Allen, "Traffic Repugnant to Humanity"; Morton, "Small Change"; Allen, "Children and European Slave Trading."

16. Lawrance powerfully argues that the "age of abolition" be understood instead as an "age of child enslavement" (*Amistad's Orphans*, 7, 266–71). For modern-day slavery, see Bales, *Disposable People*, and Quirk, "Ending Slavery in All Its Forms."

17. Adderley, *"New Negroes from Africa,"* 206.

18. Ibid., 204, 213.

19. Gann and Duignan, *Rulers of Belgian Africa*, 101. Born in a Croatian town in the Austro-Hungarian Empire, Lerman worked in Belgian civil administration from 1888 until 1894. During his Liberian stay, he visited Edward Blyden and recorded his admiration of Blyden as an "educated African."

20. "Liberia as a Civilizer on the Congo," *African Repository* 63, no. 4 (April 1889): 61–63. The anonymous author attributes the quote to Lerman's government report on Congo migrants at Boma.

21. See Adderley's critical discussion of the idea of an African "homeland," in *"New Negroes from Africa,"* 209, 213.

BIBLIOGRAPHY

Primary Sources

ARCHIVAL SOURCES

Huntington Library, San Marino, California
   Journal & Remarks on Board the U. States Frigate San Jacinto of 15 guns,
        1860, Feb. 21–1861, Sept. 28, HM30205
   Letterbook of Thomas Aloysius Dornin, 1860, May 15–1861, Sept. 16, HM 30206
   Papers of Edward Griffin Beckwith and John Laurence Fox, 1805–1909
Library of Congress, Washington, D.C.
   American Colonization Society Records, MSS10660, Manuscript Division, microfilm
        J. W. Grymes, "Report of Doctr Grymes of Wash. City, D.C.," 10 December 1860.
        Series 1.E, Miscellaneous Incoming Correspondence, folder 1860 "Liberated
        Slaves."
   Maps of Liberia, 1830–1870. Geography and Map Division, On-Line Collection,
        https://www.loc.gov/collections/maps-of-liberia-1830-to-1870/. Accessed
        19 February 2016.
Lutheran Historical Society, Lutheran Theological Seminary, Gettysburg, Pennsylvania
   Morris Officer Diary, 20 January 1860–1 October 1860. Internet Archive Digitization
        of American Theological Library Association Microtext Project, University
        of Chicago Library, https://archive.org/details/MorrisOfficerDiary18521874.
        Accessed 14 January 2016.
Mystic Seaport, Mystic, Connecticut
   Henry Eason, "Journal, 1858–September 1860," Log 902. G. W. Blunt White Library,
        Mystic Seaport Museum Inc., on-line document, http://library.mysticseaport
        .org/initiative/PageImage.cfm?BibID=32915. Accessed 12 January 2016.
National Archives and Records Administration, Washington, D.C., and College Park,
        Maryland
   Admiralty Final Record Books of the U.S. District Court for the Southern District of
        Florida (Key West), 1829–1911. Record Group 21: Records of District Courts of
        the United States.
   Box 4, U.S. v. Schooner Fenix, Sept. 1831. Record Group 60: Supreme Court Case
        Papers, 1809–1870, General Records of the Department of Justice.
   Letters Received by the Secretary of the Navy From Commanding Officers of
        Squadrons, 1841–1886. Record Group 45: Naval Records Collection of the
        Office of Naval Records and Library, 1691–1945. Microfilm M89, Reels 11–12.
   Logs of US Naval Ships, 1801–1915, Logs of Ships and Stations, 1801–1946. Record
        Group 24: Records of the Bureau of Naval Personnel.
   Log of the United States Naval Ship *Niagara*

Log of United States Steamer *Crusader*

Log of United States Steamer *Mohawk*

Log of United States Steamer *Wyandotte*

Records of the Office of the Secretary of the Interior Relating to the Suppression of the African Slave Trade and Negro Colonization, 1854–1872. Record Group 48: General Records of the Department of the Interior. Microfilm M160, 10 reels.

David M. Rubenstein Rare Book and Manuscript Library, Duke University, Durham, North Carolina

John Moore McCalla Journal, 1860–61, John M. McCalla Papers

South Carolina Historical Society, Charleston

John Grimball Family Papers

Virginia Historical Society, Richmond

William Proby Young, "Ship Log, New York to Liberia, 1860"

West Virginia and Regional History Center, West Virginia University Libraries, Morgantown

John Moore McCalla Papers

NEWSPAPERS AND PERIODICALS

African Repository

African Repository and Colonial Journal

Anglo-African Magazine

Anti-Slavery Bugle

Carolina Spartan

Charleston Daily Courier

Charleston Mercury

Colored American

De Bow's Review

Douglass' Monthly

Frank Leslie's Illustrated Newspaper

Frederick Douglass' Paper

Freedom's Journal

Harper's Weekly

Illustrated London News

Liberator

National Anti-Slavery Standard

National Era

New York Herald

New York Times

New-York Daily Tribune

Weekly Anglo-African

The World (New York)

ON-LINE DATABASES (ACCESSED 22 FEBRUARY 2016)

African Origins, http://www.african-origins.org/

Ancestry Library, http://www.ancestry.com/

Black Abolitionist Papers, 1830–1865, *Proquest*, http://www.proquest.com/products-services/blk_abol_pap.html

The Liberated Africans Project, http://www.liberatedafricans.org/

Virginia Emigrants to Liberia, http://www.vcdh.virginia.edu/liberia/index.php?page=Home

Voyages: The Trans-Atlantic Slave Trade Database (*Voyages*), http://www.slavevoyages.org/

PUBLISHED SOURCES

An Act in Addition to the Acts Prohibiting the Slave Trade. Chap. 101. 15th Cong., 2nd Sess., 3 March 1819.

An Act to Prohibit the Importation of Slaves into Any Port or Place within the Jurisdiction of the United States, from and after the First Day of January, in the Year of Our Lord, One Thousand Eight Hundred and Eight. Chap. 22. 9th Cong., 2nd Sess., 2 March 1807.

"The Africans of the Amistad." *New-Hampshire Statesman and State Journal*, 21 September 1839.

B., J. B. "Cape Mount." *Christian Advocate and Journal*, 21 April 1847, 63.

Ball, S. S. *Report on the Condition and Prospect of the Republic of Liberia*. Alton, Ill.: "Telegraph" Office, 1848.

Bentley, Rev. W. Holman. *Appendix to the Dictionary and Grammar of the Kongo Language*. London: Baptist Missionary Society, 1895.

Bibb, Henry. "Slave Hunters Baffled." *Voice of the Fugitive*, 17 June 1852.

Blyden, Edward W. "A Chapter in the History of the African Slave Trade." *Anglo-African Magazine* 1, no. 6 (June 1859): 178–84.

"The Book Trade—2. *Africa and the American Flag*." *Merchants Magazine and Commercial Review*, 1 November 1854, 651.

Bowen, T. J. *Central Africa: Adventures and Missionary Labors in Several Countries in the Interior of Africa, from 1849 to 1856*. Charleston, S.C.: Southern Baptist Publication Society, 1857.

Bridge, Horatio. *Journal of an African Cruiser: Comprising Sketches of the Canaries, the Cape De Verds, Liberia, Madeira, Sierra Leone, and Other Places of Interest on the West Coast of Africa*. Edited by Nathaniel Hawthorne. London, 1845. New York: George P. Putnam, 1853.

Burmeister, Hermann. *The Black Man: The Comparative Anatomy and Psychology of the African Negro*. Translated by Robert Tomes, Dr. Phil. of Berlin and Julius Friedlander, M.D. of New York. New York: William C. Bryant, 1853.

"Captain Canot, or Twenty Years of an African Slaver." *North American Review* 80, no. 166 (January 1855): 153–70.

"The Captain of the Slaver." *Georgia Telegraph and Macon Weekly Telegraph*, 14 September 1858.

"The Captured Slave Brig." *Daily Ohio Statesman*, 3 September 1858.

"The Captured Slaver." *Daily Ohio Statesman*, 17 September 1858.

"Capture of a Slaver." *Farmer's Cabinet*, 8 September 1858.

"Capture of the Slaver Pons." *Boston Daily Atlas*, 19 March 1846.

"Condition and Expense of the United States Agency for Recaptured Africans Taken to the Coast of Africa, Communicated to the House of Representatives, 12 March 1828." *American State Papers: Naval Affairs*, 3:143–49.

"The Congo Fever in Charleston." *Chicago Daily Press and Tribune*, 6 September 1858.

Conneau, Captain Theophilus. *A Slaver's Log Book or 20 Years' Residence in Africa: The Original 1853 Manuscript by Captain Theophilus Conneau*. Introduction by Mabel M. Smythe, ed. 1854. London: Prentice-Hall International, 1976.

Cornish, Samuel, and Theodore S. Wright. *The Colonization Scheme Considered in Its Reflection by the Colored People*. Newark: Aaron Guest, 1840.

"Correspondence with the British Commissioners, Havana, No. 99." *Colonies and Slaves: Relating to Colonies; African Captured; Jamaica; Slave Emancipation; Slave Trade, Session 14 June–20 October 1831*, 19:121–22.

Cowan, Alexander M. *Liberia, as I Found It, in 1858*. Frankfort, Ky.: A. G. Hodges, 1858.

Crowther, Samuel Ajayi. "The Narrative of Samuel Ajayi Crowther [1837, 1842]." In *Africa Remembered: Narratives by West Africans from the Era of the Slave Trade*, edited by Philip D. Curtin, 298–316. Madison: University of Wisconsin Press, 1967.

Crummell, Alexander. "Address of Rev. Alexander Crummell." *African Repository* 37, no. 9 (September 1861): 271–80.

———. "'Africa and Her People': Lecture Notes." In *Destiny and Race: Selected Writings, 1840–1898, Alexander Crummell*, edited by Wilson Jeremiah Moses. Boston: University of Massachusetts Press, 1992.

———. "The Regenerating Policy of Liberia." *African Repository* 47, no. 8 (August 1871): 225–36.

———. "Rev. Mr. Crummell on the Congo Recaptives." *African Repository* 37, no. 10 (October 1861): 312–13.

Curry, Thomas. *Reports of Cases Argued and Determined in the Supreme Court of Louisiana.* Vol. 12. New Orleans: Benjamin Levy, 1839.

Curtin, Philip D., ed. *Africa Remembered: Narratives by West Africans from the Era of the Slave Trade.* Long Grove, Ill.: Waveland Press, 1967.

Dalzel, Archibald. *The Kingdom of Dahomey: An Inland Kingdom of Africa.* London: Spilsbury and Snowhill, 1793.

"Death of John McNevin: A Man Who Sketched Battle Pictures in Two Wars." *Brooklyn Daily Eagle*, 1 March 1894.

Delany, Martin. *Blake; or, the Huts of America.* Edited by Floyd J. Miller. Reprint, Boston: Beacon Press, 1970.

"Dr. Rainey, 'Father of Bridge,' Glad Life-Work Is Completed." *Brooklyn Daily Eagle*, 12 June 1909, 38.

Douglass, Frederick. *The Claims of the Negro, Ethnologically Considered.* Rochester: Lee, Mann and Co., 1854.

———. "Freedom in the West Indies: An Address Delivered in Poughkeepsie, New York, on 2 August 1858." In *The Frederick Douglass Papers.* Series 1, *Speeches, Debates and Interviews*, edited by John W. Blassingame, 3:214–42. New Haven: Yale University Press, 1985.

———. "Slavery and the Limits of Nonintervention: An Address Delivered in Halifax, England, on 7 December 1859." In *The Frederick Douglass Papers.* Series 1, *Speeches, Debates and Interviews*, edited by John W. Blassingame, 3:276–88. New Haven: Yale University Press, 1985.

Drake, Richard, and Rev. Henry Byrd West. *Revelations of a Slave Smuggler: Being the Autobiography of Capt. Rich'd Drake, an African Trader for Fifty Years.* New York: Robert M. De Witt, 1860.

Eisami, Ali. "Ali Eisami Gazirmabe [1850]." In *Africa Remembered: Narratives by West Africans from the Era of the Slave Trade*, edited by Philip D. Curtin, 199–216. Madison: University of Wisconsin Press, 1967.

Equiano, Olaudah. *The Interesting Narrative of the Life of Olaudah Equiano, or Gustavus Vassa, the African.* 1789. Documenting the American South, University Library, University of North Carolina at Chapel Hill, 2001, http://docsouth.unc.edu/neh/equiano1/equiano1.html. Accessed 12 February 2016.

Ethiop. "The Anglo-African and the African Slave Trade." *Anglo-African Magazine* 1, no. 9 (September 1859): 283–86.

———. "What Shall We Do with the White People?" *Anglo-African Magazine* 2, no. 2 (February 1860): 41–45.

"Extracts from Letters Respecting the Capture of the Slave Ship 'Pons.'" HC10-12179. Quaker Broadsides Collection, Haverford Special Collections, Haverford College,

Haverford, Mass., http://triptych.brynmawr.edu/cdm/search/searchterm/HC10-12179. Accessed 24 January 2016.

Fairhead, James, Tim Geysbeek, Svend E. Holsoe, and Melissa Leach, eds. *African-American Exploration in West Africa: Four Nineteenth-Century Diaries*. Bloomington: Indiana University Press, 2003.

Foote, Andrew H. *Africa and the American Flag*. New York: Appleton, 1854.

Forbes, Frederick E. *Dahomey and the Dahomans: Being the Journals of Two Missions to the King of Dahomey, and Residence at His Capital, in the Years 1849 and 1850*. 2 vols. London: Longman, Brown, Green, and Longmans, 1851.

——— . *Six Months' Service in the African Blockade, from April to October, 1848, in Command of H.M.S. Bonetta*. London: Richard Bentley, 1849.

Forty-Second Annual Report of the American Colonization Society with the Proceedings of the Board of Directors and the Society: January 18, 1859. Washington, D.C.: C. Alexander, 1859.

Forty-Seventh Annual Report of the American Colonization Society with the Proceedings of the Annual Meeting and of the Board of Directors and the Society: January 19, 1864. Washington, D.C.: Colonization Society Building, 1864.

Fowler, L. N. "Phrenological Developments of Joseph Cinquez, Alias Ginqua." *American Phrenological Journal and Miscellany* 2 (1840): 136–38.

Garnet, Henry Highland. *The Past and the Present Condition, and the Destiny, of the Colored Race*. Troy, N.Y.: J. C. Kneeland, 1848.

Guannu, Joseph Saye, ed. *The Inaugural Addresses of the Presidents of Liberia: From Joseph Jenkins Roberts to William Richard Tolbert, Jr., 1848 to 1976*. Hicksville, N.Y.: Exposition Press, 1980.

"Highly Interesting from the Gulf." *Chicago Press and Tribune*, 8 June 1860.

House Special Committee on Slavery and the Slave Trade. *Report of Special Committee of the House of Representatives of South Carolina on So Much of the Message of His Excellency Gov. Jas. H. Adams*. Charleston, S.C.: Walker, Evans & Co., 1857.

——— . *Report of the Minority of the Special Committee of Seven, to Whom Was Referred So Much of His Late Excellency's Message, No. 1, as Relates to Slavery and the Slave Trade*. Columbia, S.C.: Steam Power Press Carolina Times, 1857.

Howe, Henry. *Life and Death on the Ocean: A Collection of Extraordinary Adventures*. Cincinnati: Henry Howe, 1855.

Hoyt, W. B. *Land of Hope: Reminiscences of Liberia and Cape Palmas*. Hartford, Conn.: William J. Fox and Henry B. Hoyt, 1852.

H.R. Ex. Doc. No. 7, African Slave Trade. 36th Cong., 2nd Sess. (1861), 1–648.

Hunt, James. *The Negro's Place in Nature*. New York: Van Evrie, Horton and Co., 1864.

Imhoff, Rev. Alex. J. *The Life of Rev. Morris Officer, A.M.* Dayton, Ohio: United Brethren Publishing House, 1876.

"Is the Plan of the American Union under the Constitution Anti-Slavery or Not?: A Debate between Frederick Douglass and Charles Lenox Remond in New York, New York, on 20, 21 May 1857." In *The Frederick Douglass Papers*. Series 1, *Speeches, Debates and Interviews*, edited by John W. Blassingame, 3:151–62. New Haven: Yale University Press, 1985.

Jacobs, Harriet A. *Incidents in the Life of a Slave Girl Written by Herself*. Edited by Jean Fagan Yellin. Cambridge: Harvard University Press, 1987.

Jefferson, Thomas. *Notes on the State of Virginia*. Boston: Wells and Lily, 1829.

Key of the Gulf, 14 July 1860.

"The Key West Africans." *Constitution*, 17 July 1860, 83.

Koelle, S. W. *Polyglotta Africana; or a Comparative Vocabulary of Nearly Three Hundred Words and Phrases, in More Than One Hundred Distinct African Languages*. London: Church Missionary House, 1854. Sierra Leone: Foourah Bay College, The University College of Sierra Leone, 1963.

Laman, K. E. *Grammar of the Kongo Language*. Translated by Elin Wikander. New York: Christian Alliance, 1912.

Law, Robin, and Paul Lovejoy, eds. *The Biography of Mahommah Gardo Baquaqua: His Passage from Slavery to Freedom in Africa and America*. Princeton: Markus Wiener Publishers, 2007.

Levien, Douglas A. *The Case of the Slaver Echo*. Albany, N.Y.: Week, Parsons & Company, 1859.

"Liberated Africans." *Religious Intelligencer*, 31 January 1824, 549–51.

Lindsly, Harvey. "Differences in the Intellectual Character of the Several Varieties of the Human Race." *Southern Literary Messenger* 5, no. 9 (September 1839): 616–20.

Lindsly, Webster. "Dreadful Sufferings Caused by the Slave Trade." *African Repository* 37, no. 4 (April 1861): 108–12.

Livingstone, David. *Missionary Travels and Researches in South Africa*. London: J. Murray, 1857.

Lugenbeel, J. W. "Authenticity of Captain Canot." *Home Journal*, 7 October 1854.

———. *Sketches of Liberia: Comprising a Brief Account of the Geography, Climate, Productions, and Diseases, of the Republic of Liberia*. 2nd ed. Washington, D.C.: C. Alexander, 1853.

Manning, Edward. *Six Months on a Slaver*. New York: Harper & Brothers, 1879.

Mayer, Brantz. *History of the War between Mexico and the United States, with a Preliminary View of Its Origin*. New York: Wiley and Putnam, 1848.

———. *Mexico: Aztec, Spanish, and Republican*. Vol. 1. New York: C. A. Alvord, 1850.

———, ed. *Captain Canot, or Twenty Years of an African Slaver, Being an Account of His Career and Adventures on the Coast, in the Interior, on the Shipboard, and in the West Indies*. New York: Appleton, 1854.

McCord, Louisa Susanna. "Diversity of the Races: Its Bearing Upon Negro Slavery." *Southern Quarterly Review* 3, no. 6 (April 1851): 392–419.

McCune Smith, James. "Civilization: Its Dependence on Physical Circumstances," *Anglo-African Magazine* 1, no. 1 (January 1859): 5–17.

McCune Smith, James, and John Stauffer, eds. *The Works of James McCune Smith: Black Intellectual and Abolitionist*. New York: Oxford, 2006.

"Modern Algiers." *Harper's Weekly*, 4 December 1858, 772–73.

Morton, Samuel George. *Crania Americana; or, a Comparative View of the Skulls of Various Aboriginal Nations of North and South America*. Philadelphia: J. Dobson, 1839.

Mullaly, John. *The Laying of the Cable; or the Ocean Telegraph*. New York: Appleton, 1858.

Nesbit, William. "Four Months in Liberia: Or African Colonization Exposed." 1855. In *Liberian Dreams: Back-to-Africa Narratives from the 1850s*, edited by Wilson Jeremiah Moses, 79–126. University Park: Pennsylvania State University Press, 1998.

Nott, J. C., and Geo. R. Gliddon. *Types of Mankind: Or, Ethnological Researches, Based Upon the Ancient Monuments, Paintings, Sculptures, and Crania of Races, and Upon Their Natural, Geographical, Philological and Biblical History*. Philadelphia: Lippincott, Grambo, 1854.

"On the Capture, by a United States Vessel, of the Spanish Ship Fenix, with African

Slaves on Board, Communicated to the House of Representatives, January 18, 1831." *American State Papers: Naval Affairs*, 3: 865–71.

Park, Mungo. *Travels in the Interior Districts of Africa*. Edited by Kate Ferguson Marsters. 1799. Durham, N.C.: Duke University Press, 2000.

Pennington, J. W. C. "An American Slave in England, London." *Liberator*, 18 October 1849.

———. "The Great Conflict Requires Great Faith." *Anglo-African Magazine* 1, no. 11 (November 1859): 343–45.

———. "Instructions of the Executive Committee to Mr. and Mrs. Wilson." *Union Missionary Herald* 1, no. 2 (February 1842): 65–72.

———. "Intelligence from Jamaica. Kingston, Ja., Feb. 12th, 1846." *Christian Contributor & Free Missionary* 3, no. 16 (18 June 1846): 62.

———. "A Letter from Rev. Dr. Pennington." *Frederick Douglass' Paper*, 6 April 1855.

———. *A Narrative of the Events from the Life of J. H. Banks, An Escaped Slave, From the Cotton State, Alabama, in America*. 1861. Documenting the American South, University Library, University of North Carolina at Chapel Hill, 2000, http://docsouth.unc.edu/ neh/penning/penning.html. Accessed 17 January 2016.

———. "Report on Colonization, Colored National Convention, 6–8 July 1853, Rochester, NY." In *Minutes of the Proceedings of the National Negro Conventions, 1830–1864*, edited by Howard Holman Bell, 47–57. New York: Arno Press & New York Times, 1969.

———. "A Review of Slavery and the Slave Trade." *Anglo-African Magazine* 1, no. 5 (May 1859): 93–96.

———. "The Self-Redeeming Power of the Colored Races of the World." *Anglo-African Magazine* 1, no. 10 (October 1859): 314–20.

———. "Slave Trade—Wildfire, and the Message of the 19th of May, 1860." *The World*, 13 July 1860, 6.

———. *A Two Years' Absence, or a Farewell Sermon Preached in the Fifth Congregational Church*. Hartford: H. T. Wells, 1845.

———. "Why the Guilty Slavers Are Never Punished as Pirates, as They Should Be." *World*, 20 July 1860, 6.

Pennington, James W. C. *The Fugitive Blacksmith: Or Events in the History of James W. C. Pennington, Pastor of a Presbyterian Church, New York, Formerly a Slave in the State of Maryland, United States*. 1849. Documenting the American South, University Library, University of North Carolina at Chapel Hill, 2001, http://docsouth.unc.edu/neh/ penning49/penning49.html. Accessed 17 January 2016.

———. *A Text Book of the Origin and History, &C. &C. of the Colored People*. Hartford: L. Skinner, 1841. Detroit: Negro History Press, 1969.

"A Precedent." *Pittsfield Sun*, 30 September 1858.

Rainey, Thomas. *Ocean Steam Navigation and the Ocean Post*. New York: Appleton, 1858.

Senate Ex. Doc. No. 150, Information Relative to the Operations of the United States Squadron on the West Coast of Africa. 28th Cong., 2nd Sess. (1845), 1–414.

"The Sixth Annual Report of the American Society for Colonizing the Free People of Color of the United States." *North American Review*, January 1824, 40–90.

"The Slaver Kibby and Her Captain." *Times-Picayune*, 8 August 1860.

"The Slave Trade in Alabama." *Daily Evening Bulletin*, 7 August 1860.

Southard, Samuel L. "Documents. From the Navy Department, Accompanying the President's Message." *Niles National Register*, 1 January 1825, 280.

Spratt, L. W. *The Foreign Slave Trade the Source of Political Power—of Material Progress, of Social Integrity, and of Social Emancipation to the South*. Charleston, S.C.: Steam Power Press of Walker, Evans & Co., 1858.

——— . *Speech Upon the Foreign Slave Trade before the Legislature of South Carolina*. Charleston, S.C.: Steam Power Press Southern Guardian, 1858.

Still, William. *The Underground Railroad*. Philadelphia: Porter & Coates, 1872.

"Still Another Slaver Captured." *Florida Peninsular*, 2 June 1860.

Thomas, Charles W. *Adventures and Observations on the West Coast of Africa, and Its Islands*. New York: Derby and Jackson, 1860.

Thomes, William Henry. *A Slaver's Adventure on Land and Sea*. Boston: Lee and Shepard, 1872.

Twenty-Ninth Annual Report of the Mission Society of the Methodist Church. New York: Conference Office, 1848.

Van Evrie, John H. *Negroes and Negro Slavery; the First, an Inferior Race—the Latter, Its Normal Condition*. Baltimore: John Toy, 1853.

Vermilyea, L. H. *The Slaver, the War, and around the World*. Albany: Weed, Parsons and Company, 1867.

Walker, David. "Walker's Appeal, in Four Articles; Together with a Preamble, to the Coloured Citizens of the World." 1830. Documenting the American South, University Library, University of North Carolina at Chapel Hill, 2001, http://docsouth.unc.edu/nc/walker/walker.html. Accessed 25 January 2016.

Walsh, Robert. *Notices of Brazil in 1828 and 1829*. London: Frederick Westly and A. H. Davis, 1830.

Washington, Augustus. "Liberia as It Is, 1854." 1854. In *Liberian Dreams: Back-to-Africa Narratives from the 1850s*, edited by Wilson Jeremiah Moses, 202–12. University Park: Pennsylvania State University Press, 1998.

Wiley, Bell I., ed. *Slaves No More: Letters from Liberia, 1833–1869*. Lexington: University Press of Kentucky, 1980.

Williams, Samuel. "Four Years in Liberia: A Sketch of the Life of the Rev. Samuel Williams with Remarks on the Missions, Manners and Customs of the Natives of Western Africa Together with an Answer to Nesbit's Book." 1857. In *Liberian Dreams: Back-to-Africa Narratives from the 1850s*, edited by Wilson Jeremiah Moses, 127–78. University Park: Pennsylvania State University Press, 1998.

Woodruff, J. *Report of the Trials in the Echo Cases, in Federal Court, Charleston, S.C., April, 1859; Together with Arguments of Counsel and Charge of the Court*. Columbia, S.C.: Steam-power Press of R. W. Gibbes, 1859.

Wright, Joseph. "Joseph Wright of the Egba [1839, 1841]." In *Africa Remembered: Narratives by West Africans from the Era of the Slave Trade*, edited by Philip D. Curtin, 317–33. Madison: University of Wisconsin Press, 1967.

Secondary Sources

Adderley, Rosanne Marion. *"New Negroes from Africa": Slave Trade Abolition and Free African Settlement in the Nineteenth-Century Caribbean*. Bloomington: Indiana University Press, 2006.

Afolayan, Funso. "Kingdoms of West Africa: Benin, Oyo, and Asante." In *Africa*, edited by Toyin Falola, 161–89. Durham, N.C.: Carolina Academic Press, 2000.

Akingbade, Harrison. "The Liberian Settlers and the Campaign against the Slave Trade, 1825–1865." *Africa: Rivista Trimestrale di Studi e Documentazione* 38, no. 3 (September 1983): 339–68.

Akpan, M. B. "Black Imperialism: Americo-Liberian Rule over the African Peoples of Liberia, 1841–1964." *Canadian Journal of African Studies* 7, no. 2 (1973): 217–36.

Alanamu, Temilola. "Indigenous Medical Practices and the Advent of CMS Medical Evangelism in Nineteenth-Century Yorubaland." *Church History and Religious Culture* 93 (2013): 5–27.

Alexander, Leslie M. *African or American?: Black Identity and Political Activism in New York City, 1784–1861*. Urbana: University of Illinois Press, 2008.

Allen, Richard B. "Children and European Slave Trading in the Indian Ocean during the Eighteenth and Early Nineteenth Centuries." In *Children in Slavery through the Ages*, edited by Gwyn Campbell, Suzanne Miers, and Joseph C. Miller, 35–54. Athens: Ohio University Press, 2009.

———. "A Traffic Repugnant to Humanity: Children, the Mascarene Slave Trade and British Abolitionism." *Slavery and Abolition* 27, no. 2 (August 2006): 219–36.

Allen, William E. "Liberia and the Atlantic World in the Nineteenth Century: Convergence and Effects." *History in Africa* 37 (2010): 7–49.

Alpers, Edward A. "The Other Middle Passage: The African Slave Trade in the Indian Ocean." In *Many Middle Passages: Forced Migration and the Making of the Modern World*, edited by Emma Christopher, Cassandra Pybus, and Marcus Rediker, 20–38. Berkeley: University of California Press, 2007.

Anbinder, Tyler. "Isaiah Rynders and the Ironies of Popular Democracy in Antebellum New York." In *Contested Democracy: Freedom, Race, and Power*, edited by Manisha Sinha and Penny Von Eschen, 31–53. New York: Columbia University Press, 2007.

Anderson, Richard, Alex Borucki, Daniel Domingues da Silva, David Eltis, Paul Lachance, Philip Misevich, and Olatunji Ojo. "Using African Names to Identify the Origins of Captives in the Transatlantic Slave Trade: Crowd-Sourcing and the Registers of Liberated Africans, 1808–1862." *African Studies Association* 40, no. 1 (October 2013): 165–91.

Apter, Andrew. "Yoruba Ethnogenesis from Within." *Comparative Studies in Society and History* 55, no. 2 (2013): 356–87.

Apter, Andrew, and Lauren Derby, eds. *Activating the Past: History and Memory in the Black Atlantic World*. Newcastle upon Tyne: Cambridge Scholars, 2010.

Asiegbu, Johnson U. J. *Slavery and the Politics of Liberation, 1787–1861: A Study of Liberated African Emigration and British Anti-Slavery Policy*. London: Longmans, Green, 1969.

Austen, Ralph A. "The Moral Economy of Witchcraft: An Essay in Comparative History." In *Modernity and Its Malcontents: Ritual and Power in Postcolonial Africa*, edited by Jean Comaroff and John Comaroff, 89–110. Chicago: University of Chicago Press, 1993.

———. "The Slave Trade as History and Memory: Confrontations of Slaving Voyage Documents and Communal Traditions." *William and Mary Quarterly* 58, no. 1 (2001): 229–44.

Bailey, Anne C. *African Voices of the Atlantic Slave Trade: Beyond the Silence and the Shame*. Boston: Beacon Press, 2005.

Bales, Kevin. *Disposable People: New Slavery in the Global Economy*. 3rd ed. Berkeley: University of California Press, 2012.

Ball, Erica L. *To Live an Antislavery Life: Personal Politics and the Antebellum Middle Class*. Athens: University of Georgia Press, 2012.

Bassani, Ezio. "Kongo Nail Fetishes from the Chiloango River Area." *African Arts* 10, no. 3 (April 1977): 36–40, 88.

Bastin, Marie Louise. "Arts of the Angolan Peoples. I: Chokwe / L'Art d'un Peuple d'Angola." *African Arts* 2, no. 1 (Autumn 1968): 40–47, 60–64.

Batterson, Sarah. "A Horde of Foreign Freebooters: The U.S. and the Suppression of the Slave Trade." *Diacronie: Studi di Storia Contemporanea* 13, no. 1 (2013).

Bay, Edna G. *Wives of the Leopard: Gender, Politics, and Culture in the Kingdom of Dahomey*. Charlottesville: University of Virginia Press, 1998.

Bay, Mia. *The White Image in the Black Mind: African-American Ideas about White People, 1830–1925*. New York: Oxford University Press, 1999.

Beckert, Sven. "Emancipation and Empire: Reconstructing the Worldwide Web of Cotton Production in the Age of the American Civil War." *American Historical Review* 109, no. 5 (December 2004): 1405–38.

Bender, Thomas, ed. *The Antislavery Debate: Capitalism and Abolitionism as a Problem in Historical Interpretation*. Berkeley: University of California Press, 1992.

Berlin, Ira. *Generations of Captivity: A History of African-American Slaves*. Cambridge: Harvard University Press, 2003.

Berlin, Ira, and Leslie M. Harris, eds. *Slavery in New York*. New York: New Press, 2005.

Berns, Marla C. "Ga'anda Scarification: A Model for Art and Identity." In *Marks of Civilization: Artistic Transformations of the Human Body*, edited by Arnold Rubin, 57–75. Los Angeles: Museum of Cultural History, 1988.

Blackett, R. J. M. *Building an Antislavery Wall: Black Americans in the Atlantic Abolitionist Movement, 1831–1860*. Baton Rouge: Louisiana State University Press, 1983.

———. *Beating against the Barriers: Biographical Essays in Nineteenth-Century Afro-American History*. Baton Rouge: Louisiana State University Press, 1986.

Blackett, Richard. "Martin R. Delany and Robert Campbell: Black Americans in Search of an African Colony." *Journal of Negro History* 62, no. 1 (January 1977): 1–25.

Blanchard, Pascal, Gilles Boëtsch, and Nanette Jacomijn Snoep. *Human Zoos: The Invention of the Savage*. Paris: Actes Sud, 2011.

Blier, Suzanne Preston. *African Vodun: Art, Psychology, and Power*. Chicago: University of Chicago Press, 1995.

Blight, David W. *Frederick Douglass' Civil War: Keeping Faith in Jubilee*. Baton Rouge: Louisiana State University Press, 1991.

Blum, Hester. *The View from the Masthead: Maritime Imagination and Antebellum American Sea Narratives*. Chapel Hill: University of North Carolina Press, 2008.

Bohannan, Paul. "Beauty and Scarification amongst the Tiv." In *Marks of Civilization: Artistic Transformations of the Human Body*, edited by Arnold Rubin, 76–82. Los Angeles: Museum of Cultural History, 1988.

Borucki, Alex. *From Shipmates to Soldiers: Emerging Black Identities in the Río de la Plata*. Albuquerque: University of New Mexico Press, 2015.

———. "Shipmate Networks and Black Identities in the Marriage Files of Montevideo." *Hispanic American Historical Review* 93, no. 2 (May 2013): 205–38.

Boyd, Willis D. "The American Colonization Society and the Slave Recaptives of 1860–61: An Early Example of United States–African Relations." *Journal of Negro History* 47 (April 1962): 108–26.

———. "Negro Colonization in the National Crisis, 1860–1870." Ph.D. diss., University of California, Los Angeles, 1953.

Brancaccio, Patrick. "The Black Man's Paradise: Hawthorne's Editing of the *Journal of an African Cruiser*." *New England Quarterly* 53, no. 1 (March 1980): 23–41.

Brantlinger, Patrick. *Rule of Darkness: British Literature and Imperialism, 1830–1914*. Ithaca: Cornell University Press, 1990.

———. "Victorians and Africans: The Genealogy of the Myth of the Dark Continent." *Critical Inquiry* 12, no. 1 (Autumn 1985): 166–203.

Broadhead, Susan Herlin. "Slave Wives, Free Sisters: Bakongo Women and Slavery c. 1700–1850." In *Women and Slavery in Africa*, edited by Claire C. Robertson and Martin A. Klein, 160–81. Madison: University of Wisconsin Press, 1983.

Brooks, George E. "Samuel Hodges, Jr., and the Symbiosis of Slave and 'Legitimate' Trades, 1810s–1820s." *International Journal of African Historical Studies* 41, no. 1 (2008): 101–15.

———. *West Africa and Cabo Verde, 1790s–1830s: The Symbiosis of Slave and Legitimate Trades*. Bloomington, Ind.: AuthorHouse, 2010.

Brown, Christopher L. "The British Government and the Slave Trade: Early Parliamentary Enquiries, 1714–1783." In *The British Slave Trade: Abolition, Parliament and the People*, edited by Stephen Farrell, Melanie Unwin, and James Walvin, 27–41. Edinburgh: Edinburgh University Press, 2007.

Brown, Joshua. *Beyond the Lines: Pictorial Reporting, Everyday Life, and the Crisis of Gilded Age America*. Berkeley: University of California Press, 2002.

Brown, Vincent. *The Reaper's Garden: Death and Power in the World of Atlantic Slavery*. Cambridge: Harvard University Press, 2008.

———. "Social Death and Political Life in the Study of Slavery." *American Historical Review* 114, no. 5 (December 2009): 1231–49.

Browne, Jefferson B. *Key West: The Old and the New*. Edited by Samuel Proctor. Gainesville: University of Florida Press, 1973.

Bryant, Jonathan. *Dark Places of the Earth: The Voyage of the Slave Ship Antelope*. New York: Norton, 2015.

Burin, Eric. *Slavery and the Peculiar Solution: A History of the American Colonization Society*. Gainesville: University Press of Florida, 2005.

———. "The Slave Trade Act of 1819: A New Look at Colonization and the Politics of Slavery." *American Nineteenth Century History* 13, no. 1 (March 2012): 1–14.

Burroughs, Robert. "Eyes on the Prize: Journeys in Slave Ships Taken as Prizes by the Royal Navy." *Slavery and Abolition* 31, no. 1 (March 2010): 99–115.

———. "'[T]he True Sailors of Western Africa': Kru Seafaring Identity in British Travellers' Accounts of the 1830s and 1840s." *Journal for Maritime Research* 11, no. 1 (September 2009): 51–67.

Burrowes, Carl Patrick. *Power and Press Freedom in Liberia, 1830–1970: The Impact of Globalization and Civil Society on Media-Government Relations*. Trenton, N.J.: Africa World Press, 2004.

Byrd, Alexander X. *Captives and Voyagers: Black Migrants across the Eighteenth-Century British Atlantic World*. Baton Rouge: Louisiana State University Press, 2008.

Calonius, Eric. *The Wanderer: The Last American Slave Ship and the Conspiracy That Set Its Sails.* New York: St. Martin's Press, 2006.

Camp, Stephanie M. H. *Closer to Freedom: Enslaved Women and Everyday Resistance in the Plantation South.* Chapel Hill: University of North Carolina Press, 2004.

Campbell, Gwyn, Suzanne Miers, and Joseph C. Miller. "Children in European Systems of Slavery: Introduction." *Slavery and Abolition* 27, no. 2 (August 2006): 163–82.

———, eds. *Children in Slavery through the Ages.* Athens: Ohio University Press, 2009.

———, eds. *Child Slaves in the Modern World.* Athens: Ohio University Press, 2011.

Campbell, James T. *Middle Passages: African American Journeys to Africa, 1787–2005.* New York: Penguin, 2006.

Candido, Mariana P. *An African Slaving Port and the Atlantic World: Benguela and Its Hinterland.* New York: Cambridge University Press, 2013.

———. "Tracing Benguela Identity to the Homeland." In *Crossing Memories: Slavery and African Diaspora,* edited by Ana Lucia Araujo, Mariana P. Candido, and Paul E. Lovejoy, 183–207. Trenton, N.J.: Africa World Press, 2011.

Candido, Mariana Pinho. "African Freedom Suits and Portuguese Vassal Status: Legal Mechanisms for Fighting Enslavement in Benguela, Angola, 1800–1830." *Slavery and Abolition* 32, no. 3 (2011): 447–59.

Canney, Donald L. *Africa Squadron: The U.S. Navy and the Slave Trade, 1842–1861.* Washington, D.C.: Potomac Books, 2006.

———. *The Old Steam Navy: Frigates, Sloops, and Gunboats, 1815–1885.* Vol. 1. Annapolis, Md.: West Point Naval Institute, 1990.

Carson, John. *The Measure of Merit: Talents, Intelligence, and Inequality in the French and American Republics, 1750–1940.* Princeton: Princeton University Press, 2006.

Chan, Kwok B., and David Loveridge. "Refugees 'in Transit': Vietnamese in a Refugee Camp in Hong Kong." *International Migration Review* 21, no. 3 (Autumn 1987): 745–59.

Childs, Matt D. *The 1812 Aponte Rebellion in Cuba and the Struggle against Atlantic Slavery.* Chapel Hill: University of North Carolina Press, 2006.

Christopher, Emma. *Slave Ship Sailors and Their Captive Cargoes, 1730–1807.* Cambridge: Cambridge University Press, 2006.

Christopher, Emma, Cassandra Pybus, and Marcus Rediker, eds. *Many Middle Passages: Forced Migration and the Making of the Modern World.* Berkeley: University of California Press, 2007.

Clayton, Lawrence A. *Bartolomé de las Casas: A Biography.* Translated by Janet Lloyd. Cambridge: Cambridge University Press, 2012.

Clegg, Claude A., III. *The Price of Liberty: African Americans and the Making of Liberia.* Chapel Hill: University of North Carolina Press, 2004.

Clifton, James M., ed. *Life and Labor on Argyle Island: Letters and Documents of a Savannah River Rice Plantation, 1833–1867.* Savannah: Beehive Press, 1978.

Coghe, Samuël. "The Problem of Freedom in a Mid-Nineteenth-Century Atlantic Slave Society: The Liberated Africans of the Anglo-Portuguese Mixed Commission in Luanda (1844–1870)." *Slavery and Abolition* 33, no. 3 (September 2012): 479–500.

Cole, Gibril R. "Liberated Slaves and Islam in Nineteenth-Century West Africa." In *The Yoruba Diaspora in the Atlantic World,* edited by Toyin Falola and Matt D. Childs, 383–403. Bloomington: Indiana University Press, 2004.

Conrad, Robert. "Neither Slave nor Free: The *Emancipados* of Brazil, 1818–1868." *Hispanic American Historical Review* 53, no. 1 (1973): 50–70.

Conyers, Lawrence B., and Corey Malcom. *Evidence for the African Cemetery at Higgs Beach, Key West, Florida.* Key West: Mel Fisher Heritage Society, August 2002.

Cook, James W. "Seeing the Visual in U.S. History." *Journal of American History* 95, no. 2 (September 2008): 432–41.

Cooksey, Susan, Robin Poynor, and Hein Vanhee, eds. *Kongo across the Waters.* Gainesville: University Press of Florida, 2013.

Cooper, Helene. *The House at Sugar Beach: In Search of a Lost African Childhood.* New York: Simon and Schuster, 2008.

Coquery-Vidrovitch, Catherine. "African Slaves and the Atlantic: A Cultural Overview." Introduction to *The Second Slavery: Mass Slaveries and Modernity in the Americas and in the Atlantic Basin*, edited by Michael Zeuske and Javier Lavina, 1–18. Zurich: LIT, 2014.

Cottrol, Robert J. *The Long, Lingering Shadow: Slavery, Race, and Law in the American Hemisphere.* Athens: University of Georgia Press, 2013.

Crais, Clifton, and Pamela Scully. *Sara Baartman and the Hottentot Venus: A Ghost Story and a Biography.* Princeton: Princeton University Press, 2010.

Curry, Leonard P. *The Free Black in Urban America, 1800–1850: The Shadow of the Dream.* Chicago: University of Chicago Press, 1981.

Curtin, Philip D. *The Image of Africa: British Ideas and Action, 1780–1850.* Madison: University of Wisconsin Press, 1964.

Curtin, Philip D., and Jan Vansina. "Sources of the Nineteenth Century Atlantic Slave Trade." *Journal of African History* 5, no. 2 (November 1964): 185–208.

Curto, José C. "Experiences of Enslavement in West Central Africa." *Histoire Sociale* 41, no. 82 (2008): 381–415.

Curto, José C., and Paul E. Lovejoy, eds. *Enslaving Connections: Changing Cultures of Africa and Brazil during the Era of Slavery.* Amherst, N.Y.: Humanity Books, 2004.

Dain, Bruce. *A Hideous Monster of the Mind: American Race Theory in the Early Republic.* Cambridge: Harvard University Press, 2003.

Davis, David Brion. *Inhuman Bondage: The Rise and Fall of Slavery in the New World.* New York: Oxford University Press, 2006.

Davis, Robert Ralph, Jr. "Buchanian Espionage: A Report on Illegal Slave Trading in the South in 1859." *Journal of Southern History* 37, no. 2 (May 1971): 271–78.

———. "James Buchanan and the Suppression of the Slave Trade, 1859–1861." *Pennsylvania History* 33, no. 4 (October 1966): 446–59.

Delbanco, Andrew. *The Abolitionist Imagination.* Cambridge: Harvard University Press, 2012.

DeLombard, Jeannine Marie. *In the Shadow of the Gallows: Race, Crime, and American Civic Identity.* Philadelphia: University of Pennsylvania Press, 2012.

Deyle, Steven. "An 'Abominable' New Trade: The Closing of the African Slave Trade and the Changing Patterns of U.S. Political Power, 1808–1860." *William and Mary Quarterly* 66, no. 4 (October 2009): 833–50.

———. "The Irony of Liberty: Origins of the Domestic Slave Trade." *Journal of the Early Republic* 12, no. 1 (Spring 1992): 37–62.

Diedrich, Maria, Henry Louis Gates Jr., and Carl Pedersen, eds. *Black Imagination and the Middle Passage.* New York: Oxford University Press, 1999.

Diouf, Sylviane A. *Dreams of Africa in Alabama: The Slave Ship Clotilda and the Story of the Last Africans Brought to America.* New York: Oxford University Press, 2007.

―――. *Slavery's Exiles: The Story of the American Maroons*. New York: New York University Press, 2014.

Domingues da Silva, Daniel, David Eltis, Philip Misevich, and Olatunji Ojo. "The Diaspora of Africans Liberated from Slave Ships in the Nineteenth Century." *Journal of African History* 55, no. 3 (November 2014): 347–69.

Drake, Frederick C., and R. W. Shufeldt. "Secret History of the Slave Trade to Cuba Written by an American Naval Officer, Robert Wilson Schufeldt [*sic*], 1861." *Journal of Negro History* 55, no. 3 (1970): 218–35.

Drescher, Seymour. "The Ending of the Slave Trade and the Evolution of European Scientific Racism." In *The Atlantic Slave Trade: Effects on Economies, Societies, and Peoples in Africa, the Americas, and Europe*, edited by Joseph E. Inikori and Stanley L. Engerman, 361–96. Durham, N.C.: Duke University Press, 1992.

Drewal, Henry John. "Art or Accident: Yorùbá Body Artists and Their Deity Ògún." In *Africa's Ogun: Old World and New*, edited by Sandra T. Barnes, 235–60. Bloomington: Indiana University Press, 1989.

―――. "Beauty and Being: Aesthetics and Ontology in Yoruba Body Art." In *Marks of Civilization: Artistic Transformations of the Human Body*, edited by Arnold Rubin, 83–104. Los Angeles: Museum of Cultural History, 1988.

Drewal, Henry John, and John Mason. "Ogun Mind/Body Potentiality: Yoruba Scarification and Painting Traditions in Africa and the Americas." In *Africa's Ogun: Old World and New*, edited by Sandra T. Barnes, 332–52. 2nd ed. Bloomington: Indiana University Press, 1997.

Du Bois, W. E. B. "Apologia." In *The Suppression of the African Slave-Trade, to the United States of America, 1638–1870*. New York: Social Science Press, 1954.

―――. *The Suppression of the African Slave-Trade to the United States of America, 1638–1870*. Harvard University Press, 1896. Mineola, N.Y.: Dover Publications, 1970.

Edwards, Elizabeth. Introduction to *Anthropology and Photography, 1860–1920*, edited by Elizabeth Edwards, 3–17. New Haven: Yale University Press, 1992.

Eltis, David. "The Diaspora of Yoruba Speakers, 1650–1865: Dimensions and Implications." In *The Yoruba Diaspora in the Atlantic World*, edited by Toyin Falola and Matt D. Childs, 17–39. Bloomington: Indiana University Press, 2004.

―――. *Economic Growth and the Ending of the Transatlantic Slave Trade*. New York: Oxford University Press, 1987.

Eltis, David, and Stanley L. Engerman. "Fluctuations in Sex and Age Ratios in the Transatlantic Slave Trade." *Economic History Review* 46, no. 2 (May 1993): 308–23.

―――. "Was the Slave Trade Dominated by Men?" *Journal of Interdisciplinary History* 23, no. 2 (Autumn 1992): 237–57.

Eltis, David, and David Richardson. "A New Assessment of the Transatlantic Slave Trade." In *Extending the Frontiers: Essays on the New Transatlantic Slave Trade Database*, edited by David Eltis and David Richardson, 1–60. New Haven: Yale University Press, 2008.

―――, eds. *Extending the Frontiers: Essays on the New Transatlantic Slave Trade Database*. New Haven: Yale University Press, 2008.

Erickson, Paul A. "American School of Anthropology." In *History of Physical Anthropology*, edited by Frank Spencer, 65–66. New York: Garland Publishing, 1997.

Everill, Bronwen. *Abolition and Empire in Sierra Leone and Liberia*. London: Palgrave Macmillan, 2013.

———. "'Destiny Seems to Point Me to That Country': Early Nineteenth-Century African American Migration, Emigration, and Expansion." *Journal of Global History* 7, no. 1 (March 2012): 53–77.

Fabian, Ann. *The Skull Collectors: Race, Science and America's Unburied Dead*. Chicago: University of Chicago Press, 2010.

Fabre, Geneviève. "The Slave Ship Dance." In *Black Imagination and the Middle Passage*, edited by Maria Diedrich, Henry Louis Gates Jr., and Carl Pedersen, 33–46. New York: Oxford University Press, 1999.

Falola, Toyin, and Matt D. Childs, eds. *The Yoruba Diaspora in the Atlantic World*. Bloomington: Indiana University Press, 2004.

Fanning, Sarah. *Caribbean Crossing: African Americans and the Haitian Emigration Movement*. New York: New York University Press, 2014.

Fausto-Sterling, Anne. "Gender, Race, and Nation: The Comparative Anatomy of 'Hottentot' Women in Europe, 1815–1817." In *Deviant Bodies: Critical Perspectives on Difference in Science and Popular Culture*, edited by Jennifer Terry and Jacqueline Urla, 19–48. Bloomington: Indiana University Press, 1995.

Fehrenbacher, Don Edward. *The Slaveholding Republic: An Account of the United States Government's Relations to Slavery*. Completed and edited by Ward M. McAfee. New York: Oxford University Press, 2001.

Fernández, Luis Martínez. "The Havana Anglo-Spanish Mixed Commission for the Suppression of the Slave Trade and Cuba's *Emancipados*." *Slavery and Abolition* 16, no. 2 (1995): 205–25.

Ferreira, Roquinaldo. *Cross-Cultural Exchange in the Atlantic World: Angola and Brazil during the Era of the Slave Trade*. New York: Cambridge University Press, 2014.

———. "The Suppression of the Slave Trade and Slave Departures from Angola, 1830–1860s." In *Extending the Frontiers: Essays on the New Transatlantic Slave Trade Database*, edited by David Eltis and David Richardson, 313–34. New Haven: Yale University Press, 2008.

Fett, Sharla M. "Middle Passages and Forced Migrations: Liberated Africans in U.S. Camps and Ships." *Slavery and Abolition* 31, no. 1 (March 2010): 75–98.

———. "'The Ship of Slavery': Atlantic Slave Trade Suppression, Liberated Africans, and Black Abolition Politics in Antebellum New York." In *Paths of the Atlantic Slave Trade: Interactions, Identities, and Images*, edited by Ana Lucia Araujo, 131–60. New York: Cambria, 2011.

———. *Working Cures: Healing, Health, and Power on Southern Slave Plantations*. Chapel Hill: University of North Carolina Press, 2002.

Finkelman, Paul. "Regulating the Slave Trade." *Civil War History* 54, no. 4 (December 2008): 379–405.

Fish, Peter G. "War on the Slave Trade: Changing Fortunes in Antebellum U.S. Courts of the Mid-Atlantic South." In *The Early Republic and the Sea*, edited by William S. Dudley and Michael J. Crawford, 138–89. Washington, D.C.: Brassey's, 2001.

Foner, Eric. *Gateway to Freedom: The Hidden History of the Underground Railroad*. New York: Norton, 2015.

Foner, Philip S. *Business and Slavery: The New York Merchants and the Irrepressible Conflict*. Chapel Hill: University of North Carolina Press, 1941.

Foreman, P. Gabrielle. "Who's Your Mama?: 'White' Mulatta Genealogies, Early

Photography, and Anti-Passing Narratives of Slavery and Freedom." *American Literary History* 14, no. 3 (Fall 2002): 506–39.

Foxhall, Katherine. "From Convicts to Colonists: The Health of Prisoners and the Voyage to Australia, 1823–53." *Journal of Imperial and Commonwealth History* 39, no. 1 (March 2011): 1–19.

Frohne, Andrea. *The African Burial Ground in New York City: Memory, Spirituality, and Space*. Syracuse, N.Y.: Syracuse University Press, 2015.

Fyfe, Christopher. "A. B. C. Sibthorpe: A Tribute." *History in Africa* 19 (1992): 327–52.

Fyle, C. Magbaile. "The Yoruba Diaspora in Sierra Leone's Krio Society." In *The Yoruba Diaspora in the Atlantic World*, edited by Toyin Falola and Matt D. Childs, 366–80. Bloomington: Indiana University Press, 2004.

Gann, Lewis H., and Peter Duignan. *The Rulers of Belgian Africa, 1884–1914*. Princeton: Princeton University Press, 1979.

Gigantino, James J., II. *The Ragged Road to Abolition: Slavery and Freedom in New Jersey, 1775–1865*. Philadelphia: University of Pennsylvania Press, 2015.

Gilliland, C. Herbert. *Voyage to a Thousand Cares: Master's Mate Lawrence with the African Squadron, 1844–1846*. Annapolis, Md.: Naval Institute Press, 2004.

Gomez, Michael A. *Exchanging Our Country Marks: The Transformation of African Identities in the Colonial and Antebellum South*. Chapel Hill: University of North Carolina Press, 1998.

Gordon, David M. "The Abolition of the Slave Trade and the Transformation of the South-Central African Interior during the Nineteenth Century." *William and Mary Quarterly* 66, no. 4 (October 2009): 915–38.

Gould, Eliga H. *Among the Powers of the Earth: The American Revolution and the Making of a New World Empire*. Cambridge: Harvard University Press, 2012.

———. "Entangled Histories, Entangled Worlds: The English-Speaking Atlantic as a Spanish Periphery." *American Historical Review* 112, no. 3 (June 2007): 764–86.

Gould, Stephen Jay. *The Mismeasure of Man*. Rev. and expanded ed. New York: Norton, 1996.

Graden, Dale T. *Disease, Resistance, and Lies: The Demise of the Transatlantic Slave Trade to Brazil and Cuba*. Baton Rouge: Louisiana State University Press, 2014.

Guyer, Jane I. "Wealth in People, Wealth in Things." *Journal of African History* 36, no. 1 (March 1995): 83–90.

Hall, Gwendolyn Midlo. *Slavery and African Ethnicities in the Americas: Restoring the Links*. Chapel Hill: University of North Carolina Press, 2005.

Halttunen, Karen. "Humanitarianism and the Pornography of Pain in Anglo-American Culture." *American Historical Review* 100, no. 2 (April 1995): 303–34.

———. *Murder Most Foul: The Killer and the American Gothic Imagination*. Cambridge: Harvard University Press, 1998.

Handler, Jerome S. "The Middle Passage and the Material Culture of Captive Africans." *Slavery and Abolition* 30, no. 1 (March 2009): 1–26.

———. "A Prone Burial from a Plantation Slave Cemetery in Barbados, West Indies: Possible Evidence for an African-Type Witch or Other Negatively Viewed Person." *Historical Archaeology* 30, no. 3 (1996): 76–86.

Harmon, Judd Scott. "Suppress and Protect: The United States Navy, the African Slave Trade, and Maritime Commerce, 1794–1862." Ph.D. diss., College of William and Mary, 1977.

Harms, Robert. *River of Wealth, River of Sorrow: The Central Zaire Basin in the Era of the Slave and Ivory Trade, 1500–1891*. New Haven: Yale University Press, 1981.

———. "Sustaining the System: Trading Towns along the Middle Zaire." In *Women and Slavery in Africa*, edited by Claire C. Robertson and Martin A. Klein, 95–110. Madison: University of Wisconsin Press, 1983.

Harris, John. "New York Merchants and the Illegal Slave Trade to Cuba, 1850–1866." OAH Meeting conference paper, Atlanta, Georgia, 11 April 2014, cited with permission.

———. "Voyage of the *Echo*: The Trials of an Illegal Trans-Atlantic Slave Ship." Lowcountry Digital Library: Lowcountry Digital History Initiative, http://ldhi .library.cofc.edu/exhibits/show/voyage-of-the-echo-the-trials. Accessed 10 June 2015.

Harris, Leslie M. *In the Shadow of Slavery: African Americans in New York City, 1626–1863*. Chicago: University of Chicago Press, 2003.

Hartman, Saidiya V. *Scenes of Subjection: Terror, Slavery, and Self-Making in Nineteenth-Century America*. New York: Oxford University Press, 1997.

Hartnell, Anna. "Katrina Tourism and a Tale of Two Cities: Visualizing Race and Class in New Orleans." *American Quarterly* 61, no. 3 (September 2009): 723–47.

Hawthorne, Walter. "'Being Now, as It Were, One Family': Shipmate Bonding on the Slave Vessel *Emilia*, in Rio De Janeiro and throughout the Atlantic World." *Luso-Brazilian Review* 45, no. 1 (2008): 53–77.

———. *From Africa to Brazil: Culture, Identity, and an Atlantic Slave Trade, 1600–1830*. Cambridge: Cambridge University Press, 2010.

———. "Gorge: An African Seaman and His Flights from 'Freedom' Back to 'Slavery' in the Early Nineteenth Century." *Slavery and Abolition* 31, no. 3 (September 2010): 411–28.

Herlin, Susan J. "Brazil and the Commercialization of Kongo, 1840–1870." In *Enslaving Connections: Changing Cultures of Africa and Brazil during the Era of Slavery*, edited by José C. Curto and Paul E. Lovejoy, 261–84. Amherst, N.Y.: Humanity Books, 2004.

Hersak, Dunja. "There Are Many Congo Worlds: Particularities of Magico-Religious Beliefs among the Vili and Yombe of Congo Brazzaville." *Africa: Journal of the African International Institute* 71, no. 4 (2001): 614–60.

Heywood, Linda M. "Portuguese into African: The Eighteenth-Century African Background to Atlantic Creole Cultures." In *Central Africans and Cultural Transformations in the American Diaspora*, edited by Linda M. Heywood, 91–113. Cambridge: Cambridge University Press, 2002.

———. "Slavery and Forced Labor in the Changing Political Economy of Central Angola, 1850–1949." In *The End of Slavery in Africa*, edited by Suzanne Miers and Richard Roberts, 415–36. Madison: University of Wisconsin Press, 1988.

———. "Slavery and Its Transformation in the Kingdom of Kongo, 1491–1800." *Journal of African History* 50, no. 1 (March 2009): 1–22.

———, ed. *Central Africans and Cultural Transformations in the American Diaspora*. Cambridge: Cambridge University Press, 2002.

Hilton, Anne. *The Kingdom of Kongo*. Oxford: Clarendon Press, 1985.

Hodges, Graham Russell. *Root and Branch: African Americans in New York and East Jersey, 1613–1863*. Chapel Hill: University of North Carolina Press, 1999.

Hodges, Graham Russell Gao. *David Ruggles: A Radical Black Abolitionist and the Underground Railroad in New York City*. Chapel Hill: University of North Carolina Press, 2010.

Hoefte, Rosemarijn. *In Place of Slavery: A Social History of British Indian and Javanese Laborers in Surinam*. Gainesville: University Press of Florida, 1998.

Holsoe, Svend E. "Theodore Canot at Cape Mount, 1841–1847." *Liberian Studies Journal* 4, no. 2 (1971–72): 163–81.

Holt, Thomas C. "Marking: Race, Race-Making, and the Writing of History." *American Historical Review* 100, no. 1 (February 1995): 1–20.

Horne, Gerald. *The Deepest South: The United States, Brazil, and the African Slave Trade*. New York: New York University Press, 2007.

Horsman, Reginald. *Josiah Nott of Mobile: Southerner, Physician, and Racial Theorist*. Baton Rouge: Louisiana State University Press, 1987.

———. *Race and Manifest Destiny: The Origins of American Racial Anglo-Saxonism*. Cambridge: Harvard University Press, 1981.

Howard, Allen M. "Nineteenth-Century Coastal Slave Trading and the British Abolition Campaign in Sierra Leone." *Slavery and Abolition* 27, no. 1 (April 2006): 23–49.

Howard, Warren S. *American Slavers and the Federal Law, 1837–1862*. Berkeley: University of California Press, 1963.

Hu-DeHart, Evelyn. "La Trata Amarilla: The 'Yellow Trade' and the Middle Passage, 1847–1884." In *Many Middle Passages: Forced Migration and the Making of the Modern World*, edited by Emma Christopher, Cassandra Pybus, and Marcus Rediker, 166–83. Berkeley: University of California Press, 2007.

Hurston, Zora Neale. "Cudjo's Own Story of the Last American Slaver." *Journal of Negro History* 12, no. 4 (October 1927): 648–63.

Inikori, Joseph E., and Stanley L. Engerman, eds. *The Atlantic Slave Trade: Effects on Economies, Societies, and Peoples in Africa, the Americas, and Europe*. Durham, N.C.: Duke University Press, 1992.

Jackson, Debra. "'A Cultural Stronghold': The *Anglo-African* Newspaper and the Black Community of New York." *New York History* 85, no. 4 (Summer 2004): 331–57.

Jalland, Pat. *Death in the Victorian Family*. New York: Oxford University Press, 2000.

Jamieson, Ross W. "Material Culture and Social Death: African-American Burial Practices." *Historical Archaeology* 29, no. 4 (1995): 39–58.

Janzen, John M. "Ideologies and Institutions in Precolonial Western Equatorial African Therapeutics." In *The Social Basis of Health and Healing in Africa*, edited by Steven Feierman and John M. Janzen, 195–211. Berkeley: University of California Press, 1992.

———. *Lemba, 1650–1930: A Drum of Affliction in Africa and the New World*. New York: Garland, 1982.

———. *The Quest for Therapy in Lower Zaire*. Berkeley: University of California Press, 1978.

Johnson, Samuel. *The History of the Yorubas: From the Earliest Times to the Beginning of the British Protectorate*. Lagos: C.M.S. Bookshops, 1921.

Johnson, Walter. *River of Dark Dreams: Slavery and Empire in the Cotton Kingdom*. Cambridge: Harvard University Press, 2013.

———. "White Lies: Human Property and Domestic Slavery aboard the Slave Ship *Creole*." *Atlantic Studies* 5, no. 2 (August 2008): 237–63.

Jones, Adam. "New Light on the Liberated Africans and Their Origins: A List of Children Named after Benefactors, 1821–4." Paper presented at the Fifth Birmingham Sierra Leone Studies Symposium, Fircroft College, Birmingham, 1988.

———. "Recaptive Nations: Evidence Concerning the Demographic Impact of the

Atlantic Slave Trade in the Early Nineteenth Century." *Slavery and Abolition* 11, no. 1 (May 1990): 42–57.

———. "Théophile Conneau at Galinhas and New Sestos, 1836–1841: A Comparison of the Sources." *History in Africa* 8 (1981): 89–106.

Kaplan, Amy. "'Left Alone with America': The Absence of Empire in the Study of American Culture." In *Cultures of United States Imperialism*, edited by Amy Kaplan and Donald E. Pease, 3–21. Durham, N.C.: Duke University Press, 1993.

Karasch, Mary C. *Slave Life in Rio de Janeiro, 1808–1850*. Princeton: Princeton University Press, 1987.

Kaye, Anthony E. "The Second Slavery: Modernity in the Nineteenth-Century South and the Atlantic World." *Journal of Southern History* 73, no. 3 (August 2009): 627–50.

Kerber, Linda. "The Stateless as the Citizen's Other: A View from the United States." *American Historical Review* 112, no. 1 (February 2007): 1–34.

King, Wilma. *Stolen Childhood: Slave Youth in Nineteenth-Century America*. Bloomington: Indiana University Press, 1995.

Klein, Herbert S. "African Women in the Atlantic Slave Trade." In *Women and Slavery in Africa*, edited by Claire C. Robertson and Martin A. Klein, 29–48. Madison: University of Wisconsin Press, 1983.

Krauss, Taylor. "In the Ghost Forest: Listening to Tutsi Rescapés." In *Listening on the Edge: Oral History in the Aftermath of Crisis*, edited by Mark Cave and Stephen M. Sloan, 91–109. New York: Oxford University Press, 2014.

Kunz, E. F. "The Refugee in Flight: Kinetic Models and Forms of Displacement." *International Migration Review* 7, no. 2 (Summer 1973): 125–46.

Lai, Walton Look. *Indentured Labor, Caribbean Sugar: Chinese and Indian Migrants to the British West Indies, 1838–1918*. Baltimore: Johns Hopkins University Press, 1993.

Landers, Jane L. *Black Society in Spanish Florida*. Urbana-Champaign: University of Illinois Press, 1999.

Langley, Joan, and Wright Langley. *Key West: Images of the Past*. Key West, Fla.: Belland and Swift, 1982.

Lapansky-Werner, Emma J., and Margaret Hope Bacon, eds. *Back to Africa: Benjamin Coates and the Colonization Movement in America, 1848–1880*. University Park: Pennsylvania State University Press, 2008.

Larson, Pier M. "Horrid Journeying: Narratives of Enslavement and the Global African Diaspora." *Journal of World History* 19, no. 4 (December 2008): 431–64.

Law, Robin. "Abolition and Imperialism: International Law and the British Suppression of the Atlantic Slave Trade." In *Abolitionism and Imperialism in Britain, Africa, and the Atlantic*, edited by Derek R. Peterson, 150–74. Athens: Ohio University Press, 2010.

———. *Ouidah: The Social History of a West African Slaving "Port," 1727–1892*. Athens: Ohio University Press, 2004.

———. "Yoruba Liberated Slaves Who Returned to West Africa." In *The Yoruba Diaspora in the Atlantic World*, edited by Toyin Falola and Matt D. Childs, 349–65. Bloomington: Indiana University Press, 2004.

———, ed. *From Slave Trade to "Legitimate" Commerce: The Commercial Transition in Nineteenth-Century West Africa*. Cambridge: Cambridge University Press, 1995.

Lawrance, Benjamin N. *Amistad's Orphans: An Atlantic Story of Children, Slavery, and Smuggling*. New Haven: Yale University Press, 2014.

Lee, Debbie. *Slavery and the Romantic Imagination*. Philadelphia: University of Pennsylvania Press, 2002.

Lehuu, Isabelle. *Carnival on the Page: Popular Print Media in Antebellum America*. Chapel Hill: University of North Carolina Press, 2000.

Lennon, John, and Malcolm Foley. *Dark Tourism: The Attraction of Death and Disaster*. London: Continuum, 2000.

Lindsay, Lisa A. "Atlantic Bonds: A Nineteenth-Century Odyssey from America to Africa." Manuscript, 2016.

———. "The Boundaries of Slavery in Mid-Nineteenth-Century Liberia." In *Borderlands in World History, 1700–1914*, edited by Paul Readman, Cynthia Radding, and Chad Bryant, 258–78. New York: Palgrave Macmillan, 2014.

———. "'To Return to the Bosom of Their Fatherland': Brazilian Immigrants in Nineteenth-Century Lagos." *Slavery and Abolition* 15, no. 1 (April 1994): 22–50.

Lively, Adam. *Masks: Blackness, Race, and the Imagination*. New York: Oxford University Press, 2000.

Lovejoy, Paul. "The Children of Slavery—the Transatlantic Phase." *Slavery and Abolition* 27, no. 2 (August 2006): 197–217.

———. "Pawnship, Debt, and 'Freedom' in Atlantic Africa during the Era of the Slave Trade: A Reassessment." *Journal of African History* 55, no. 1 (March 2014): 55–78.

———. "Scarification and the Loss of History in the African Diaspora." In *Activating the Past: History and Memory in the Black Atlantic World*, edited by Andrew Apter and Lauren Derby, 99–138. Newcastle upon Tyne: Cambridge Scholars, 2010.

———. *Transformations in Slavery: A History of Slavery in Africa*. 2nd ed. Cambridge: Cambridge University Press, 2000.

———. "The Yoruba Factor in the Trans-Atlantic Slave Trade." In *The Yoruba Diaspora in the Atlantic World*, edited by Toyin Falola and Matt D. Childs, 40–55. Bloomington: Indiana University Press, 2004.

Luse, Christopher A. "Slavery's Champions Stood at Odds: Polygenesis and the Defense of Slavery." *Civil War History* 53, no. 4 (2007): 379–412.

MacGaffey, Wyatt. *Astonishment and Power: The Eyes of Understanding: Kongo Minkisi*. Washington, D.C.: Smithsonian Institution, 1993.

———. "Economic and Social Dimensions of Kongo Slavery." In *Slavery in Africa*, edited by Suzanne Miers and I. Kopytoff, 242–43. Madison: University of Wisconsin Press, 1977.

———. *Religion and Society in Central Africa: The Bakongo of Lower Zaire*. Chicago: University of Chicago Press, 1986.

MacMaster, Richard. "United States Navy and African Exploration, 1851–1860." *Mid-America: An Historical Review* 46, no. 3 (1964): 187–203.

Maffitt, Emma Martin. *The Life and Services of John Newland Maffitt*. New York: Neale, 1906.

Malcom, Corey. "Cemeteries at South Beach, Key West, Florida." https://www.academia.edu/4349925/Cemeteries_at_South_Beach_Key_West_Florida. Accessed 19 January 2015.

———. "Key West and the Slave Ships of 1860." https://www.academia.edu/4690762/Key_West_and_the_Slave_Ships_of_1860. Accessed 14 July 2014.

———. "Transporting African Refugees from Key West to Liberia." *Florida Keys Sea Heritage Journal* 19, no. 2 (Winter 2008/2009): 1–6.

Malcom, Corey, and Lawrence B. Conyers. "Evidence for the African Cemetery at Higgs Beach, Key West, Florida." *Florida Keys Sea Heritage Journal* 13 (Fall 2002): 1, 8–15.

Mamigonian, Beatriz G. "In the Name of Freedom: Slave Trade Abolition, the Law and the Brazilian Branch of the African Emigration Scheme (Brazil–British West Indies, 1830s–1850s)." *Slavery and Abolition* 30, no. 1 (March 2009): 41–66.

Mamigonian, Beatriz Gallotti. "To Be a Liberated African in Brazil: Labour and Citizenship in the Nineteenth Century." Ph.D. diss., University of Waterloo, 2002.

Mann, Kristin. *Slavery and the Birth of an African City: Lagos, 1760–1900.* Bloomington: Indiana University Press, 2007.

Manning, Patrick. *Slavery and African Life: Occidental, Oriental, and African Slave Trades.* Cambridge: Cambridge University Press, 1990.

Marques, Leonardo. "The Contraband Slave Trade of the Second Slavery." Pre-circulated paper, cited with permission, at "Ever Closer to Freedom: The Work and Legacies of Stephanie M. H. Camp," University of Washington, Seattle, 7 May 2015.

———. "The United States and the Transatlantic Slave Trade to the Americas, 1776–1867." Ph.D. diss., Emory University, 2013.

Martin, Phyllis M. "Cabinda and Cabindans: Some Aspects of an African Maritime Society." In *Africa and the Sea: Proceedings of a Colloquium at the University of Aberdeen,* edited by Jeffrey C. Stone, 80–96. Aberdeen: Aberdeen University African Studies Group, 1985.

———. *The External Trade of the Loango Coast, 1576–1870.* New York: Oxford University Press, 1972.

Mason, John Edwin. *Social Death and Resurrection: Slavery and Emancipation in South Africa.* Charlottesville: University of Virginia Press, 2003.

Mason, Matthew. "The Battle of the Slaveholding Liberators: Great Britain, the United States, and Slavery in the Early Nineteenth Century." *William and Mary Quarterly* 59, no. 3 (July 2002): 665–96.

———. "Keeping Up Appearances: The International Politics of Slave Trade Abolition in the Nineteenth-Century Atlantic World." *William and Mary Quarterly* 66, no. 4 (October 2009): 809–32.

———. *Slavery and Politics in the Early American Republic.* Chapel Hill: University of North Carolina Press, 2006.

———. "Slavery Overshadowed: Congress Debates Prohibiting the Atlantic Slave Trade to the United States, 1806–1807." *Journal of the Early Republic* 20, no. 1 (Spring 2000): 59–81.

McCarthy, Timothy Patrick, and John Stauffer, eds. *Prophets of Protest: Reconsidering the History of American Abolitionism.* New York: New Press, 2006.

McHenry, Elizabeth. *Forgotten Readers: Recovering the Lost History of African American Literary Societies.* Durham, N.C.: Duke University Press, 2002.

Melish, Joanne Pope. "The 'Condition' Debate and Racial Discourse in the Antebellum North." *Journal of the Early Republic* 19, no. 4 (Winter 1999): 651–72.

———. *Disowning Slavery: Gradual Emancipation and "Race" in New England, 1780–1860.* Ithaca: Cornell University Press, 1998.

Merrill, Lisa. "Exhibiting Race 'under the World's Huge Glass Case': William and Ellen Craft and William Wells Brown at the Great Exhibition in Crystal Palace, London, 1851." *Slavery and Abolition* 33, no. 2 (June 2012): 321–36.

Meyer, Iysle E. "T. J. Bowen and Central Africa: A Nineteenth-Century Missionary Delusion." *International Journal of African Historical Studies* 15, no. 2 (1982): 247–60.

Miller, Joseph C. "Atlantic Ambiguities of British and American Abolition." *William and Mary Quarterly* 66, no. 4 (October 2009): 677–704.

——. "Central Africa during the Era of the Slave Trade, c. 1490s–1850s." In *Central Africans and Cultural Transformations in the American Diaspora*, edited by Linda M. Heywood, 21–69. Cambridge: Cambridge University Press, 2002.

——. *The Problem of Slavery as History: A Global Approach*. New Haven: Yale University Press, 2012.

——. "Retention, Reinvention, and Remembering: Restoring Identities through Enslavement in Africa and under Slavery in Brazil." In *Enslaving Connections: Changing Cultures of Africa and Brazil during the Era of Slavery*, edited by José C. Curto and Paul E. Lovejoy, 81–121. Amherst, N.Y.: Humanity Books, 2004.

——. "Slave Prices in the Portuguese Southern Atlantic, 1600–1830." In *Africans in Bondage: Studies in Slavery and the Slave Trade*, edited by Paul E. Lovejoy, 43–77. Madison: African Studies Program, University of Wisconsin, 1986.

——. *Way of Death: Merchant Capitalism and the Angolan Slave Trade, 1730–1830*. Madison: University of Wisconsin Press, 1988.

Mintz, Sidney W., and Richard Price. *The Birth of African-American Culture: An Anthropological Perspective*. Boston: Beacon Press, 1976; rpt. 1992.

Moráguez, Oscar Grandío. "The African Origins of Slaves Arriving in Cuba, 1789–1865." In *Extending the Frontiers: Essays on the New Transatlantic Slave Trade Database*, edited by David Eltis and David Richardson, 176–201. New Haven: Yale University Press, 2008.

Morgan, Jennifer L. *Laboring Women: Reproduction and Gender in New World Slavery*. Philadelphia: University of Pennsylvania Press, 2004.

Morgan, Philip D. *Slave Counterpoint: Black Culture in the Eighteenth-Century Chesapeake and Lowcountry*. Chapel Hill: University of North Carolina Press, 1998.

Morton, Fred. "Small Change: Children in the Nineteenth-Century East African Slave Trade." In *Children in Slavery through the Ages*, edited by Gwyn Campbell, Suzanne Miers, and Joseph C. Miller, 55–70. Athens: Ohio University Press, 2009.

Moses, Wilson Jeremiah. *Creative Conflict in African American Thought: Frederick Douglass, Alexander Crummell, Booker T. Washington, W. E. B. Du Bois, and Marcus Garvey*. New York: Cambridge University Press, 2004.

——. *The Golden Age of Black Nationalism, 1850–1925*. Hamden, Conn.: Archon, 1978.

——, ed. *Classical Black Nationalism: From the American Revolution to Marcus Garvey*. New York: New York University Press, 1996.

——, ed. *Liberian Dreams: Back-to-Africa Narratives from the 1850s*. University Park: Pennsylvania State University Press, 1998.

Mouser, Bruce L. "The Baltimore/Pongo Connection: American Entrepreneurism, Colonial Expansionism, or African Opportunism?" *International Journal of African Historical Studies* 33, no. 2 (2000): 313–33.

——. "Baltimore's African Experiment, 1822–1827." *Journal of Negro History* 80, no. 3 (Summer 1995): 113–30.

——. "Théophilus Conneau: The Saga of a Tale." *History in Africa* 6 (1979): 97–107.

Mudimbe, V. Y. *The Invention of Africa*. Bloomington: University of Indiana Press, 1988.

Mustakeem, Sowande' M. *Slavery at Sea: Terror, Sex, and Sickness in the Middle Passage*. Urbana: University of Illinois Press, 2016.

New-England Historic Genealogical Society. *Memorial Biographies of the New-England Historic Genealogical Society*. Vol. 7. Boston: New-England Historic Genealogical Society, Stanhope Press, 1907.

Newman, Debra Lynn. "The Emergence of Liberian Women in the Nineteenth Century." Ph.D. diss., Howard University, 1984.

Nichols, John B. *History of the Medical Society of the District of Columbia, 1817–1909*. Washington, D.C.: Medical Society of the District of Columbia, 1909.

Noonan, John T. *The Antelope: The Ordeal of the Recaptured Africans in the Administrations of James Monroe and John Quincy Adams*. Berkeley: University of California Press, 1977.

Northrup, David. "Becoming African: Identity Formation among Liberated Slaves in Nineteenth-Century Sierra Leone." *Slavery and Abolition* 27, no. 1 (April 2006): 1–21.

——. *Indentured Labor in the Age of Imperialism, 1834–1922*. New York: Cambridge University Press, 1995.

Nwokeji, G. Ugo. "African Conceptions of Gender and the Slave Traffic." *William and Mary Quarterly* 58, no. 1 (January 2001): 47–68.

——. *The Slave Trade and Culture in the Bight of Biafra: An African Society in the Atlantic World*. Cambridge: Cambridge University Press, 2010.

Nwokeji, G. Ugo, and David Eltis. "The Roots of the African Diaspora: Methodological Considerations in the Analysis of Names in the Liberated African Registers of Sierra Leone and Havana." *History in Africa* 29 (2002): 365–79.

Obadele-Starks, Ernest. *Freebooters and Smugglers: The Foreign Slave Trade in the United States after 1808*. Fayetteville: University of Arkansas Press, 2007.

O'Hear, Ann. "The Enslavement of Yoruba." In *The Yoruba Diaspora in the Atlantic World*, edited by Toyin Falola and Matt D. Childs, 56–73. Bloomington: Indiana University Press, 2004.

Ojo, Olatunji. "Beyond Diversity: Women, Scarification, and Yoruba Identity." *History in Africa* 35 (2008): 347–74.

Page, Robert. "A Case of Opportunity: Privateers, Slaves, Georgians, and the Case of the *Tentativa*." *Journal of the Georgia Association of Historians* 19 (1998): 219–40.

Pandora, Katherine. "Popular Science in National and Transnational Perspective: Suggestions from the American Context." *Isis* 100, no. 2 (June 2009): 346–58.

Park, Eunjin. *"White" Americans in "Black" Africa: Black and White American Methodist Missionaries in Liberia, 1820–1875*. New York: Routledge, 2001.

Patterson, Orlando. *Slavery and Social Death: A Comparative Study*. Cambridge: Harvard University Press, 1982.

——. *The Sociology of Slavery*. London: MacGibbon and Kee, 1967.

Pearson, Andrea G. "*Frank Leslie's Illustrated Newspaper* and *Harper's Weekly*: Innovation and Imitation in Nineteenth-Century American Pictorial Reporting." *Journal of Popular Culture* 23, no. 4 (Spring 1990): 81–111.

Pearson, Andrew. *Distant Freedom: St Helena and the Abolition of the Slave Trade, 1840–1872*. Liverpool: Liverpool University Press, 2016.

Pearson, Andrew, Ben Jeffs, Annsofie Witkin, and Helen MacQuarrie. *Infernal Traffic: Excavation of a Liberated African Graveyard in Rupert's Valley, St Helena*. London: Council for British Archeology, 2011.

Pearson, Susan J. "'Infantile Specimens': Showing Babies in Nineteenth-Century America." *Journal of Social History* 42, no. 2 (Winter 2008): 341–70.

Peel, J. D. Y. *Religious Encounter and the Making of the Yoruba*. Indianapolis: Indiana University Press, 2000.

Penningroth, Dylan C. *The Claims of Kinfolk: African American Property and Community in the Nineteenth-Century South*. Chapel Hill: University of North Carolina Press, 2003.

Pentangelo, John. "Sailors and Slaves: USS *Constellation* and the Transatlantic Slave Trade." *Sea History* 32, no. 32 (Autumn 2010): 10–14.

Peterson, John. *Province of Freedom: A History of Sierra Leone, 1787–1870*. London: Faber and Faber, 1969.

Petridis, Constantine. "Of Mothers and Sorcerers: A Luluwa Maternity Figure." *Art Institute of Chicago Museum Studies* 23, no. 2 (1997): 182–95, 198–200.

Pettitt, Clare. *Dr. Livingstone, I Presume?: Missionaries, Journalists, Explorers, and Empire*. Cambridge: Harvard University Press, 2007.

Poignant, Roslyn. *Professional Savages: Captive Lives and Western Spectacle*. New Haven: Yale University Press, 2004.

———. "Surveying the Field of View: The Making of the Rai Photographic Collection." In *Anthropology and Photography, 1860–1920*, edited by Elizabeth Edwards, 42–73. New Haven: Yale University Press, 1992.

Poole, Deborah. *Vision, Race, and Modernity: A Visual Economy of the Andean Image World*. Princeton: Princeton University Press, 1997.

Power-Green, Ousmane K. *Against Wind and Tide: The African American Struggle against the Colonization Movement*. New York: New York University Press, 2014.

Premo, Bianca. *Children of the Father King: Youth, Authority, and Legal Minority in Colonial Lima*. Chapel Hill: University of North Carolina Press, 2005.

Pybus, Cassandra. *Epic Journeys of Freedom: Runaway Slaves of the American Revolution and Their Global Quest for Liberty*. Boston: Beacon Press, 2006.

Quarles, Benjamin. *Black Abolitionists*. New York: Oxford University Press, 1969.

Quigley, David. "Southern Slavery in a Free City: Economy, Politics, and Culture." In *Slavery in New York*, edited by Ira Berlin and Leslie M. Harris, 263–88. New York: New Press, 2005.

Quirk, Joel. "Ending Slavery in All Its Forms: Legal Abolition and Effective Emancipation in Historical Perspective." *International Journal of Human Rights* 12, no. 4 (September 2008): 529–54.

Rael, Patrick. *Black Identity and Black Protest in the Antebellum North*. Chapel Hill: University of North Carolina Press, 2002.

———. "A Common Nature, a United Destiny: African American Responses to Racial Science from the Revolution to the Civil War." In *Prophets of Protest: Reconsidering the History of American Abolitionism*, edited by Timothy Patrick McCarthy and John Stauffer, 183–99. New York: New Press, 2006.

Ravenel, Mrs. St. Julien. *Charleston: The Place and the People*. London: Macmillan, 1912.

Rediker, Marcus. *The Amistad Rebellion: An Atlantic Odyssey of Slavery and Freedom*. New York: Viking, 2012.

———. *The Slave Ship: A Human History*. New York: Viking, 2007.

Reichlin, Elinor. "Faces of Slavery: A Historical Find." *American Heritage* 28, no. 4 (June 1977): 4–11.

Reilly, Timothy F. "The Conscience of a Colonizationist: Parson Clapp and the Slavery Dilemma." *Louisiana History* 39, no. 4 (Autumn 1998): 411–41.

———. "The Louisiana Colonization Society and the Protestant Missionary, 1830–1860." *Louisiana History* 43, no. 4 (Autumn 2002): 433–77.

Reis, João José. *Death Is a Festival: Funeral Rites and Rebellion in Nineteenth-Century Brazil.* Translated by H. Sabrina Gledhill. Chapel Hill: University of North Carolina Press, 2003.

Reis, João José, and Beatriz Gallotti Mamigonian. "Nagô and Mina: The Yoruba Diaspora in Brazil." In *The Yoruba Diaspora in the Atlantic World*, edited by Toyin Falola and Matt D. Childs, 77–110. Bloomington: Indiana University Press, 2004.

Reiss, Benjamin. *The Showman and the Slave: Race, Death, and Memory in Barnum's America.* Cambridge: Harvard University Press, 2001.

Renda, Mary A. *Taking Haiti: Military Occupation and the Culture of U.S. Imperialism, 1915–1940.* Chapel Hill: University of North Carolina Press, 2001.

Rice, Alan J., and Martin Crawford, eds. *Liberating Sojourn: Frederick Douglass and Transatlantic Reform.* Athens: University of Georgia Press, 1999.

Richardson, David. "Shipboard Revolts, African Authority, and the Atlantic Slave Trade." *William and Mary Quarterly* 58, no. 1 (January 2001): 69–92.

Roberts, Neil. *Freedom as Marronage.* Chicago: University of Chicago Press, 2015.

Robertson, Claire C., and Martin A. Klein, eds. *Women and Slavery in Africa.* Madison: University of Wisconsin Press, 1983.

Rogers, Molly. *Delia's Tears: Race, Science, and Photography in Nineteenth-Century America.* New Haven: Yale University Press, 2010.

———. "The Slave Daguerreotypes of the Peabody Museum: Scientific Meaning and Utility." *History of Photography* 30, no. 1 (Spring 2006): 38–54.

Rothman, Adam. *Slave Country: American Expansion and the Origins of the Deep South.* Cambridge: Harvard University Press, 2005.

Rubin, Arnold, ed. *Marks of Civilization: Artistic Transformations of the Human Body.* Los Angeles: Museum of Cultural History, 1988.

Rugemer, Edward. *The Problem of Emancipation: The Caribbean Roots of the American Civil War.* Baton Rouge: Louisiana State University Press, 2008.

Samuels, Ellen. "Examining Millie and Christine McKoy: Where Enslavement and Enfreakment Meet." *Signs* 37, no. 1 (Autumn 2011): 53–81.

Sanneh, Lamin. *Abolitionists Abroad: American Blacks and the Making of Modern West Africa.* Cambridge: Harvard University Press, 1999.

Saunders, Christopher. "Liberated Africans in Cape Colony in the First Half of the Nineteenth Century." *International Journal of African Historical Studies* 18, no. 2 (1985): 223–39.

Sawyer, Amos. *The Emergence of Autocracy in Liberia: Tragedy and Challenges.* San Francisco: Institute for Contemporary Studies, 1992.

Schoeppner, Michael A. "Status across Borders: Roger Taney, Black British Subjects, and a Diplomatic Antecedent to the Dred Scott Decision." *Journal of American History* 100, no. 1 (June 2013): 46–67.

Schuler, Monica. *Alas! Alas! Kongo: A Social History of Liberated African Immigration to Jamaica, 1841–1865.* Baltimore: Johns Hopkins University Press, 1980.

———. "Enslavement, the Slave Voyage, and Astral and Aquatic Journeys in African Diaspora Discourse." In *Africa and the Americas: Interconnections during the Slave Trade*, edited by José C. Curto and Renée Soulodre-La France, 185–211. Trenton, N.J.: Africa World Press, 2005.

———. *Liberated Africans in Nineteenth Century Guyana*. Mona, Jamaica: Department of History, University of the West Indies, Mona, 1992.

———. "Liberated Central Africans in Nineteenth-Century Guyana." In *Central Africans and Cultural Transformations in the American Diaspora*, edited by Linda M. Heywood, 319–52. Cambridge: Cambridge University Press, 2002.

———. "The Recruitment of African Indentured Labourers for European Colonies in the Nineteenth Century." In *Colonialism and Migration: Indentured Labour before and after Slavery*, edited by P. C. Emmer, 125–61. Boston: Martinus Nijhoff, 1986.

Scott, Rebecca J. *Degrees of Freedom: Louisiana and Cuba after Slavery*. Cambridge: Harvard University Press, 2005.

———. "Paper Thin: Freedom and Re-Enslavement in the Diaspora of the Haitian Revolution." *Law and History Review* 29, no. 4 (November 2011): 1061–87.

———. *Was Freedom Portable?: Wartime Journeys from Saint-Domingue to Jamaica to Cuba to Louisiana*. Kingston, Jamaica: Department of History and Archaeology, University of the West Indies, Mona, 2013.

Sharpley, Richard, and Philip R. Stone, eds. *The Darker Side of Travel: The Theory and Practice of Dark Tourism*. Buffalo: Channel View Publications, 2009.

Shaw, Caroline Emily. "The British, Persecuted Foreigners, and the Emergence of the Refugee Category in Nineteenth-Century Britain." *Immigrants and Minorities* 30, no. 2–3 (July/November 2012): 239–62.

Shick, Tom W. *Behold the Promised Land: A History of Afro-American Settler Society in Nineteenth-Century Liberia*. Baltimore: Johns Hopkins University Press, 1980.

Sidbury, James. *Becoming African in America: Race and Nation in the Early Black Atlantic*. New York: Oxford University Press, 2007.

Sidbury, James, and Jorge Cañizares-Esguerra. "Mapping Ethnogenesis in the Early Modern Atlantic." *William and Mary Quarterly* 68, no. 2 (April 2011): 181–208.

Sinha, Manisha. "An Alternative Tradition of Radicalism: African American Abolitionists and the Metaphor of Revolution." In *Contested Democracy: Freedom, Race, and Power*, edited by Manisha Sinha and Penny Von Eschen, 9–30. New York: Columbia University Press, 2007.

———. "Black Abolitionism: The Assault on Southern Slavery and the Struggle for Racial Equality." In *Slavery in New York*, edited by Ira Berlin and Leslie M. Harris, 239–62. New York: New Press, 2005.

———. "Coming of Age: The Historiography of Black Abolitionism." In *Prophets of Protest: Reconsidering the History of American Abolitionism*, edited by Timothy Patrick McCarthy and John Stauffer, 23–38. New York: New Press, 2006.

———. *The Counterrevolution of Slavery: Politics and Ideology in Antebellum South Carolina*. Chapel Hill: University of North Carolina Press, 2000.

———. "Judicial Nullification: The South Carolinian Movement to Reopen the African Slave Trade in the 1850s." In *Black Imagination and the Middle Passage*, edited by Maria Diedrich, Henry Louis Gates Jr., and Carl Pederson, 127–43. New York: Oxford University Press, 1999.

———. *The Slave's Cause: A History of Abolition*. New Haven: Yale University Press, 2016.

Sinha, Manisha, and Penny Von Eschen, eds. *Contested Democracy: Freedom, Race, and Power in American History*. New York: Columbia University Press, 2007.

Sinnema, Peter W. *Dynamics of the Pictured Page: Representing the Nation in the Illustrated London News*. London: Ashgate, 1998.

Slenes, Robert W. "African Abrahams, Lucretias, and Men of Sorrows: Allegory and Allusion in the Brazilian Anti-Slavery Lithographs (1827–1835) of Johann Moritz Rugendas." *Slavery and Abolition* 23, no. 2 (August 2002): 147–68.

———. "'Malungu, Ngoma's Coming!': Africa Hidden and Discovered in Brazil." In *Mostra do Redescobrimento: Negro de Corpo e Alma (Black in Body and Soul)*, edited by Nelson Aguilar, 221–29. São Paulo: Fundação Bienal de São Paulo, 2000.

Smallwood, Stephanie E. "Commodified Freedom: Interrogating the Limits of Anti-Slavery Ideology in the Early Republic." *Journal of the Early Republic* 24, no. 2 (Summer 2004): 289–98.

———. *Saltwater Slavery: A Middle Passage from Africa to American Diaspora*. Cambridge: Harvard University Press, 2007.

Smith, Justin E. H. *Nature, Human Nature, and Human Difference: Race in Early Modern Philosophy*. Princeton: Princeton University Press, 2015.

Smith, Mark. "Engineering Slavery: The U.S. Army Corps of Engineers and Slavery at Key West." *Florida Historical Quarterly* 86, no. 4 (Spring 2008): 498–526.

Snyder, Terri L. *The Power to Die: Slavery and Suicide in British North America*. Chicago: University of Chicago Press, 2015.

Soodalter, Ron. *Hanging Captain Gordon: The Life and Trial of an American Slave Trader*. New York: Atria, 2006.

Stanton, William. *The Leopard's Spots: Scientific Attitudes toward Race in America, 1815–1859*. Chicago: University of Chicago Press, 1960.

Staudenraus, P. J. *The African Colonization Movement, 1816–1865*. New York: Columbia University Press, 1961.

Stauffer, John. *The Black Hearts of Men: Radical Abolitionists and the Transformation of Race*. Cambridge: Harvard University Press, 2002.

———. "Fighting the Devil with His Own Fire." In *The Abolitionist Imagination*, by Andrew Delbanco, 59–79. Cambridge: Harvard University Press, 2012.

———, ed. *The Works of James McCune Smith*. New York: Oxford University Press, 2006.

Stebbins, Consuelo E. *City of Intrigue, Nest of Revolution: A Documentary History of Key West in the Nineteenth Century*. Gainesville: University Press of Florida, 2007.

Stepan, Nancy Leys. *Picturing Tropical Nature*. London: Reaktion Books, 2001.

Stephens, Lester D. *Science, Race, and Religion in the American South: John Bachman and the Charleston Circle of Naturalists, 1815–1895*. Chapel Hill: University of North Carolina Press, 2000.

Stewart, David J. "Burial at Sea: Separating and Placing the Dead during the Age of Sail." *Mortality* 10, no. 4 (November 2005): 276–85.

Stocking, George W., Jr. *Victorian Anthropology*. New York: Free Press, 1987.

Streeby, Shelley. "American Sensations: Empire, Amnesia, and the US-Mexican War." *American Literary History* 13, no. 1 (Spring 2001): 1–40.

Sundiata, Ibrahim K. *From Slaving to Neoslavery: The Bight of Biafra and Fernando Po in the Era of Abolition, 1827–1930*. Madison: University of Wisconsin Press, 1996.

Sundquist, Eric. *To Wake the Nations: Race in the Making of American Literature*. Cambridge: Harvard University Press, 1993.

Swanson, Gail. "The African Cemetery on Higgs Beach, Key West, Florida." *South Florida History* 32, no. 1 (March 2004): 24–28.

———. *Slave Ship Guerrero*. West Conshohocken, Pa.: Infinity, 2005.

Sweet, James H. "Defying Social Death: The Multiple Configurations of African Slave

Family in the Atlantic World." *William and Mary Quarterly* 70, no. 2 (April 2013): 251–72.

———. *Domingos Álvares, African Healing, and the Intellectual History of the Atlantic World.* Chapel Hill: University of North Carolina Press, 2011.

———. "The Quiet Violence of Ethnogenesis." *William and Mary Quarterly* 68, no. 2 (April 2011): 209–14.

———. *Recreating Africa: Culture, Kinship, and Religion in the African-Portuguese World, 1441–1770.* Chapel Hill: University of North Carolina Press, 2003.

———. "Teaching the Modern African Diaspora: A Case Study of the Atlantic Slave Trade." *Radical History Review* 77 (Spring 2000): 106–22.

Swift, David E. *Black Prophets of Justice: Activist Clergy before the Civil War.* Baton Rouge: Louisiana State University Press, 1989.

Takaki, Ronald T. *A Pro-Slavery Crusade: The Agitation to Reopen the African Slave Trade.* New York: Free Press, 1971.

Temperley, Howard. *White Dreams, Black Africa: The Antislavery Expedition to the Niger River, 1841–1842.* New Haven: Yale University Press, 1991.

Thornton, John. *Africa and Africans in the Making of the Atlantic World, 1400–1680.* Cambridge: Cambridge University Press, 1992.

———. "African Dimensions of the Stono Rebellion." *American Historical Review* 96, no. 4 (October 1991): 1101–13.

———. "Cannibals, Witches, and Slave Traders in the Atlantic World." *William and Mary Quarterly* 60, no. 2 (April 2003): 273–94.

———. "Religious and Ceremonial Life in the Kongo and Mbundu Areas, 1500–1700." In *Central Africans and Cultural Transformations in the American Diaspora*, edited by Linda M. Heywood, 71–90. Cambridge: Cambridge University Press, 2002.

Thurs, Daniel Patrick. *Science Talk: Changing Notions of Science in American Culture.* New Brunswick: Rutgers University Press, 2007.

Tomek, Beverly C. *Colonization and Its Discontents: Emancipation, Emigration, and Antislavery in Antebellum Pennsylvania.* New York: New York University Press, 2011.

Tomich, Dale. "The 'Second Slavery': Bonded Labor and the Transformation of the Nineteenth-Century World Economy." In *Rethinking the Nineteenth Century: Contradictions and Movements*, edited by Francisco O. Ramirez, 103–17. New York: Greenwood Press, 1988.

Trouillot, Michel-Rolph. *Global Transformations: Anthropology and the Modern World.* New York: Palgrave Macmillan, 2003.

Tucker, Spencer C. "Lieutenant Andrew H. Foote and the African Slave Trade." *American Neptune* 60, no. 1 (2000): 31–48.

Tyler-McGraw, Marie. *An African Republic: Black and White Virginians in the Making of Liberia.* Chapel Hill: University of North Carolina Press, 2007.

Vansina, Jan. "Ambaca Society and the Slave Trade, c. 1760–1845." *Journal of African History* 46, no. 1 (March 2005): 1–27.

———. Foreword to *Central Africans and Cultural Transformations in the American Diaspora*, edited by Linda M. Heywood, xi–xiii. Cambridge: Cambridge University Press, 2002.

———. *Paths in the Rainforest: Toward a History of Political Tradition in Equatorial Africa.* Madison: University of Wisconsin Press, 1990.

Vinson, Robert Trent. "The Law as Lawbreaker: The Promotion and Encouragement of the Atlantic Slave Trade by the New York Judiciary System, 1857–1862." *Afro-Americans in New York Life and History* 20, no. 2 (July 1996): 35–58.

Volk, Kyle G. *Moral Minorities and the Making of American Democracy*. New York: Oxford University Press, 2014.

Voorsanger, Catherine Hoover, and John K. Howat, eds. *Art and the Empire City, New York, 1825–1861*. New York: Metropolitan Museum of Art, 2013.

Vos, Jelmer. "Kongo, North America, and the Slave Trade." In *Kongo across the Waters*, edited by Susan Cooksey, Robin Poynor, and Hein Vanhee, 40–49. Gainesville: University Press of Florida, 2013.

———. "'Without the Slave Trade, No Recruitment': From Slave Trading to 'Migrant Recruitment' in the Lower Kongo, 1830–1890." In *Trafficking in Slavery's Wake: Law and the Experience of Women and Children in Africa*, edited by Benjamin N. Lawrance and Richard L. Roberts, 45–64. Athens: Ohio University Press, 2012.

Wallis, Brian. "Black Bodies, White Science: Louis Agassiz's Slave Daguerreotypes." *American Art* 9, no. 2 (Summer 1995): 38–61.

Warner, Faith R. "Social Support and Distress among Q'eqchi' Refugee Women in Maya Tecún, Mexico." *Medical Anthropology Quarterly* 21, no. 2 (June 2007): 193–217.

Watson, R. L. "'Prize Negroes' and the Development of Racial Attitudes in the Cape Colony." *South African Historical Journal* 43, no. 1 (November 2000): 138–62.

Webber, Christopher L. *American to the Backbone: The Life of James W. C. Pennington, the Fugitive Slave Who Became One of the First Black Abolitionists*. New York: Pegasus, 2011.

Weiner, Marli F., with Mazie Hough. *Sex, Sickness, and Slavery: Illness in the Antebellum South*. Urbana: University of Illinois Press, 2012.

Wells, Tom Henderson. *The Slave Ship Wanderer*. Athens: University of Georgia Press, 1967.

Westerlund, David. "Pluralism and Change: A Comparative and Historical Approach to African Disease Etiologies." In *Culture, Experience, and Pluralism: Essays on African Ideas of Illness and Healing*, edited by Anita Jacobson-Widding and David Westerlund, 179–218. Stockholm: Uppsala, 1989.

White, Ashli. *Encountering Revolution: Haiti and the Making of the Early Republic*. Baltimore: Johns Hopkins University Press, 2010.

White, E. Frances. *Dark Continent of Our Bodies: Black Feminism and the Politics of Respectability*. Philadelphia: Temple University Press, 2001.

White, Shane. *Stories of Freedom in Black New York*. Cambridge: Harvard University Press, 2002.

Wilder, Craig Steven. *In the Company of Black Men: The African Influence on African American Culture in New York City*. New York: New York University Press, 2001.

Will, Thomas E. "The American School of Ethnology: Science and Scripture in the Proslavery Argument." *Southern Historian* 19 (1998): 14–34.

Williams, Patricia J. *The Alchemy of Race and Rights: Diary of a Law Professor*. Cambridge: Harvard University Press, 1991.

Wolf, Eric. *Europe and the People without History*. Berkeley: University of California Press, 1982.

Wong, Edlie L. *Neither Fugitive nor Free: Atlantic Slavery, Freedom Suits, and the Legal Culture of Travel*. New York: New York University Press, 2009.

Wood, Marcus. *Blind Memory: Visual Representations of Slavery in England and America, 1780–1865*. New York: Routledge, 2000.

————. *Slavery, Empathy, and Pornography.* Cambridge: Oxford University Press, 2003.

Wright, Marcia. *Strategies of Slaves and Women: Life-Stories from East/Central Africa.* New York: Lilian Barber Press, 1993.

Young, Jason R. *Rituals of Resistance: African Atlantic Religion in Kongo and the Lowcountry South in the Era of Slavery.* Baton Rouge: Louisiana State University Press, 2011.

Younger, Karen Fisher. "Liberia and the Last Slave Ships." *Civil War History* 54, no. 4 (December 2008): 424–42.

Yun, Lisa. *The Coolie Speaks: Chinese Indentured Laborers and African Slaves in Cuba.* Philadelphia: Temple University Press, 2008.

Zboray, Ronald J. "Antebellum Reading and the Ironies of Technical Innovation." *American Quarterly* 40, no. 1 (March 1988): 65–82.

Zeuske, Michael. *Amistad: A Hidden Network of Slavers and Merchants.* Translated by Steven Rendell. Princeton: Markus Wiener Publishers, 2014.

Zeuske, Michael, and Javier Lavina, eds. *The Second Slavery: Mass Slaveries and Modernity in the Americas and in the Atlantic Basin.* Zurich: LIT, 2014.

INDEX